THACKRAY'S
2012
INVESTOR'S
GUIDE

Brooke Thackray MBA, CIM, CFP

Published in 2011 by: MountAlpha Media:

alphamountain.com

ISBN13: 978-0-9782200-6-8

Printed and Bound by Webcom
10 9 8 7 6 5 4 3 2 1

June 4th low

Thackray's 2012 Investor's Guide

To my wife Jane

Acknowledgements

This book is the product of many years of research and could not have been written without the help of many people. I would like to thank my wife, Jane Steer-Thackray, and my children Justin, Megan, Carly and Madeleine, for the help they have given me and their patience during the many hours that I have devoted to writing this book. Credit must be given to Don Vialoux and Jon Vialoux. The three of us work together with the Horizons AlphaPro Seasonal Rotation ETF (ticker HAC:TSX) and many of the ideas and strategies that we have shared have found their way into this book. I would also like to thank the proofreaders and editors, Amanda ODonnell and Jane Stiegler. Special mention goes to Jane for the countless hours she spent helping with writing, formatting and editing. This book could not have been written without her help.

INTRODUCTION

2012 THACKRAY'S INVESTOR'S GUIDE

Every year I try and add new features and strategies to the latest edition of the Investor's Guide. Many of the new features are based upon reader feedback – thank you.

Single Stock Investing

ETFs are a very valuable tool and are great building blocks for seasonal portfolios. It makes sense that if a stock ETF has a seasonal trend, the stocks that make up the ETF will also have seasonal trends. The seasonal performance of an ETF is essentially a blended average of all the underlying stocks.

The seasonal trends for stocks are very often driven by the timing of earnings announcements or other events that happen at approximately the same time each year. The result is that one company can have a positive seasonal trend at one time of the year and a second company in the same sector of the market, can have a different seasonal trend. That is not to say that the companies will have two totally different seasonal trends, in fact there is typically some overlap. The start or end dates of the seasonal periods may be different, but the bulk of the middle holding period is usually the same.

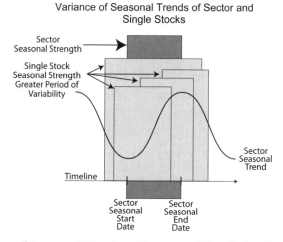

Variance of Seasonal Trends of Sector and Single Stocks

The *Variance of Seasonal Trends of Sector and Single Stocks* diagram illustrates the relationship of several individual stocks in a sector and the sector. The sector's seasonal period of strength is represented by the darker shaded area: the underlying individual stocks' period of seasonal strength in the sector is represented by the lighter shaded area. Each lightly shaded box represents a stock. Some stocks start their seasonal period before the sector and others later. Some stocks end their period of seasonal strength before the sector and others later. Overall, using individual stocks can increase the amount of time to take advantage of a seasonal sector trend.

Using individual stocks for seasonal investing allows for the implementation of a strategy that maximizes the benefits of the seasonal performance for each stock, without averaging in the inferior performance of other stocks in the same sector. Rotating between stocks in the same sector, depending on their individual seasonal entry and exit dates, will theoretically outperform the sector. For example, investing in a retail stock and then a media stock and then an auto stock, all within their seasonal periods will typcially outperform investing in a consumer discretionary ETF during its seasonal period.

Another benefit from investing in individual stocks on a seasonal basis is the potential for greater returns. Stocks have more volatility than a sector ETF, which is good and bad. If you choose the right stock it will provide superior returns compared with a sector ETF. If you choose the wrong stock it will underperform the ETF. By selecting individual stocks that have strong seasonal profiles, supported by positive technical indicators the probability of superior returns is increased.

A good strategy is to use ETFs in conjunction with stocks: buy a sector ETF during is seasonal period and buy three different stocks that are part of the sector at approximately the same time, but varying the entry and exit dates according to seasonality for each stock. To reduce risk the position in the ETF should typically be larger than the three stocks combined.

The stocks chosen to be part of this book are typically large blue-chip bellwether stocks from various sectors of the market. Generally, large blue-chip companies have stronger seasonality patterns than small companies and do not pose the same level risk.

THACKRAY'S 2012 INVESTOR'S GUIDE

You can choose great companies to invest in and still underperform the market. Unless you are in the market at the right time and in the best sectors, your investment expertise can be all for naught.

Successful investors know when they should be in the market. Very successful investors know when they should be in the market, and the best sectors in which to invest. *Thackray's 2012 Investor's Guide* is designed to provide investors with the knowledge of when and what to buy, and when to sell.

The goal of this book is to help investors capture extra profits by taking advantage of the seasonal trends in the markets. This book is straightforward. There are no complicated rules and there are no complex algorithms. The strategies put forward are intuitive and easy to understand.

It does not matter if you are a short-term or long-term investor, this book can be used to help establish entry and exit points. For the short-term investor, specific periods are identified that can provide profitable opportunities. For the long-term investor best buy dates are identified to launch new investments on a sound footing.

The stock market has its seasonal rhythms. Historically, the broad markets, such as the S&P 500, have a seasonal trend of outperforming during certain times of the year. Likewise, different sectors of the market have their own seasonal trends of outperformance. When oil stocks tend to do well in the springtime before "driving season," health care stocks tend to underperform the market. When utilities do well in the summertime, industrials do not. With different markets and different sectors having a tendency to outperform at different times of the year, there is always a place to invest.

Until recently, investors did not have access to the information necessary to analyze and create sector strategies. In recent years there have been a great number of sector Exchange Traded Funds (ETFs) and sector indexes introduced into the market. For the first time, investors are now able to easily implement a sector rotation strategy. This book provides a seasonal road map of what sectors tend to do well at different times of the year. It is a first of its kind, revealing new sector-based strategies that have never before been published.

In terms of market timing there are ample strategies in this book to help determine the times when equities should be over or underweight. During a favorable time for the market, investments can be purchased to overweight equities relative to their target weight in a portfolio (staying within risk tolerances). During an unfavorable time, investments can be sold to underweight equities relative to their target.

A large part of the book is devoted to sector seasonality – the underpinnings for a sector rotation strategy. The most practical rotation strategy is to create a core part of a portfolio that represents the broad market and then set aside an allocation to be rotated between favored sectors from one time period to the next.

It does not makes sense to apply any investment strategy only once with a large investment. Seasonal strategies are no exception. The best way to apply an investment strategy is to use a disciplined methodology that allows for diversification and a large enough number of investments to help remove the anomalies of the market. This reduces risk and increases the probability of a long term gain.

Following the specific buy and sell dates put forth in this book would have netted an investor large, above market returns. To "turbo-charge" gains, an investor can combine seasonality with technical analysis. As the seasonal periods are never exactly the same, technical analysis can help investors capture the extra gains when a sector turns up early, or momentum extends the trend.

IMPORTANT: Strategy Buy and Sell Dates
The beginning date of every strategy period in this book represents a full day in the market; therefore, investors should buy at the end of the preceding market day. For example the *Biotech Summer Solstice* seasonal period of strength is from June 23rd to September 13th. To be in the sector for the full seasonal period, an investor would enter the market before the closing bell on June 22nd. If the buy date landed on a weekend or holiday, then the buy would occur at the end of the preceding trading day.

The last day of a trading strategy is the sell date. For example, the Biotech sector investment would be sold at the end of the day on September 13th. If the sell date is a holiday or weekend, then the investment would be sold at the close on the preceding trading day.

What is Seasonal Investing?

In order to properly understand seasonal investing in the stock market, it is important to look briefly at its evolution. It may surprise investors to know that seasonal investing at the broad market level, i.e. Dow Jones or S&P 500, has been around for a long time. The initial seasonal strategies were written by Fields (1931, 1934) and Watchel (1942), who focused on the *January Effect*. Coincidentally, this strategy is still bantered about in the press every year.

Yale Yirsch Senior has been largely responsible for the next stage in the evolution, producing the *Stock Trader's Almanac* for more than forty years. This publication focuses on broad market trends such as the best six months of the year and tendencies of the market to do well depending on the political party in power and holiday trades.

In 1999, Brooke Thackray and Bruce Lindsay wrote, *Time In Time Out: Outsmart the Market Using Calendar Investment Strategies*. This work focused on a comprehensive analysis of the six month seasonal cycle and other shorter seasonal cycles in the broad markets such as the S&P 500.

Don Vialoux, considered the patriarch of seasonal investing in Canada, has written many articles on seasonal investing. His writings on this topic have developed a large following, via his free newsletter available at www.timingthemarket.ca.

Seasonal investing has changed over time. The focus has shifted from broad market strategies to taking advantage of sector rotation opportunities – investing in different sectors at different times of the year, depending on their seasonal strength. This has created a whole new set of investment opportunities. Rather than just being "in or out" of the market, investors can now always be invested by shifting between different sectors and asset classes, taking advantage of both up and down markets.

Definition – Seasonal investing is a method of investing in the market at the time of the year when it typically does well, or investing in a sector of the market when it typically outperforms the broad market such as the S&P 500.

The term seasonal investing is somewhat of a misnomer, and it is easy to see why some investors might believe that the discipline relates to investing based upon the seasons of the year – winter, spring, summer and autumn. Other than some agricultural commodities where the price is often correlated to growing seasons, generally seasonal investment strategies use the calendar as a reference for buy and sell dates. It is usually a specific event, i.e.

Christmas sales, that occurs on a recurring annual basis that creates the seasonal opportunity.

The discipline of seasonal investing is not restricted to the stock market. It has been used successfully for a number of years in the commodities market. The opportunities in this market tend to be based upon changes in supply and/or demand that occur on a yearly basis. Most commodities, especially the agricultural commodities, tend to have cyclical supply cycles, i.e., crops are harvested only at certain times of the year. The supply bulge that occurs at the same time every year provides seasonal investors with profit opportunities. Recurring increased seasonal demand for commodities also plays a major part in providing opportunities for seasonal investors. This applies to most metals and many other commodities, whether the end-product is industrial or consumer based.

Seasonal investment strategies can be used with a lot of different types of investments. The premise is the same, outperformance during a certain period of the year based upon a repeating event in the markets or economy. In my past writings I have developed seasonal strategies that have been used successfully in the stock, commodity, bond and foreign exchange markets. Seasonal investing is still relatively new for most markets with a lot of new opportunities waiting to be discovered.

How Does Seasonal Investing Work?

Most stock market sector seasonal trends are the result of a recurring annual catalyst: an event that affects the sector positively. These events can range from a seasonal spike in demand, seasonal inventory lows, weather effects, conferences and other events. Mainstream investors very often anticipate a move in a sector and incorrectly try to take a position just before an event takes place that is supposed to drive a sector higher. A good example of this would be investors buying oil just before the cold weather sets in. Unfortunately, their efforts are usually unsuccessful as they are too late to the party and the opportunity has already passed.

By the time the anticipated event occurs, a substantial amount of investors have bought into the sector – fully pricing in the expected benefit. At this time there is little potential left in the short-term. Unless there is a strong positive surprise, the sector's outperformance tends to slowly roll over. If the event produces less than its desired result, the sector can be severely punished.

So how does the seasonal investor take advantage of this opportunity? "Be there" before the mainstream investors, and get out before they do. Seasonal investors usually enter a sector two or three months before an event is anticipated to have a positive effect on a sector and get out before the actual event takes place. In essence, seasonal investors are benefiting from the mainstream investor's tendency to "buy in" too late.

Seasonality in the markets occurs because of three major reasons: money flow, changing market analyst expectations and the *Anticipation-Realization Cycle*. First, money flows vary throughout the year and at different times of the month. Generally, money flows increase at the end of the year and into the start of the next year. This is a result of year end bonuses and tax related investments. In addition, money flows increase at month end from money managers "window dressing" their portfolios. As a result of these money flows, the months around the end of the year and the days around the end of the month, tend to have a stronger performance than the other times of the year.

Second, the analyst expectations cycle tends to push markets up at the end of the year and the beginning of the next year. Stock market analysts tend to be a positive bunch – the large investment houses pay them to be positive. They start the year with aggressive earnings for all of their favorite companies. As the year progresses, they generally back off their earnings forecast, which decreases their support for the market. After a lull in the summer and early autumn months, they start to focus on the next year with another rosy forecast. As a result, the stock market tends to rise once again at the end of the year.

Third, at the sector level, sectors of the market tend to be greatly influenced by the *Anticipation-Realization Cycle*. Although some investors may not be familiar with the term "anticipation-realization," they probably are familiar with the concept of "buy the rumor – sell the fact," or in the famous words of Lord Rothschild "Buy on the sound of the war-cannons; sell on the sound of the victory trumpets."

The *Anticipation-Realization Cycle* as it applies to human behavior has been much studied in psychology journals. In the investment world, the premise of this cycle rests on investors anticipating a positive event in the market to drive prices higher and buying in ahead of the event. When the event takes place, or is realized, upward pressure on prices decreases as there is very little impetus for further outperformance.

A good example of the *Anticipation-Realization Cycle* takes place with the "conference effect." Very often large industries have major conferences that occur at approximately the same time every year. Major companies in the industry often hold back positive announce-

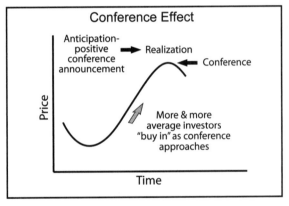

ments and product introductions to be released during the conference.

Two to three months prior to the conference, seasonal investors tend to buy into the sector. Shortly afterwards, the mainstream investors anticipate "good news" from the conference and start to buy in. As a result, prices are pushed up. Just before the conference starts, seasonal investors capture their profits by exiting their positions. As the conference unfolds, company announcements are made (realized), but as the potential good news has already been priced into the sector, there is little to push prices higher and the sector typically starts to rolls over.

The same *Anticipation-Realization Cycle* takes place with increased demand for oil to meet the "summer driving season", increased sales of goods at Christmas time, increased demand for gold jewellery to meet the autumn and winter demand, and many other events that tend to drive the outperformance of different sectors.

Does Seasonal Investing ALWAYS Work?

The simple answer to the above question is "No." There is not any investment system in the world that works all of the time. When following any investment system, it is probability of success that counts. It has often been said that "being correct in the markets 60% of the time will make you rich." Investors tend to forget this and become too emotionally attached to their losses. Just about every investment trading book states that investors typically fail to let their profits run and cut their losses quickly. I concur. In my many years in the investment industry, the biggest mistake that I have found with investors is not being able to cut their losses. Everyone wants to be right, that is how we have been raised. Investors feel that if they sell at a loss they have failed, and as a result, often suffer bigger losses by waiting for their position to trade at profit.

With any investment system, investors should let probability work for them. This means that investors should be able to enter and exit positions capturing both gains and losses without becoming emotionally attached to any positions. Emotional attachment clouds judgement, which leads to errors. When all of the trades are put together, the goal is for profits to be larger than losses in a way that minimizes risks and beats the market.

If we examine the winter oil stock trade, my favorite seasonal trade, we can see how probability has worked in an investor's favor. This trade is based upon the premise that at the tail end of winter, the refineries drive up demand for oil in order to produce enough gas for the approaching "driving season" that starts in the spring. As a result, oil stocks tend to increase and outperform the market (from February 25th to May 9th).

XOI vs S&P 500 1984 to 2011			
Feb 25		positive	
to May 9	S&P 500	XOI	Diff
1984	1.7 %	5.6 %	3.9 %
1985	1.4	4.9	3.5
1986	6.0	7.7	1.7
1987	3.7	25.5	21.8
1988	-3.0	5.6	8.6
1989	6.3	8.1	1.8
1990	5.8	-0.6	-6.3
1991	4.8	6.8	2.0
1992	0.9	5.8	4.9
1993	0.3	6.3	6.0
1994	-4.7	3.2	7.9
1995	7.3	10.3	3.1
1996	-2.1	2.2	4.3
1997	1.8	4.7	2.9
1998	7.5	9.8	2.3
1999	7.3	35.4	28.1
2000	4.3	22.2	17.9
2001	0.8	10.2	9.4
2002	-1.5	5.3	6.9
2003	12.1	5.7	-6.4
2004	-3.5	4.0	7.5
2005	-1.8	-1.0	0.8
2006	2.8	9.4	6.6
2007	4.2	10.1	5.8
2008	2.6	7.6	5.0
2009	20.2	15.8	-4.4
2010	0.5	-2.3	-2.8
2011	3.1	-0.6	-3.7
Avg	3.3 %	7.7 %	4.4 %
Fq > 0	79 %	86 %	82 %

The oil stock sector, represented by the Amex Oil Index (XOI), has been very successful at this time of year, producing an average return of 7.7% and beating the S&P 500 by 4.4%, from 1984 to 2011. In addition it has been positive 24 out of 28 times. Not all seasonal trades are created equal: this strategic sector trade is at the top of the list. Investors should always evaluate the strength of seasonal trades before applying them to their own portfolios.

If an investor started using the seasonal investment discipline in 1984 and chose to invest in the winter-oil trade, they would have been very happy with the results. If they had chosen almost any other year to start the winter-oil trade in the last 28 years, they would have also been very pleased with the results. The exception to this occurs in the years 1990, 2005, 2010 and 2011. These years produced nominal losses of 0.6%, 1.0%, 2.3% and 0.6% respectively.

Does this mean the system does not work? No. An investor can start any methodology of trading at the "wrong time," and be unsuccessful for a particular trade. In fact, if the investor started the oil-winter trade in 1990 and had given up in the same year, they would have missed the following successful twelve years. They would have also missed all of the other successful seasonal trades that took place in the year. Investors have to remember that it is the final score that counts, after all of the gains have been weighed against the losses.

In practical terms, investors should not put all of their investment strategies in one basket. If one or two large investments were made based upon seasonal strategies, it is possible that the seasonal methodology might be inappropriately evaluated and its use discontinued. A much more prudent strategy is to use a larger number of strategic seasonal investments with smaller investments. The end result will be to put the seasonal probability to work with a much greater chance of success.

Measuring Seasonal Performance

How do you determine if a seasonal strategy has been successful? Many people feel that ten years of data is a good sample size, others feel that fifteen years is better, and yet others feel that the more data the better. I tend to fall into the camp that, if possible, it is best to use fifteen or twenty years of data for sectors and more data for the broad markets, such as the S&P 500. Although the most recent data in almost any analytical framework is the most relevant, it is important to get enough data to reflect a sector's performance across different economic conditions. Given that historically the economy has performed on an eight year cycle, four years of expansion and then four years of contraction, using a short data set does not provide for enough exposure to different economic conditions.

A data set that is too long can run into the problem of older data having too much of an influence on the numbers when fundamental factors affecting a sector have changed. It is important to look at trends over time and assess if there has been a change that should be considered in determining the dates for a seasonal cycle. Each sector should be judged on its own merit. The analysis tables in this book illustrate the performance level for each year in order to provide the opportunity for readers to determine any relevant changes.

In order to determine if a seasonal strategy is effective there are two possible benchmarks, absolute and relative performance. Absolute performance measures if a profit is made and relative performance measures the performance of a sector in relationship to a major market. Both measurements have their merits and depending on your investment style, one measurement may be more valuable than another. This book provides both sets of measurement in tables and graphs.

It is not just the average percent gain of a sector over a certain time period that determines success. It is possible that one or two spectacular years of performance skew the results substantially (particularly with a small data set). The frequency of success is also very important: the higher the percentage of success the better. Also, the fewer large drawdowns the better. There is no magic number (percent success rate) per se of what constitutes a successful strategy. The success rate should be above fifty percent, otherwise it would be better to just invest in the broad market. Ideally speaking a strategy should have a high percentage success rate on both an absolute and relative basis. Some strategies are stronger than others, but that does not mean that the weaker strategies should not be used. Prudence should be used in determining the ideal portfolio allocation.

Illustrating the strength of a sector's seasonal performance can be accomplished through either an absolute yearly average performance graph, or a relative yearly average performance graph. The absolute graph shows the average yearly cumulative gain for a set number of years. It lets a reader visually identify the strong periods during the year. The relative graph shows the average yearly cumulative gain for the sector relative to the benchmark index.

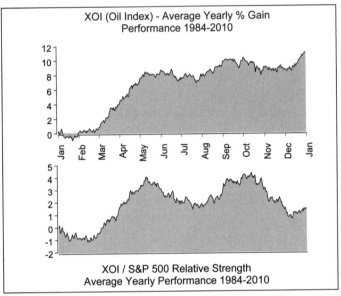

Both graphs are useful in determining the strength of a particular seasonal strategy. In the above diagram, the top graph illustrates the average year for the XOI (Oil Index) from 1984 to 2010. Essentially it illustrates the cumulative average gain if an investment were made in the index. The steep rising line starting in January/February shows the overall price rise that typically occurs in this sector at this time of year. In May the line flattens out and then rises very modestly starting in July.

The bottom graph is a ratio graph, illustrating the strength of the XOI Index relative to the S&P 500. It is derived by dividing the average year of the XOI by the average year of the S&P 500. When the line in the graph is rising, the XOI is outperforming the S&P 500, and vise versa when it is declining. This is an important graph and should be used in considering seasonal investments because the S&P 500 is a viable alternative to the energy sector. If both markets are increasing, but the S&P 500 is increasing at a faster rate, the S&P 500 represents a more attractive opportunity. This is particularly true when measuring the risk of a volatile sector relative to the broad market. If both investments were expected to produce the same rate of return, generally the broad market is a better investment because of its diversification.

Who Can Use Seasonal Investing?

Any investor from novice to expert, from short-term trader to long-term investor can benefit from using seasonal analysis. Seasonal investing is unique because it is an easy to understand system that can be used by itself or as a complement to another investment discipline. For the novice it provides an easy to follow strategy that makes intuitive sense. For the expert it can be used as a stand-alone system or as a complement to an existing system.

Seasonal investing is easily understood by all levels of investors, which allows investors to make rational decisions. This may seem obvious, but it is very common for investors to listen to a "guru of the market", be impressed and blindly follow his advice. When the advice works there is no problem. When the advice does not work investors wonder why they made the investment in the first place. When investors do not understand their investments it causes stress, bad decisions and a lack of "stick-to-it ness" with any investment discipline. Even expert investors realize the importance of understanding your investments. Michael Lynch of Fidelity Investments used to say "Never invest in any idea that you can't illustrate with a crayon." Investors do not need to go that far, but they should understand their investments.

Novice investors find seasonal strategies very easy to understand because they are intuitive. They do not have to be investing for years to understand why seasonal strategies work. They understand that an increase in demand for gold every year at the same time causes a ripple effect in the stock market pushing up gold stocks at the same time every year.

Most expert investors use information from a variety of sources in making their decisions. Even experts that primarily use fundamental analysis can benefit from using seasonal trends to get an edge in the market. Fundamental analysis is a very crude tool and provides very little in the way of timing an investment. Using seasonal trends can help with the timing of the buy and sell decisions and produce extra profit.

Seasonal investing can be used by both short-term and long-term investors, but in different ways. For short-term investors it provides a complete trade – buy and sell dates. For long-term investors it can provide a buy date for a sector of interest.

Combining Seasonal Analysis with other Investment Disciplines

Seasonal investing used by itself has historically produced above average market returns. Depending on an investor's particular style, it can be combined with one of the other three investment disciplines: fundamental, quantitative and technical analysis. There are two basic ways to combine seasonal analysis with other investment methodologies – as the primary or secondary method. If it is used as a primary method, seasonally strong time periods are established for a number of sectors and then appropriate sectors are chosen based upon fundamental, quantitative or technical screens. If it is used as a secondary method, sector selections are first made based upon one of three methods and then final sectors are chosen based upon which ones are in their seasonally strong period.

Technical analysis is an ideal mate for seasonal analysis. Unlike fundamental and quantitative analysis, which are very blunt timing tools at best, seasonal and technical analysis can provide specific trigger points to buy and sell. The combination can turbo-charge investment strategies, adding extra profits by fine-tuning entry and exit dates.

Seasonal analysis provides both buy and sell dates. Although a sector in the market can sometimes bottom on the exact seasonal buy date, it more often bottoms a bit early or a bit late. After all, the seasonal buy date is based upon an average of historical performance. Depending on the sector, buying opportunities start to develop approximately one month before and after the seasonal buy date. Using technical analysis gives an investor the advantage of buying into a sector when it turns up early or waiting when it turns up late. Likewise, technical analysis can be used to trigger a sell signal when the market turns down before or after the sell date.

The sell decision can be extended with the help of a trailing stop-loss order. If a sector has strong momentum and the technical tools do not provide a sell signal, it is possible to let the sector "run." When a trailing stop-loss is used, a profitable sell point is established. If the price continues to run, then the selling point is raised. If, on the other hand, the price falls through the stop-loss point, the position is sold.

Sectors of the Market

Standard & Poor's has done an excellent job in categorizing the U.S. stock market into its different parts. Although the demand for this service initially came from institutional investors, many individual investors now seek the same information. Knowing the sector breakdown in the market allows investors to see how different their portfolio is relative to the market. As a result, they are able to make conscious decisions on what parts of the stock market to overweight based upon their beliefs of which sectors will outperform. It also helps control the amount of desired risk.

Standard & Poor's uses four levels of detail in its Global Industry Classification Standard (GICS$^{©}$) to categorize stock markets around the world. From the most specific, it classifies companies into sub-industries, industries, industry groups and finally economic sectors. All companies in the Standard & Poor's global family of indices are classified according to the GICS structure.

This book focuses on the U.S. market, analyzing the trends of the venerable S&P 500 index and its economic sectors and industry groups. The following diagram illustrates the index classified according to its economic sectors.

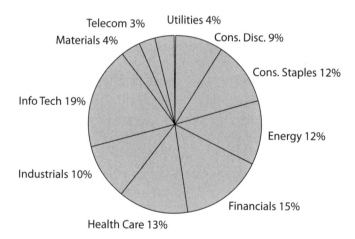

Standard and Poor's, Understanding Sectors, June 30, 2010

For more information on Standard and Poor's Global Industry Classification Standard (GICS$^{©}$), refer to www.standardandpoors.com

Investment Products – Which One Is The Right One?

There are many ways to take advantage of the seasonal trends at the broad stock market and sector levels. Regardless of the investment products that you currently use, whether exchange traded funds, mutual funds, stocks or options, all can be used with the strategies in this book. Different investments offer different risk-reward relationships and return potential.

Exchange Traded Funds (ETFs)

Exchange Traded Funds (ETFs) offer the purest method of seasonal investment. The broad market ETFs are designed to track the major indices and the sector ETFs are designed to track specific sectors without using active management. Relatively new, ETFs are a great way to capture both market and sector trends. They were originally introduced into the Canadian market in 1993 to represent the Toronto stock market index. Shortly afterward they were introduced to the U.S. market and there are now hundreds of ETFs to represent almost every market, sector, style of investing and company capitalization. Originally ETFs were mainly of interest to institutional investors, but individual investors have fast realized the merits of ETF investing and have made some of the broad market ETFs the most heavily traded securities in the world.

An ETF is a single security that represents a market, such as the S&P 500; a sector of the market, such as the financial sector; or a commodity, such as gold. In the case of the S&P 500, an investor buying one security is buying all 500 stocks in the index. By investing into a financial ETF, an investor is buying the companies that make up the financial sector of the market. By investing into gold commodity ETF, an investor is buying a security that represents the price of gold.

ETFs trade on the open market just like stocks. They have a bid and an ask, can be shorted and many are option eligible. They are a very low cost, tax efficient method of targeting specific parts of the market.

Mutual Funds

Mutual funds are a good way to combine market or sector investing with active management. In recent years, many mutual fund companies have added sector funds to accommodate an increasing appetite in this area.

As the seasonal strategies put forward in this book have a short-term nature, it is important to make sure that there are no fees (or a nominal charge) for getting into and out of a position in the market.

Stocks

Stocks provide an opportunity to make better returns than the market or sector. If the market increases during its seasonal period, some stocks will increase dramatically more than the index. Choosing one of the outperforming stocks will greatly enhance returns; choosing one of the underperforming stocks can create substantial loses. Using stocks requires increased attention to diversification and security selection.

Options

Disclaimer: Options involve risk and are not suitable for every investor. Because they are cash-settled, investors should be aware of the special risks associated with index options and should consult a tax advisor. Prior to buying or selling options, a person must receive a copy of Characteristics and Risks of Standardized Options and should thoroughly understand the risks involved in any use of options. Copies may be obtained from The Options Clearing Corporation, 440 S. LaSalle Street, Chicago, IL 60605.

Options, for more sophisticated investors, are a good tool to take advantage of both market and sector opportunities. An option position can be established with either stocks or ETFs. There are many different ways to use options for seasonal trends: establish a long position on the market during its seasonally strong period, establish a short position during its seasonally weak period, or create a spread trade to capture the superior gains of a sector over the market.

THACKRAY'S 2012 INVESTOR'S GUIDE

CONTENTS

JANUARY

	MONDAY	TUESDAY	WEDNESDAY
WEEK 01	**2** 29 CAN Market Closed- New Year's Day USA Market Closed- New Year's Day	**3** 28	**4** 27
WEEK 02	**9** 22	**10** 21	**11** 20
WEEK 03	**16** 15 USA Market Closed- Martin Luther King Jr. Day	**17** 14	**18** 13
WEEK 04	**23** 8	**24** 7	**25** 6
WEEK 05	**30** 1	**31**	1

THURSDAY		FRIDAY	
5	26	**6**	25
12	19	**13**	18
19	12	**20**	11
26	5	**27**	4
2		3	

FEBRUARY

M	T	W	T	F	S	S
		1	2	3	4	5
6	7	8	9	10	11	12
13	14	15	16	17	18	19
20	21	22	23	24	25	26
27	28	29				

MARCH

M	T	W	T	F	S	S
			1	2	3	4
5	6	7	8	9	10	11
12	13	14	15	16	17	18
19	20	21	22	23	24	25
26	27	28	29	30	31	

APRIL

M	T	W	T	F	S	S
						1
2	3	4	5	6	7	8
9	10	11	12	13	14	15
16	17	18	19	20	21	22
23	24	25	26	27	28	29
30						

MAY

M	T	W	T	F	S	S
	1	2	3	4	5	6
7	8	9	10	11	12	13
14	15	16	17	18	19	20
21	22	23	24	25	26	27
28	29	30	31			

JANUARY SUMMARY

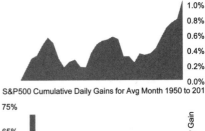

S&P500 Cumulative Daily Gains for Avg Month 1950 to 2011

	Dow Jones	S&P 500	Nasdaq	TSX Comp
Month Rank	6	5	1	4
# Up	40	38	26	16
# Down	22	24	14	11
% Pos	65	61	65	59
% Avg. Gain	1.0	1.1	2.6	1.0

Dow & S&P 1950-June 2011, Nasdaq 1972-June 2011, TSX 1985-June 2011

♦ Traditionally, January tends to be a positive month for the stock market and it often sets the sentiment for the rest of the year (see *January Predictor* strategy). For three years in a row (2008-2010) January produced large losses. In 2011, it got back on track producing a gain of 2.3% in the S&P 500. ♦ The *retail* sector starts its seasonal trend in January- it has been positive over the last four years. ♦ Both platinum and silver start their seasonal trades in January (see *Platinum Records Solid Results* and *Silver- Best Three Periods* strategies).

BEST / WORST JANUARY BROAD MKTS. 2002-2011

BEST JANUARY MARKETS
♦ Russell 2000 (2006) 8.9%
♦ TSX Comp (2006) 6.0%
♦ Nasdaq (2006) 4.6%

WORST JANUARY MARKETS
♦ Russell 3000 Value (2009) -11.9%
♦ Russell 2000 (2009) -11.2%
♦ Nasdaq (2008) -9.9%

Index Values End of Month

	2002	2003	2004	2005	2006	2007	2008	2009	2010	2011
Dow	9,920	8,054	10,488	10,490	10,865	12,622	12,650	8,001	10,067	11,892
S&P 500	1,130	856	1,131	1,181	1,280	1,438	1,379	826	1,074	1,286
Nasdaq	1,934	1,321	2,066	2,062	2,306	2,464	2,390	1,476	2,147	2,700
TSX	7,648	6,569	8,521	9,204	11,946	13,034	13,155	8,695	11,094	13,552
Russell 1000	1,147	873	1,163	1,219	1,341	1,507	1,444	860	1,133	1,371
Russell 2000	1,201	925	1,443	1,551	1,822	1,989	1,773	1,102	1,496	1,942
Russell 3000 Growth	1,944	1,378	1,872	1,871	2,066	2,238	2,214	1,386	1,879	2,330
Russell 3000 Value	2,051	1,668	2,229	2,450	2,717	3,151	2,883	1,638	2,100	2,507

Percent Gain for January

	2002	2003	2004	2005	2006	2007	2008	2009	2010	2011
Dow	-1.0	-3.5	0.3	-2.7	1.4	1.3	-4.6	-8.8	-3.5	2.7
S&P 500	-1.6	-2.7	1.7	-2.5	2.5	1.4	-6.1	-8.6	-3.7	2.3
Nasdaq	-0.8	-1.1	3.1	-5.2	4.6	2.0	-9.9	-6.4	-5.4	1.8
TSX	-0.5	-0.7	3.7	-0.5	6.0	1.0	-4.9	-3.3	-5.5	0.8
Russell 1000	-1.4	-2.5	1.8	-2.6	2.7	1.8	-6.1	-8.3	-3.7	2.3
Russell 2000	-1.1	-2.9	4.3	-4.2	8.9	1.6	-6.9	-11.2	-3.7	-0.3
Russell 3000 Growth	-1.9	-2.5	2.2	-3.5	2.4	2.5	-8.0	-5.1	-4.4	2.2
Russell 3000 Value	-0.8	-2.6	1.7	-2.1	4.1	1.1	-4.2	-11.9	-3.0	1.9

January Market Avg. Performance 2002 to 2011[1]

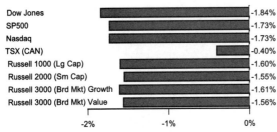

		-1.84%
Dow Jones		-1.84%
SP500		-1.73%
Nasdaq		-1.73%
TSX (CAN)		-0.40%
Russell 1000 (Lg Cap)		-1.60%
Russell 2000 (Sm Cap)		-1.55%
Russell 3000 (Brd Mkt) Growth		-1.61%
Russell 3000 (Brd Mkt) Value		-1.56%

Interest Corner Jan[2]

	Fed Funds %[3]	3 Mo. T-Bill %[4]	10 Yr %[5]	20 Yr %[6]
2011	0.25	0.15	3.42	4.33
2010	0.25	0.08	3.63	4.38
2009	0.25	0.24	2.87	3.86
2008	3.00	1.96	3.67	4.35
2007	5.25	5.12	4.83	5.02

(1) Russell Data provided by Russell (2) Federal Reserve Bank of St. Louis- end of month values (3) Target rate set by FOMC (4)(5)(6) Constant yield maturities.

THACKRAY SECTOR THERMOMETER

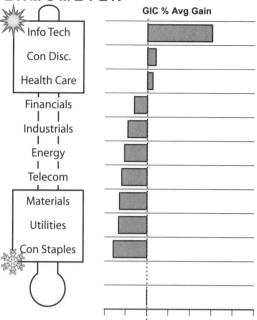

GIC(2) % Avg Gain	Fq % Gain >S&P 500	
SP GIC SECTOR 1990-2010(1)		
3.0 %	76 %	Information Technology
0.4	52	Consumer Discretionary
0.3	62	Health Care
-0.6	62	Financials
-0.9	29	Industrials
-1.1	38	Energy
-1.2	48	Telecom
-1.3	43	Materials
-1.3	33	Utilities
-1.6 %	29 %	Consumer Staples
0.0 %	N/A %	S&P 500

Sector Commentary

♦ On average from 1990 to 2010, January has been the month for *information technology*, returning an average 3.0% and beating the S&P 500, 76% of the time. ♦ In 2011, the *information technology* sector performed well, producing a gain of 4.2% (tied for second best sector in January with the *industrial* sector). ♦ In January 2011, the *energy* sector produced the strongest performance with 7.3%. ♦ All three of the bottom sectors of the TST (Thackray Sector Thermometer) performed below market, with *consumer staples* and *materials* producing losses.

Sub-Sector Commentary

♦ In January 2011, *agriculture* made it to the top of the sub-sector list with a gain of 8.6%. This sub-sector usually outperforms the market until the end of December, but it still managed to perform very well in January. ♦ The *integrated oil and gas* sub-sector also uncharacteristically performed very well in January with a 7.1% return, benefiting from rising oil prices at the time. ♦ The next two best performing sub-sectors are usually at the top of the sub-sector TST: the *semiconductor* and *software & services*, producing returns of 6.9% and 2.8% respectively.

SELECTED SUB-SECTORS 1990-2010(3)		
3.7 %	50 %	Semiconductor (SOX) 95-2010
2.3	67	Software & Services
1.7	50	Biotech (93-2010)
1.4	57	Auto & Components
0.9	57	Gold (London PM)
-0.1	57	Pharmaceuticals
-0.2	52	Banks
-0.2	48	Transportation
-0.2	52	Retail
-0.4	41	Agriculture Products (94-2010)
-0.7	43	Gold (XAU)
-1.0	48	Metals & Mining
-1.3	43	Integrated Oil & Gas
-2.3	38	Airlines

(1) Sector data provided by Standard and Poors (2) GIC is short form for Global Industry Classification (3) Sub Sector data provided by Standard and Poors, except where marked by symbol.

THACKRAY SECTOR THERMOMETER PORTFOLIO (TSTP) BEATS MARKET BY 14% per year (avg.) (1990-2010)

Investing in the three sectors (S&P GIC) that have averaged the best monthly performance over the long-term, has significantly rewarded investors.

From a portfolio perspective, funds are divided up evenly amongst the three top sectors at the beginning of the starting month. At the end of the month, the three sectors are sold and the proceeds are invested in the top three sectors for the next month. The process repeats itself with the accumulated funds being invested at the start of each month. Funds are accumulated month by month until the end of the time period.

For each month, the same sectors are used from year to year, over the study period. For example the same three sectors would be used every January.

TSTP Avg. Gain of 22% vs. 8% for S&P 500

Following the Thackray Sector Thermometer Portfolio (TSTP) strategy from 1990 to 2010 has produced an average return of 22%, compared with the S&P 500 which produced an average return of 8% over the same period. To illustrate how much of an impact investing in different sectors of the market can have on a portfolio, the same sector selection process was used for the three worst performing sectors. Investing in the three worst sectors from 1990 to 2010 has produced an average loss of 3% per year.

Most investors get caught up investing in a certain stock or company. There is a lot of research proving that it is much more important to pick the appropriate asset class or sector of the market compared to picking stocks.

Hot and Cold Box Sector Portfolios

The *Hot Box* refers to the top three sectors on the Thackray Sector Thermometer tagged with an image of the sun.

The *Cold Box* refers to the bottom three sectors tagged with an image of a snowflake.

Monthly results for each sector in the Hot and Cold Boxes are posted on the Monthly Sector Performance pages beside the Thackray Sector Thermometer (TST).

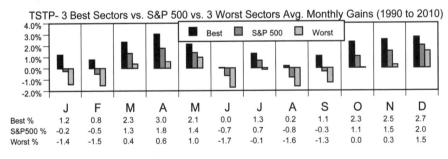

TSTP- 3 Best Sectors vs. S&P 500 vs. 3 Worst Sectors Avg. Monthly Gains (1990 to 2010)

	J	F	M	A	M	J	J	A	S	O	N	D	Avg. Year Gain
Best %	1.2	0.8	2.3	3.0	2.1	0.0	1.3	0.2	1.1	2.3	2.5	2.7	22.0%
S&P500 %	-0.2	-0.5	1.3	1.8	1.4	-0.7	0.7	-0.8	-0.3	1.1	1.5	2.0	8.0%
Worst %	-1.4	-1.5	0.4	0.6	1.0	-1.7	-0.1	-1.6	-1.3	0.0	0.3	1.5	-2.9%

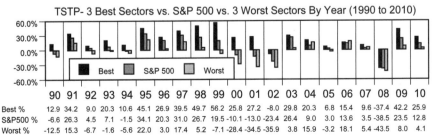

TSTP- 3 Best Sectors vs. S&P 500 vs. 3 Worst Sectors By Year (1990 to 2010)

	90	91	92	93	94	95	96	97	98	99	00	01	02	03	04	05	06	07	08	09	10	Total Period Gain
Best %	12.9	34.2	9.0	20.3	10.6	45.1	26.9	39.5	49.7	56.2	25.8	27.2	-8.0	29.8	20.3	6.8	15.4	9.6	-37.4	42.2	25.9	4496%
S&P500 %	-6.6	26.3	4.5	7.1	-1.5	34.1	20.3	31.0	26.7	19.5	-10.1	-13.0	-23.4	26.4	9.0	3.0	13.6	3.5	-38.5	23.5	12.8	256%
Worst %	-12.5	15.3	-6.7	-1.6	-5.6	22.0	3.0	17.4	5.2	-7.1	-28.4	-34.5	-35.9	3.8	15.9	-3.2	18.1	5.4	-43.5	8.0	4.1	-65%

2 MONDAY	002 / 364	**3** TUESDAY	003 / 363

4 WEDNESDAY	004 / 362	**5** THURSDAY	005 / 361

6 FRIDAY   006 / 360

Market Indices & Rates
Weekly Values**

Stock Markets	2010	2011
Dow	10,591	11,691
S&P500	1,139	1,273
Nasdaq	2,307	2,698
TSX	11,908	13,346
FTSE	5,523	6,015
DAX	6,034	6,967
Nikkei	10,710	10,462
Hang Seng	22,217	23,667

Commodities	2010	2011
Oil	82.37	89.53
Gold	1,126.4	1,373.0

Bond Yields	2010	2011
USA 5 Yr Treasury	2.60	2.04
USA 10 Yr T	3.83	3.40
USA 20 Yr T	4.60	4.26
Moody's Aaa	5.30	5.01
Moody's Baa	6.34	6.09
CAN 5 Yr T	2.74	2.48
CAN 10 Yr T	3.61	3.20

Money Market	2010	2011
USA Fed Funds	0.25	0.25
USA 3 Mo T-B	0.06	0.14
CAN tgt overnight rate	0.25	1.00
CAN 3 Mo T-B	0.18	0.98

Foreign Exchange	2010	2011
USD/EUR	1.44	1.31
USD/GBP	1.60	1.55
CAN/USD	1.04	1.00
JPY/USD	92.52	82.70

JANUARY

M	T	W	T	F	S	S
						1
2	3	4	5	6	7	8
9	10	11	12	13	14	15
16	17	18	19	20	21	22
23	24	25	26	27	28	29
30	31					

FEBRUARY

M	T	W	T	F	S	S
	1	2	3	4	5
6	7	8	9	10	11	12
13	14	15	16	17	18	19
20	21	22	23	24	25	26
27	28	29				

MARCH

M	T	W	T	F	S	S
			1	2	3	4
5	6	7	8	9	10	11
12	13	14	15	16	17	18
19	20	21	22	23	24	25
26	27	28	29	30	31	

2010 Strategy Performance

TSTP 2010 Best 3 Sectors vs. S&P 500 vs. Worst 3 Sectors

	J	F	M	A	M	J	J	A	S	O	N	D	Total Year Gain
Best %	-3.7	2.9	6.5	3.0	-7.0	-2.8	8.9	-0.8	8.6	3.0	-0.9	6.8	25.9%
S&P500 %	-3.7	2.9	5.9	1.5	-8.2	-5.4	6.9	-4.7	8.8	3.7	-0.2	6.5	12.8%
Worst %	-5.0	-1.0	4.3	-2.3	-6.6	-7.6	7.7	-1.6	10.2	3.0	0.2	4.5	4.1%

The year 2010 ended up being a very good year for the market with the S&P 500 producing a final gain of 12.8%. More amazingly, the TSTP best three sectors (see previous page for details), doubled the S&P 500 gain, producing a return of 25.9%. The TSTP managed to perform at market or better 7 out of 12 months. To reference the monthly statistics for the TSTP and to see the sectors that were used each month, refer to the Thackray Sector Thermometer on the Monthly Sector Performance page, found at the beginning of each month.

** Weekly avg closing values- except Fed Funds & CAN overnight tgt rate weekly closing values.

PLATINUM RECORDS SOLID RESULTS
January 1st to May 31st

Most investors focus on gold in the precious metals sector, some look at silver, but few notice platinum. Platinum outperforms gold starting at the beginning of the year until the end of May.

A large portion of the platinum produced each year is consumed by catalytic converters, mainly used in the automotive sector to control exhaust emissions. Approximately 40% of platinum is used for jewellery, 37% for catalytic converters and the rest is used for other industrial purposes.

6.9% extra and 76% of the time better than Gold

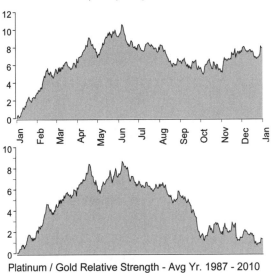

Platinum (Metal) - Avg. Year 1987 to 2010

Platinum / Gold Relative Strength - Avg Yr. 1987 - 2010

Platinum vs. Gold 1987 to 2011*

Jan 1 to May 31	Gold	Positive Platinum	Diff
1987 %	16.0 %	22.1 %	6.1 %
1988	-5.9	13.8	19.7
1989	-11.8	-2.6	9.2
1990	-8.9	-0.9	8.0
1991	-6.7	-4.9	1.8
1992	-4.4	4.5	9.0
1993	12.6	9.0	-3.6
1994	-1.1	2.0	3.1
1995	0.3	3.5	3.2
1996	0.9	-0.2	-1.2
1997	-6.4	10.5	16.9
1998	1.2	0.1	-1.0
1999	-6.7	0.4	7.1
2000	-6.2	23.4	29.6
2001	-2.5	-0.6	2.0
2002	18.1	14.8	-3.4
2003	4.1	7.6	3.5
2004	-5.5	2.9	8.4
2005	-4.9	0.5	5.3
2006	27.3	32.6	5.3
2007	4.3	13.7	9.4
2008	6.2	31.2	24.9
2009	12.2	29.4	17.3
2010	11.0	6.9	-4.1
2011	9.3	4.2	-5.2
Avg.	2.1 %	9.0 %	6.9 %
Fq > 0	52 %	80 %	76 %

num in auto catalyst usage, platinum is a more effective agent with diesel emissions. Currently, approximately 50% of Europe's automobiles are diesel powered. As higher fuel prices change North American driving patterns (a small fraction of autos are currently powered by diesel), it is expected that the automotive industry will offer a greater selection of diesel powered autos. This should help increase overall platinum demand.

In addition, China is adding more and more demand for cars. It was not too long ago that rush hour in Beijing was crowded with bikes, now it is cars. China has recently started to outpace America in auto sales. In August of 2010, the Chinese purchased more cars than Americans (*Gartman 2010, September*). Increasing demand for cars translates into an increase in the demand for platinum.

Platinum does well at the beginning of the year as it benefits from positive worldwide economic forecasts that dominate the market at the time. Strong economic forecasts translates into healthy worldwide auto production, which in turn translates into healthy platinum demand. Later in the year as economic forecasts are curtailed, platinum tends to lose its upwards momentum. In recent years, platinum has been in a strong bull market because of increasing inflation expectations, increasing jewellery usage, more stringent automotive emission requirements and supply problems in the South African mines.

Although palladium, a cheaper metal in the Platinum Group of Metals (PGM) can be substituted for plati-

* *Platinum based upon Bloomberg closing prices & Gold based upon London PM price.*

09 MONDAY 009 / 357

10 TUESDAY 010 / 356

11 WEDNESDAY 011 / 355

12 THURSDAY 012 / 354

13 FRIDAY 013 / 353

Market Indices & Rates
Weekly Values**

Stock Markets	2010	2011
Dow	10,658	11,717
S&P500	1,143	1,281
Nasdaq	2,301	2,731
TSX	11,822	13,394
FTSE	5,493	6,009
DAX	5,962	7,004
Nikkei	10,876	10,528
Hang Seng	21,972	23,987

Commodities	2010	2011
Oil	80.07	91.03
Gold	1139.6	1373.9

Bond Yields	2010	2011
USA 5 Yr Treasury	2.51	1.96
USA 10 Yr T	3.77	3.36
USA 20 Yr T	4.55	4.26
Moody's Aaa	5.24	5.01
Moody's Baa	6.25	6.07
CAN 5 Yr T	2.69	2.52
CAN 10 Yr T	3.56	3.23

Money Market	2010	2011
USA Fed Funds	0.25	0.25
USA 3 Mo T-B	0.05	0.15
CAN tgt overnight rate	0.25	1.00
CAN 3 Mo T-B	0.18	0.96

Foreign Exchange	2010	2011
USD/EUR	1.45	1.32
USD/GBP	1.62	1.57
CAN/USD	1.03	0.99
JPY/USD	91.28	82.93

2010-11 Strategy Performance

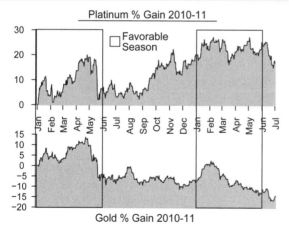

Platinum % Gain 2010-11

Gold % Gain 2010-11

In 2010, platinum rallied in its seasonal period, but corrected substantially at the beginning of May when global economic concerns brought the stock markets around the world tumbling down. In the end, the sector still managed to produce a positive gain during its seasonal period. In 2011, the platinum trade was mediocre and under performed gold. Economic concerns were starting to creep into the market, holding platinum back. Once again, it corrected in April with the stock market.

** Weekly avg closing values- except Fed Funds & CAN overnight tgt rate weekly closing values.

JANUARY

M	T	W	T	F	S	S
						1
2	3	4	5	6	7	8
9	10	11	12	13	14	15
16	17	18	19	20	21	22
23	24	25	26	27	28	29
30	31					

FEBRUARY

M	T	W	T	F	S	S
		1	2	3	4	5
6	7	8	9	10	11	12
13	14	15	16	17	18	19
20	21	22	23	24	25	26
27	28	29				

MARCH

M	T	W	T	F	S	S
			1	2	3	4
5	6	7	8	9	10	11
12	13	14	15	16	17	18
19	20	21	22	23	24	25
26	27	28	29	30	31	

RETAIL – POST HOLIDAY BARGAIN
1st of II Retail Strategies for the Year
SHOP Jan 21st and RETURN Your Investment Apr 12th

A few weeks after the Christmas holidays, retail stocks go on sale, representing a good buying opportunity in mid to late January. The opportunity coincides with the earnings season.

Historically, the retail sector has outperformed from January 21st until April 12th - the start of the next earnings season. From 1990 to 2011, during its seasonally strong period, the retail sector has averaged 8.6%, compared with the S&P 500 which has averaged 2.0%. Not only has the retail sector had greater gains than the broad market, but it has also outperformed it on a fairly regular basis: 82% of the time.

6.6% extra & 82% of the time
better than the S&P 500

Retail Sector vs. S&P 500 1990 to 2011			
Jan 21 to Apr 12	S&P 500	Positive Retail	Diff
1990	1.5 %	9.7 %	8.1 %
1991	14.5	29.9	15.4
1992	-2.9	-2.7	0.2
1993	3.5	-0.6	-4.0
1994	-5.8	2.0	7.8
1995	9.1	7.4	-1.8
1996	4.1	19.7	15.7
1997	-5.0	6.0	11.0
1998	13.5	20.1	6.6
1999	8.1	23.4	15.2
2000	1.5	5.8	4.3
2001	-11.8	-0.5	11.3
2002	-1.5	6.7	8.2
2003	-3.7	6.5	10.3
2004	0.6	6.7	6.1
2005	1.1	-1.6	-2.7
2006	2.1	3.4	1.3
2007	1.2	-0.7	-1.9
2008	0.6	3.5	3.0
2009	6.4	25.1	18.7
2010	5.1	15.5	10.4
2011	2.7	4.4	1.7
Avg.	2.0 %	8.6 %	6.6 %
Fq > 0	73 %	77 %	82 %

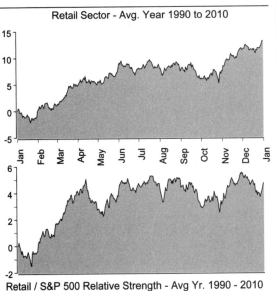

Retail Sector - Avg. Year 1990 to 2010

Retail / S&P 500 Relative Strength - Avg. Yr. 1990 - 2010

proximately 2/3 of the GDP. The retail sector benefits from the optimistic forecasts and tends to outperform.

Surprisingly, there have only been minimal drawdowns (losses) over the last twenty years during the retail seasonal period. The worst loss was 2.7% in 1992, and even in this year the retail sector beat the S&P 500.

From a seasonal basis, investors have been best served by exiting the Retail sector in April and then returning to it later at the end of October (see *Retail Shop Early* strategy).

Most investors think the best time to invest in retail stocks is before Black Friday in November. Yes, there is a positive seasonal cycle at this time, but it is not nearly as strong as the cycle from January to April.

The January retail bounce coincides with the "rosy" stock market analysts' forecasts that tend to occur at the beginning of the year. These forecasts generally rely on healthy consumer spending as it makes up ap-

(i) *Retail SP GIC Sector # 2550:*
An index designed to represent a cross section of retail companies
For more information on the retail sector, see www.standardandpoors.com.

16 MONDAY   016 / 350

17 TUESDAY   017 / 349

18 WEDNESDAY   018 / 348

19 THURSDAY   019 / 347

20 FRIDAY   020 / 346

WEEK 03

Market Indices & Rates
Weekly Values**

Stock Markets	2010	2011
Dow	10,473	11,839
S&P500	1,124	1,285
Nasdaq	2,271	2,721
TSX	11,601	13,406
FTSE	5,413	5,957
DAX	5,838	7,078
Nikkei	10,763	10,458
Hang Seng	21,203	24,122

Commodities	2010	2011
Oil	76.67	89.77
Gold	1116.0	1358.2

Bond Yields	2010	2011
USA 5 Yr Treasury	2.42	2.01
USA 10 Yr T	3.66	3.42
USA 20 Yr T	4.42	4.32
Moody's Aaa	5.22	5.07
Moody's Baa	6.16	6.12
CAN 5 Yr T	2.55	2.57
CAN 10 Yr T	3.43	3.28

Money Market	2010	2011
USA Fed Funds	0.25	0.25
USA 3 Mo T-B	0.06	0.16
CAN tgt overnight rate	0.25	1.00
CAN 3 Mo T-B	0.16	0.97

Foreign Exchange	2010	2011
USD/EUR	1.42	1.34
USD/GBP	1.63	1.59
CAN/USD	1.04	0.99
JPY/USD	90.69	82.57

JANUARY

M	T	W	T	F	S	S
						1
2	3	4	5	6	7	8
9	10	11	12	13	14	15
16	17	18	19	20	21	22
23	24	25	26	27	28	29
30	31					

FEBRUARY

M	T	W	T	F	S	S
		1	2	3	4	5
6	7	8	9	10	11	12
13	14	15	16	17	18	19
20	21	22	23	24	25	26
27	28	29				

MARCH

M	T	W	T	F	S	S
			1	2	3	4
5	6	7	8	9	10	11
12	13	14	15	16	17	18
19	20	21	22	23	24	25
26	27	28	29	30	31	

2010-11 Strategy Performance

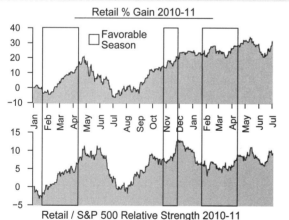

Retail % Gain 2010-11

Retail / S&P 500 Relative Strength 2010-11

At times the strength of the consumer can be mind boggling. Despite a high unemployment rate at the beginning of 2010 and a weak housing market, consumers continued to spend money, leading to the retail sector strongly outperforming the S&P 500. In 2011, the retail sector once again outperformed, but not by such a wide margin. Year after year this trade works. In the past when it has not worked, the losses have been relatively small. The above graph also includes the Retail trade in November (see *Retail – Shop Early* strategy for details).

** Weekly avg closing values- except Fed Funds & CAN overnight tgt rate weekly closing values.

TJX TJX Companies Inc.
January 22nd to March 30th

TJX is an off-price apparel and home fashions retailer that typically reports its fourth quarter earnings in approximately the third week of February. The company, like the retail sector, benefits from investors expecting positive results and a busy holiday season.

TJX has a very similar period of seasonal strength as the retail sector. The best seasonal period for investing in TJX has been from January 22nd to March 30th. From 1990 to 2011, investing in this period has produced an average gain of 14.4%, which is substantially better than the 1.4% performance of the S&P 500. It is also important to note that the stock has been positive more than three-quarters of the time during this period.

14.4% & positive 77% of the time

Equally impressive is the amount of times TJX has produced a large gain, versus a large loss. In the last twenty-two years, TJX has only had one loss of 10% or greater. This compares to eleven times where the company had gains of 10% or greater.

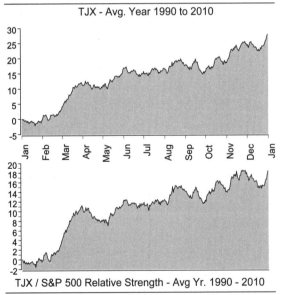

TJX vs. Retail vs. S&P 500
1990 to 2011

Jan 22 to Mar 30	S&P 500	Retail	TJX
		Positive	
1990	0.2%	6.3%	8.9%
1991	13.3	21.7	65.2
1992	-2.3	1.7	19.5
1993	3.8	3.0	21.7
1994	-6.1	-0.1	-0.5
1995	8.1	9.7	-5.4
1996	5.5	19.7	44.7
1997	-1.1	10.4	8.0
1998	12.6	19.7	25.8
1999	5.3	16.5	19.1
2000	3.2	5.1	33.6
2001	-13.6	1.7	16.5
2002	1.8	4.7	3.0
2003	-2.7	6.6	-6.6
2004	-1.8	5.4	3.6
2005	1.2	-0.6	-1.4
2006	3.1	4.5	4.0
2007	-0.7	-2.7	-10.0
2008	-0.8	1.4	13.4
2009	-6.3	8.1	29.6
2010	5.1	12.5	17.6
2011	3.5	3.5	6.4
Avg	1.4%	7.2%	14.4%
Fq > 0	59%	86%	77%

TJX - Avg. Year 1990 to 2010

TJX / S&P 500 Relative Strength - Avg Yr. 1990 - 2010

It is interesting to note that the seasonally strong period for TJX ends before one of the strongest months of the year, April. It is possible that by the end of March, after a typical strong run for one month after its fourth quarter earnings, that the full value of TJX's earnings report has already been priced into the stock and investors are looking to invest in companies that can provide more "juice." This is particularly true if the market is in good shape and showing signs of positive momentum.

On the other hand, if the market is starting to shows signs of weakening, then TJX is typically one of the better choices in the retail sector because of its price sensitive target market. When consumers are questioning the strength of the economy, consumers will "trade down," benefiting companies such as TJX. In a soft economy, investors anticipate consumers trading down and favor companies such as TJX. In this scenario, investors can hang on to TJX a bit longer than the end of March, but investors should still favor the March 30th date.

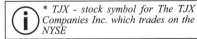
TJX - stock symbol for The TJX Companies Inc. which trades on the NYSE

23 MONDAY	023 / 343	**24** TUESDAY	024 / 342

25 WEDNESDAY	025 / 341	**26** THURSDAY	026 / 340

27 FRIDAY 027 / 339

WEEK 04

Market Indices & Rates
Weekly Values**

Stock Markets	2010	2011
Dow	10,163	11,951
S&P500	1,089	1,291
Nasdaq	2,192	2,724
TSX	11,286	13,384
FTSE	5,218	5,935
DAX	5,619	7,103
Nikkei	10,340	10,410
Hang Seng	20,244	23,766

Commodities	2010	2011
Oil	73.97	86.82
Gold	1090.0	1329.7

Bond Yields	2010	2011
USA 5 Yr Treasury	2.39	1.98
USA 10 Yr T	3.66	3.40
USA 20 Yr T	4.42	4.29
Moody's Aaa	5.28	5.06
Moody's Baa	6.23	6.08
CAN 5 Yr T	2.46	2.55
CAN 10 Yr T	3.36	3.29

Money Market	2010	2011
USA Fed Funds	0.25	0.25
USA 3 Mo T-B	0.07	0.16
CAN tgt overnight rate	0.25	1.00
CAN 3 Mo T-B	0.16	0.96

Foreign Exchange	2010	2011
USD/EUR	1.40	1.37
USD/GBP	1.61	1.59
CAN/USD	1.06	1.00
JPY/USD	90.03	82.40

2010-11 Strategy Performance

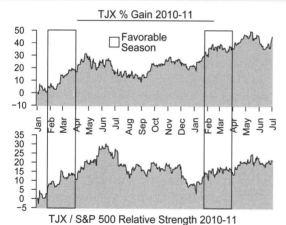

TJX % Gain 2010-11

TJX / S&P 500 Relative Strength 2010-11

In 2011, TJX started to outperform right on schedule at the beginning of its seasonally strong period in January. The company continued to produce positive returns into late April when the market started to turn down. Relative to the S&P 500, TJX maintained its outperformance into the beginning of June. Given the weakness in the market, this was not totally unexpected as investors were attracted to retail companies, such as TJX, that benefited from consumers "trading down."

** Weekly avg closing values- except Fed Funds & CAN overnight tgt rate weekly closing values.

JANUARY

M	T	W	T	F	S	S
						1
2	3	4	5	6	7	8
9	10	11	12	13	14	15
16	17	18	19	20	21	22
23	24	25	26	27	28	29
30	31					

FEBRUARY

M	T	W	T	F	S	S
	1	2	3	4	5
6	7	8	9	10	11	12
13	14	15	16	17	18	19
20	21	22	23	24	25	26
27	28	29				

MARCH

M	T	W	T	F	S	S
			1	2	3	4
5	6	7	8	9	10	11
12	13	14	15	16	17	18
19	20	21	22	23	24	25
26	27	28	29	30	31	

JANUARY PREDICTOR
Predicting the Rest of the Year

January has an uncanny trait of predicting the rest of the year. "As January goes, the rest of the year goes." In other words, if January is positive, the rest of the year tends to be positive, and if January is negative, the rest of the year tends to be negative.

72% accuracy predicting S&P 500 direction 1950 to 2010

There have been quite a few different theories as to why January is a good predictor for the rest of the year. Generally speaking, the explanation that makes the most sense is that investors and money managers are setting up their expectations for the rest of the year.

If money managers are expecting a good year, they are more inclined to move more money into the market in January, boosting the performance of January and the rest of the year. If money managers are expecting a sub-performance year, they are more inclined to hold back on funds in January, producing a negative January and rest of the year.

It is important to note, however, that January is much better at predicting a positive remainder of the year, as compared to a negative remainder.

Since 1950 it has correctly predicted positive "rest of the years," 33 out of 37 years or 89% of the time. This compares to predicting negative "rest of the years," 11 out of 24 times, or 48% of the time.

In other words, it is really a flip of the coin when January is negative. Investors should pay more attention to positive January performances, rather than negative performances in considering the future direction of the markets during the year.

> ⚠ *Basing a yearly investment decision on one month's returns is not considered to be a reasonable portfolio investment strategy and large returns can be missed. For example, in 2003 the January Predictor forecasted a negative rest of year return. The market returned an astonishing 30%.*

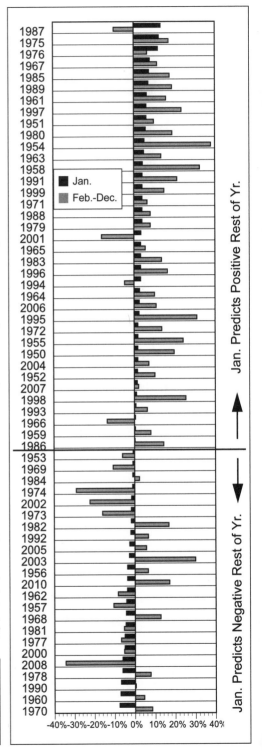

30 MONDAY 030 / 336

31 TUESDAY 031 / 335

1 WEDNESDAY 032 / 334

2 THURSDAY 033 / 333

3 FRIDAY 034 / 332

WEEK 05

Market Indices & Rates
Weekly Values**

Stock Markets	2010	2011
Dow	10,153	12,026
S&P500	1,084	1,303
Nasdaq	2,164	2,745
TSX	11,294	13,716
FTSE	5,197	5,960
DAX	5,601	7,171
Nikkei	10,279	10,389
Hang Seng	20,249	23,613

Commodities	2010	2011
Oil	74.59	90.68
Gold	1090.8	1335.7

Bond Yields	2010	2011
USA 5 Yr Treasury	2.33	2.10
USA 10 Yr T	3.66	3.54
USA 20 Yr T	4.42	4.41
Moody's Aaa	5.29	5.19
Moody's Baa	6.25	6.17
CAN 5 Yr T	2.46	2.62
CAN 10 Yr T	3.38	3.38

Money Market	2010	2011
USA Fed Funds	0.25	0.25
USA 3 Mo T-B	0.10	0.15
CAN tgt overnight rate	0.25	1.00
CAN 3 Mo T-B	0.17	0.95

Foreign Exchange	2010	2011
USD/EUR	1.38	1.37
USD/GBP	1.58	1.61
CAN/USD	1.07	0.99
JPY/USD	90.06	81.75

FEBRUARY

M	T	W	T	F	S	S
		1	2	3	4	5
6	7	8	9	10	11	12
13	14	15	16	17	18	19
20	21	22	23	24	25	26
27	28	29				

MARCH

M	T	W	T	F	S	S
			1	2	3	4
5	6	7	8	9	10	11
12	13	14	15	16	17	18
19	20	21	22	23	24	25
26	27	28	29	30	31	

APRIL

M	T	W	T	F	S	S
						1
2	3	4	5	6	7	8
9	10	11	12	13	14	15
16	17	18	19	20	21	22
23	24	25	26	27	28	29
30						

2010-2011 Strategy Performance

January Predictor S&P 500 (2010 & 2011)

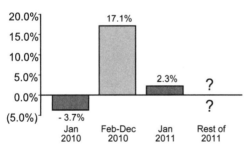

The press loves to publish yearly forecasts at the beginning of the year and often cites the Yale Hirsch's January Barometer from the *Stock Trader's Almanac*. The *January Predictor* is mainly added to this book because of investor interest, but investors should realize that basing an investment strategy on a one month indicator is risky and other factors should be considered in managing a portfolio.

The January results of the S&P 500 gaining 2.3% in 2011 predicted a positive rest of the year. At the time of writing this book, the S&P 500 is substantially lower than its close of 1286 at the end of January. As a result, there is only a very small chance that the *January Predictor* will be correct this year.

** Weekly avg closing values- except Fed Funds & CAN overnight tgt rate weekly closing values.

FEBRUARY

	MONDAY	TUESDAY	WEDNESDAY
WEEK 05	30	31	1 28
WEEK 06	6 23	7 22	8 21
WEEK 07	13 16	14 15	15 14
WEEK 08	20 9 CAN Market Closed - Family Day USA Market Closed - Presidents' Day	21 8	22 7
WEEK 09	27 2	28 1	29

THURSDAY		FRIDAY	
2	27	**3**	26
9	20	**10**	19
16	13	**17**	12
23	6	**24**	5
1		2	

MARCH

M	T	W	T	F	S	S
			1	2	3	4
5	6	7	8	9	10	11
12	13	14	15	16	17	18
19	20	21	22	23	24	25
26	27	28	29	30	31	

APRIL

M	T	W	T	F	S	S
						1
2	3	4	5	6	7	8
9	10	11	12	13	14	15
16	17	18	19	20	21	22
23	24	25	26	27	28	29
30						

MAY

M	T	W	T	F	S	S
	1	2	3	4	5	6
7	8	9	10	11	12	13
14	15	16	17	18	19	20
21	22	23	24	25	26	27
28	29	30	31			

JUNE

M	T	W	T	F	S	S
				1	2	3
4	5	6	7	8	9	10
11	12	13	14	15	16	17
18	19	20	21	22	23	24
25	26	27	28	29	30	

FEBRUARY
SUMMARY

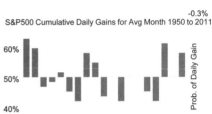

0.3%

0.1%

-0.1%

-0.3%

S&P500 Cumulative Daily Gains for Avg Month 1950 to 2011

	Dow Jones	S&P 500	Nasdaq	TSX Comp
Month Rank	9	11	9	6
# Up	35	33	20	15
# Down	27	29	20	12
% Pos	56	53	50	56
% Avg. Gain	0.0	-0.2	0.3	0.9

Dow & S&P 1950-June 2011, Nasdaq 1972-June 2011, TSX 1985-June 2011

♦ From 1950 to 2010, February has been the second worst month (S&P 500), producing a loss of 0.2% and positive only 52% of the time ♦ In February 2011, the S&P 500 uncharacteristically performed extremely well, producing a gain of 3.2% ♦ The *oil sector* and *oil stocks* tend to either do well in February or bottom towards the end of the month with a strong move into May ♦ For Canadian investors, *Suncor* starts its seasonal trend in February.

BEST / WORST FEBRUARY BROAD MKTS. 2002-2011

BEST FEBRUARY MARKETS

♦ Russell 2000 (2011) 5.4%
♦ TSX Comp (2005) 5.0%
♦ TSX Comp (2010) 4.8%

WORST FEBRUARY MARKETS

♦ Russell 3000 Value (2009) -13.8%
♦ Russell 2000 (2009) -12.3%
♦ Dow (2009) -11.7%

Index Values End of Month

	2002	2003	2004	2005	2006	2007	2008	2009	2010	2011
Dow	10,106	7,891	10,584	10,766	10,993	12,269	12,266	7,063	10,325	12,226
S&P 500	1,107	841	1,145	1,204	1,281	1,407	1,331	735	1,104	1,327
Nasdaq	1,731	1,338	2,030	2,052	2,281	2,416	2,271	1,378	2,238	2,782
TSX	7,638	6,555	8,788	9,668	11,688	13,045	13,583	8,123	11,630	14,131
Russell 1000	1,122	858	1,178	1,244	1,341	1,478	1,396	768	1,168	1,415
Russell 2000	1,166	896	1,455	1,576	1,816	1,972	1,705	967	1,562	2,046
Russell 3000 Growth	1,858	1,367	1,880	1,889	2,059	2,195	2,165	1,276	1,942	2,407
Russell 3000 Value	2,051	1,619	2,272	2,522	2,725	3,094	2,755	1,412	2,164	2,596

Percent Gain for February

	2002	2003	2004	2005	2006	2007	2008	2009	2010	2011
Dow	1.9	-2.0	0.9	2.6	1.2	-2.8	-3.0	-11.7	2.6	2.8
S&P 500	-2.1	-1.7	1.2	1.9	0.0	-2.2	-3.5	-11.0	2.9	3.2
Nasdaq	-10.5	1.3	-1.8	-0.5	-1.1	-1.9	-5.0	-6.7	4.2	3.0
TSX	-0.1	-0.2	3.1	5.0	-2.2	0.1	3.3	-6.6	4.8	4.3
Russell 1000	-2.1	-1.7	1.2	2.0	0.0	-1.9	-3.3	-10.7	3.1	3.3
Russell 2000	-2.8	-3.1	0.8	1.6	-0.3	-0.9	-3.8	-12.3	4.4	5.4
Russell 3000 Growth	-4.4	-0.7	0.5	1.0	-0.3	-1.9	-2.2	-7.9	3.3	3.3
Russell 3000 Value	0.0	-3.0	1.9	2.9	0.3	-1.8	-4.5	-13.8	3.0	3.6

February Market Avg. Performance 2002 to 2011[(1)]

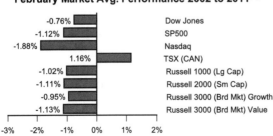

	-0.76%	Dow Jones
	-1.12%	SP500
-1.88%		Nasdaq
	1.16%	TSX (CAN)
	-1.02%	Russell 1000 (Lg Cap)
	-1.11%	Russell 2000 (Sm Cap)
	-0.95%	Russell 3000 (Brd Mkt) Growth
	-1.13%	Russell 3000 (Brd Mkt) Value

Interest Corner Feb[(2)]

	Fed Funds % [(3)]	3 Mo. T-Bill % [(4)]	10 Yr % [(5)]	20 Yr % [(6)]
2011	0.25	0.15	3.42	4.25
2010	0.25	0.13	3.61	4.40
2009	0.25	0.26	3.02	3.98
2008	3.00	1.85	3.53	4.37
2007	5.25	5.16	4.56	4.78

(1) Russell Data provided by Russell (2) Federal Reserve Bank of St. Louis- end of month values (3) Target rate set by FOMC (4)(5)(6) Constant yield maturities.

THACKRAY SECTOR THERMOMETER

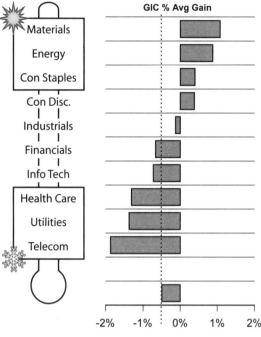

		GIC% Avg Gain
Materials		
Energy		
Con Staples		
Con Disc.		
Industrials		
Financials		
Info Tech		
Health Care		
Utilities		
Telecom		

-2% -1% 0% 1% 2%

GIC(2) % Avg Gain	Fq % Gain >S&P 500	SP GIC SECTOR 1990-2010(1)
1.1 %	67 %	Materials
0.9	48	Energy
0.4	52	Consumer Staples
0.4	71	Consumer Discretionary
-0.1	57	Industrials
-0.7	67	Financials
-0.7	52	Information Technology
-1.3	38	Health Care
-1.4	24	Utilities
-1.9 %	38 %	Telecom
-0.5 %	N/A %	S&P 500

Sector Commentary

♦ Although February is typically a mediocre month, there are four sectors that have produced positive results from 1990 to 2010: *materials, energy, consumer discretionary* and *consumer staples*. ♦ In 2011 (not included in results of TST), *energy* was the strongest sector producing a 6.8% gain, followed by the *consumer discretionary* which produced a gain of 5.8%. ♦ In 2011, the worst performing sector was utilities, producing a gain of 0.8%. The second worst sector was *information technology* with a gain of 1.8%. Both of these sectors are typically in the bottom four sectors for the month.

Sub-Sector Commentary

♦ In February 2011, *agriculture* performed well with a 13.8% gain, along with the *integrated oil & gas* sector with a 7.2% gain. ♦ *gold* stocks usually perform well in February (better than gold bullion) and in 2011, *gold stocks* (XAU) produced a gain of 7.7%. ♦ The *semiconductor* and *retail* sectors usually perform well in February, and in 2011 they maintained their strong performance with returns of 4.1% and 3.0% respectively.

		SELECTED SUB-SECTORS 1990-2010(3)
2.2 %	56 %	Semiconductor (SOX) 95-2010
1.8	62	Metals & Mining
1.6	71	Gold (XAU)
1.4	76	Retail
0.9	57	Airlines
0.8	48	Gold (London PM)
0.6	48	Integrated Oil & Gas
0.2	62	Transportation
0.0	48	Auto & Components
-0.4	62	Banks
-0.7	48	Software & Services
-1.4	47	Agriculture Products (94-2010)
-1.4	38	Pharmaceuticals
-1.8	56	Biotech (93-2010)

(1) Sector data provided by Standard and Poors (2) GIC is short form for Global Industry Classification (3) Sub Sector data provided by Standard and Poors, except where marked by symbol.

DuPont
January 28th to May 14th

DuPont is a diversified chemicals company that operates in seven segments: Agriculture & Nutrition, Electronics & Communications, Performance Chemicals, Performance Coatings, Performance Materials, Safety & Protection, and Pharmaceuticals.

The chemicals sector is a large part of the U.S. materials sector, which has a seasonally strong period from January 23rd to May 5th. DuPont has a similar seasonal trend that starts a few days later on January 28th. Investors can use technical analysis to determine if an earlier position in DuPont should be taken.

11.2% & positive 95% of the time

The DuPont seasonal trade has worked very well since 1990. It has produced an average gain of 11.2% and has been positive 95% of the time. It has also beaten the S&P 500, 82% of the time. Over this time period DuPont recorded only one large loss during its seasonal period. In 2000, Dupont lost 16.2% from January 28th to May 14th.

Jan 28 to May 14	S&P 500	DD	Diff
1990	3.9%	0.3%	-3.5%
1991	13.3	19.6	6.3
1992	0.5	11.7	11.3
1993	1.5	15.2	13.8
1994	-5.4	6.6	12.0
1995	10.6	21.6	11.0
1996	3.2	6.3	3.0
1997	8.5	4.6	-3.9
1998	15.1	34.9	19.7
1999	8.4	32.6	24.2
2000	2.4	-16.2	-18.6
2001	-6.5	12.8	19.3
2002	-5.3	3.2	8.4
2003	9.3	11.3	2.0
2004	-2.0	2.5	4.5
2005	-0.2	2.6	2.8
2006	3.3	13.4	10.1
2007	5.9	4.2	-1.7
2008	5.8	11.1	5.4
2009	6.9	24.9	18.1
2010	6.2	15.3	9.0
2011	2.7	7.2	4.4
Avg	4.0%	11.2%	7.2%
Fq > 0	77%	95%	82%

DuPont vs. S&P 500 — 1990 to 2011 (Positive)

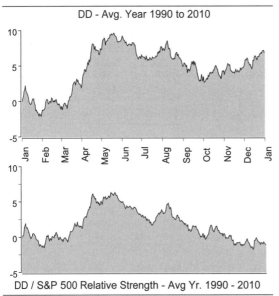

DD - Avg. Year 1990 to 2010

DD / S&P 500 Relative Strength - Avg Yr. 1990 - 2010

which has produced a gain of 4.2% and has been positive 71% of the time.

The materials sector tends to outperform the S&P 500 from October 28th to January 6th (see *Material Stocks - Material Gains* strategy). During this same time period, DuPont has produced approximately the same gain as the S&P 500 and has been positive less often.

If investors are interested in purchasing DuPont, on a seasonal basis it is clear that they should concentrate their efforts on the February to May seasonal period.

Investors should be aware that DuPont not does perform as well as the broad market from May 6th to the end of the of the year. In fact, on average it generated a loss of 1.8% and was only positive 43% of the time from 1990 to 2010. This compares to the S&P 500

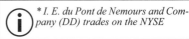
I. E. du Pont de Nemours and Company (DD) trades on the NYSE

6 MONDAY	037 / 329

7 TUESDAY	038 / 328

8 WEDNESDAY	039 / 327

9 THURSDAY	040 / 326

10 FRIDAY	041 / 325

WEEK 06

Market Indices & Rates
Weekly Values**

Stock Markets	2010	2011
Dow	10,050	12,227
S&P500	1,070	1,323
Nasdaq	2,157	2,794
TSX	11,316	13,819
FTSE	5,128	6,056
DAX	5,505	7,328
Nikkei	9,985	10,613
Hang Seng	19,965	23,148

Commodities	2010	2011
Oil	73.91	86.69
Gold	1072.6	1358.7

Bond Yields	2010	2011
USA 5 Yr Treasury	2.34	2.36
USA 10 Yr T	3.69	3.68
USA 20 Yr T	4.48	4.52
Moody's Aaa	5.36	5.28
Moody's Baa	6.36	6.22
CAN 5 Yr T	2.49	2.75
CAN 10 Yr T	3.42	3.46

Money Market	2010	2011
USA Fed Funds	0.25	0.25
USA 3 Mo T-B	0.11	0.14
CAN tgt overnight rate	0.25	1.00
CAN 3 Mo T-B	0.17	0.96

Foreign Exchange	2010	2011
USD/EUR	1.37	1.36
USD/GBP	1.57	1.61
CAN/USD	1.06	0.99
JPY/USD	89.73	82.74

FEBRUARY

M	T	W	T	F	S	S
	1	2	3	4	5	
6	7	8	9	10	11	12
13	14	15	16	17	18	19
20	21	22	23	24	25	26
27	28	29				

MARCH

M	T	W	T	F	S	S
			1	2	3	4
5	6	7	8	9	10	11
12	13	14	15	16	17	18
19	20	21	22	23	24	25
26	27	28	29	30	31	

APRIL

M	T	W	T	F	S	S
						1
2	3	4	5	6	7	8
9	10	11	12	13	14	15
16	17	18	19	20	21	22
23	24	25	26	27	28	29
30						

2010-11 Strategy Performance

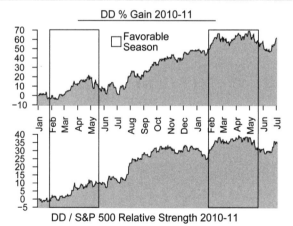

DD % Gain 2010-11

Favorable Season

DD / S&P 500 Relative Strength 2010-11

DuPont performed very well during its seasonally strong period in 2010 and 2011. It produced positive returns and outperformed the S&P 500 in both periods. Outside the seasonal period, during the summer and autumn of 2010, DuPont uncharacteristically outperformed the market. During this period, the market had a strong run and the cyclical stocks performed extremely well.

** Weekly avg closing values- except Fed Funds & CAN overnight tgt rate weekly closing values.

OIL – WINTER/SPRING STRATEGY
Ist of II Oil Stock Strategies for the Year
February 25th to May 9th

The *Oil- Winter/Spring Strategy* is one of the strongest seasonal outperformance trends. From 1984 to 2011, for the two and half months starting on February 25th and ending May 9th, the energy sector (XOI) has outperformed the S&P 500 by an average 4.4%.

What is even more impressive are the positive returns 24 out of 28 times, and the outperformance of the S&P 500, 23 out of 28 times.

> **4.4% extra and 24 out of 28 times positive, in just over two months**

XOI vs S&P 500 1984 to 2011			
Feb 25 to May 9	positive		
	S&P 500	XOI	Diff
1984	1.7 %	5.6 %	3.9 %
1985	1.4	4.9	3.5
1986	6.0	7.7	1.7
1987	3.7	25.5	21.8
1988	-3.0	5.6	8.6
1989	6.3	8.1	1.8
1990	5.8	-0.6	-6.3
1991	4.8	6.8	2.0
1992	0.9	5.8	4.9
1993	0.3	6.3	6.0
1994	-4.7	3.2	7.9
1995	7.3	10.3	3.1
1996	-2.1	2.2	4.3
1997	1.8	4.7	2.9
1998	7.5	9.8	2.3
1999	7.3	35.4	28.1
2000	4.3	22.2	17.9
2001	0.8	10.2	9.4
2002	-1.5	5.3	6.9
2003	12.1	5.7	-6.4
2004	-3.5	4.0	7.5
2005	-1.8	-1.0	0.8
2006	2.8	9.4	6.6
2007	4.2	10.1	5.8
2008	2.6	7.6	5.0
2009	20.2	15.8	-4.4
2010	0.5	-2.3	-2.8
2011	3.1	-0.6	-3.7
Avg	3.3 %	7.7 %	4.4 %
Fq > 0	79 %	86 %	82 %

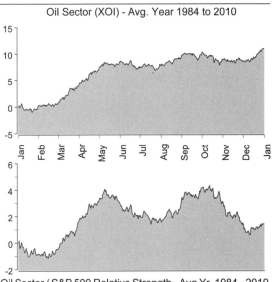

Oil Sector (XOI) - Avg. Year 1984 to 2010

Oil Sector / S&P 500 Relative Strength - Avg Yr. 1984 - 2010

A lot of investors assume that the time to buy oil stocks is just before the winter cold sets in. The rationale is that oil will climb in price as the temperature drops.

The results in the market have not supported this assumption. The dynamic of the price for a barrel of oil has more to do with oil inventory. Refineries have a choice: they can produce either gasoline or heating oil. As the winter progresses, refineries start to convert their operations from heating oil to gasoline.

During this switch-over time, low inventory levels of both heating oil and gasoline can drive up the price of a barrel of oil and oil stocks. In early May, before the kick-off of the driving season (Memorial Day in May), the refineries have finished their conversion to gasoline. The price of oil and oil stocks tend to decline.

Investors are given another chance for above average gains in the energy sector, when the second seasonal for oil stocks takes place in late July (*see Oil – Summer Autumn Strategy*). Although this seasonal cycle is not as strong as the February to May cycle, it is definitely worth while for seasonal investors to investigate.

> (i) *Amex Oil Index (XOI):*
> *An index designed to represent a cross section of widely held oil corporations involved in various phases of the oil industry.*
> *For more information on the XOI index, see www.cboe.com*

13 MONDAY	044 / 322	**14** TUESDAY	045 / 321

15 WEDNESDAY	046 / 320	**16** THURSDAY	047 / 319

17 FRIDAY 048 / 318

WEEK 07

Market Indices & Rates
Weekly Values**

Stock Markets	2010	2011
Dow	10,343	12,298
S&P500	1,103	1,336
Nasdaq	2,232	2,823
TSX	11,656	14,032
FTSE	5,274	6,071
DAX	5,631	7,409
Nikkei	10,163	10,792
Hang Seng	20,283	23,215

Commodities	2010	2011
Oil	78.30	85.34
Gold	1112.7	1374.3

Bond Yields	2010	2011
USA 5 Yr Treasury	2.42	2.34
USA 10 Yr T	3.74	3.60
USA 20 Yr T	4.56	4.45
Moody's Aaa	5.44	5.26
Moody's Baa	6.45	6.15
CAN 5 Yr T	2.54	2.78
CAN 10 Yr T	3.48	3.48

Money Market	2010	2011
USA Fed Funds	0.25	0.25
USA 3 Mo T-B	0.10	0.11
CAN tgt overnight rate	0.25	1.00
CAN 3 Mo T-B	0.16	0.96

Foreign Exchange	2010	2011
USD/EUR	1.36	1.36
USD/GBP	1.56	1.61
CAN/USD	1.05	0.99
JPY/USD	90.95	83.45

2010-11 Strategy Performance*

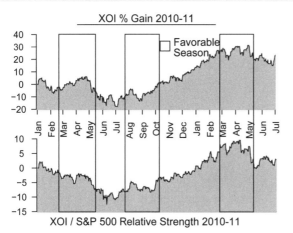

XOI % Gain 2010-11

XOI / S&P 500 Relative Strength 2010-11

FEBRUARY

M	T	W	T	F	S	S
		1	2	3	4	5
6	7	8	9	10	11	12
13	14	15	16	17	18	19
20	21	22	23	24	25	26
27	28	29				

MARCH

M	T	W	T	F	S	S
			1	2	3	4
5	6	7	8	9	10	11
12	13	14	15	16	17	18
19	20	21	22	23	24	25
26	27	28	29	30	31	

APRIL

M	T	W	T	F	S	S
						1
2	3	4	5	6	7	8
9	10	11	12	13	14	15
16	17	18	19	20	21	22
23	24	25	26	27	28	29
30						

The energy sector performed very well in its 2010 summer seasonal period (*Oil - Summer Strategy*) from late July to early October and continued to rally past its seasonal period with strong momentum. The rally lasted right up until the start of its second seasonal period in late February 2011. At that point, it had nothing left and was relatively flat for the remainder of its winter seasonal period.

** Weekly avg closing values- except Fed Funds & CAN overnight tgt rate weekly closing values.

SU [CA][US] Suncor Energy
February 18th to May 9th

Suncor is a Canadian premier integrated energy company, trading in both the Canadian and U.S. markets. For investors, it is often synonymous with the oil sands as that is where it derives most of its revenue.

The primary period of seasonal strength for Suncor is very similar to the energy sector trend in the U.S., starting in late February and lasting into early May. From 1993 to 2011 during the periods of February 18th to May 9th, Suncor has produced an average return of 13.7% and has been positive 89% of the time. This is substantially better than the 3.3% average return of the S&P TSX Composite.

13.7% & 84% of the time better than the S&P TSX Composite

During its seasonal period from 1990 to 2011, Suncor has produced returns of 10% or greater, nine times. This compares to the largest loss of 8.7%. In addition, it has outperformed the S&P TSX Composite sixteen out of nineteen times.

Suncor vs. S&P/TSX Composite
1993 to 2011

Feb 18 to May 9	TSX Comp.	Energy (Cdn)**	SU
1993	10.6%	21.4%	34.8%
1994	-5.2	4.1	2.6
1995	4.4	15.9	15.3
1996	2.3	0.8	3.3
1997	0.2	1.1	20.5
1998	10.6	5.2	5.6
1999	10.0	37.2	33.7
2000	-1.8	24.6	7.9
2001	-3.8	3.7	17.2
2002	1.6	14.9	13.9
2003	1.3	-1.4	-7.4
2004	-5.6	6.7	1.2
2005	-0.6	3.4	6.8
2006	4.9	6.6	13.5
2007	4.4	8.2	6.0
2008	9.8	22.6	29.9
2009	22.2	33.5	63.3
2010	0.5	-3.2	1.5
2011	-3.3	-4.9	-8.7
Avg	3.3%	10.5%	13.7%
Fq > 0	68%	84%	89%

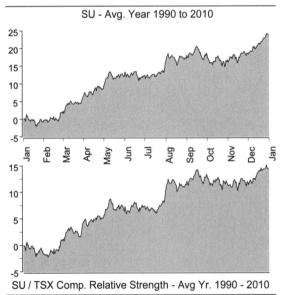

SU - Avg. Year 1990 to 2010

SU / TSX Comp. Relative Strength - Avg Yr. 1990 - 2010

It is not just Suncor that does well at this time of year, but also the Canadian energy sector. During the same time period, the sector produced an average return of 10.5% and was positive 84% of the time.

The driving price behind companies in the energy sector is ultimately the price of oil. Although there are operational issues with energy companies, in general if the price of oil increases, the stock prices of energy companies increase and vice versa. Interestingly, although Canadian and U.S. energy companies have similar seasonal patterns, Canadian energy companies will sometimes lead the way and start their seasonal outperformance before U.S. companies. It is possible that this can be attributed to different earnings release dates. Nevertheless, it is something that is attention worthy for investors.

Investors should also note that the broad energy sector also has a secondary seasonal cycle from late July to mid-September. Suncor mirrors this secondary cycle, outperforming the market at this time. As mentioned in the *Oil Winter/Spring Strategy*, this cycle tends not to be as strong as the February to May cycle.

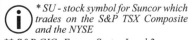

(i) * SU - stock symbol for Suncor which trades on the S&P TSX Composite and the NYSE

** S&P GICs Energy Sector Level 2

20 MONDAY 051 / 315

21 TUESDAY 052 / 314

22 WEDNESDAY 053 / 313

23 THURSDAY 054 / 312

24 FRIDAY 055 / 311

Market Indices & Rates
Weekly Values**

Stock Markets	2010	2011
Dow	10,337	12,129
S&P500	1,103	1,312
Nasdaq	2,233	2,750
TSX	11,589	13,960
FTSE	5,329	5,971
DAX	5,608	7,230
Nikkei	10,236	10,616
Hang Seng	20,495	22,999

Commodities	2010	2011
Oil	79.22	95.71
Gold	1105.6	1405.5

Bond Yields	2010	2011
USA 5 Yr Treasury	2.37	2.18
USA 10 Yr T	3.69	3.46
USA 20 Yr T	4.48	4.31
Moody's Aaa	5.31	5.17
Moody's Baa	6.33	6.06
CAN 5 Yr T	2.53	2.61
CAN 10 Yr T	3.44	3.32

Money Market	2010	2011
USA Fed Funds	0.25	0.25
USA 3 Mo T-B	0.12	0.13
CAN tgt overnight rate	0.25	1.00
CAN 3 Mo T-B	0.16	0.95

Foreign Exchange	2010	2011
USD/EUR	1.36	1.37
USD/GBP	1.54	1.62
CAN/USD	1.05	0.98
JPY/USD	89.91	82.40

FEBRUARY

M	T	W	T	F	S	S
			1	2	3	4	5
6	7	8	9	10	11	12
13	14	15	16	17	18	19
20	21	22	23	24	25	26
27	28	29				

MARCH

M	T	W	T	F	S	S
			1	2	3	4
5	6	7	8	9	10	11
12	13	14	15	16	17	18
19	20	21	22	23	24	25
26	27	28	29	30	31	

APRIL

M	T	W	T	F	S	S
						1
2	3	4	5	6	7	8
9	10	11	12	13	14	15
16	17	18	19	20	21	22
23	24	25	26	27	28	29
30						

2010 Strategy Performance

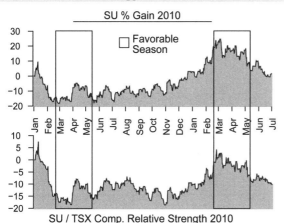

SU % Gain 2010

Favorable Season

SU / TSX Comp. Relative Strength 2010

Suncor's performance during its seasonally strong period in 2011 shows that company earnings do not always matter in the short-term. Suncor came out with stronger than expected earnings on both February 2nd and May 3rd, but under performed the S&P/TSX Composite during its seasonally strong period.

Earnings are very important, but in this case a pull back in the price of crude and exposure to Libyan oil operations had a dampening effect on the stock price.

** Weekly avg closing values- except Fed Funds & CAN overnight tgt rate weekly closing values.

PRESIDENTIAL ELECTION CYCLE
4th Year — 2nd Best Year

As 2012 is the fourth year of the Presidential election cycle, it is important to note that it is the second strongest year of the four year cycle.

Historically, the first two years of the cycle tend to be weak and the last two years tend to be strong. This pattern tends to repeat as the President makes tough decisions to bring the economy back on track in the first and second years of his term and in the third and fourth years, he creates policies that help get him re-elected.

2nd Best year of Presidential Cycle

The fourth year has been the second best year of the Presidential Cycle, having produced an average annual return of 7.5% and has been positive 67% of the time from 1901 to 2008. Since 1901

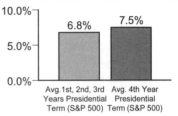

Avg. 4th Year Presidential Term vs. 1st, 2nd, 3rd Years S&P 500 1901 to 2008

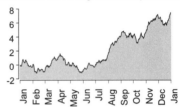

Dow Jones 4th Yr. Avg. % Growth (1903-2007)

the fourth year of the cycle has only been negative nine times.

This is in comparison to the average of the other years of the election cycle where the S&P 500 has returned 5.0% in the first year, 2.8% in the second year and 12.6% in the third year.

Given the persistent weak state of the economy, large government deficits and the economic crisis, the current President will have his work cut out for him. Obama has endeavored to spend his way out of the recession and if the history of the Presidential Cycle is any guide, the spending trend will continue. In the past, the government spending has helped to stimulate the economy and the stock market. The difference this time is that the government has record high deficits and investors are starting to worry about the long-term economic impact. Nevertheless, the fourth year of the cycle points to a higher finish.

President	1st Year	2nd Year	3rd Year	4th Year
1901 McKinley (R)	-8.7 %	-0.4 %	-23.6 %	41.7 %
1905 T. Roosevelt (R)	38.2	-1.9	-37.7	46.6
1909 Taft (R)	15.0	-17.9	0.4	7.6
1913 Wilson (D)	-10.3	-30.7	81.7	-4.2
1917 Wilson (D)	-21.7	10.5	30.5	-32.9
1921 Harding (R)	12.7	21.7	-3.3	26.2
1925 Coolidge (R)	30.0	0.3	28.8	48.2
1929 Hoover (R)	-17.2	-33.8	-52.7	-23.1
1933 Roosevelt (R)	66.8	4.1	38.6	24.8
1937 Roosevelt (R)	-32.8	28.0	-3.0	-12.7
1941 Roosevelt (R)	-15.3	7.6	13.8	12.1
1945 Roosevelt (R)	26.7	-8.1	2.3	-2.2
1949 Truman (D)	12.9	17.6	14.4	8.4
1953 Eisenhower (R)	-3.8	44.0	20.8	2.3
1957 Eisenhower (R)	-12.8	34.0	16.4	-9.3
1961 Kennedy (D)	18.7	-10.8	17.0	14.6
1965 Johnson (D)	10.9	-18.9	15.2	4.3
1969 Nixon (R)	-15.2	4.8	6.1	14.6
1973 Nixon (R)	-16.6	-27.6	38.3	17.9
1977 Carter (D)	-17.3	-3.2	4.2	14.9
1981 Reagan (R)	-9.2	19.6	20.3	-3.7
1985 Reagan (R)	27.7	22.6	2.3	11.9
1989 G. H. Bush (R)	27.0	-4.3	20.3	4.2
1993 Clinton (D)	13.7	2.1	33.5	26.0
1997 Clinton (D)	22.6	16.1	25.2	-6.2
2001 G.W. Bush (R)	-7.1	-16.8	25.3	3.1
2005 G.W. Bush (R)	-0.6	16.3	6.4	-33.8
Average Return	5.0	2.8	12.6	7.5
% of Years Positive	48 %	56 %	82 %	67 %

4 Year President Cycle- Dow Jones

(i) *The Presidential Cycle is closely aligned with the well known and closely followed 4 Year Cycle. In this cycle the market tends to bottom approximately every four years. The bottom is typically predicted to occur towards the end of the 2nd year in the Presidential Cycle at the time of mid-term elections.*

27 MONDAY	058 / 308	**28** TUESDAY	059 / 307

29 WEDNESDAY	060 / 306	**1** THURSDAY	061 / 305

2 FRIDAY		062 / 304

WEEK 09

Market Indices & Rates
Weekly Values**

Stock Markets	2010	2011
Dow	10,443	12,156
S&P500	1,123	1,319
Nasdaq	2,291	2,770
TSX	11,842	14,174
FTSE	5,510	5,968
DAX	5,796	7,216
Nikkei	10,232	10,630
Hang Seng	20,841	23,263

Commodities	2010	2011
Oil	80.19	101.03
Gold	1129.3	1423.2

Bond Yields	2010	2011
USA 5 Yr Treasury	2.29	2.17
USA 10 Yr T	3.63	3.47
USA 20 Yr T	4.43	4.31
Moody's Aaa	5.24	5.14
Moody's Baa	6.26	6.05
CAN 5 Yr T	2.61	2.69
CAN 10 Yr T	3.42	3.33

Money Market	2010	2011
USA Fed Funds	0.25	0.25
USA 3 Mo T-B	0.14	0.13
CAN tgt overnight rate	0.25	1.00
CAN 3 Mo T-B	0.18	0.95

Foreign Exchange	2010	2011
USD/EUR	1.36	1.39
USD/GBP	1.50	1.63
CAN/USD	1.03	0.97
JPY/USD	89.15	82.06

2nd Year Presidential Cycle Strategy Performance

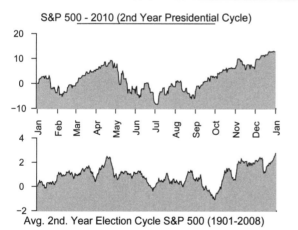

S&P 500 - 2010 (2nd Year Presidential Cycle)

Avg. 2nd. Year Election Cycle S&P 500 (1901-2008)

The second year of the Presidential Cycle (2010) tends to be the weakest year in the cycle. Since 1901 the second year has produced an average return of 2.8%. Although the magnitude in gains between the S&P 500 in 2010 and the average second year of the Presidential Cycle was substantially different (S&P 500 produced a gain of 12.8% in 2010), the patterns were similar – a peak in April, correction in the summer and then a rally at the end of the year.

** Weekly avg closing values- except Fed Funds & CAN overnight tgt rate weekly closing values.

MARCH

M	T	W	T	F	S	S
			1	2	3	4
5	6	7	8	9	10	11
12	13	14	15	16	17	18
19	20	21	22	23	24	25
26	27	28	29	30	31	

APRIL

M	T	W	T	F	S	S
						1
2	3	4	5	6	7	8
9	10	11	12	13	14	15
16	17	18	19	20	21	22
23	24	25	26	27	28	29
30						

MAY

M	T	W	T	F	S	S
	1	2	3	4	5	6
7	8	9	10	11	12	13
14	15	16	17	18	19	20
21	22	23	24	25	26	27
28	29	30	31			

MARCH

	MONDAY	TUESDAY	WEDNESDAY
WEEK 09	27	28	29
WEEK 10	**5** 26	**6** 25	**7** 24
WEEK 11	**12** 19	**13** 18	**14** 17
WEEK 12	**19** 12	**20** 11	**21** 10
WEEK 13	**26** 5	**27** 4	**28** 3

THURSDAY	FRIDAY
1 30	**2** 29
8 23	**9** 22
15 16	**16** 15
22 9	**23** 8
29 2	**30** 1

APRIL

M	T	W	T	F	S	S
						1
2	3	4	5	6	7	8
9	10	11	12	13	14	15
16	17	18	19	20	21	22
23	24	25	26	27	28	29
30						

MAY

M	T	W	T	F	S	S
	1	2	3	4	5	6
7	8	9	10	11	12	13
14	15	16	17	18	19	20
21	22	23	24	25	26	27
28	29	30	31			

JUNE

M	T	W	T	F	S	S
				1	2	3
4	5	6	7	8	9	10
11	12	13	14	15	16	17
18	19	20	21	22	23	24
25	26	27	28	29	30	

JULY

M	T	W	T	F	S	S
						1
2	3	4	5	6	7	8
9	10	11	12	13	14	15
16	17	18	19	20	21	22
23	24	25	26	27	28	29
30	31					

MARCH
S U M M A R Y

	Dow Jones	S&P 500	Nasdaq	TSX Comp
Month Rank	5	4	7	3
# Up	40	40	25	17
# Down	22	22	15	10
% Pos	65	65	63	63
% Avg. Gain	1.1	1.1	0.6	1.3

Dow & S&P 1950-June 2011, Nasdaq 1972-June 2011, TSX 1985-June 2011

S&P500 Cumulative Daily Gains for Avg Month 1950 to 2011

♦ In March 2011, the S&P 500 corrected mid-month after a strong January and February, ending up with a gain of 1.3%. ♦ One of the main causes of the mid-month correction was the global economic slowdown as the result of the devastating tsunami that occurred on March 11th. Although Japan continued to suffer economic hardship, global concerns faded. A sector shift took place in the market at this time, with the defensives starting to uncharacteristically perform strongly at this time of the year- foreshadowing a possible future correction.

BEST / WORST MARCH BROAD MKTS. 2002-2011

BEST MARCH MARKETS
- ♦ Nasdaq (2009) 10.9%
- ♦ Russell 3000 Gr (2009) 8.7%
- ♦ Russell 2000 (2009) 8.7%

WORST MARCH MARKETS
- ♦ TSX Comp (2003) -3.2%
- ♦ Russell 2000 (2005) -3.0%
- ♦ Nasdaq (2005) -2.6%

Index Values End of Month

	2002	2003	2004	2005	2006	2007	2008	2009	2010	2011
Dow	10,404	7,992	10,358	10,504	11,109	12,354	12,263	7,609	10,857	12,320
S&P 500	1,147	848	1,126	1,181	1,295	1,421	1,323	798	1,169	1,326
Nasdaq	1,845	1,341	1,994	1,999	2,340	2,422	2,279	1,529	2,398	2,781
TSX	7,851	6,343	8,586	9,612	12,111	13,166	13,350	8,720	12,038	14,116
Russell 1000	1,167	866	1,160	1,222	1,359	1,492	1,385	834	1,238	1,417
Russell 2000	1,259	906	1,467	1,529	1,902	1,990	1,710	1,051	1,687	2,096
Russell 3000 Growth	1,928	1,391	1,847	1,850	2,094	2,206	2,149	1,387	2,054	2,414
Russell 3000 Value	2,150	1,620	2,252	2,481	2,765	3,137	2,733	1,529	2,304	2,604

Percent Gain for March

	2002	2003	2004	2005	2006	2007	2008	2009	2010	2011
Dow	2.9	1.3	-2.1	-2.4	1.1	0.7	0.0	7.7	5.1	0.8
S&P 500	3.7	0.8	-1.6	-1.9	1.1	1.0	-0.6	8.5	5.9	-0.1
Nasdaq	6.6	0.3	-1.8	-2.6	2.6	0.2	0.3	10.9	7.1	0.0
TSX	2.8	-3.2	-2.3	-0.6	3.6	0.9	-1.7	7.4	3.5	-0.1
Russell 1000	4.0	0.9	-1.5	-1.7	1.3	0.9	-0.8	8.5	6.0	0.1
Russell 2000	7.9	1.1	0.8	-3.0	4.7	0.9	0.3	8.7	8.0	2.4
Russell 3000 Growth	3.7	1.7	-1.8	-2.1	1.7	0.5	-0.7	8.7	5.8	0.3
Russell 3000 Value	4.8	0.0	-0.9	-1.6	1.5	1.4	-0.8	8.3	6.5	0.3

March Market Avg. Performance 2002 to 2011[1]

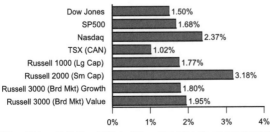

- Dow Jones: 1.50%
- SP500: 1.68%
- Nasdaq: 2.37%
- TSX (CAN): 1.02%
- Russell 1000 (Lg Cap): 1.77%
- Russell 2000 (Sm Cap): 3.18%
- Russell 3000 (Brd Mkt) Growth: 1.80%
- Russell 3000 (Brd Mkt) Value: 1.95%

Interest Corner Mar[2]

	Fed Funds %[3]	3 Mo. T-Bill %[4]	10 Yr %[5]	20 Yr %[6]
2011	0.25	0.09	3.47	4.29
2010	0.25	0.16	3.84	4.55
2009	0.25	0.21	2.71	3.61
2008	2.25	1.38	3.45	4.30
2007	5.25	5.04	4.65	4.92

(1) Russell Data provided by Russell (2) Federal Reserve Bank of St. Louis- end of month values (3) Target rate set by FOMC (4)(5)(6) Constant yield maturities.

THACKRAY SECTOR THERMOMETER

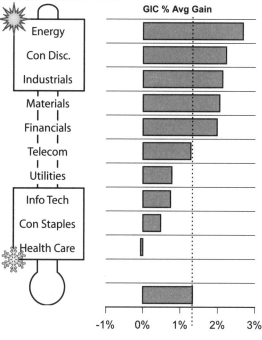

GIC[2] % Avg Gain	Fq % Gain >S&P 500	SP GIC SECTOR 1990-2010[1]
2.7 %	62 %	Energy
2.2	76	Consumer Discretionary
2.1	71	Industrials
2.0	52	Materials
2.0	57	Financials
1.3	57	Telecom
0.8	48	Utilities
0.7	43	Information Technology
0.5	48	Consumer Staples
-0.1 %	24 %	Health Care
1.3 %	N/A %	S&P 500

Sector Commentary

♦ Once again in March 2011 the *industrials* sector was one of the top performing sectors, producing a 1.7% gain. ♦ The *health care* sector was definitely the big surprise of the month. Typically this sector is at the bottom of the pack, but as investors started to become more concerned with market valuations, they started to switch over to some of the defensive sectors - *health care* was the first sector to benefit and ended up producing a gain of 1.7% in March.

Sub-Sector Commentary

♦ The *airlines, biotech* and *transportation* sub-sectors were at the top of the list in performance for March 2011, producing gains of 6.8%, 6.7% and 3.2% respectively. ♦ The *airlines* and *transportation* sub-sectors are usually at the top of the list. *Biotech* is typically one of the worst performing, sectors but with the *health care* sector performing well, *biotech* responded. ♦ The *retail* sector is typically one of the best performing sub-sectors, but it only managed to achieve a mediocre 0.6% gain.

SELECTED SUB-SECTORS 1990-2010[3]		
3.9 %	76 %	Retail
3.6	62	Airlines
2.6	57	Integrated Oil & Gas
2.3	71	Transportation
1.7	62	Software & Services
1.6	44	Semiconductor (SOX) 95-2010
1.4	52	Auto & Components
1.4	43	Metals & Mining
1.3	48	Banks
0.2	29	Agriculture Products (94-2010)
0.2	38	Gold (XAU)
0.1	24	Pharmaceuticals
-0.9	38	Gold (London PM)
-1.0	28	Biotech (93-2010)

(1) Sector data provided by Standard and Poors (2) GIC is short form for Global Industry Classification (3) Sub Sector data provided by Standard and Poors, except where marked by symbol.

AMD vs. INTC
AMD vs. Intel
Feb 24 to May 5 & May 6 to Jul 29

The two heavy weight semiconductor fabricators, AMD and Intel, have benefited immensely from the proliferation of low cost computers, particularly in the 1990's. Since 2000 the stock price of both companies has lost ground. Despite the ups and downs of the semiconductor market, both Intel and AMD have still exhibited seasonal trends.

Generally, from the end of February to the beginning of May, AMD has shown a fairly strong positive seasonal trend. From February 24th to May 5th, for the time period 1990 to 2011, AMD has produced an average return of 20.5% and has been positive 64% of the time. The frequency level of positive returns is acceptable, but it is not extraordinarily high. Given that the size of the losses are relatively small compared to the gains during this time period, AMD is still a stock worth considering at this time.

47% extra & 82% of the time positive

From May 6th to July 29th, AMD and Intel have very different seasonal patterns – AMD tends to decrease and INTC tends to increase. This is the makings of a great pair trade. On average AMD has produced a loss of 17.8% and INTC has produced a gain of 3.2%. The frequency of success for both trades is 82% and 64% respectively.

Putting the two trades together, Feb-May (long AMD) and May-Jul (long INTC and short AMD) has produced an average gain of 47.4% and has been positive 82% of the time.

Investors should also know that there are other profitable time periods to trade both INTC and AMD. Both stocks tend to have a weak September and have a strong October and November. The strength of the February to July strategy is the positive frequency of the pair trade.

 Intel (INTC) trades on the Nasdaq. Advanced Micro Devices Inc. (AMD) trades on the NYSE.

Long AMD & Short INTC - Feb 24 to May 5
Short AMD & Long INTC - May 6 to July 29

	Pos. when Long		
	Neg. when Short		

Year	Feb 24 to May 5 Pos. AMD	May 6 to Jul 29 Neg. AMD	May 6 to Jul 29 Pos. INTC	Compound Growth
1990	8.1 %	-14.9 %	3.0 %	27.4 %
1991	56.5	-15.5	-6.2	71.0
1992	-7.7	-52.1	8.0	47.8
1993	38.0	-19.1	4.4	70.4
1994	14.3	8.0	0.3	5.5
1995	17.4	-4.0	23.6	49.7
1996	-4.9	-37.8	6.1	36.9
1997	28.4	-22.7	8.5	68.4
1998	24.1	-39.1	3.4	76.8
1999	-7.7	1.1	8.6	-0.7
2000	124.1	-22.8	4.7	185.6
2001	40.2	-43.0	-5.4	92.9
2002	-14.0	-26.2	-28.9	-16.3
2003	40.5	-3.4	30.9	88.7
2004	2.6	-17.5	-7.5	12.8
2005	-11.2	36.2	11.9	-32.8
2006	-14.8	-44.5	-6.8	17.4
2007	-7.9	2.5	7.5	-3.3
2008	-2.7	-35.5	-4.4	27.6
2009	113.9	-14.1	20.1	186.9
2010	10.1	-9.3	-5.2	14.7
2011	3.7	-17.3	-5.4	16.0
Avg.	20.5 %	-17.8 %	3.2 %	47.4 %

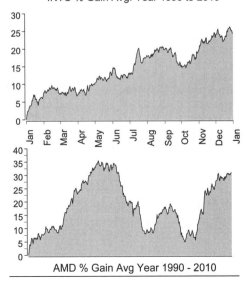

INTC % Gain Avg. Year 1990 to 2010

AMD % Gain Avg Year 1990 - 2010

5 MONDAY	065 / 301	**6** TUESDAY	066 / 300

7 WEDNESDAY	067 / 299	**8** THURSDAY	068 / 298

9 FRIDAY	069 / 297

Market Indices & Rates
Weekly Values**

Stock Markets	2010	2011
Dow	10,584	12,109
S&P500	1,145	1,310
Nasdaq	2,354	2,736
TSX	11,967	13,861
FTSE	5,619	5,912
DAX	5,914	7,101
Nikkei	10,627	10,462
Hang Seng	21,210	23,540

Commodities	2010	2011
Oil	81.76	103.74
Gold	1114.5	1423.9

Bond Yields	2010	2011
USA 5 Yr Treasury	2.39	2.14
USA 10 Yr T	3.72	3.46
USA 20 Yr T	4.51	4.33
Moody's Aaa	5.28	5.17
Moody's Baa	6.30	6.08
CAN 5 Yr T	2.81	2.74
CAN 10 Yr T	3.52	3.33

Money Market	2010	2011
USA Fed Funds	0.25	0.25
USA 3 Mo T-B	0.16	0.10
CAN tgt overnight rate	0.25	1.00
CAN 3 Mo T-B	0.20	0.95

Foreign Exchange	2010	2011
USD/EUR	1.37	1.39
USD/GBP	1.51	1.61
CAN/USD	1.02	0.97
JPY/USD	90.37	82.49

2010-11 Strategy Performance

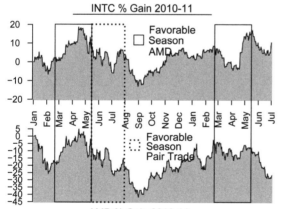

INTC % Gain 2010-11

AMD % Gain 2010-11

MARCH

M	T	W	T	F	S	S
			1	2	3	4
5	6	7	8	9	10	11
12	13	14	15	16	17	18
19	20	21	22	23	24	25
26	27	28	29	30	31	

APRIL

M	T	W	T	F	S	S
						1
2	3	4	5	6	7	8
9	10	11	12	13	14	15
16	17	18	19	20	21	22
23	24	25	26	27	28	29
30						

MAY

M	T	W	T	F	S	S
	1	2	3	4	5	6
7	8	9	10	11	12	13
14	15	16	17	18	19	20
21	22	23	24	25	26	27
28	29	30	31			

In 2010 and 2011, AMD increased from late February to early May and then decreased from early May to July. Intel also decreased in the May to July cycles for both years. Overall, the AMD vs. Intel trade worked because the gains in the short position of AMD offset the loses in the long position of Intel.

Investors should be careful with a short position in AMD in 2012 from May to July as the company is expected to launch the long awaited energy efficient Bulldozer semiconductors in late 2011.

** Weekly avg closing values- except Fed Funds & CAN overnight tgt rate weekly closing values.

WITCHES' HANGOVER
Day After Witching Day – Worst Day of the Month

Double, double toil and trouble;
Fire burn and cauldron bubble.
(Shakespeare, *Macbeth*, Act IV, Scene 1)

Looking for a negative day to establish a long position, or even short the market? In our book *Time In Time Out, Outsmart the Market Using Calendar Investment Strategies*, Bruce Lindsay and I coined the term "Witches' Hangover" (WH) to describe the most negative day of the month. It is aptly coined because it is the trading day after Witching Day (WD).

WH avg. loss 0.16%

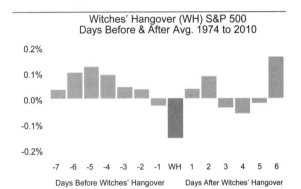

Witches' Hangover (WH) S&P 500
Days Before & After Avg. 1974 to 2010

Days Before Witches' Hangover   Days After Witches' Hangover

Witching Day (WD), the third Friday of every month, has a track record of volatility and negative performance. This is the day that stock options and futures expire.

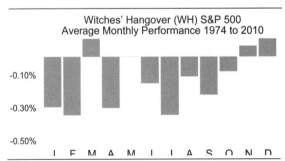

Witches' Hangover (WH) S&P 500
Average Monthly Performance 1974 to 2010

Although investors have been led to believe that Witching Day is the worst day of the month, Witches' Hangover has produced a bigger negative performance. This may be a result of investors, after a Friday of volatility and poor performance, suffering a stock market hangover and selling into the market on the Monday. In the

	Daily Avg. Gains for WD & WH S&P 500 1974 to 2010	
	Negative	
	WD	WH
1974	-0.54 %	-0.64 %
1975	-0.13	-0.23
1976	-0.01	0.03
1977	-0.07	-0.26
1978	-0.35	-0.04
1979	-0.16	0.03
1980	-0.14	-0.13
1981	0.16	-0.19
1982	0.32	0.24
1983	-0.09	-0.07
1984	-0.33	-0.20
1985	0.04	0.27
1986	0.23	0.07
1987	-0.02	-1.81
1988	0.62	-0.27
1989	0.22	-0.56
1990	0.02	-0.69
1991	-0.11	-0.33
1992	0.15	-0.24
1993	-0.13	-0.12
1994	-0.19	-0.34
1995	-0.02	0.08
1996	0.27	0.09
1997	-0.46	0.10
1998	0.37	0.55
1999	0.06	0.07
2000	-0.81	-0.44
2001	-0.72	0.45
2002	-0.26	-0.55
2003	0.30	-0.86
2004	-0.03	-0.12
2005	-0.05	-0.08
2006	-0.13	-0.02
2007	0.28	0.00
2008	1.03	0.36
2009	-0.10	-0.16
2010	-0.33	0.25
Avg.	-0.03 %	-0.16 %

graph "Witches' Hangover (WH) - Days Before & After Avg" the average daily performance of Witches' Hangover is marked WH and is the darker column. Witching Day (WD) is the previous day. WH is clearly the worst day. Together they make a wicked pair.

Witches' Hangover is a one day strategy and the average investor should not make investment portfolio decisions on one day performances.

MARCH

12 MONDAY	072 / 294	**13** TUESDAY	073 / 293

14 WEDNESDAY	074 / 292	**15** THURSDAY	075 / 291

16 FRIDAY	076 / 290

WEEK 11

**Market Indices & Rates
Weekly Values****

Stock Markets	2010	2011
Dow	10,717	11,819
S&P500	1,160	1,278
Nasdaq	2,379	2,653
TSX	12,037	13,645
FTSE	5,630	5,697
DAX	5,979	6,670
Nikkei	10,778	9,098
Hang Seng	21,238	22,662

Commodities	2010	2011
Oil	81.46	99.77
Gold	1115.8	1409.7

Bond Yields	2010	2011
USA 5 Yr Treasury	2.42	1.95
USA 10 Yr T	3.68	3.29
USA 20 Yr T	4.43	4.18
Moody's Aaa	5.21	5.07
Moody's Baa	6.21	5.98
CAN 5 Yr T	2.79	2.52
CAN 10 Yr T	3.47	3.18

Money Market	2010	2011
USA Fed Funds	0.25	0.25
USA 3 Mo T-B	0.16	0.09
CAN tgt overnight rate	0.25	1.00
CAN 3 Mo T-B	0.22	0.91

Foreign Exchange	2010	2011
USD/EUR	1.37	1.40
USD/GBP	1.52	1.61
CAN/USD	1.02	0.98
JPY/USD	90.42	80.28

2010 Strategy Performance

Witches' Hangover Performance by Month S&P 500 (2010)

Although the day after Witching day had a positive average performance in 2010, buried in the average number are some large moves up and down. January, September and October produced large positive results. In these months the market was rallying strongly, and overcame the negative effects of Witches' Hangover.

In 2010 Witching Day produced an average negative return. Pairing Witching Day and Witches' Hangover proved to be successful.

Although the day after Witches' Hangover is the most negative day of the month, it is important for investors to remember that large macro trends can overwhelm the strength of the strategy.

** Weekly avg closing values- except Fed Funds & CAN overnight tgt rate weekly closing values.

MARCH

M	T	W	T	F	S	S
			1	2	3	4
5	6	7	8	9	10	11
12	13	14	15	16	17	18
19	20	21	22	23	24	25
26	27	28	29	30	31	

APRIL

M	T	W	T	F	S	S
						1
2	3	4	5	6	7	8
9	10	11	12	13	14	15
16	17	18	19	20	21	22
23	24	25	26	27	28	29
30						

MAY

M	T	W	T	F	S	S
	1	2	3	4	5	6
7	8	9	10	11	12	13
14	15	16	17	18	19	20
21	22	23	24	25	26	27
28	29	30	31			

SUPER SEVEN DAYS
7 Best Days of the Month

The end of the month tends to be an excellent time to invest: portfolio managers "window dress" (adjust their portfolios to look good for month end reports), investors stop procrastinating and invest their extra cash, and brokers try to increase their commissions by investing their client's extra cash.

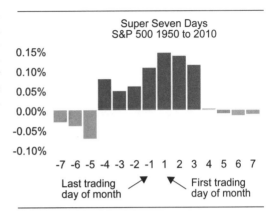

*From 1950 to 2010
All 7 days better
than market average*

All of these factors tend to produce above average returns in the market during the days around month end.

The above graph illustrates the strength of the Super Seven days. The Super Seven days are the last four trading days of the month and the first three trading days of the next month represented by the dark columns from day -4 to day 3. All of the Super Seven days have daily average gains above the daily market average gain of 0.03% (since 1950).

% Gain Super Seven Day Period From 2001 to 2010

	2001	2002	2003	2004	2005	2006	2007	2008	2009	2010	Avg.
Jan	-0.2 %	-3.8 %	-1.1 %	-2.5 %	1.8 %	-0.1 %	1.6 %	-4.5	-0.5	0.0	-0.9 %
Feb	-0.9	5.2	-0.3	0.9	2.2	-0.4	-5.6	-2.8	4.1	1.0	-0.5
Mar	-4.3	-2.0	0.2	3.7	0.9	0.8	0.1	1.2	3.5	2.0	0.6
Apr	3.2	-1.8	1.7	-1.2	1.2	0.0	1.5	1.3	4.3	-3.8	0.6
May	-0.7	-3.1	5.7	1.9	0.2	0.5	1.6	0.1	5.0	2.7	1.4
Jun	0.1	-3.6	0.2	-2.1	0.3	1.9	1.8	-3.9	-0.2	-4.2	-1.0
Jul	2.0	-0.5	-3.3	1.3	1.3	0.9	-5.6	2.2	2.1	1.1	0.1
Aug	-6.2	-7.3	3.4	0.8	1.7	0.4	0.8	-2.4	-2.4	4.7	-0.6
Sep	6.9	0.0	2.0	2.9	-1.6	1.8	1.4	-7.3	-1.0	1.1	0.6
Oct	0.2	2.0	2.0	4.4	2.0	-1.3	-0.8	12.2	-1.9	1.0	2.0
Nov	1.1	-2.6	2.8	1.2	-0.3	1.0	5.5	8.8	-0.6	3.7	2.1
Dec	2.4	4.1	2.7	-1.8	0.4	-0.1	-5.7	7.7	0.9	1.5	1.2
Avg.	0.3	-1.1	1.3	0.8	0.8	0.0	0.0	1.1	0.4	0.9	0.5

Although the Super Seven has done extremely well, there have been two trouble spots of negative performance. First, in 1998 when the *Asian Financial Flu* currency crisis struck the market; the market had three separate declines of more than 10%, which in turn resulted in three negative performances of the Super Seven greater than 5% at month ends.

> ⚠ *Historically it has been best not to use the Super Seven for July and August. Both of these months have negative average performances and have been negative more often than positive over the last ten years.*

The months affected were July, August and September. Second, 2002 was a disastrous year for the market. The first major decline started on March 12 and pushed the market down more than 30%. The second major decline started on August 22 and pushed the market down more than 15%. Both of these declines had a large effect on the results of the Super Seven for the year. Despite these negative periods, the Super Seven has outperformed the broad market over the last ten years.

19 MONDAY	079 / 287	**20** TUESDAY	080 / 286

---

21 WEDNESDAY	081 / 285	**22** THURSDAY	082 / 284

---

23 FRIDAY
083 / 283

WEEK 12

Market Indices & Rates
Weekly Values**

Stock Markets	2010	2011
Dow	10,840	12,106
S&P500	1,168	1,303
Nasdaq	2,400	2,711
TSX	11,978	14,034
FTSE	5,685	5,825
DAX	6,059	6,856
Nikkei	10,854	9,507
Hang Seng	20,952	22,888

Commodities	2010	2011
Oil	80.68	104.32
Gold	1095.8	1436.1

Bond Yields	2010	2011
USA 5 Yr Treasury	2.55	2.10
USA 10 Yr T	3.79	3.38
USA 20 Yr T	4.53	4.22
Moody's Aaa	5.30	5.10
Moody's Baa	6.28	6.00
CAN 5 Yr T	2.84	2.60
CAN 10 Yr T	3.51	3.21

Money Market	2010	2011
USA Fed Funds	0.25	0.25
USA 3 Mo T-B	0.14	0.09
CAN tgt overnight rate	0.25	1.00
CAN 3 Mo T-B	0.24	0.91

Foreign Exchange	2010	2011
USD/EUR	1.34	1.42
USD/GBP	1.49	1.62
CAN/USD	1.02	0.98
JPY/USD	91.62	81.05

MARCH

M	T	W	T	F	S	S
			1	2	3	4
5	6	7	8	9	10	11
12	13	14	15	16	17	18
19	20	21	22	23	24	25
26	27	28	29	30	31	

APRIL

M	T	W	T	F	S	S
						1
2	3	4	5	6	7	8
9	10	11	12	13	14	15
16	17	18	19	20	21	22
23	24	25	26	27	28	29
30						

MAY

M	T	W	T	F	S	S
	1	2	3	4	5	6
7	8	9	10	11	12	13
14	15	16	17	18	19	20
21	22	23	24	25	26	27
28	29	30	31			

2010 Strategy Performance

Super Seven Days By Month S&P 500 (2010)

The Super Seven strategy was positive in 2010 mainly as a result of the gains in March, April and May. On average in 2010 all of the gains for the strategy were made in the first few days of the month, rather than the last few days of the preceding month. This phenomenon often happens in consolidating or bear markets – where fewer days produce most of the gain, particularly the first few days of the month. In addition the first day of the month tends to be the strongest (see *First Day of the Month* strategy).

** Weekly avg closing values- except Fed Funds & CAN overnight tgt rate weekly closing values.

CANADIANS GIVE 3 CHEERS FOR AMERICAN HOLIDAYS

When I used to work on the retail side of the investment business I was always amazed at how often the Canadian market increased on American holidays, when the Canadian stock market was open and the American market was closed.

The holiday always had light volume, tended not to have large increases or decreases, but nevertheless usually ended the day with a gain.

1% average gain from 1977 to 2010 and 94% of the time positive

How the trade works

For the three big holidays in the United States that do not exist in Canada (Memorial, Independence and U.S. Thanksgiving Days), buy at the end of the market day before the holiday (TSX Composite) and sell at the end of the U.S. holiday when the U.S markets are closed.

For U.S. investors to take advantage of this trade they must have access to the TSX Composite. Unfortunately, as of the current time SEC regulations do not allow Americans to purchase foreign ETFs.

Generally, markets perform well around most major American holidays, hence the trading strategies for American holidays included in this book. The typical U.S. holiday trade is to get into the stock market the day before the holiday and then exit the day after the holiday.

The main reason for the strong performance around these holidays is a lack of institutional involvement in the markets, allowing bullish retail investors to push up the markets.

On the actual holidays, there are no economic news releases in America and very seldom is there anything released in Canada of significance. During market hours, without any influences the market tends to float, preferring to wait until the next day before making any significant moves.

Despite this laxidasical action during the day, the TSX Comp tends to end the day on a gain. This is true for the three major holidays that are covered in this book: Memorial, Independence and Thanksgiving Day.

From a theoretical perspective a lot of the gain that is captured on the U.S. holiday is realized on the next day that the markets are open in the United States. This does not invalidate the *Canadians Give 3 Cheers* trade – it presents more alternatives for the astute investor.

For example, an investor can allocate a portion of money to a standard American holiday trade and another portion to the *Canadian Give 3 Cheers* version. By spreading out the exit days, the overall risk in the trade is reduced.

S&P/TSX Comp
Gain 1977-2010   Positive

	Memorial	Independence	Thanksgiving	Compound Growth
1977	0.10 %	-0.08 %	0.61 %	0.63 %
1978	-0.05	-0.16	0.57	0.36
1979	1.11	0.23	0.58	1.93
1980	1.64	0.76	0.89	3.32
1981	0.51	-0.15	1.03	1.40
1982	-0.18	-0.01	0.35	0.17
1983	0.29	0.53	0.15	0.97
1984	0.86	-0.11	0.73	1.48
1985	0.61	0.31	0.31	1.24
1986	0.23	-0.02	0.22	0.44
1987	-0.11	1.08	1.57	2.55
1988	0.44	0.08	0.58	1.11
1989	0.10	-0.12	-0.11	-0.13
1990	0.11	0.43	0.02	0.57
1991	0.02	0.18	-0.09	0.11
1992	-0.06	0.35	0.36	0.65
1993	0.42	-0.18	0.14	0.38
1994	-0.19	0.70	0.91	1.43
1995	0.14	0.25	0.29	0.68
1996	0.11	0.25	0.54	0.90
1997	1.08	-0.04	-0.85	0.18
1998	0.56	0.18	0.51	1.25
1999	0.57	1.63	1.14	3.39
2000	0.43	1.04	0.91	2.40
2001	-0.02	-0.23	0.70	0.45
2002	-0.01	0.08	0.38	0.45
2003	0.03	0.03	0.26	0.31
2004	0.84	-0.02	0.55	1.39
2005	0.56	0.39	1.48	2.45
2006	0.70	1.04	0.70	2.46
2007	0.35	-0.03	0.76	1.08
2008	0.24	-0.94	1.28	0.56
2009	0.76	0.36	-1.29	-0.18
2010	0.78	-0.92	0.34	0.19
Avg	0.38 %	0.20 %	0.49 %	1.08 %
Fq > 0	79 %	59 %	88 %	94 %

26 MONDAY	086 / 280	**27** TUESDAY	087 / 279

28 WEDNESDAY	088 / 278	**29** THURSDAY	089 / 277

30 FRIDAY		090 / 276

Market Indices & Rates
Weekly Values**

Stock Markets	2010	2011
Dow	10,897	12,305
S&P500	1,174	1,323
Nasdaq	2,404	2,767
TSX	12,066	14,031
FTSE	5,702	5,941
DAX	6,172	7,030
Nikkei	11,141	9,622
Hang Seng	21,347	23,382

Commodities	2010	2011
Oil	83.29	105.54
Gold	1113.4	1423.4

Bond Yields	2010	2011
USA 5 Yr Treasury	2.60	2.23
USA 10 Yr T	3.89	3.47
USA 20 Yr T	4.60	4.29
Moody's Aaa	5.36	5.15
Moody's Baa	6.35	6.05
CAN 5 Yr T	2.90	2.74
CAN 10 Yr T	3.57	3.32

Money Market	2010	2011
USA Fed Funds	0.25	0.25
USA 3 Mo T-B	0.16	0.09
CAN tgt overnight rate	0.25	1.00
CAN 3 Mo T-B	0.28	0.92

Foreign Exchange	2010	2011
USD/EUR	1.35	1.41
USD/GBP	1.51	1.60
CAN/USD	1.02	0.97
JPY/USD	93.43	82.85

MARCH

M	T	W	T	F	S	S
			1	2	3	4
5	6	7	8	9	10	11
12	13	14	15	16	17	18
19	20	21	22	23	24	25
26	27	28	29	30	31	

APRIL

M	T	W	T	F	S	S
						1
2	3	4	5	6	7	8
9	10	11	12	13	14	15
16	17	18	19	20	21	22
23	24	25	26	27	28	29
30						

MAY

M	T	W	T	F	S	S
	1	2	3	4	5	6
7	8	9	10	11	12	13
14	15	16	17	18	19	20
21	22	23	24	25	26	27
28	29	30	31			

2010 Strategy Performance

Holiday Strategy S&P/TSX Comp 2010

```
1.0%
        0.8%
                              0.3%
0.0%
                   -0.9%
-1.0%
     Memorial  Independence  Thanksgiving
```

In 2010, both Memorial Day and U.S. Thanksgiving Day propelled the *Canadians Give 3 Cheers* strategy to positive results. Independence Day was uncharacteristically negative.

The Independence Day loss was less than the gains of the other two holidays, producing a gain for the overall strategy. This strategy has a very good track record and investors on both sides of the U.S./Canada border should consider using it.

** Weekly avg closing values- except Fed Funds & CAN overnight tgt rate weekly closing values.

APRIL

	MONDAY	TUESDAY	WEDNESDAY
WEEK 14	**2** 28	**3** 27	**4** 26
WEEK 15	**9** 21	**10** 20	**11** 19
WEEK 16	**16** 14	**17** 13	**18** 12
WEEK 17	**23** 7	**24** 6	**25** 5
WEEK 18	**30**	1	2

THURSDAY		FRIDAY	
5	25	**6**	24
		USA Market Closed- Good Friday CAN Market Closed- Good Friday	
12	18	**13**	17
19	11	**20**	10
26	4	**27**	3
3		4	

MAY

M	T	W	T	F	S	S
	1	2	3	4	5	6
7	8	9	10	11	12	13
14	15	16	17	18	19	20
21	22	23	24	25	26	27
28	29	30	31			

JUNE

M	T	W	T	F	S	S
				1	2	3
4	5	6	7	8	9	10
11	12	13	14	15	16	17
18	19	20	21	22	23	24
25	26	27	28	29	30	

JULY

M	T	W	T	F	S	S
						1
2	3	4	5	6	7	8
9	10	11	12	13	14	15
16	17	18	19	20	21	22
23	24	25	26	27	28	29
30	31					

AUGUST

M	T	W	T	F	S	S
		1	2	3	4	5
6	7	8	9	10	11	12
13	14	15	16	17	18	19
20	21	22	23	24	25	26
27	28	29	30	31		

APRIL SUMMARY

	Dow Jones	S&P 500	Nasdaq	TSX Comp
Month Rank	1	3	4	7
# Up	40	43	26	16
# Down	22	19	14	11
% Pos	65	69	65	59
% Avg. Gain	2.0	1.5	1.5	0.8

Dow & S&P 1950-June 2011, Nasdaq 1972-June 2011, TSX 1985-June 2011

S&P500 Cumulative Daily Gains for Avg Month 1950 to 2011

Prob. of Daily Gain

♦ From 1950 to 2010, April was the third best month of the year (average gain of 1.5%). ♦ April has recently turned out to be a pivotal month. Although the S&P 500 has done well over the last two years during April, 1.5% in 2010 and 2.8% in 2011, the market has peaked late in the month. Investors should be watching for the same trend to take place in 2012. ♦ The *energy* and *materials* sectors tend to perform well in April. ♦ The Canadian dollar also has a strong track record of outperforming the U.S. dollar in the month of April (see *Canadian Dollar Strong April* strategy).

BEST / WORST APRIL BROAD MKTS. 2002-2011

BEST APRIL MARKETS
- ♦ Russell 2000 (2009) 15.3%
- ♦ Nasdaq (2009) 12.3%
- ♦ Russell 3000 Value (2009) 10.9%

WORST APRIL MARKETS
- ♦ Nasdaq (2002) -8.5%
- ♦ Russell 3000 Gr (2002) -7.8%
- ♦ S&P500 (2002) -6.1%

Index Values End of Month

	2002	2003	2004	2005	2006	2007	2008	2009	2010	2011
Dow	9,946	8,480	10,226	10,193	11,367	13,063	12,820	8,168	11,009	12,811
S&P 500	1,077	917	1,107	1,157	1,311	1,482	1,386	873	1,187	1,364
Nasdaq	1,688	1,464	1,920	1,922	2,323	2,525	2,413	1,717	2,461	2,874
TSX	7,663	6,586	8,244	9,369	12,204	13,417	13,937	9,325	12,211	13,945
Russell 1000	1,100	934	1,138	1,198	1,373	1,553	1,453	917	1,259	1,458
Russell 2000	1,269	991	1,391	1,440	1,900	2,024	1,780	1,212	1,781	2,150
Russell 3000 Growth	1,778	1,495	1,820	1,807	2,090	2,305	2,261	1,524	2,081	2,494
Russell 3000 Value	2,084	1,759	2,188	2,426	2,825	3,241	2,858	1,696	2,369	2,667

Percent Gain for April

	2002	2003	2004	2005	2006	2007	2008	2009	2010	2011
Dow	-4.4	6.1	-1.3	-3.0	2.3	5.7	4.5	7.3	1.4	4.0
S&P 500	-6.1	8.1	-1.7	-2.0	1.2	4.3	4.8	9.4	1.5	2.8
Nasdaq	-8.5	9.2	-3.7	-3.9	-0.7	4.3	5.9	12.3	2.6	3.3
TSX	-2.4	3.8	-4.0	-2.5	0.8	1.9	4.4	6.9	1.4	-1.2
Russell 1000	-5.8	7.9	-1.9	-2.0	1.1	4.1	5.0	10.0	1.8	2.9
Russell 2000	0.8	9.4	-5.2	-5.8	-0.1	1.7	4.1	15.3	5.6	2.6
Russell 3000 Growth	-7.8	7.5	-1.5	-2.3	-0.2	4.5	5.2	9.9	1.3	3.3
Russell 3000 Value	-3.0	8.6	-2.8	-2.2	2.1	3.3	4.6	10.9	2.8	2.4

April Market Avg. Performance 2002 to 2011[1]

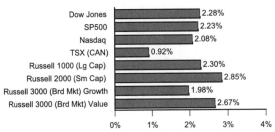

	Dow Jones	2.28%
	SP500	2.23%
	Nasdaq	2.08%
	TSX (CAN)	0.92%
	Russell 1000 (Lg Cap)	2.30%
	Russell 2000 (Sm Cap)	2.85%
	Russell 3000 (Brd Mkt) Growth	1.98%
	Russell 3000 (Brd Mkt) Value	2.67%

Interest Corner Apr[2]

	Fed Funds %[3]	3 Mo. T-Bill %[4]	10 Yr %[5]	20 Yr %[6]
2011	0.25	0.04	3.32	4.15
2010	0.25	0.16	3.69	4.36
2009	0.25	0.14	3.16	4.10
2008	2.00	1.43	3.77	4.49
2007	5.25	4.91	4.63	4.88

(1) Russell Data provided by Russell (2) Federal Reserve Bank of St. Louis- end of month values (3) Target rate set by FOMC (4)(5)(6) Constant yield maturities.

THACKRAY SECTOR THERMOMETER

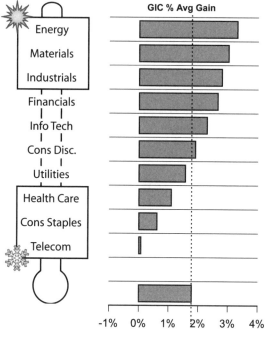

GIC[2] % Avg Gain	Fq % Gain >S&P 500	
SP GIC SECTOR 1990-2010[1]		
3.3 %	71 %	Energy
3.0	52	Materials
2.8	67	Industrials
2.7	57	Financials
2.3	52	Information Technology
1.9	52	Consumer Discretionary
1.6	43	Utilities
1.1	43	Health Care
0.6	38	Consumer Staples
0.1 %	29 %	Telecom
1.8 %	N/A %	S&P 500

Sector Commentary

♦ In April 2011, the defensive sectors were the best performers- *health care, consumer staples* and *utilities* produced returns of 6.4%, 5.1% and 3.8%, respectively. If the defensive sectors outperform when they typically underperform, it often forecasts a downturn. ♦ In the beginning of April 2011, the defensive sectors outperformed, signifying a possible correction. The market corrected later in the month.

Sub-Sector Commentary

♦ *Pharmaceuticals, biotech* and *gold* are typically in the bottom half of the sub-sector list for April, but in 2011 the three sub-sectors were at the top of the list producing gains of 7.2%, 6.7% and 5.1% respectively. ♦ *Pharmaceuticals* and *biotech* benefited from investors moving into defensive sub-sectors, including *health care*. ♦ *Gold* (London PM) benefited from the world losing faith in the fiat currencies as the economies of both Europe and the U.S. were coming into question, raising the possibility of printing more money.

SELECTED SUB-SECTORS 1990-2010[3]		
7.6 %	57 %	Auto & Components
5.1	69	Semiconductor (SOX) 95-2010
3.4	57	Banks
2.9	71	Integrated Oil & Gas
2.7	57	Transportation
2.3	57	Airlines
1.8	43	Metals & Mining
1.6	43	Software & Services
1.6	48	Pharmaceuticals
0.5	38	Retail
0.4	43	Gold (London PM)
-0.3	59	Agriculture Products (94-2010)
-0.4	33	Biotech (93-2010)
-0.7	33	XAU Gold

(1) Sector data provided by Standard and Poors (2) GIC is short form for Global Industry Classification (3) Sub Sector data provided by Standard and Poors, except where marked by symbol.

18 DAY EARNINGS MONTH EFFECT
Markets Outperform 1st 18 Calendar Days of Earnings Months

Earnings season occurs the first month of every quarter. At this time, public companies report their financials for the previous quarter and often give guidance on future expectations. As a result investors tend to bid up stocks, anticipating good earnings.

Earnings are a major driver of stock market prices as investors generally like to get in the stock market early in anticipation of favorable results, which helps to run up stock prices in the first half of the month.

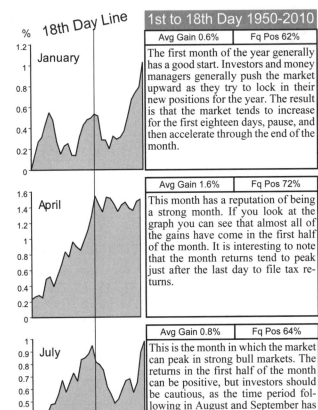

1st to 18th Day 1950-2010

January — Avg Gain 0.6% | Fq Pos 62%

The first month of the year generally has a good start. Investors and money managers generally push the market upward as they try to lock in their new positions for the year. The result is that the market tends to increase for the first eighteen days, pause, and then accelerate through the end of the month.

April — Avg Gain 1.6% | Fq Pos 72%

This month has a reputation of being a strong month. If you look at the graph you can see that almost all of the gains have come in the first half of the month. It is interesting to note that the month returns tend to peak just after the last day to file tax returns.

July — Avg Gain 0.8% | Fq Pos 64%

This is the month in which the market can peak in strong bull markets. The returns in the first half of the month can be positive, but investors should be cautious, as the time period following in August and September has a tendency towards negative returns.

October — Avg Gain 0.7% | Fq Pos 64%

This is the month with a bad reputation. Once again, the first part of the month tends to do well. It is the middle segment, centered around the notorious Black Monday, that brings down the results. Toward the end of the month investors realize that the world has not ended and start to buy stocks again, providing a strong finish to the month.

	1st to 18th Day Gain S&P500			
	JAN	APR	JUL	OCT
1950	0.54 %	4.28 %	-3.56 %	2.88 %
1951	4.85	3.41	4.39	1.76
1952	2.02	-3.57	-0.44	-1.39
1953	-2.07	-2.65	0.87	3.38
1954	2.50	3.71	2.91	-1.49
1955	-3.28	4.62	3.24	-4.63
1956	-2.88	-1.53	4.96	2.18
1957	-4.35	2.95	2.45	-4.93
1958	2.78	1.45	1.17	2.80
1959	1.09	4.47	1.23	0.79
1960	-3.34	2.26	-2.14	1.55
1961	2.70	1.75	-0.36	2.22
1962	-4.42	-1.84	2.65	0.12
1963	3.30	3.49	-1.27	2.26
1964	2.05	1.99	2.84	0.77
1965	2.05	2.31	1.87	1.91
1966	1.64	2.63	2.66	2.77
1967	6.80	1.84	3.16	-1.51
1968	-0.94	7.63	1.87	2.09
1969	-1.76	-0.27	-2.82	3.37
1970	-1.24	-4.42	6.83	-0.02
1971	1.37	3.17	0.42	-1.01
1972	1.92	2.40	-1.22	-2.13
1973	0.68	0.02	2.00	1.46
1974	-2.04	0.85	-2.58	13.76
1975	3.50	3.53	-2.09	5.95
1976	7.55	-2.04	0.38	-3.58
1977	-3.85	2.15	0.47	-3.18
1978	-4.77	4.73	1.40	-2.00
1979	3.76	0.11	-1.19	-5.22
1980	2.90	-1.51	6.83	4.83
1981	-0.73	-0.96	-0.34	2.59
1982	-4.35	4.33	1.33	13.54
1983	4.10	4.43	-2.20	1.05
1984	1.59	-0.80	-1.16	1.20
1985	2.44	0.10	1.32	2.72
1986	-1.35	1.46	-5.77	3.25
1987	9.96	-1.64	3.48	-12.16
1988	1.94	0.12	-1.09	2.75
1989	3.17	3.78	4.20	-2.12
1990	-4.30	0.23	1.73	-0.10
1991	0.61	3.53	3.83	1.20
1992	0.42	3.06	1.83	-1.45
1993	0.26	-0.60	-1.06	2.07
1994	1.67	-0.74	2.46	1.07
1995	2.27	0.93	2.52	0.52
1996	-1.25	-0.29	-4.04	3.42
1997	4.78	1.22	3.41	-0.33
1998	-0.92	1.90	4.67	3.88
1999	1.14	2.54	3.36	-2.23
2000	-0.96	-3.80	2.69	-6.57
2001	2.10	6.71	-1.36	2.66
2002	-1.79	-2.00	-10.94	8.48
2003	2.50	5.35	1.93	4.35
2004	2.51	0.75	-3.46	-0.05
2005	-1.32	-2.93	2.50	-4.12
2006	2.55	1.22	0.51	3.15
2007	1.41	4.33	-3.20	1.48
2008	-9.75	5.11	-1.51	19.36
2009	-5.88	8.99	2.29	2.89
2010	1.88	1.94	3.32	3.81
Avg	0.55 %	1.55 %	0.79 %	0.71 %

2 MONDAY	093 / 273	**3** TUESDAY	094 / 272

4 WEDNESDAY	095 / 271	**5** THURSDAY	096 / 270

6 FRIDAY 097 / 269

WEEK 14

Market Indices & Rates
Weekly Values**

Stock Markets	2010	2011
Dow	10,953	12,402
S&P500	1,188	1,333
Nasdaq	2,438	2,791
TSX	12,149	14,202
FTSE	5,757	6,026
DAX	6,224	7,192
Nikkei	11,257	9,656
Hang Seng	22,001	24,278

Commodities	2010	2011
Oil	85.93	109.75
Gold	1143.8	1451.9

Bond Yields	2010	2011
USA 5 Yr Treasury	2.67	2.28
USA 10 Yr T	3.94	3.54
USA 20 Yr T	4.63	4.35
Moody's Aaa	5.38	5.19
Moody's Baa	6.38	6.10
CAN 5 Yr T	3.03	2.82
CAN 10 Yr T	3.66	3.41

Money Market	2010	2011
USA Fed Funds	0.25	0.25
USA 3 Mo T-B	0.17	0.05
CAN tgt overnight rate	0.25	1.00
CAN 3 Mo T-B	0.28	0.97

Foreign Exchange	2010	2011
USD/EUR	1.34	1.43
USD/GBP	1.53	1.63
CAN/USD	1.00	0.96
JPY/USD	93.62	84.82

2010 Strategy Performance

First 18 Days of Earnings Months S&P 500 (2010)

The *18 Day Earnings Month Effect* worked extremely well in 2010. Without taking into account compounding effects and just adding up the returns from the earnings months in 2010, the returns were 10.9%. Interestingly, the returns for the S&P 500 in 2010 were 12.8%. In other words, almost all of the returns came in the first eighteen days of the earnings months.

When strong earnings are expected, investors should favor the first eighteen days of earnings months.

APRIL

M	T	W	T	F	S	S
						1
2	3	4	5	6	7	8
9	10	11	12	13	14	15
16	17	18	19	20	21	22
23	24	25	26	27	28	29
30						

MAY

M	T	W	T	F	S	S
	1	2	3	4	5	6
7	8	9	10	11	12	13
14	15	16	17	18	19	20
21	22	23	24	25	26	27
28	29	30	31			

JUNE

M	T	W	T	F	S	S
				1	2	3
4	5	6	7	8	9	10
11	12	13	14	15	16	17
18	19	20	21	22	23	24
25	26	27	28	29	30	

** Weekly avg closing values- except Fed Funds & CAN overnight tgt rate weekly closing values.

CONSUMER SWITCH
SELL CONSUMER DISCRETIONARY
BUY CONSUMER STAPLES
Consumer Staples Outperform Apr 23 to Oct 27

The *Consumer Switch* strategy has allowed investors to use a set portion of their account to switch between the two related consumer sectors. To use this strategy, investors would invest in the consumer discretionary sector from October 28th to April 22nd, and then use the proceeds to invest in the consumer staples sector from April 23rd to October 27th, and then repeat the cycle.

The end result has been outperformance compared with buying and holding both consumer sectors, or buying and holding the broad market.

2079% total aggregate gain compared with 303% for the S&P 500

The basic premise of the strategy is that the consumer discretionary sector tends to outperform during the favorable six months when more money flows into the market, pushing up stock prices. On the other hand, the consumer staples sector tends to outperform when investors are looking for safety and stability of earnings in the six months when the market tends to move into a defensive mode.

Consumer Staples & Discretionary Switch Strategy*			
Investment Period	Buy @ Beginning of Period	% Gain @ End of Period	% Gain Cumulative
90 Apr23 - 90 Oct29	Staples	7.7%	8%
90 Oct29 - 91 Apr23	Discretionary	41.7	53
91 Apr23 - 91 Oct28	Staples	2.1	56
91 Oct28 - 92 Apr23	Discretionary	15.9	81
92 Apr23 - 92 Oct27	Staples	6.3	92
92 Oct27 - 93 Apr23	Discretionary	6.3	104
93 Apr23 - 93 Oct27	Staples	5.8	116
93 Oct27 - 94 Apr25	Discretionary	-3.7	108
94 Apr25 - 94 Oct27	Staples	10.2	129
94 Oct27 - 95 Apr24	Discretionary	4.4	139
95 Apr24 - 95 Oct27	Staples	15.3	176
95 Oct27 - 96 Apr23	Discretionary	17.3	227
96 Apr23 - 96 Oct27	Staples	12.6	265
96 Oct27 - 97 Apr23	Discretionary	5.1	283
97 Apr23 - 97 Oct27	Staples	2.5	293
97 Oct27 - 98 Apr23	Discretionary	35.9	434
98 Apr23 - 98 Oct27	Staples	-0.7	423
98 Oct27 - 99 Apr23	Discretionary	41.8	651
99 Apr23 - 99 Oct27	Staples	-9.7	578
99 Oct27 - 00 Apr24	Discretionary	11.9	659
00 Apr24 - 00 Oct27	Staples	16.5	785
00 Oct27 - 01 Apr23	Discretionary	9.8	872
01 Apr23 - 01 Oct29	Staples	4.0	910
01 Oct29 - 02 Apr23	Discretionary	16.1	1073
02 Apr23 - 02 Oct28	Staples	-13.9	910
02 Oct28 - 03 Apr23	Discretionary	3.0	941
03 Apr23 - 03 Oct27	Staples	8.4	1028
03 Oct27 - 04 Apr23	Discretionary	9.6	1137
04 Apr23 - 04 Oct27	Staples	-7.4	1045
04 Oct27 - 05 Apr25	Discretionary	-2.0	1021
05 Apr25 - 05 Oct27	Staples	-0.5	1016
05 Oct27 - 06 Apr24	Discretionary	9.2	1119
06 Apr24 - 06 Oct27	Staples	10.6	1249
06 Oct27 - 07 Apr23	Discretionary	6.3	1334
07 Apr23 - 07 Oct29	Staples	4.6	1400
07 Oct29 - 08 Apr23	Discretionary	-13.7	1194
08 Apr23 - 08 Oct27	Staples	-21.5	916
08 Oct27 - 09 Apr23	Discretionary	17.7	1096
09 Apr23 - 09 Oct27	Staples	20.6	1342
09 Oct27 - 10 Apr23	Discretionary	29.7	1770
10 Apr23 - 10 Oct27	Staples	2.4	1815
10 Oct27 - 11 Apr25	Discretionary	13.7	2079

* If buy date lands on weekend or holiday, then date used is next trading date

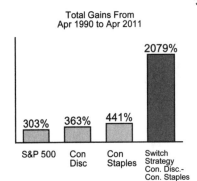

Total Gains From Apr 1990 to Apr 2011

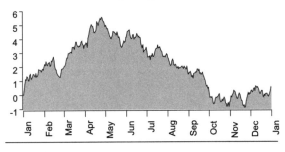

Consumer Discretionary / Consumer Staples Relative Strength Avg. Year 1990 - 2010

9 MONDAY	100 / 266	**10** TUESDAY	101 / 265

11 WEDNESDAY	102 / 264	**12** THURSDAY	103 / 263

13 FRIDAY	104 / 262

WEEK 15

Market Indices & Rates
Weekly Values**

Stock Markets	2010	2011
Dow	11,062	12,309
S&P500	1,202	1,317
Nasdaq	2,485	2,761
TSX	12,147	13,851
FTSE	5,781	5,998
DAX	6,246	7,162
Nikkei	11,199	9,632
Hang Seng	22,077	24,087

Commodities	2010	2011
Oil	84.60	108.21
Gold	1153.4	1463.7

Bond Yields	2010	2011
USA 5 Yr Treasury	2.57	2.22
USA 10 Yr T	3.85	3.51
USA 20 Yr T	4.54	4.33
Moody's Aaa	5.28	5.16
Moody's Baa	6.26	6.07
CAN 5 Yr T	3.11	2.78
CAN 10 Yr T	3.69	3.39

Money Market	2010	2011
USA Fed Funds	0.25	0.25
USA 3 Mo T-B	0.16	0.06
CAN tgt overnight rate	0.25	1.00
CAN 3 Mo T-B	0.27	0.95

Foreign Exchange	2010	2011
USD/EUR	1.36	1.45
USD/GBP	1.54	1.63
CAN/USD	1.00	0.96
JPY/USD	92.97	83.73

2010-11 Strategy Performance

Consumer Discretionary vs. Consumer Staples 2010-11

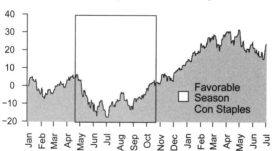

The above graph is a relative strength graph between the consumer discretionary and staples sectors. When the line is rising, the discretionary sector is outperforming and when it is falling, the staples sector is outperforming.

In 2010 the discretionary sector outperformed the staples sector in its seasonally strong period, the staples sector outperformed the discretionary sector during the summer months and then the discretionary sector outperformed in the autumn of 2010 into the spring of 2011. In other words, all parts of the seasonal cycle worked.

** Weekly avg closing values- except Fed Funds & CAN overnight tgt rate weekly closing values.

APRIL

M	T	W	T	F	S	S
						1
2	3	4	5	6	7	8
9	10	11	12	13	14	15
16	17	18	19	20	21	22
23	24	25	26	27	28	29
30						

MAY

M	T	W	T	F	S	S
	1	2	3	4	5	6
7	8	9	10	11	12	13
14	15	16	17	18	19	20
21	22	23	24	25	26	27
28	29	30	31			

JUNE

M	T	W	T	F	S	S
				1	2	3
4	5	6	7	8	9	10
11	12	13	14	15	16	17
18	19	20	21	22	23	24
25	26	27	28	29	30	

1/2 and 1/2
First 1/2 of April – Financial Stocks
Second 1/2 of April – Information Technology Stocks

The half and half strategy is a short-term switch combination that takes advantage of the superior performance of financial stocks in the first part of April and information technology stocks in the second half.

The opportunity exists because technology stocks tend to increase at the same time financial stocks tend to decrease, creating an ideal switch opportunity.

3.3% extra & 17 times out of 22 better than the S&P 500

Why do financial stocks tend to start their decline relative to the broad market at mid-month? Is it a coincidence that the rate on the three month T-Bill tends to bottom out at the same time?

The common denominator that affects both of these markets is liquidity. Basically, investors sell-off their money market positions to cover their taxes, decreasing short-term money market rates.

Decreasing short-term yields are good for financial stocks, particularly banks. Banks tend to make more money with a steeper yield curve. They borrow short-term money (your savings account) and lend out long-term (mortgages). The steeper the curve, the more money banks make.

The end result is that financial stocks benefit from this trend in the first half of April.

On the flip side, investors stop selling their money market positions to cover taxes by mid-month. At this time, yields tend to increase and financial stocks decrease.

Fortunately, information technology stocks tend to present a good opportunity at this time. By mid-April, tech-

nology stocks tend to become oversold as technology stocks typically start to correct after a strong January (see *Information Technology - Use It or Lose It* strategy).

The correction becomes magnified by investors selling off their holdings to pay their tax bill in mid-April. Investors typically sell off information technology stocks rather than the staid blue chip companies.

Financials & Info Tech & 1/2 & 1/2 > S&P 500

Year	April 1st to April 15th		April 16th to April 30		April Compound Growth	
	S&P 500	Finan cials	S&P 500	Info Tech	S&P 500	1/2 & 1/2
1990	1.3%	1.3%	-3.9%	-1.9%	-2.7%	-0.7%
1991	1.6	2.3	-1.5	-3.1	0.0	-0.9
1992	3.1	1.0	-0.3	-1.3	2.8	-0.3
1993	-0.7	3.5	-1.8	-2.2	-2.5	1.3
1994	0.1	4.9	1.1	3.5	1.2	8.6
1995	1.7	2.9	1.1	5.8	2.8	8.8
1996	-0.5	-2.3	1.8	8.2	1.3	5.8
1997	-0.3	0.3	6.2	11.3	5.8	11.6
1998	1.6	5.5	-0.7	4.3	0.9	10.0
1999	2.8	5.0	0.9	1.3	3.8	6.4
2000	-9.5	-7.0	7.1	14.8	-3.1	6.8
2001	2.0	0.2	5.6	8.3	7.7	8.5
2002	-3.9	-1.6	-2.3	-3.5	-6.1	-5.1
2003	5.0	9.3	2.9	5.3	8.1	15.1
2004	0.2	-3.0	-1.9	-5.0	-1.7	-7.8
2005	-3.2	-2.6	1.2	2.3	-2.0	-0.4
2006	-0.4	-0.3	1.7	-1.3	1.2	-1.6
2007	2.3	0.5	2.0	2.7	4.3	3.2
2008	0.9	-0.6	3.8	6.8	4.8	6.2
2009	6.8	23.0	2.4	5.8	9.4	30.1
2010	3.6	6.5	-2.1	-2.9	1.5	3.4
2011	-0.5	-1.6	3.3	4.6	2.9	2.9
Avg.	0.6%	2.1%	1.2%	2.9%	1.8%	5.1%

Alternate Strategy—
The first few days in May tend to produce gains. An alternate strategy is to hold the information technology position for the first three trading days in May.

The SP GICS Financial Sector # 40 encompasses a wide range financial based companies.
The SP GICS Information Technology Sector # 45 encompasses a wide range information technology based companies.
For more information on the information technology sector, see www.standardandpoors.com

16 MONDAY	107 / 259	**17** TUESDAY	108 / 258

18 WEDNESDAY	109 / 257	**19** THURSDAY	110 / 256

20 FRIDAY 111 / 255

WEEK 16

Market Indices & Rates
Weekly Values**

Stock Markets	2010	2011
Dow	11,135	12,357
S&P500	1,207	1,321
Nasdaq	2,507	2,776
TSX	12,150	13,827
FTSE	5,725	5,952
DAX	6,217	7,153
Nikkei	10,953	9,594
Hang Seng	21,448	23,846

Commodities	2010	2011
Oil	83.07	109.46
Gold	1139.5	1497.1

Bond Yields	2010	2011
USA 5 Yr Treasury	2.56	2.12
USA 10 Yr T	3.81	3.41
USA 20 Yr T	4.50	4.23
Moody's Aaa	5.25	5.16
Moody's Baa	6.20	5.98
CAN 5 Yr T	3.15	2.68
CAN 10 Yr T	3.70	3.28

Money Market	2010	2011
USA Fed Funds	0.25	0.25
USA 3 Mo T-B	0.16	0.06
CAN tgt overnight rate	0.25	1.00
CAN 3 Mo T-B	0.34	0.96

Foreign Exchange	2010	2011
USD/EUR	1.34	1.44
USD/GBP	1.54	1.64
CAN/USD	1.00	0.96
JPY/USD	93.25	82.31

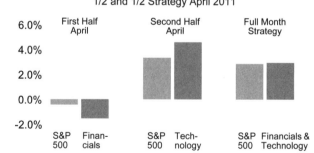

2011 Strategy Performance

1/2 and 1/2 Strategy April 2011

In 2011, the *1/2 and 1/2* strategy worked, producing a gain of 2.9% which was a fraction more than the S&P 500. The financial sector produced a larger loss than the S&P 500 in the first half of the month. The European debt situation at the time was weighing on the markets, particularly the financial sector. In the second half of the month the technology sector was able to outperform the S&P 500, despite a pullback in the markets towards the end of the month.

APRIL

M	T	W	T	F	S	S
						1
2	3	4	5	6	7	8
9	10	11	12	13	14	15
16	17	18	19	20	21	22
23	24	25	26	27	28	29
30						

MAY

M	T	W	T	F	S	S
	1	2	3	4	5	6
7	8	9	10	11	12	13
14	15	16	17	18	19	20
21	22	23	24	25	26	27
28	29	30	31			

JUNE

M	T	W	T	F	S	S
				1	2	3
4	5	6	7	8	9	10
11	12	13	14	15	16	17
18	19	20	21	22	23	24
25	26	27	28	29	30	

** Weekly avg closing values- except Fed Funds & CAN overnight tgt rate weekly closing values.

CANADIAN DOLLAR STRONG APRIL

Since the year 2000 when the price of oil started its ascent, the Canadian dollar has been labelled as a petro currency by foreign investors.

All other things being equal, if oil increases in price, investors favor the Canadian dollar over the U.S. dollar. They do so with good reason, as Canada is a net exporter of oil and benefits from its rising price.

Oil tends to do well in the month of April as this is the heart of one of the strongest seasonal strategies – oil and oil stocks outperform from February 25th to May 9th (see *Oil Winter/Spring Strategy*). With the rising price of oil in April the Canadian dollar gets a free ride upwards.

April has been a strong month for the Canadian dollar relative to the U.S. dollar. The largest losses have had a tendency to occur in years when the Fed Reserve has been aggressively hiking their target rate.

At some point during the years 1987, 2000, 2004 and 2005, the Fed increased their target rate by a total of at least 1% in each year. Since 1971 three of these years (1987, 2004 and 2005) were three of the biggest losers for the Canadian dollar in the month of April.

The Canadian dollar has been strong in April regardless of the long-term trend

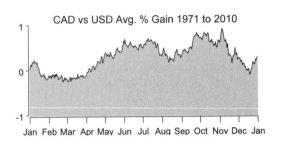

CAD vs USD Avg. % Gain 1971 to 2010

of the dollar moving either up or down. The Canadian dollar started at approximately par in 1971 and reached a low in 2002 of $0.62 and then reached a recent high of $1.09 in 2007.

In both the ups and downs of the economy, the Canadian dollar has outperformed the U.S. dollar in April.

CAD vs USD Apr. % Gain 1971-2011   Positive

		1980	0.44%	1990	0.44%	2000	-2.09%	2010	-0.26%
1971	-0.10%	1981	-0.74	1991	0.65	2001	2.65	2011	2.70
1972	0.53	1982	0.89	1992	-0.48	2002	1.74		
1973	-0.41	1983	0.36	1993	-1.02	2003	2.60		
1974	1.08	1984	-0.62	1994	0.09	2004	-4.58		
1975	-1.56	1985	0.04	1995	3.17	2005	-3.81		
1976	0.55	1986	1.69	1996	-0.15	2006	4.62		
1977	0.91	1987	-2.38	1997	-0.97	2007	3.99		
1978	0.09	1988	0.41	1998	-0.78	2008	1.73		
1979	1.61	1989	0.60	1999	3.42	2009	5.68		
Avg.	0.30%		-0.02%		0.44%		1.25%		1.22%

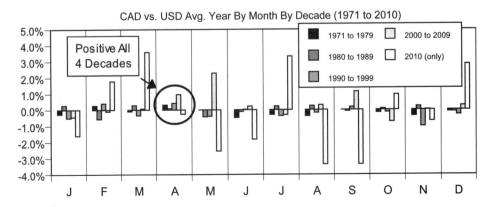

CAD vs. USD Avg. Year By Month By Decade (1971 to 2010)

Positive All 4 Decades

1971 to 1979 | 1980 to 1989 | 1990 to 1999 | 2000 to 2009 | 2010 (only)

23 MONDAY	114 / 252	**24** TUESDAY	115 / 251

25 WEDNESDAY	116 / 250	**26** THURSDAY	117 / 249

27 FRIDAY   118 / 248

WEEK 17

Market Indices & Rates
Weekly Values**

Stock Markets	2010	2011
Dow	11,084	12,668
S&P500	1,196	1,352
Nasdaq	2,488	2,858
TSX	12,183	13,910
FTSE	5,623	6,069
DAX	6,171	7,438
Nikkei	11,090	9,693
Hang Seng	21,137	23,857

Commodities	2010	2011
Oil	84.24	112.73
Gold	1162.2	1514.7

Bond Yields	2010	2011
USA 5 Yr Treasury	2.50	2.04
USA 10 Yr T	3.76	3.36
USA 20 Yr T	4.43	4.18
Moody's Aaa	5.20	5.13
Moody's Baa	6.14	5.93
CAN 5 Yr T	3.06	2.62
CAN 10 Yr T	3.65	3.23

Money Market	2010	2011
USA Fed Funds	0.25	0.25
USA 3 Mo T-B	0.16	0.06
CAN tgt overnight rate	0.25	1.00
CAN 3 Mo T-B	0.38	0.98

Foreign Exchange	2010	2011
USD/EUR	1.33	1.47
USD/GBP	1.53	1.66
CAN/USD	1.01	0.95
JPY/USD	93.83	81.65

2010-11 Strategy Performance

Canadian Dollar vs. U.S. Dollar 2010-11

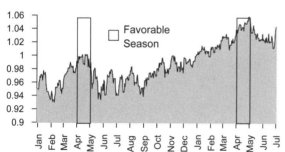

In 2010 the Canadian dollar had a strong run in February, March and the beginning of April, bringing it up to parity in mid-April. It bounced off the resistance level at parity and produced a minor loss for April.

Later in 2010 the Canadian dollar rallied starting in September as the U.S. embarked upon a second round of quantitative easing which caused their dollar to devalue. The rally lasted until the end of April 2011. During April 2011 the Canadian dollar appreciated 2.7% relative to the U.S. dollar. As the market started to move into a risk averse scenario in May, fearing tough times ahead investors were once again attracted to the U.S. dollar.

** Weekly avg closing values- except Fed Funds & CAN overnight tgt rate weekly closing values.

APRIL

M	T	W	T	F	S	S
						1
2	3	4	5	6	7	8
9	10	11	12	13	14	15
16	17	18	19	20	21	22
23	24	25	26	27	28	29
30						

MAY

M	T	W	T	F	S	S
	1	2	3	4	5	6
7	8	9	10	11	12	13
14	15	16	17	18	19	20
21	22	23	24	25	26	27
28	29	30	31			

JUNE

M	T	W	T	F	S	S
				1	2	3
4	5	6	7	8	9	10
11	12	13	14	15	16	17
18	19	20	21	22	23	24
25	26	27	28	29	30	

MAY

	MONDAY	TUESDAY	WEDNESDAY
WEEK 18	30	1 30	2 29
WEEK 19	7 24	8 23	9 22
WEEK 20	14 17	15 16	16 15
WEEK 21	21 10 CAN Market Closed- Victoria Day	22 9	23 8
WEEK 22	28 3 USA Market Closed- Memorial Day	29 2	30 1

THURSDAY		FRIDAY	
3	28	**4**	27
10	21	**11**	20
17	14	**18**	13
24	7	**25**	6
31		1	

JUNE

M	T	W	T	F	S	S
				1	2	3
4	5	6	7	8	9	10
11	12	13	14	15	16	17
18	19	20	21	22	23	24
25	26	27	28	29	30	

JULY

M	T	W	T	F	S	S
						1
2	3	4	5	6	7	8
9	10	11	12	13	14	15
16	17	18	19	20	21	22
23	24	25	26	27	28	29
30	31					

AUGUST

M	T	W	T	F	S	S
		1	2	3	4	5
6	7	8	9	10	11	12
13	14	15	16	17	18	19
20	21	22	23	24	25	26
27	28	29	30	31		

SEPTEMBER

M	T	W	T	F	S	S
					1	2
3	4	5	6	7	8	9
10	11	12	13	14	15	16
17	18	19	20	21	22	23
24	25	26	27	28	29	30

MAY
S U M M A R Y

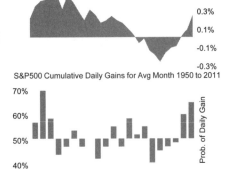

0.7%
0.5%
0.3%
0.1%
-0.1%
-0.3%

S&P500 Cumulative Daily Gains for Avg Month 1950 to 2011

	Dow Jones	S&P 500	Nasdaq	TSX Comp
Month Rank	8	8	5	2
# Up	31	35	24	18
# Down	31	27	16	9
% Pos	50	56	60	67
% Avg. Gain	0.0	0.2	1.0	1.9

Dow & S&P 1950-June 2011, Nasdaq 1972-June 2011, TSX 1985-June 2011

♦ The beginning of May is often the time that investors should start to become cautious and defensive. ♦ On average, at this time of the year the market peaks or at least flattens out. In May 2011, the S&P 500 fell 1.4% compared with 2010 when it fell 8.2%. ♦ The days around Memorial Day tend to provide a positive boost to the markets at the end of the month (see *Memorial Day Strategy*). ♦ Overall, investors at the beginning of the month should consider using the three R's - reduce equities, reduce beta and reallocate into seasonally strong sectors.

BEST / WORST MAY BROAD MKTS. 2002-2011

BEST MAY MARKETS
♦ TSX Comp (2009) 11.2%
♦ Russell 2000 (2003) 10.6%
♦ Nasdaq (2003) 9.0%

WORST MAY MARKETS
♦ Russell 3000 Value (2010) -8.5%
♦ Nasdaq (2010) -8.3%
♦ S&P500 (2010) -8.2%

Index Values End of Month

	2002	2003	2004	2005	2006	2007	2008	2009	2010	2011
Dow	9,925	8,850	10,188	10,467	11,168	13,628	12,638	8,500	10,137	12,570
S&P 500	1,067	964	1,121	1,192	1,270	1,531	1,400	919	1,089	1,345
Nasdaq	1,616	1,596	1,987	2,068	2,179	2,605	2,523	1,774	2,257	2,835
TSX	7,656	6,860	8,417	9,607	11,745	14,057	14,715	10,370	11,763	13,803
Russell 1000	1,088	986	1,152	1,239	1,330	1,605	1,477	965	1,157	1,439
Russell 2000	1,211	1,096	1,412	1,533	1,792	2,105	1,860	1,247	1,644	2,108
Russell 3000 Growth	1,729	1,574	1,852	1,895	2,009	2,386	2,344	1,596	1,920	2,461
Russell 3000 Value	2,084	1,873	2,206	2,486	2,742	3,348	2,853	1,790	2,169	2,632

Percent Gain for May

	2002	2003	2004	2005	2006	2007	2008	2009	2010	2011
Dow	-0.2	4.4	-0.4	2.7	-1.7	4.3	-1.4	4.1	-7.9	-1.9
S&P 500	-0.9	5.1	1.2	3.0	-3.1	3.3	1.1	5.3	-8.2	-1.4
Nasdaq	-4.3	9.0	3.5	7.6	-6.2	3.1	4.6	3.3	-8.3	-1.3
TSX	-0.1	4.2	2.1	2.5	-3.8	4.8	5.6	11.2	-3.7	-1.0
Russell 1000	-1.0	5.5	1.3	3.4	-3.2	3.4	1.6	5.3	-8.1	-1.3
Russell 2000	-4.5	10.6	1.5	6.4	-5.7	4.0	4.5	2.9	-7.7	-2.0
Russell 3000 Growth	-2.7	5.3	1.8	4.9	-3.9	3.5	3.7	4.7	-7.7	-1.3
Russell 3000 Value	0.0	6.4	0.8	2.5	-2.9	3.3	-0.2	5.5	-8.5	-1.3

May Market Avg. Performance 2002 to 2011[1]

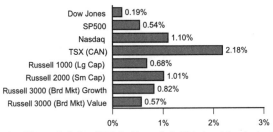

Dow Jones 0.19%
SP500 0.54%
Nasdaq 1.10%
TSX (CAN) 2.18%
Russell 1000 (Lg Cap) 0.68%
Russell 2000 (Sm Cap) 1.01%
Russell 3000 (Brd Mkt) Growth 0.82%
Russell 3000 (Brd Mkt) Value 0.57%

0%   1%   2%   3%

Interest Corner May[2]

	Fed Funds % [3]	3 Mo. T-Bill % [4]	10 Yr % [5]	20 Yr % [6]
2011	0.25	0.06	3.05	3.91
2010	0.25	0.16	3.31	4.05
2009	0.25	0.14	3.47	4.34
2008	2.00	1.89	4.06	4.74
2007	5.25	4.73	4.90	5.10

(1) Russell Data provided by Russell (2) Federal Reserve Bank of St. Louis- end of month values (3) Target rate set by FOMC (4)(5)(6) Constant yield maturities.

THACKRAY SECTOR THERMOMETER

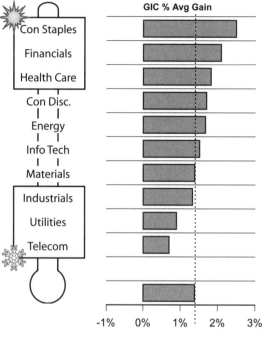

	GIC(2) % Avg Gain	Fq % Gain >S&P 500	
	SP GIC SECTOR 1990-2010(1)		
Con Staples	2.5 %	62 %	Consumer Staples
Financials	2.1	48	Financials
Health Care	1.8	48	Health Care
Con Disc.	1.7	52	Consumer Discretionary
Energy	1.7	38	Energy
Info Tech	1.5	57	Information Technology
Materials	1.4	38	Materials
Industrials	1.3	38	Industrials
Utilities	0.9	43	Utilities
Telecom	0.7 %	48 %	Telecom
	1.4 %	N/A %	S&P 500

GIC % Avg Gain axis: -1% 0% 1% 2% 3%

Sector Commentary

♦ In May of 2011, the defensive sectors outperformed across the board. ♦ The *consumer staples* sector produced the strongest return of 2.4%. This sector is typically the strongest sector in the month and also has the highest frequency of being positive. The sector starts to outperform its counterpart, *Consumer Discretionary* in late April (see *Consumer Switch Strategy*). ♦ *Health care*, which is also part of the May TST best three sectors, generated a 2.2% gain for the month. Interestingly, the two sectors that are at the bottom of the TST, *utilities* and *telecom*, moved to the top of the pack producing gains of 1.6%. ♦ All of the remaining sectors produced negative returns. When defensive sectors jump to the top of the pack out of season, investors should be wary of a market correction ahead.

Sub-Sector Commentary

♦ *Biotech* and *pharmaceuticals* took the top two spots in the sub-sector list in April 2011, with gains of 4.5% and 2.2% respectively. Once again, these two sectors benefited from investors' appetite to move into the defensive *health care* sector.

		SELECTED SUB-SECTORS 1990-2010(3)
4.5 %	67 %	Gold (XAU)
3.3	53	Agriculture Products (94-2010)
2.5	48	Banks
2.3	57	Metals & Mining
2.2	62	Retail
2.0	61	Biotech (93-2010)
1.6	43	Pharmaceuticals
1.3	38	Integrated Oil & Gas
1.0	33	Software & Services
1.0	57	Gold (London PM)
0.7	43	Transportation
0.3	29	Auto & Components
0.3	50	Semiconductor (SOX) 95-2010
-0.6	29	Airlines

(1) Sector data provided by Standard and Poors (2) GIC is short form for Global Industry Classification (3) Sub Sector data provided by Standard and Poors, except where marked by symbol.

1ST DAY OF THE MONTH
Best Day of the Month

Not all days are equal. There is one day of the month that has typically been the best – the first trading day. This day benefits from portfolio managers finishing off their window dressing (making their portfolios look good on the books) and retail investors buying up new positions to start the month on a favorable footing.

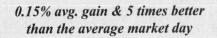

0.15% avg. gain & 5 times better than the average market day

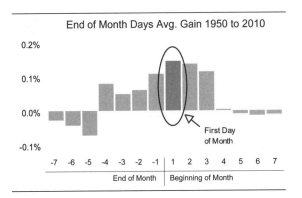

End of Month Days Avg. Gain 1950 to 2010

First Day of Month

End of Month | Beginning of Month

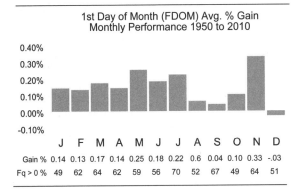

1st Day of Month (FDOM) Avg. % Gain
Monthly Performance 1950 to 2010

	J	F	M	A	M	J	J	A	S	O	N	D
Gain %	0.14	0.13	0.17	0.14	0.25	0.18	0.22	0.6	0.04	0.10	0.33	-.03
Fq > 0 %	49	62	64	62	59	56	70	52	67	49	64	51

From 1950 to 2010, the first day of the month (FDOM) has produced an average return of 0.15% and has been positive 59% of the time. This compares to the average market day (all trading days of the year) over the same time period, which has produced a return of 0.03% and has been positive 53% of the time.

The interesting result is that the average daily gain of the first day of the month was almost five times better than the average market day, and yet it had only a slightly higher frequency of being positive. What this means is that when the first day is positive, it has a much higher likelihood of producing an extraordinarily large gain. Examining the returns on a monthly basis, only the "first day" of December has performed below the average market day from 1950 to 2010.

On the other hand, the best "first day" of the month has clearly been November: the traditional start of the six month favorable time period to invest and also one of the best months for a stock market gain.

It is interesting to note that a high frequency positive first day of the month does not necessarily mean that the average gain is high. For example, the first day in September has been positive 67% of the time from 1950 to 2010. Yet, although the first day has a high frequency of being positive, it is the second worst month for a first day return. In other words, the first day of September has a a high frequency of being positive, but its average return is low.

This indicates that the first day in September has a wide range of returns, with some large down days, but most of the time is positive.

As a side note, the month of September has also proved unfriendly to the market and has produced an average negative return from 1950 to 2010.

> **CAUTION:**
> Generally, it is not a wise strategy to invest for just one day: the expected rate of return, combined with the risk from volatility do not justify the expected returns.

30 MONDAY 121 / 245   **1 TUESDAY** 122 / 244

2 WEDNESDAY 123 / 243   **3 THURSDAY** 124 / 242

4 FRIDAY 125 / 241

WEEK 18

Market Indices & Rates
Weekly Values**

Stock Markets	2010	2011
Dow	10,769	12,712
S&P500	1,156	1,348
Nasdaq	2,382	2,835
TSX	11,927	13,652
FTSE	5,284	5,991
DAX	5,951	7,454
Nikkei	10,530	9,932
Hang Seng	20,391	23,342

Commodities	2010	2011
Oil	80.22	106.16
Gold	1184.4	1519.7

Bond Yields	2010	2011
USA 5 Yr Treasury	2.29	1.92
USA 10 Yr T	3.56	3.24
USA 20 Yr T	4.20	4.07
Moody's Aaa	5.00	5.00
Moody's Baa	5.98	5.82
CAN 5 Yr T	2.85	2.53
CAN 10 Yr T	3.54	3.17

Money Market	2010	2011
USA Fed Funds	0.25	0.25
USA 3 Mo T-B	0.14	0.03
CAN tgt overnight rate	0.25	1.00
CAN 3 Mo T-B	0.36	0.97

Foreign Exchange	2010	2011
USD/EUR	1.29	1.47
USD/GBP	1.50	1.65
CAN/USD	1.03	0.96
JPY/USD	93.01	80.70

MAY

M	T	W	T	F	S	S
	1	2	3	4	5	6
7	8	9	10	11	12	13
14	15	16	17	18	19	20
21	22	23	24	25	26	27
28	29	30	31			

JUNE

M	T	W	T	F	S	S
				1	2	3
4	5	6	7	8	9	10
11	12	13	14	15	16	17
18	19	20	21	22	23	24
25	26	27	28	29	30	

JULY

M	T	W	T	F	S	S
						1
2	3	4	5	6	7	8
9	10	11	12	13	14	15
16	17	18	19	20	21	22
23	24	25	26	27	28	29
30	31					

2011 Strategy Performance

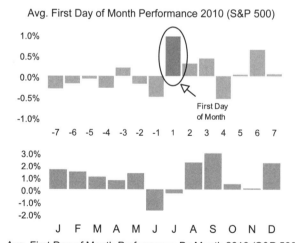

Avg. First Day of Month Performance 2010 (S&P 500)

Avg. First Day of Month Performance By Month 2010 (S&P 500)

The *First Day of the Month* strategy was extremely successful in 2010. On average, the first day of the month produced very strong gains compared to any other day of the month and was positive ten out of twelve months.

** Weekly avg closing values- except Fed Funds & CAN overnight tgt rate weekly closing values.

Being out of the market feels good when it is going down. And the market has a habit of going down after the beginning of May. Although sometimes a strong market can continue into July and less frequently into autumn, it has historically made sense to reduce your equity exposure in May.

$1,057,851 gain on $10,000

The accompanying table uses the S&P 500 to compare the returns made from Oct 28th to May 5th (favorable six months), to the returns made during the remainder of the year (unfavorable six months). From 1950 to 2010, the October to May time period has produced stunning results.

Starting with $10,000 and investing from October 28th to May 5th every year (1950 to 2010) has produced a gain of $1,057,851. On the flip side, being invested from May 6th to October 27th, has actually lost money. An initial investment of $10,000 has lost $3,273 over the same time period.

Investors often worry about being out of the market at a time when the market is rallying, and missing out on profits. The S&P 500 in the last sixty-one years, during the unfavorable six months, has only had gains of greater than 10%, eight times. This compares with twenty-five times in the favorable six months. Being out of the markets during the unfavorable six months has proven to be a wiser strategy than being out of the markets during the other six months.

S&P 500 Non-Favorable 6 Month Avg. Gain vs Favorable 6 Month Avg. Gain (1950-2011)

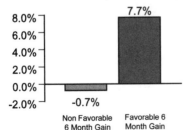

The above growth rates are geometric averages in order to represent the cumulative growth of a dollar investment over time. These figures differ from the arithmetic mean calculations used in the Six 'N' Six Take a Break Strategy, which are used to represent an average year.

	S&P 500 % May 6 to Oct 27	$10,000 Start	S&P 500 % Oct 28 to May 5	$10,000 Start
1950/51	8.5%	10,851	15.2%	11,517
1951/52	0.2	10,870	3.7	11,947
1952/53	1.8	11,067	3.9	12,413
1953/54	-3.1	10,727	16.6	14,475
1954/55	13.2	12,141	18.1	17,097
1955/56	11.4	13,528	15.1	19,681
1956/57	-4.6	12,903	0.2	19,711
1957/58	-12.4	11,302	7.9	21,265
1958/59	15.1	13,013	14.5	24,356
1959/60	-0.6	12,939	-4.5	23,270
1960/61	-2.3	12,647	24.1	28,869
1961/62	2.7	12,993	-3.1	27,982
1962/63	-17.7	10,698	28.4	35,929
1963/64	5.7	11,306	9.3	39,264
1964/65	5.1	11,882	5.5	41,440
1965/66	3.1	12,253	-5.0	39,388
1966/67	-8.8	11,180	17.7	46,364
1967/68	0.6	11,241	3.9	48,171
1968/69	5.6	11,872	0.2	48,249
1969/70	-6.2	11,141	-19.7	38,722
1970/71	5.8	11,782	24.9	48,346
1971/72	-9.6	10,647	13.7	54,965
1972/73	3.7	11,046	0.3	55,154
1973/74	0.3	11,084	-18.0	45,205
1974/75	-23.2	8,513	28.5	58,073
1975/76	-0.4	8,480	12.4	65,290
1976/77	0.9	8,554	-1.6	64,231
1977/78	-7.8	7,890	4.5	67,146
1978/79	-2.0	7,732	6.4	71,476
1979/80	-0.1	7,723	5.8	75,605
1980/81	20.2	9,283	1.9	77,047
1981/82	-8.5	8,498	-1.4	76,001
1982/83	15.0	9,769	21.4	92,293
1983/84	0.3	9,803	-3.5	89,085
1984/85	3.9	10,183	8.9	97,057
1985/86	4.1	10,604	26.8	123,044
1986/87	0.4	10,651	23.7	152,196
1987/88	-21.0	8,409	11.0	168,904
1988/89	7.1	9,010	10.9	187,380
1989/90	8.9	9,814	1.0	189,242
1990/91	-10.0	8,837	25.0	236,498
1991/92	0.9	8,916	8.5	256,590
1992/93	0.4	8,952	6.2	272,550
1993/94	4.5	9,356	-2.8	264,789
1994/95	3.2	9,656	11.6	295,636
1995/96	11.5	10,762	10.7	327,219
1996/97	9.2	11,757	18.5	387,591
1997/98	5.6	12,419	27.2	493,003
1998/99	-4.5	11,860	26.5	623,489
1999/00	-3.8	11,415	10.5	688,842
2000/01	-3.7	10,992	-8.2	632,435
2001/02	-12.8	9,586	-2.8	614,583
2002/03	-16.4	8,016	3.2	634,369
2003/04	11.3	8,921	8.8	689,985
2004/05	0.3	8,952	4.2	718,942
2005/06	0.5	9,000	12.5	808,503
2006/07	3.9	9,350	9.3	883,804
2007/08	2.0	9,534	-8.3	810,240
2008/09	-39.7	5,750	6.5	862,619
2009/10	17.7	6,766	9.7	934,470
2010/11	1.4	6,862	12.9	1,067,851
Total Gain (Loss)	**($3,138)**			**$1,057,851**

7 MONDAY	128 / 238

8 TUESDAY	129 / 237

9 WEDNESDAY	130 / 236

10 THURSDAY	131 / 235

11 FRIDAY	132 / 234

Market Indices & Rates
Weekly Values**

Stock Markets	2010	2011
Dow	10,767	12,673
S&P500	1,156	1,346
Nasdaq	2,383	2,850
TSX	12,055	13,501
FTSE	5,360	5,962
DAX	6,110	7,451
Nikkei	10,484	9,769
Hang Seng	20,271	23,244

Commodities	2010	2011
Oil	74.97	100.65
Gold	1226.1	1503.8

Bond Yields	2010	2011
USA 5 Yr Treasury	2.25	1.87
USA 10 Yr T	3.54	3.20
USA 20 Yr T	4.23	4.05
Moody's Aaa	5.07	4.98
Moody's Baa	6.12	5.83
CAN 5 Yr T	2.89	2.54
CAN 10 Yr T	3.55	3.22

Money Market	2010	2011
USA Fed Funds	0.25	0.25
USA 3 Mo T-B	0.16	0.03
CAN tgt overnight rate	0.25	1.00
CAN 3 Mo T-B	0.38	0.97

Foreign Exchange	2010	2011
USD/EUR	1.26	1.43
USD/GBP	1.48	1.63
CAN/USD	1.02	0.96
JPY/USD	92.88	80.81

MAY

M	T	W	T	F	S	S
	1	2	3	4	5	6
7	8	9	10	11	12	13
14	15	16	17	18	19	20
21	22	23	24	25	26	27
28	29	30	31			

JUNE

M	T	W	T	F	S	S
				1	2	3
4	5	6	7	8	9	10
11	12	13	14	15	16	17
18	19	20	21	22	23	24
25	26	27	28	29	30	

JULY

M	T	W	T	F	S	S
						1
2	3	4	5	6	7	8
9	10	11	12	13	14	15
16	17	18	19	20	21	22
23	24	25	26	27	28	29
30	31					

2009-11 Strategy Performance

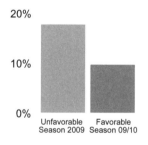

Favorable vs. Unfavorable Seasons 2009-2011 (S&P 500)

Unfavorable Season 2009 · Favorable Season 09/10 · Unfavorable Season 2010 · Favorable Season 10/11

Staying out of the market for the unfavourable six months from May 6th to October 27th, paid off handsomely in 2009 as a quantitative easing program helped propel the markets higher.

In 2010, the unfavorable season had a small gain of 1.4%. This is in spite of a large gut-wrenching correction that occurred during the summer months. The announcement that the Fed was considering another quantitative easing program was largely responsible for the recovery.

** Weekly avg closing values- except Fed Funds & CAN overnight tgt rate weekly closing values.

In analysing long-term trends for the broad markets such as the S&P 500 or the TSX Composite, a large data set is preferable because it incorporates various economic cycles. The daily data set for the TSX Composite starts in 1977.

Over this time period investors have been rewarded for following the six month cycle of investing from October 28th to May 5th, versus the other unfavorable six months, May 6th to October 27th.

Starting with an investment of $10,000 in 1977, investing in the unfavorable six months has produced a loss of $3,326, versus investing in the favorable six months which has produced a gain of $190,778.

$190,778 gain on $10,000 since 1977

The TSX Composite Average Year 1977 to 2010 (graph below) indicates that the market tended to peak in mid-July or the end of August. In our book *Time In Time Out, Outsmart the Stock Market Using Calendar Investment Strategies*, Bruce Lindsay and I analysed a number of market trends and peaks over different decades.

What we found was that the markets tend to peak at the beginning of May or mid-July. The mid-July peak was usually the result of a strong bull market in place that had a lot of momentum.

The main reason that the TSX Composite data shows a peak occurring in July-August is that the data is primarily from the biggest bull market in history, starting in 1982.

Does a later average peak in the stock market mean that the best six month cycle does not work? No. Dividing the year up into six month intervals, the period from October to May is far superior compared with the other half of the year.

The table below illustrates the superiority of the best six months over the worst six months. Going down the table year by year, the period from October 28 to May 5th outperforms the period from May 6th to October 27.

In a strong bull market investors always have the choice of using a stop loss or technical indicators to help extend the exit point past the May date.

	TSX Comp May 6 to Oct 27	$10,000 Start	TSX Comp Oct 28 to May 5	$10,000 Start
1977/78	-3.9 %	9,608	13.1 %	11,313
1978/79	12.1	10,775	21.3	13,728
1979/80	2.9	11,084	23.0	16,883
1980/81	22.5	13,579	-2.4	16,479
1981/82	-17.0	11,272	-18.2	13,488
1982/83	16.6	13,138	34.6	18,150
1983/84	-0.9	13,015	-1.9	17,811
1984/85	1.6	13,226	10.7	19,718
1985/86	0.5	13,299	16.5	22,978
1986/87	-1.9	13,045	24.8	28,666
1987/88	-23.4	9,992	15.3	33,050
1988/89	2.7	10,260	5.7	34,939
1989/90	7.9	11,072	-13.3	30,294
1990/91	-8.4	10,148	13.1	34,266
1991/92	-1.6	9,982	-2.0	33,571
1992/93	-2.3	9,750	15.3	38,704
1993/94	10.8	10,801	1.7	39,365
1994/95	-0.1	10,792	0.3	39,483
1995/96	1.3	10,936	18.2	46,671
1996/97	8.3	11,843	10.8	51,725
1997/98	7.3	12,707	17.0	60,510
1998/99	-22.3	9,870	17.1	70,871
1999/00	-0.2	9,853	36.9	97,009
2000/01	-2.9	9,570	-14.4	83,062
2001/02	-12.2	8,399	9.4	90,875
2002/03	-16.4	7,020	4.0	94,476
2003/04	15.1	8,079	10.3	104,252
2004/05	3.9	8,398	7.8	112,379
2005/06	8.1	9,080	19.8	134,587
2006/07	0.0	9,079	12.2	151,053
2007/08	3.8	9,426	-0.2	150,820
2008/09	-40.2	5,638	15.7	174,551
2009/10	11.9	6,307	7.4	187,526
2010/11	5.8	6,674	7.1	200,778
Total Gain (Loss)	**($-3,326)**			**$190,778**

TSX Comp. - Avg. Year 1977 to 2010

14 MONDAY 135 / 231

15 TUESDAY 136 / 230

16 WEDNESDAY 137 / 229

17 THURSDAY 138 / 228

18 FRIDAY 139 / 227

WEEK 20

Market Indices & Rates
Weekly Values**

Stock Markets	2010	2011
Dow	10,369	12,541
S&P500	1,106	1,335
Nasdaq	2,281	2,801
TSX	11,634	13,543
FTSE	5,173	5,923
DAX	5,982	7,315
Nikkei	10,096	9,603
Hang Seng	19,696	23,047

Commodities	2010	2011
Oil	69.08	98.46
Gold	1203.9	1491.9

Bond Yields	2010	2011
USA 5 Yr Treasury	2.10	1.83
USA 10 Yr T	3.33	3.15
USA 20 Yr T	4.04	3.99
Moody's Aaa	4.87	4.93
Moody's Baa	6.00	5.76
CAN 5 Yr T	2.68	2.50
CAN 10 Yr T	3.40	3.19

Money Market	2010	2011
USA Fed Funds	0.25	0.25
USA 3 Mo T-B	0.17	0.05
CAN tgt overnight rate	0.25	1.00
CAN 3 Mo T-B	0.37	0.96

Foreign Exchange	2010	2011
USD/EUR	1.24	1.42
USD/GBP	1.44	1.62
CAN/USD	1.05	0.97
JPY/USD	91.24	81.44

2010-11 Strategy Performance

Favorable Season S&P/TSX 2010

In 2010, the S&P/TSX Composite produced a small gain in the beginning of the year during its favorable season. At the start of the unfavorable season the market started to correct, along with the U.S. stock market. With both oil and gold performing well during their seasonal periods in July, the S&P/TSX Composite started to improve. With the help of "Helicopter" Ben Bernanke dumping liquidity into the markets the Canadian market performed well until the end of the year.

MAY

M	T	W	T	F	S	S
	1	2	3	4	5	6
7	8	9	10	11	12	13
14	15	16	17	18	19	20
21	22	23	24	25	26	27
28	29	30	31			

JUNE

M	T	W	T	F	S	S
				1	2	3
4	5	6	7	8	9	10
11	12	13	14	15	16	17
18	19	20	21	22	23	24
25	26	27	28	29	30	

JULY

M	T	W	T	F	S	S
						1
2	3	4	5	6	7	8
9	10	11	12	13	14	15
16	17	18	19	20	21	22
23	24	25	26	27	28	29
30	31					

** Weekly avg closing values- except Fed Funds & CAN overnight tgt rate weekly closing values.

⚡ JUNE – LEADERLESS MONTH
No Sector Consistently Leads the Pack

June is on average a leaderless month. One year, one sector leads the market, and the next year another sector leads the market. This is somewhat evident by looking at the Thackray Sector Thermometer for the month of June. Out of the ten S&P GIC sectors, from 1990 to 2010 the technology sector has been the top sector five times and the worst sector four times.

This is a disproportionate amount of highs and lows for one sector. Almost all of the top sector performances for information technology occurred in the late 90's and early 2000's, during the technology bubble. Although the other sectors may not have such top and bottom results as the technology sector, they are nevertheless dispersed throughout the ranks.

The June S&P GIC Top/Bottom 3 Ranking Table illustrates the frequency of the GIC sectors placing in the top or bottom three sectors. Other than health care and financials having the largest ratios of both top and bottom placement in the ranks, there is little to give investors guidance of the possible best sectors.

Very often you can judge the strength of a market by which sector is leading. Investors often look to the financial sector to be a leader, and when it is not one of the top sectors, they tend to be cautious. Other investors look at the strength of the semiconductor sector to be a leader. The belief is that if the sector is strong, then investors are bullish on the economy and the stock market.

Using the top ten S&P GIC sectors, there does not seem to be a significant predictive trend in June. When the technology sector has been a top sector, the subsequent period has been both positive and negative. Likewise, when it has been in the bottom sector, the subsequent period has been positive and negative.

A possible explanation for the lack of leadership in June is that the month is a transition month. As described in the "Six'n'Six" strategy, the market often peaks at the beginning of May. On the other hand, typically in bull markets, the market can peak mid-July. June acts as a bridge month between the two seasonal peak months of May and July, and as a result a higher degree of sector rotation takes place.

With a lot of sectors finishing their period of strength in May, and investors trying to push them higher, there is a struggle with some of the defensive and commodity sectors that are trying to start their rallies. As a result, different sectors of the market lead in different years depending on the extent and nature of the struggle.

The lack of leadership in June is significant for investors as it means there is a lack of seasonal investment opportunities. Although there are sector opportunities in June, there are just not a lot of them. If investors desire market exposure in June, typically they should not over commit to one or two sectors and they should use fundamental and technical analysis to assist in making entry and exit decisions.

June Best / Worst S&P GIC Sectors (1990-2011)		
	Best Sector	Worst Sector
1990	Health Care	Telecom
1991	Telecom	Info Tech
1992	Financials	Health Care
1993	Telecom	Health Care
1994	Telecom	Info Tech
1995	Info Tech	Energy
1996	Utilities	Materials
1997	Health Care	Info Tech
1998	Info Tech	Materials
1999	Info Tech	Utilities
2000	Info Tech	Materials
2001	Info Tech	Utilities
2002	Energy	Telecom
2003	Health Care	Energy
2004	Industrials	Health Care
2005	Energy	Industrials
2006	Telecom	Info Tech
2007	Energy	Utilities
2008	Energy	Financials
2009	Utilities	Materials
2010	Telecom	Consumer Disc.
2011	Consumer Disc.	Financials

June Sector Frequency Top/Bottom 3 S&P GIC Sectors (1990-2011)		
	Top 3	Bottom 3
Energy	7	6
Materials	5	8
Industrials	5	6
Consumer Disc	4	4
Consumer Staples	2	5
Health Care	10	6
Financials	5	11
Telecom	10	4
Info Tech	7	9
Utilities	11	7

21 MONDAY · 142 / 224

22 TUESDAY · 143 / 223

23 WEDNESDAY · 144 / 222

24 THURSDAY · 145 / 221

25 FRIDAY · 146 / 220

WEEK 21

Market Indices & Rates
Weekly Values**

Stock Markets	2010	2011
Dow	10,096	12,395
S&P500	1,082	1,322
Nasdaq	2,231	2,769
TSX	11,621	13,730
FTSE	5,086	5,877
DAX	5,823	7,144
Nikkei	9,629	9,489
Hang Seng	19,410	22,842

Commodities	2010	2011
Oil	70.65	99.58
Gold	1203.2	1523.1

Bond Yields	2010	2011
USA 5 Yr Treasury	2.08	1.77
USA 10 Yr T	3.25	3.10
USA 20 Yr T	3.99	3.96
Moody's Aaa	4.91	4.95
Moody's Baa	6.10	5.74
CAN 5 Yr T	2.61	2.38
CAN 10 Yr T	3.31	3.08

Money Market	2010	2011
USA Fed Funds	0.25	0.25
USA 3 Mo T-B	0.17	0.06
CAN tgt overnight rate	0.25	1.00
CAN 3 Mo T-B	0.45	0.95

Foreign Exchange	2010	2011
USD/EUR	1.23	1.41
USD/GBP	1.45	1.63
CAN/USD	1.06	0.98
JPY/USD	90.51	81.60

MAY

M	T	W	T	F	S	S
	1	2	3	4	5	6
7	8	9	10	11	12	13
14	15	16	17	18	19	20
21	22	23	24	25	26	27
28	29	30	31			

JUNE

M	T	W	T	F	S	S
				1	2	3
4	5	6	7	8	9	10
11	12	13	14	15	16	17
18	19	20	21	22	23	24
25	26	27	28	29	30	

JULY

M	T	W	T	F	S	S
						1
2	3	4	5	6	7	8
9	10	11	12	13	14	15
16	17	18	19	20	21	22
23	24	25	26	27	28	29
30	31					

2011 Strategy Performance

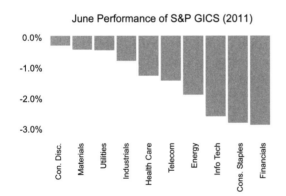

June Performance of S&P GICS (2011)

June was not a good month for the stock market in 2011. As a result, the defensive sectors outperformed the cyclical sectors. Generally when the market is pushing strongly to the downside, the defensive sectors will outperform on a relative basis and when the market is in a rally mode, the cyclicals will outperform.

** Weekly avg closing values- except Fed Funds & CAN overnight tgt rate weekly closing values.

MEMORIAL DAY – BE EARLY & STAY LATE
Positive 2 Market Days Before Memorial Day to 5 Market Days into June

A lot of strategies that focus on investing around holidays concentrate on the market performance the day before and the day after a holiday.

Not all holidays were created equal. The typical Memorial Day trade is to invest the day before the holiday and sell the day after. If you invested the stock market just for these two days you would be missing out on a lot of gains.

> *1.1% average gain and positive 66% of the time*

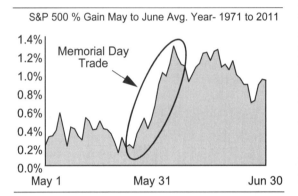

S&P 500 % Gain May to June Avg. Year- 1971 to 2011

Memorial Day Trade

Historically, the best strategy has been to invest two market days before Memorial Day and hold until five market days into June. Extending the investment into June makes sense. The first few days in June tend to be positive– so why sell early?

The graph shows the performance of the S&P 500 on a calendar basis for the months of May and June from 1971 to 2011.

The increase from the end of May into June represents the opportunity with the *"Memorial Day - Be Early & Stay Late"* trade. The graph clearly shows a spike in the market that occurs at the end of the month and carries on into June.

Investors using the typical Memorial Day trade, miss out on the majority of the gain. The *Memorial Day - Be Early & Stay Late* strategy has produced an average gain of 1.1% and has been positive 66% of the time (S&P 500, 1971 to 2011). Not a bad gain for being invested an average of ten market days.

The *Memorial Day - Be Early & Stay Late* trade can be extended into June primarily because the first days in the market tend to be positive. These days are part of the end of the month effect. (see *Super Seven* strategy).

(i) *History of Memorial Day:*
Originally called Decoration Day in remembrance of those who died in the nation's service. Memorial day was first observed on May 30th 1868 when flowers were placed on the graves of Union and Confederate soldiers at Arlington National Cemetery. The South acknowledged the day after World War I, when the holiday changed from honoring just those who died fighting in the Civil War to honoring Americans who died fighting in any war. In 1971 Congress passed the National Holiday Act recognizing Memorial Day as the last Monday in May.

2 Market Days Before Memorial Day to
5 Market Days Into June - S&P 500   Positive [ ]

		1980	5.1 %	1990	1.1 %	2000	5.2 %	2010	-1.6 %
1971	1.5 %	1981	0.2	1991	0.9	2001	-0.9	2011	-2.6
1972	-2.4	1982	-2.6	1992	-0.5	2002	-5.4		
1973	1.7	1983	-2.1	1993	-1.3	2003	7.0		
1974	6.3	1984	1.2	1994	0.4	2004	2.3		
1975	3.8	1985	4.3	1995	0.9	2005	0.6		
1976	-0.7	1986	4.3	1996	0.0	2006	-0.2		
1977	1.0	1987	5.5	1997	2.2	2007	-2.1		
1978	3.1	1988	4.5	1998	-0.5	2008	-2.2		
1979	1.9	1989	2.4	1999	2.3	2009	4.1		
Avg.	1.8 %		2.3 %		0.6 %		0.8 %		-2.1 %

28 MONDAY	149 / 217	**29** TUESDAY	150 / 216

30 WEDNESDAY	151 / 215	**31** THURSDAY	152 / 214

1 FRIDAY			153 / 213

WEEK 22

Market Indices & Rates
Weekly Values**

Stock Markets	2010	2011
Dow	10,115	12,315
S&P500	1,084	1,318
Nasdaq	2,256	2,778
TSX	11,699	13,640
FTSE	5,163	5,905
DAX	5,984	7,171
Nikkei	9,780	9,593
Hang Seng	19,660	23,340

Commodities	2010	2011
Oil	72.89	100.99
Gold	1215.3	1537.4

Bond Yields	2010	2011
USA 5 Yr Treasury	2.10	1.63
USA 10 Yr T	3.31	3.01
USA 20 Yr T	4.05	3.89
Moody's Aaa	4.98	4.95
Moody's Baa	6.23	5.70
CAN 5 Yr T	2.66	2.28
CAN 10 Yr T	3.34	3.03

Money Market	2010	2011
USA Fed Funds	0.25	0.25
USA 3 Mo T-B	0.15	0.05
CAN tgt overnight rate	0.45	1.00
CAN 3 Mo T-B	0.50	0.96

Foreign Exchange	2010	2011
USD/EUR	1.22	1.44
USD/GBP	1.46	1.64
CAN/USD	1.05	0.98
JPY/USD	91.79	80.93

2010-11 Strategy Performance

S&P 500 Memorial Day Trades 2010-11

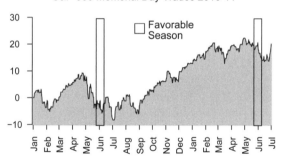

May 2010, was a disastrous month. The "flash crash" occurred on May 6th, driving some blue chip names down to a few dollars in less than half an hour and the possibility of a global economic slowdown was brought to the forefront. This negative sentiment carried forward for the Memorial Day trade, producing a loss of 1.6%. The Memorial Day trade in 2011 was also negative due to strong negative sentiment in the market. The trade produced a loss of 2.6%.

As the Memorial Day trade carries forward into June, investors should be wary of strong negative sentiment in the markets.

** Weekly avg closing values- except Fed Funds & CAN overnight tgt rate weekly closing values.

JUNE

M	T	W	T	F	S	S
				1	2	3
4	5	6	7	8	9	10
11	12	13	14	15	16	17
18	19	20	21	22	23	24
25	26	27	28	29	30	

JULY

M	T	W	T	F	S	S
						1
2	3	4	5	6	7	8
9	10	11	12	13	14	15
16	17	18	19	20	21	22
23	24	25	26	27	28	29
30	31					

AUGUST

M	T	W	T	F	S	S
	1	2	3	4	5	
6	7	8	9	10	11	12
13	14	15	16	17	18	19
20	21	22	23	24	25	26
27	28	29	30	31		

JUNE

	MONDAY	TUESDAY	WEDNESDAY
WEEK 22	28	29	30
WEEK 23	**4** 26	**5** 25	**6** 24
WEEK 24	**11** 19	**12** 18	**13** 17
WEEK 25	**18** 12	**19** 11	**20** 10
WEEK 26	**25** 5	**26** 4	**27** 3

THURSDAY	FRIDAY
31	1 29
7 23	8 22
14 16	15 15
21 9	22 8
28 2	29 1

JULY

M	T	W	T	F	S	S
						1
2	3	4	5	6	7	8
9	10	11	12	13	14	15
16	17	18	19	20	21	22
23	24	25	26	27	28	29
30	31					

AUGUST

M	T	W	T	F	S	S
		1	2	3	4	5
6	7	8	9	10	11	12
13	14	15	16	17	18	19
20	21	22	23	24	25	26
27	28	29	30	31		

SEPTEMBER

M	T	W	T	F	S	S
					1	2
3	4	5	6	7	8	9
10	11	12	13	14	15	16
17	18	19	20	21	22	23
24	25	26	27	28	29	30

OCTOBER

M	T	W	T	F	S	S
1	2	3	4	5	6	7
8	9	10	11	12	13	14
15	16	17	18	19	20	21
22	23	24	25	26	27	28
29	30	31				

JUNE
S U M M A R Y

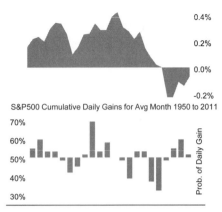

S&P500 Cumulative Daily Gains for Avg Month 1950 to 2011

	Dow Jones	S&P 500	Nasdaq	TSX Comp
Month Rank	11	10	6	11
# Up	28	31	23	12
# Down	34	31	17	15
% Pos	45	50	58	44
% Avg. Gain	-0.4	-0.1	0.7	-0.3

Dow & S&P 1950-June 2011, Nasdaq 1972-June 2011, TSX 1985-June 2011

♦ On average, June is not a strong month. From 1950 to 2010, June has been the third worst month of the year, producing a average loss of 0.1% and positive 51% of the time. ♦ In 2011, the May correction continued into June with the first half of the month being negative. In the end, this set up for a strong rally at month end and into the beginning part of July (see *Independence Day Strategy* and *Earnings Month 18 Calendar Day Strategy*).

BEST / WORST JUNE BROAD MKTS. 2002-2011

BEST JUNE MARKETS
♦ Russell 2000 (2004) 4.1%
♦ Russell 2000 (2005) 3.7%
♦ Nasdaq (2009) 3.4%

WORST JUNE MARKETS
♦ Dow (2008) -10.2%
♦ Russell 3000 Value (2008) -9.8%
♦ Nasdaq (2002) -9.4%

Index Values End of Month

	2002	2003	2004	2005	2006	2007	2008	2009	2010	2011
Dow	9,243	8,985	10,435	10,275	11,150	13,409	11,350	8,447	9,774	12,414
S&P 500	990	975	1,141	1,191	1,270	1,503	1,280	919	1,031	1,321
Nasdaq	1,463	1,623	2,048	2,057	2,172	2,603	2,293	1,835	2,109	2,774
TSX	7,146	6,983	8,546	9,903	11,613	13,907	14,467	10,375	11,294	13,301
Russell 1000	1,007	998	1,171	1,242	1,330	1,573	1,352	966	1,091	1,412
Russell 2000	1,150	1,114	1,470	1,590	1,801	2,072	1,714	1,263	1,515	2,056
Russell 3000 Growth	1,569	1,595	1,876	1,892	2,000	2,350	2,175	1,613	1,810	2,421
Russell 3000 Value	1,967	1,894	2,258	2,515	2,757	3,265	2,574	1,773	2,037	2,572

Percent Gain for June

	2002	2003	2004	2005	2006	2007	2008	2009	2010	2011
Dow	-6.9	1.5	2.4	-1.8	-0.2	-1.6	-10.2	-0.6	-3.6	-1.2
S&P 500	-7.2	1.1	1.8	0.0	0.0	-1.8	-8.6	0.0	-5.4	-1.8
Nasdaq	-9.4	1.7	3.1	-0.5	-0.3	0.0	-9.1	3.4	-6.5	-2.2
TSX	-6.7	1.8	1.5	3.1	-1.1	-1.1	-1.7	0.0	-4.0	-3.6
Russell 1000	-7.5	1.2	1.7	0.3	0.0	-2.0	-8.5	0.1	-5.7	-1.9
Russell 2000	-5.1	1.7	4.1	3.7	0.5	-1.6	-7.8	1.3	-7.9	-2.5
Russell 3000 Growth	-9.3	1.3	1.3	-0.1	-0.5	-1.5	-7.2	1.1	-5.7	-1.6
Russell 3000 Value	-5.6	1.1	2.4	1.2	0.5	-2.5	-9.8	-0.9	-6.1	-2.3

June Market Avg. Performance 2002 to 2011[1]

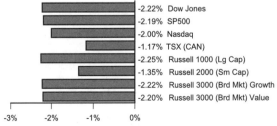

-2.22% Dow Jones
-2.19% SP500
-2.00% Nasdaq
-1.17% TSX (CAN)
-2.25% Russell 1000 (Lg Cap)
-1.35% Russell 2000 (Sm Cap)
-2.22% Russell 3000 (Brd Mkt) Growth
-2.20% Russell 3000 (Brd Mkt) Value

Interest Corner Jun[2]

	Fed Funds % [3]	3 Mo. T-Bill % [4]	10 Yr % [5]	20 Yr % [6]
2011	0.25	0.03	3.18	4.09
2010	0.25	0.18	2.97	3.74
2009	0.25	0.19	3.53	4.30
2008	2.00	1.90	3.99	4.59
2007	5.25	4.82	5.03	5.21

(1) Russell Data provided by Russell (2) Federal Reserve Bank of St. Louis- end of month values (3) Target rate set by FOMC (4)(5)(6) Constant yield maturities.

THACKRAY SECTOR THERMOMETER

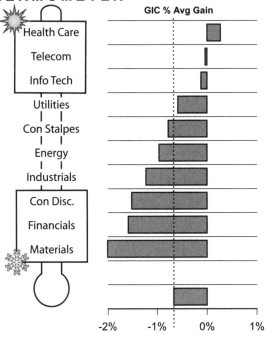

GIC[2] % Avg Gain	Fq % Gain >S&P 500	SP GIC SECTOR 1990-2010[1]
0.3 %	57 %	Health Care
0.0	62	Telecom
-0.1	43	Information Technology
-0.6	48	Utilities
-0.8	38	Consumer Staples
-1.0	38	Energy
-1.2	38	Industrials
-1.5	43	Consumer Discretionary
-1.6	38	Financials
-2.0 %	29 %	Materials
-0.7 %	N/A %	S&P 500

Sector Commentary

♦ As described in the *June – Leaderless Month* strategy, the sectors that lead one year to the next vary depending on market conditions. Overall, the defensive sectors have averaged the best gains in June from 1990 to 2010.
♦ In June 2011, once again defensive sectors were at the top of the sector pack. Although all of the sectors were negative in June, the defensive sectors were generally the least negative (*health care* -1.3%, *telecom* -1.5% and *utilities* -0.5%). The exception to this trend was the *consumer staples* sector which was one of the worst performing sectors. It produced a large loss of 2.9%, compared with S&P 500 which produced a loss of 1.8%.

Sub-Sector Commentary

♦ After a weak May 2011, June followed with a negative performance. There was only one sub-sector that produced a positive performance – *biotech*, which ended up with a gain of 0.3%. *Biotech* had been performing well over the last few months. It usually starts its seasonal outperformance in late June (see *Biotech Summer Solstice* strategy). All of the other sectors in the sub-sector list produced losses in June.

		SELECTED SUB-SECTORS 1990-2010[3]
2.6 %	76 %	Software & Services
0.4	62	Pharmaceuticals
-0.1	52	Gold (London PM)
-0.7	38	Integrated Oil & Gas
-0.8	57	Retail
-1.0	31	Semiconductor (SOX) 95-2010
-1.1	52	Metals & Mining
-1.1	43	Airlines
-1.1	35	Agriculture Products (94-2010)
-1.1	48	Gold (XAU)
-1.2	39	Biotech (93-2010)
-1.6	48	Auto & Components
-1.6	29	Transportation
-3.0	24	Banks

(1) Sector data provided by Standard and Poors (2) GIC is short form for Global Industry Classification (3) Sub Sector data provided by Standard and Poors, except where marked by symbol.

BIOTECH SUMMER SOLSTICE
June 23rd to Sep 13th

The *Biotech Summer Solstice* trade starts on June 23rd and lasts until September 13th. The trade is aptly named as its outperformance starts approximately on the day of that summer solstice starts– the longest day of the year.

There are two main drivers of the trade: biotech is a good substitute for technology stocks in the summer, and investors want to take a position in the biotech sector before the autumn conferences.

11.8% extra & 84% of the time better than the S&P 500

Biotech vs. S&P 500 1992 to 2010

Jun 23 to Sep 13	S&P 500	Biotech	Diff
Performance > S&P 500			
1992	4.0 %	17.9 %	13.8 %
1993	3.6	3.6	0.0
1994	3.2	24.2	21.0
1995	5.0	31.5	26.5
1996	2.1	7.0	4.9
1997	2.8	-18.9	-21.7
1998	-8.5	20.6	29.1
1999	0.6	64.3	63.7
2000	2.3	7.6	5.4
2001	-10.8	-3.6	7.2
2002	-10.0	8.1	18.2
2003	2.3	6.4	4.1
2004	-0.8	8.9	9.6
2005	1.4	26.0	24.5
2006	5.8	7.4	1.6
2007	-1.2	6.0	7.2
2008	-5.0	11.4	16.5
2009	16.8	7.7	-9.1
2010	2.4	2.8	0.4
Avg	0.8 %	12.6 %	11.8 %
Fq>0	68 %	89 %	84 %

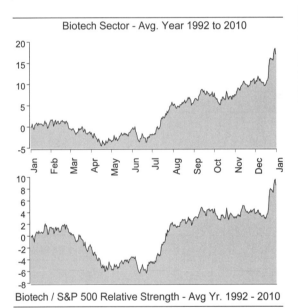

Biotech Sector - Avg. Year 1992 to 2010

Biotech / S&P 500 Relative Strength - Avg Yr. 1992 - 2010

As a result, in the softer summer months, investors are more willing to commit speculative money into the biotech sector, compared with the technology sector.

The biotech sector is one of the few sectors that starts its outperformance in June. This is in part because of the biotech conferences that occur in autumn. With positive announcements in autumn, the price of biotech companies on the stock market can increase dramatically. As a result, investors try to lock in positions early.

The biotechnology sector is often considered the cousin of the technology sector, a good place for speculative investments. The sectors are similar as both include concept companies (companies without a product but with good potential).

Despite their similarity, investors view the sectors differently. The technology sector is viewed as being largely dependent on the economy and conversely the biotech sector as being much less dependent on the economy. The end product of biotechnology companies is mainly medicine, which is not economically sensitive.

> (i) *Biotech SP GIC Sector # 352010: Companies primarily engaged in the research, development, manufacturing and/or marketing of products based on genetic analysis and genetic engineering. This includes companies specializing in protein-based therapeutics to treat human diseases.*

| **4** MONDAY | 156 / 210 |
| **5** TUESDAY | 157 / 209 |

| **6** WEDNESDAY | 158 / 208 |
| **7** THURSDAY | 159 / 207 |

| **8** FRIDAY | 160 / 206 |

WEEK 23

Market Indices & Rates
Weekly Values

Stock Markets	2010	2011
Dow	10,008	12,057
S&P500	1,069	1,282
Nasdaq	2,193	2,682
TSX	11,555	13,225
FTSE	5,096	5,832
DAX	5,973	7,096
Nikkei	9,549	9,451
Hang Seng	19,598	22,640

Commodities	2010	2011
Oil	73.41	100.01
Gold	1226.4	1539.8

Bond Yields	2010	2011
USA 5 Yr Treasury	2.01	1.58
USA 10 Yr T	3.22	3.00
USA 20 Yr T	3.96	3.90
Moody's Aaa	4.90	4.97
Moody's Baa	6.23	5.73
CAN 5 Yr T	2.66	2.24
CAN 10 Yr T	3.36	3.01

Money Market	2010	2011
USA Fed Funds	0.25	0.25
USA 3 Mo T-B	0.10	0.05
CAN tgt overnight rate	0.50	1.00
CAN 3 Mo T-B	0.53	0.94

Foreign Exchange	2010	2011
USD/EUR	1.20	1.45
USD/GBP	1.45	1.64
CAN/USD	1.04	0.98
JPY/USD	91.42	80.15

2010 Strategy Performance

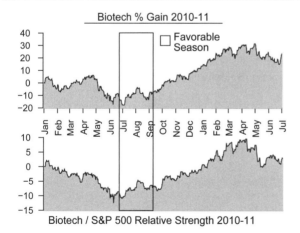

Biotech % Gain 2010-11 / Favorable Season / Biotech / S&P 500 Relative Strength 2010-11

JUNE

M	T	W	T	F	S	S
				1	2	3
4	5	6	7	8	9	10
11	12	13	14	15	16	17
18	19	20	21	22	23	24
25	26	27	28	29	30	

JULY

M	T	W	T	F	S	S
						1
2	3	4	5	6	7	8
9	10	11	12	13	14	15
16	17	18	19	20	21	22
23	24	25	26	27	28	29
30	31					

AUGUST

M	T	W	T	F	S	S
		1	2	3	4	5
6	7	8	9	10	11	12
13	14	15	16	17	18	19
20	21	22	23	24	25	26
27	28	29	30	31		

The biotech sector put in a positive performance during its seasonal period, and marginally outperformed the S&P 500.

From a technical basis it would have been better to start the trade a bit later in the month of June and as a result the returns would have been greater.

** Weekly avg closing values- except Fed Funds & CAN overnight tgt rate weekly closing values.

PotashCorp
Fertilize Your Profits - June 23rd to Jan 11th

Fertilizer stocks have displayed a strong seasonal trend from the end of June to the beginning of January. The stock prices of fertilizer companies are highly correlated to grain prices which often rise in the second half of the year (the main harvest season for the northern hemisphere).

In addition, fertilizer companies benefit from the spending patterns of farmers. In order to reduce taxes at the end of the year farmers will often make large purchases, including fertilizer. This helps to drive up the price of fertilizer stocks.

23.1% & positive 86% of the time

PotashCorp, the world's largest fertilizer company by capacity, has a profitable seasonal trend from June 23rd to January 11th. During this time period, from 1990/91 to 2010/11, it has produced an average return of 23.1% and has been positive 86% of the time (S&P TSX). These results far exceed the S&P TSX Composite which has produced an average return of 3.6% and has only been positive 57% of the time during the same period.

June 23 to Jan 11	TSX Comp	POT	Diff
1990/91	-8.8%	6.9%	15.7%
1991/92	2.2	19.3	17.2
1992/93	-0.9	4.6	5.5
1993/94	13.0	31.6	18.6
1994/95	3.3	43.2	39.8
1995/96	5.2	35.7	30.5
1996/97	18.6	35.8	17.3
1997/98	-3.7	8.3	12.0
1998/99	-4.1	-4.5	-0.4
1999/00	21.4	9.1	-12.3
2000/01	-12.5	41.4	53.9
2001/02	-0.5	11.7	12.2
2002/03	-4.7	6.8	11.5
2003/04	18.1	29.3	11.2
2004/05	5.9	44.9	39.0
2005/06	15.6	-16.2	-31.8
2006/07	12.5	72.1	59.6
2007/08	-2.5	72.2	74.7
2008/09	-37.7	-56.9	-19.2
2009/10	21.5	25.9	4.4
2010/11	13.6	63.0	49.4
Avg	3.6%	23.1%	19.5%
Fq > 0	57%	86%	81%

Potash Corp vs. S&P/TSX Composite 1990/91 to 2010/11 — Positive

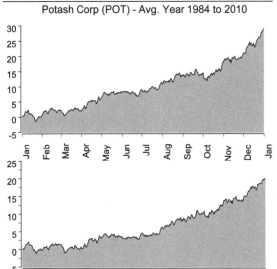

Potash Corp (POT) - Avg. Year 1984 to 2010

POT /TSX Comp Relative Strength - Avg Yr. 1990 - 2010

Since 1990 there have only been two seasonally strong periods that produced a loss of greater than 10%; 2005/06 and 2008/09. The negative performance in 2005/06 was largely a correction to a very impressive increase in price during 2004 and 2005. In 2008 with the world suffering an economic slowdown farmers around the world reduced their fertilizer ap-

plication. The result was a decrease in fertilizer prices and the stock price of fertilizer companies. In the short-term reducing the application of fertilizer helps with cash flow, but the lack of fertilizer will eventually catch up with a lower crop output. Over time as yields drop off, farmers become more motivated to apply fertilizer. In the last two years we have seen this "catch up" process take place, pushing up fertilizer prices.

Up until recently it was not possible to invest directly in the fertilizer company sector via an ETF. That changed with the launch of the Global X Fertilizers/Potash ETF (SOIL), trading in the U.S. It is expected that SOIL will have a similar seasonal trend to the fertilizer stocks.

(i) * PotashCorp (POT) trades on both the S&P TSX Composite and NYSE. It is the world's largest fertilizer company by capacity.

11 MONDAY	163 / 203	**12** TUESDAY	164 / 202

Market Indices & Rates
Weekly Values**

Stock Markets	2010	2011
Dow	10,378	11,978
S&P500	1,111	1,273
Nasdaq	2,295	2,638
TSX	11,874	12,931
FTSE	5,233	5,747
DAX	6,186	7,136
Nikkei	9,966	9,467
Hang Seng	20,135	22,199

13 WEDNESDAY	165 / 201	**14** THURSDAY	166 / 200

Commodities	2010	2011
Oil	76.74	95.89
Gold	1236.9	1526.6

Bond Yields	2010	2011
USA 5 Yr Treasury	2.06	1.58
USA 10 Yr T	3.26	2.99
USA 20 Yr T	4.00	3.90
Moody's Aaa	4.93	4.98
Moody's Baa	6.32	5.73
CAN 5 Yr T	2.71	2.22
CAN 10 Yr T	3.37	2.98

15 FRIDAY		167 / 199

Money Market	2010	2011
USA Fed Funds	0.25	0.25
USA 3 Mo T-B	0.09	0.05
CAN tgt overnight rate	0.50	1.00
CAN 3 Mo T-B	0.53	0.94

Foreign Exchange	2010	2011
USD/EUR	1.23	1.43
USD/GBP	1.48	1.63
CAN/USD	1.03	0.98
JPY/USD	91.24	80.47

2010-11 Strategy Performance

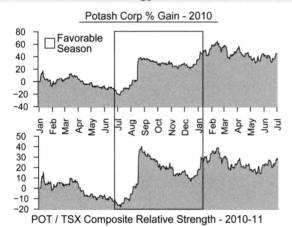

Potash Corp % Gain - 2010

POT / TSX Composite Relative Strength - 2010-11

JUNE

M	T	W	T	F	S	S
				1	2	3
4	5	6	7	8	9	10
11	12	13	14	15	16	17
18	19	20	21	22	23	24
25	26	27	28	29	30	

JULY

M	T	W	T	F	S	S
						1
2	3	4	5	6	7	8
9	10	11	12	13	14	15
16	17	18	19	20	21	22
23	24	25	26	27	28	29
30	31					

In 2010, POT started its seasonal rise at the beginning of July. It had a large spike in August when BHP Billiton made a take over offer in August. Even after the offer was withdrawn in November POT still managed to put in a solid performance at yearend. Over the total seasonal period from June 23rd 2010 to January 11th 2011, POT gained 63%.

AUGUST

M	T	W	T	F	S	S
		1	2	3	4	5
6	7	8	9	10	11	12
13	14	15	16	17	18	19
20	21	22	23	24	25	26
27	28	29	30	31		

** Weekly avg closing values- except Fed Funds & CAN overnight tgt rate weekly closing values.

INDEPENDENCE DAY – THE FULL TRADE
PROFIT BEFORE & AFTER FIREWORKS
Two Market Days Before June Month End
To 5 Market Days After Independence Day

The beginning of July is a time for celebration and the markets tend to agree.

Based on previous market data, the best way to take advantage of this trend is to be invested for the two market days prior to the June month end and hold until five market days after Independence Day. This time period has produced above average returns on a fairly consistent basis.

0.8% avg. gain &
71% of the time positive

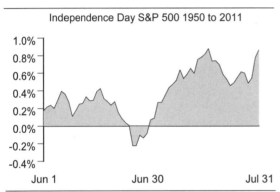

Independence Day S&P 500 1950 to 2011

The typical Independence Day trade put forward by quite a few pundits has been to invest one or two days before the holiday and take profits one or two days after the holiday.

Although this strategy has produced profits, it has left a lot of money on the table. This strategy misses out on the positive days at the end of June and on the full slate of positive days after Independence Day.

The beginning part of the *Independence Day* positive trend is driven by two combining factors.

First, portfolio managers "window dress" (buying stocks that have a favorable perception in the market); thereby pushing stock prices up at the end of the month.

Second, investors have become "wise" to the *Independence Day Trade* and try to jump in before everyone else.

Depending on market conditions at the time, investors should consider extending the exit date until eighteen calendar days in July. With July being an earnings month, the market can continue to rally until mid-month (see *18 Day Earnings Month Strategy*).

> (i) *History of Independence Day:*
> *Independence Day is celebrated on July 4th because that is the day when the Continental Congress adopted the final draft of the Declaration of Independence in 1776. Independence Day was made an official holiday at the end of the War of Independence in 1783. In 1941 Congress declared the 4th of July a federal holiday.*

S&P 500, 2 Market Days Before June Month End To 5 Market Days after Independence Day % Gain 1950 to 2011   Positive ☐

1950	-4.4 %	1960	-0.1 %	1970	1.5 %	1980	1.4 %	1990	1.7 %	2000	1.8 %	2010	0.4 %
1951	1.5	1961	1.7	1971	3.2	1981	-2.4	1991	1.4	2001	-2.6	2011	1.8
1952	0.9	1962	9.8	1972	0.3	1982	-0.6	1992	2.8	2002	-4.7		
1953	0.8	1963	0.5	1973	2.1	1983	1.5	1993	-0.6	2003	1.2		
1954	2.9	1964	2.3	1974	-8.8	1984	-0.7	1994	0.4	2004	-1.7		
1955	4.9	1965	5.0	1975	-0.2	1985	1.5	1995	1.8	2005	1.5		
1956	3.4	1966	2.1	1976	2.4	1986	-2.6	1996	-2.8	2006	2.1		
1957	3.8	1967	1.3	1977	-0.6	1987	0.4	1997	3.7	2007	0.8		
1958	2.0	1968	2.3	1978	0.6	1988	-0.6	1998	2.7	2008	-3.4		
1959	3.3	1969	-1.5	1979	1.3	1989	0.9	1999	5.1	2009	-4.3		
Avg.	1.9 %		2.3 %		0.2 %		-0.1 %		1.8 %		-0.9 %		1.1 %

18 MONDAY	170 / 196	**19** TUESDAY	171 / 195

20 WEDNESDAY	172 / 194	**21** THURSDAY	173 / 193

22 FRIDAY   174 / 192

WEEK 25

Market Indices & Rates
Weekly Values**

Stock Markets	2010	2011
Dow	10,266	12,073
S&P500	1,090	1,283
Nasdaq	2,249	2,665
TSX	11,784	12,974
FTSE	5,174	5,723
DAX	6,191	7,197
Nikkei	9,988	9,544
Hang Seng	20,802	21,848

Commodities	2010	2011
Oil	77.13	92.63
Gold	1241.5	1535.8

Bond Yields	2010	2011
USA 5 Yr Treasury	1.96	1.52
USA 10 Yr T	3.17	2.96
USA 20 Yr T	3.92	3.87
Moody's Aaa	4.84	4.95
Moody's Baa	6.22	5.72
CAN 5 Yr T	2.56	2.15
CAN 10 Yr T	3.25	2.94

Money Market	2010	2011
USA Fed Funds	0.25	0.25
USA 3 Mo T-B	0.13	0.02
CAN tgt overnight rate	0.50	1.00
CAN 3 Mo T-B	0.54	0.89

Foreign Exchange	2010	2011
USD/EUR	1.23	1.43
USD/GBP	1.49	1.61
CAN/USD	1.03	0.98
JPY/USD	90.07	80.34

2010-11 Strategy Performance

S&P 500 Independence Day Trades 2010-11

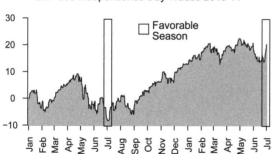

The *Independence Day Trade* in 2010 was not stellar, but it was positive. The end of June was decidedly negative, giving the trade a bad start into the beginning of July, but a sharp rise in the markets at the beginning of July brought the trade back into positive territory.

In 2011, the market rallied into the end of the month and set up a strong beginning of the month. The *Independence Day Trade* ended up with a large gain of 1.8%.

JUNE

M	T	W	T	F	S	S
				1	2	3
4	5	6	7	8	9	10
11	12	13	14	15	16	17
18	19	20	21	22	23	24
25	26	27	28	29	30	

JULY

M	T	W	T	F	S	S
						1
2	3	4	5	6	7	8
9	10	11	12	13	14	15
16	17	18	19	20	21	22
23	24	25	26	27	28	29
30	31					

AUGUST

M	T	W	T	F	S	S
		1	2	3	4	5
6	7	8	9	10	11	12
13	14	15	16	17	18	19
20	21	22	23	24	25	26
27	28	29	30	31		

** Weekly avg closing values- except Fed Funds & CAN overnight tgt rate weekly closing values.

Johnson & Johnson
July 14th to October 21st

The health care sector by nature is defensive and attracts investors when they become concerned with stock market valuations or an economic slowdown. The advantage of investing in Johnson and Johnson during its strong seasonal period is that this period coincides with the weak period of the broad stock market.

The stock market often peaks mid-month July, just as the earnings season is getting underway– the same time as JNJ's seasonal period starts.

JNJ is not only attractive because of its lack of sensitivity to discretionary spending, but also because it has a higher than average dividend yield.

6.3% & positive 71% of the time

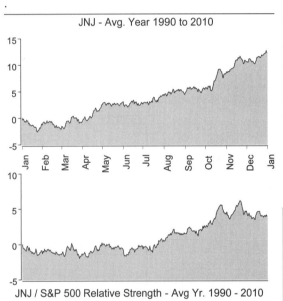

JNJ - Avg. Year 1990 to 2010

JNJ / S&P 500 Relative Strength - Avg Yr. 1990 - 2010

JNJ has a strong track record of performing well from July 14th to October 21st. During this time period, from 1990 to 2010, JNJ produced an average gain of 6.3% and was both positive 71% of the time. It also outperformed the S&P 500 71% of the time. The maximum drawdown for JNJ during this time period was 5.5%. This compares to the S&P 500 which had six periods with greater losses.

It is also important to note that all of the times when JNJ in its seasonally strong period, under performed the S&P 500, occurred when the S&P 500 produced a

JNJ vs. S&P 500
1990 to 2010

Jul 14 to Oct 21	S&P 500	JNJ	Diff (Positive)
1990	-14.9%	-4.1%	10.9%
1991	2.6	1.9	-0.7
1992	0.2	7.5	7.3
1993	3.9	4.9	1.1
1994	3.6	28.9	25.3
1995	4.7	19.7	15.0
1996	9.9	7.4	-2.4
1997	6.1	-5.5	-11.6
1998	-8.2	12.5	20.7
1999	-7.9	8.2	16.1
2000	-6.6	-3.5	3.1
2001	-11.7	10.1	21.8
2002	-2.4	21.0	23.4
2003	4.8	-2.0	-6.8
2004	-0.8	4.3	5.1
2005	-3.6	-0.5	3.0
2006	10.2	13.9	3.7
2007	-3.3	1.3	4.6
2008	-23.0	-3.9	19.0
2009	20.0	4.5	-15.5
2010	7.8	5.8	-2.0
Avg	-0.4%	6.3%	6.7%
Fq > 0	52%	71%	71%

positive return, typically over 5%. Large returns for the S&P 500 are not typical during this time of the year, making JNJ an attractive holding in a seasonal portfolio.

⊙ Seasonal HotSpot
JNJ typically releases its Q3 earnings mid-October and as a result, on average the company performs particularly well from October 11th to the 21st. October tends to be a volatile month and investors focus on stable companies that have the potential to report solid earnings. During the seasonal HotSpot, from 1990 to 2010, JNJ produced an average gain of 4.1% and was positive 76% of the time. It outperformed the S&P 500 by 2.3% and 67% of the time.

ⓘ *Johnson and Johnson (JNJ) is a diversified health care company that operates in three segments: Consumer, Pharmaceutical, and Medical Devices and Diagnostics. JNJ trades on the NYSE.*

25 MONDAY	177 / 189

26 TUESDAY	178 / 188

27 WEDNESDAY	179 / 187

28 THURSDAY	180 / 186

29 FRIDAY	181 / 185

WEEK 26

Market Indices & Rates
Weekly Values**

Stock Markets	2010	2011
Dow	9,840	12,298
S&P500	1,039	1,309
Nasdaq	2,132	2,750
TSX	11,340	13,140
FTSE	4,909	5,856
DAX	5,953	7,274
Nikkei	9,409	9,742
Hang Seng	20,252	22,141

Commodities	2010	2011
Oil	74.98	93.73
Gold	1235.0	1498.0

Bond Yields	2010	2011
USA 5 Yr Treasury	1.80	1.67
USA 10 Yr T	2.99	3.11
USA 20 Yr T	3.76	4.05
Moody's Aaa	4.69	5.11
Moody's Baa	6.06	5.88
CAN 5 Yr T	2.36	2.24
CAN 10 Yr T	3.10	3.04

Money Market	2010	2011
USA Fed Funds	0.25	0.25
USA 3 Mo T-B	0.17	0.02
CAN tgt overnight rate	0.50	1.00
CAN 3 Mo T-B	0.51	0.92

Foreign Exchange	2010	2011
USD/EUR	1.24	1.44
USD/GBP	1.51	1.60
CAN/USD	1.06	0.97
JPY/USD	88.35	80.84

JUNE

M	T	W	T	F	S	S
				1	2	3
4	5	6	7	8	9	10
11	12	13	14	15	16	17
18	19	20	21	22	23	24
25	26	27	28	29	30	

JULY

M	T	W	T	F	S	S
						1
2	3	4	5	6	7	8
9	10	11	12	13	14	15
16	17	18	19	20	21	22
23	24	25	26	27	28	29
30	31					

AUGUST

M	T	W	T	F	S	S
		1	2	3	4	5
6	7	8	9	10	11	12
13	14	15	16	17	18	19
20	21	22	23	24	25	26
27	28	29	30	31		

2010 Strategy Performance

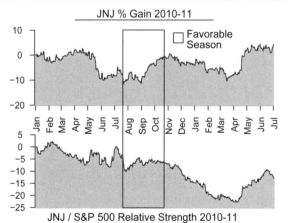

JNJ % Gain 2010-11

JNJ / S&P 500 Relative Strength 2010-11

In 2010, Johnson and Johnson was outperforming the S&P 500 up until the end of August when Bernanke leaked his intentions to launch another quantitative easing program. At that time the market started an upward trajectory. Although JNJ produced a positive return over its seasonal period, it under performed the S&P 500.

** Weekly avg closing values- except Fed Funds & CAN overnight tgt rate weekly closing values.

JULY

	MONDAY	TUESDAY	WEDNESDAY
WEEK 27	**2** 29 CAN Market Closed- Canada Day	**3** 28	**4** 27 USA Market Closed - Independence Day
WEEK 28	**9** 22	**10** 21	**11** 20
WEEK 29	**16** 15	**17** 14	**18** 13
WEEK 30	**23** 8	**24** 7	**25** 6
WEEK 31	**30** 1	**31**	1

THURSDAY	FRIDAY
5 26	**6** 25
12 19	**13** 18
19 12	**20** 11
26 5	**27** 4
2	3

AUGUST

M	T	W	T	F	S	S
		1	2	3	4	5
6	7	8	9	10	11	12
13	14	15	16	17	18	19
20	21	22	23	24	25	26
27	28	29	30	31		

SEPTEMBER

M	T	W	T	F	S	S
					1	2
3	4	5	6	7	8	9
10	11	12	13	14	15	16
17	18	19	20	21	22	23
24	25	26	27	28	29	30

OCTOBER

M	T	W	T	F	S	S
1	2	3	4	5	6	7
8	9	10	11	12	13	14
15	16	17	18	19	20	21
22	23	24	25	26	27	28
29	30	31				

NOVEMBER

M	T	W	T	F	S	S
			1	2	3	4
5	6	7	8	9	10	11
12	13	14	15	16	17	18
19	20	21	22	23	24	25
26	27	28	29	30		

JULY
S U M M A R Y

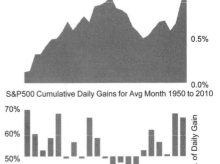

S&P500 Cumulative Daily Gains for Avg Month 1950 to 2010

	Dow Jones	S&P 500	Nasdaq	TSX Comp
Month Rank	4	6	11	5
# Up	38	33	20	17
# Down	23	28	19	9
% Pos	62	54	51	65
% Avg. Gain	1.2	1.0	0.1	0.9

Dow & S&P 1950-June 2011, Nasdaq 1972-June 2011, TSX 1985-June 2011

♦ When a summer rally occurs, the bulk of the gains are usually made in July. ♦ In the last half of the month the *energy, gold* and *utility stocks* tend to start their seasonal rallies (see strategies in this month). ♦ In 2011, the market performed well in the first part of July as investors expected solid earnings reports (see *18 Day Earnings Month Strategy*). With the start of earnings season the market started to fade as earnings were not stellar and weak economic numbers started to roll in.

BEST / WORST JULY BROAD MKTS. 2001-2010

BEST JULY MARKETS
- ♦ Russell 2000 (2009) 9.5%
- ♦ Dow (2009) 8.6%
- ♦ Russell 3000 Value (2009) 8.2%

WORST JULY MARKETS
- ♦ Russell 2000 (2002) -15.2%
- ♦ Russell 3000 Value (2002) -9.9%
- ♦ Nasdaq (2002) -9.2%

Index Values End of Month

	2001	2002	2003	2004	2005	2006	2007	2008	2009	2010
Dow	10,523	8,737	9,234	10,140	10,641	11,186	13,212	11,378	9,172	10,466
S&P 500	1,211	912	990	1,102	1,234	1,277	1,455	1,267	987	1,102
Nasdaq	2,027	1,328	1,735	1,887	2,185	2,091	2,546	2,326	1,979	2,255
TSX	7,690	6,605	7,258	8,458	10,423	11,831	13,869	13,593	10,787	11,713
Russell 1000	1,225	931	1,016	1,129	1,288	1,331	1,523	1,334	1,038	1,165
Russell 2000	1,205	975	1,183	1,370	1,689	1,741	1,929	1,776	1,384	1,618
Russell 3000 Growth	2,084	1,471	1,639	1,764	1,988	1,955	2,305	2,139	1,727	1,937
Russell 3000 Value	2,166	1,773	1,922	2,216	2,589	2,809	3,099	2,570	1,920	2,172

Percent Gain for July

	2001	2002	2003	2004	2005	2006	2007	2008	2009	2010
Dow	0.2	-5.5	2.8	-2.8	3.6	0.3	-1.5	0.2	8.6	7.1
S&P 500	-1.1	-7.9	1.6	-3.4	3.6	0.5	-3.2	-1.0	7.4	6.9
Nasdaq	-6.2	-9.2	6.9	-7.8	6.2	-3.7	-2.2	1.4	7.8	6.9
TSX	-0.6	-7.6	3.9	-1.0	5.3	1.9	-0.3	-6.0	4.0	3.7
Russell 1000	-1.5	-7.5	1.8	-3.6	3.8	0.1	-3.2	-1.3	7.5	6.8
Russell 2000	-5.5	-15.2	6.2	-6.8	6.3	-3.3	-6.9	3.6	9.5	6.8
Russell 3000 Growth	-3.0	-6.2	2.8	-6.0	5.0	-2.2	-1.9	-1.6	7.1	7.0
Russell 3000 Value	-0.5	-9.9	1.5	-1.9	2.9	1.9	-5.1	-0.2	8.2	6.6

July Market Avg. Performance 2001 to 2010[1]

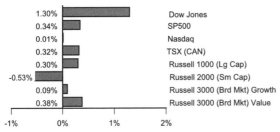

1.30%	Dow Jones
0.34%	SP500
0.01%	Nasdaq
0.32%	TSX (CAN)
0.30%	Russell 1000 (Lg Cap)
-0.53%	Russell 2000 (Sm Cap)
0.09%	Russell 3000 (Brd Mkt) Growth
0.38%	Russell 3000 (Brd Mkt) Value

Interest Corner Jul[2]

	Fed Funds % [3]	3 Mo. T-Bill % [4]	10 Yr % [5]	20 Yr % [6]
2010	0.25	0.15	2.94	3.74
2009	0.25	0.18	3.52	4.29
2008	2.00	1.68	3.99	4.63
2007	5.25	4.96	4.78	5.00
2006	5.25	5.10	4.99	5.17

(1) Russell Data provided by Russell (2) Federal Reserve Bank of St. Louis- end of month values (3) Target rate set by FOMC (4)(5)(6) Constant yield maturities.

THACKRAY SECTOR THERMOMETER

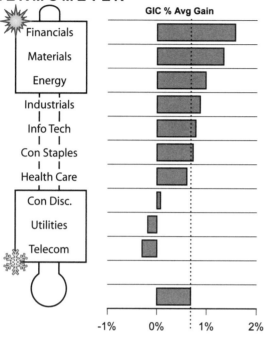

	GIC(2) % Avg Gain	Fq % Gain >S&P 500	
	SP GIC SECTOR 1990-2010(1)		
Financials	1.6 %	52 %	Financials
Materials	1.3	67	Materials
Energy	1.0	62	Energy
Industrials	0.9	52	Industrials
Info Tech	0.8	48	Information Technology
Con Staples	0.7	57	Consumer Staples
Health Care	0.6	43	Health Care
Con Disc.	0.1	48	Consumer Discretionary
Utilities	-0.2	43	Utilities
Telecom	-0.3 %	48 %	Telecom
	0.7 %	N/A %	S&P 500

Sector Commentary

♦ July's performance is really the tale of two half months. In the first half of the month, the broad market tends to do very well (see *18 Day Earnings Month Effect*). In the second half the performance tends to wither away. ♦ In July 2010, earnings were better than expected and rumours started floating around about another quantitative easing program being launched. As a result the S&P 500 gained 6.9%. All sectors did well in the month. The best sector was *materials* with a 12.2% gain and the worst sector was *health care* with a 1.3% gain.

Sub-Sector Commentary

♦ The *auto & components* sub-sector is the second highest rated sector in the sub-sector thermometer with an average gain of 2.2% from 1990 to 2010. In 2009, it gained 29.2% as the economy rebounded and car companies that not too long ago were bound for the scrap yard were emerging with strong prospects. ♦ In 2010, the *auto* sector took off once again in July, with a gain of 19.7% ♦ The *biotech* sub-sector has the best long-term average gain and has the highest frequency of beating the S&P 500. In 2010, *biotech* managed to outperform the S&P 500 with a gain of 7.6%, versus the S&P 500 with a gain of 6.9%.

SELECTED SUB-SECTORS 1990-2010(3)		
6.9 %	83 %	Biotech (93-2010)
2.2	57	Auto & Components
1.5	48	Airlines
1.5	52	Transportation
1.5	62	Banks
1.1	57	Integrated Oil & Gas
0.8	50	Semiconductor (SOX) 95-2010
0.5	52	Metals & Mining
0.5	52	Retail
0.0	48	Pharmaceuticals
-0.3	48	Gold (London PM)
-1.3	38	Gold (XAU)
-1.5	41	Agriculture Products (94-2010)
-2.2	24	Software & Services

(1) Sector data provided by Standard and Poors (2) GIC is short form for Global Industry Classification (3) Sub Sector data provided by Standard and Poors, except where marked by symbol.

UTILITIES – SUMMER BOUNCE
July 17th to Oct 3rd

Utility stocks are a long forgotten part of the market. Very seldom do you hear pundits singing their virtues. They lost out to the hype of tech stocks in the 90's and are still shunned by a large number of investors because of the fear of rising interest rates. Despite the environment of neglect, utility stocks have managed to outperform the S&P 500 on a fairly consistent basis from July 17th to October 3rd.

2.6% extra and positive at a time when the S&P 500 has been negative

Utilities' outperformance from the end of July to the beginning of October fits in very well with the theme of investors taking a defensive position during this time of year. At this time the broad market tends to produce a negative return and investors are looking for a safe place to invest. Utilities fit the bill.

Jul 17 to Oct 3	S&P 500	Positive Utilities	Diff
1990	-15.6 %	-3.4 %	12.2 %
1991	0.8	9.2	8.5
1992	-1.7	-0.9	0.8
1993	3.5	3.6	0.1
1994	1.7	-1.6	-3.3
1995	4.0	6.6	2.5
1996	10.3	-0.9	-11.2
1997	3.0	2.6	-0.4
1998	-15.3	6.8	22.1
1999	-9.6	-5.5	4.1
2000	-5.5	23.0	28.5
2001	-10.8	-13.6	-2.8
2002	-9.1	-12.0	-2.9
2003	3.6	7.2	3.6
2004	2.7	5.1	2.4
2005	-0.1	6.0	6.1
2006	7.9	5.3	-2.6
2007	-0.6	0.6	1.2
2008	-11.7	-17.6	-5.9
2009	9.0	1.1	-7.9
2010	7.6	6.3	-1.3
Avg.	-1.2 %	1.3 %	2.6 %
Fq > 0	52 %	62 %	57 %

S&P Utilities Sector vs. S&P 500 1990 to 2010

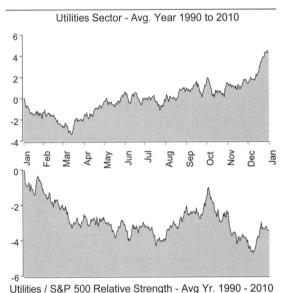

Utilities Sector - Avg. Year 1990 to 2010

Utilities / S&P 500 Relative Strength - Avg. Yr. 1990 - 2010

From July 17th to October 3rd, during the years 1990 to 2010, the utilities sector has produced an average return of 1.3%, while the S&P 500 has reached into the negative territory with an average loss of 1.2%. Utilities have produced 2.6% more when the S&P 500 has typically been negative. Also, during this time period the utilities sector beat the S&P 500, 12 out of 21 times. Not bad for a defensive sector. The utilities sector is considered defensive because it is a slow growth mature industry that has stable income from long term contracts. When the market gets "spooked," investors typically switch their money into companies with stable earnings. There is an added bonus of investing in utilities – dividends. Because the sector is mature with stable earnings they tend to pay out a higher dividend yield.

In the last two decades there have been two periods of two back-to-back years of negative performance. In 1996 and 1997 the utilities sector under performed as dividends and defensive positions did not matter much. In 2001 and 2002, the utilities sector under performed as a few scandal ridden utilities companies hit the newspaper headlines. The most notorious being Enron.

It appears the utilities trade is once again back on track as the companies have "cleaned house" and moved back to their core business: providing utilities services.

 Utilities SP GIC Sector 55: An index designed to represent a cross section of utility companies.
For more information on the utilities sector, see www.standardandpoors.com.

2 MONDAY	184 / 182

3 TUESDAY	185 / 181

4 WEDNESDAY	186 / 180

5 THURSDAY	187 / 179

6 FRIDAY	188 / 178

WEEK 27

Market Indices & Rates
Weekly Values**

Stock Markets	2009	2010
Dow	8,440	10,025
S&P500	917	1,059
Nasdaq	1,830	2,156
TSX	10,345	11,339
FTSE	4,271	5,008
DAX	4,805	5,970
Nikkei	9,875	9,401
Hang Seng	18,322	20,043

Commodities	2009	2010
Oil	69.36	74.40
Gold	934.1	1199.7

Bond Yields	2009	2010
USA 5 Yr Treasury	2.50	1.80
USA 10 Yr T	3.53	3.02
USA 20 Yr T	4.30	3.79
Moody's Aaa	5.40	4.72
Moody's Baa	7.18	6.08
CAN 5 Yr T	2.45	2.42
CAN 10 Yr T	3.37	3.15

Money Market	2009	2010
USA Fed Funds	0.25	0.25
USA 3 Mo T-B	0.18	0.16
CAN tgt overnight rate	0.25	0.50
CAN 3 Mo T-B	0.23	0.50

Foreign Exchange	2009	2010
USD/EUR	1.40	1.26
USD/GBP	1.64	1.51
CAN/USD	1.16	1.05
JPY/USD	96.21	87.99

2010 Strategy Performance

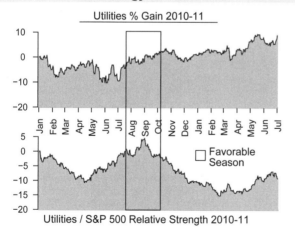

Utilities % Gain 2010-11

Utilities / S&P 500 Relative Strength 2010-11

JULY

M	T	W	T	F	S	S
						1
2	3	4	5	6	7	8
9	10	11	12	13	14	15
16	17	18	19	20	21	22
23	24	25	26	27	28	29
30	31					

AUGUST

M	T	W	T	F	S	S
		1	2	3	4	5
6	7	8	9	10	11	12
13	14	15	16	17	18	19
20	21	22	23	24	25	26
27	28	29	30	31		

SEPTEMBER

M	T	W	T	F	S	S
					1	2
3	4	5	6	7	8	9
10	11	12	13	14	15	16
17	18	19	20	21	22	23
24	25	26	27	28	29	30

Although the utilities sector produced a positive 6.3% return during its 2010 seasonally strong period, it under performed the S&P 500.

When the market is really strong, generally the defensive utilities sector under performs. The year 2010 was no exception. Investors were more interested in sectors with higher betas that could provide them with bigger returns.

** Weekly avg closing values- except Fed Funds & CAN overnight tgt rate weekly closing values.

GOLD SHINES

(Metal) Gold (Metal) Outperforms – July 12th to October 9th

"Foul cankering rust the hidden treasure frets, but gold that's put to use more gold begets."

(William Shakespeare, *Venus and Adonis*)

For many years gold was thought to be a dead investment. It was only the "gold bugs" that espoused the virtues of investing in the precious metal. Investors were mesmerized with technology stocks and central bankers, confident of their currencies, were selling gold, "left, right and center."

3.9% gain & positive 67% of the time

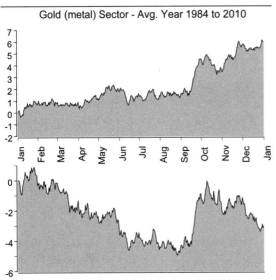

Gold (metal) Sector - Avg. Year 1984 to 2010

Gold / S&P 500 Relative Strength - Avg Yr. 1984 - 2010

Gold (Metal) London PM vs S&P 500
1984 to 2010

Jul 12 to Oct 9th	S&P 500	Positive Gold	Diff
1984	7.4 %	0.5 %	-6.9 %
1985	-5.4	4.1	9.5
1986	-2.6	25.2	27.8
1987	0.9	3.9	3.0
1988	2.8	-7.5	-10.3
1989	9.4	-4.2	-13.6
1990	-15.5	12.1	27.6
1991	0.0	-2.9	-2.8
1992	-2.9	0.4	3.3
1993	2.7	-8.8	-11.5
1994	1.6	1.6	0.0
1995	4.3	-0.1	-4.3
1996	7.9	-0.4	-8.3
1997	5.9	4.4	-1.5
1998	-15.5	2.8	18.2
1999	-4.8	25.6	30.4
2000	-5.3	-4.5	0.8
2001	-10.5	8.4	18.8
2002	-16.2	1.7	17.9
2003	4.1	7.8	3.8
2004	0.8	3.8	2.9
2005	-1.9	11.4	13.4
2006	6.1	-8.8	-14.9
2007	3.1	11.0	8.0
2008	-26.6	-8.2	18.4
2009	21.9	15.2	- 6.7
2010	8.1	11.0	2.9
Avg.	-0.8 %	3.9 %	4.7 %
Fq > 0	59 %	67 %	59 %

Times have changed and investors have taken a shine to gold (metal). In the last few years gold has substantially outperformed the stock market. On a seasonal basis, on average from 1984 to 2010, gold has done well relative to the stock market from July 12th to October 9th. The reasons for gold's seasonal changes in price, are related to jewellery production and European Central banks selling cycles (see *Golden Times* strategy page).

The movement of gold stock prices, represented by the index (XAU) on the Philadelphia Exchange, coincides closely with the price of gold (metal). Although there is a strong correlation between gold and gold stocks, there are other factors, such as company operations and hedging policies which determine each company's price in the market. Gold (metal) has typically started its seasonal strong period a few weeks earlier than gold stocks and finished just after gold stocks have turned down.

Investors should know that gold can have a run from November 1st to the end of the year. Although this is a positive time for gold, on average it does not perform as well as the S&P 500. From November 1st to Dec. 31st (1984 to 2010), gold has an average return of 2.2% and has been positive 59% of the time. In this time period it has only outperformed the S&P 500 41% of the time, which has averaged a return of 3.2%. Investors should use technical analysis to determine the relative strength of gold at this time.

ⓘ Source: Bank of England
London PM is recognized as the world benchmark for gold prices. London PM represents the close value of gold in afternoon trading in London.

9 MONDAY	191 / 175	**10** TUESDAY	192 / 174

Market Indices & Rates
Weekly Values**

Stock Markets	2009	2010
Dow	8,199	10,281
S&P500	884	1,086
Nasdaq	1,758	2,224
TSX	9,809	11,634
FTSE	4,162	5,212
DAX	4,606	6,134
Nikkei	9,466	9,595
Hang Seng	17,812	20,393

11 WEDNESDAY	193 / 173	**12** THURSDAY	194 / 172

Commodities	2009	2010
Oil	61.48	76.38
Gold	918.3	1205.2

Bond Yields	2009	2010
USA 5 Yr Treasury	2.31	1.81
USA 10 Yr T	3.42	3.05
USA 20 Yr T	4.22	3.83
Moody's Aaa	5.34	4.75
Moody's Baa	7.10	6.08
CAN 5 Yr T	2.41	2.51
CAN 10 Yr T	3.31	3.23

13 FRIDAY	195 / 171

Money Market	2009	2010
USA Fed Funds	0.25	0.25
USA 3 Mo T-B	0.19	0.15
CAN tgt overnight rate	0.25	0.50
CAN 3 Mo T-B	0.23	0.53

Foreign Exchange	2009	2010
USD/EUR	1.39	1.28
USD/GBP	1.62	1.52
CAN/USD	1.16	1.04
JPY/USD	93.74	87.95

2010 Strategy Performance

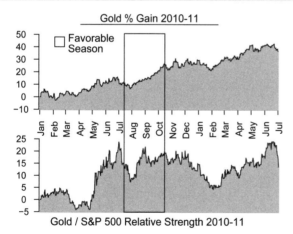

Gold % Gain 2010-11

Gold / S&P 500 Relative Strength 2010-11

JULY

M	T	W	T	F	S	S
						1
2	3	4	5	6	7	8
9	10	11	12	13	14	15
16	17	18	19	20	21	22
23	24	25	26	27	28	29
30	31					

AUGUST

M	T	W	T	F	S	S
	1	2	3	4	5
6	7	8	9	10	11	12
13	14	15	16	17	18	19
20	21	22	23	24	25	26
27	28	29	30	31		

SEPTEMBER

M	T	W	T	F	S	S
					1	2
3	4	5	6	7	8	9
10	11	12	13	14	15	16
17	18	19	20	21	22	23
24	25	26	27	28	29	30

In 2010, gold had a good run in its seasonal period with an 11.0% gain, and managed to outperform the S&P 500.

After gold went "flat" (did not make a gain or loss) from October 2010 to February 2011, investors started to flock back to the precious metal at the beginning of February, as a result of the debt problems in Europe and the U.S.

** Weekly avg closing values- except Fed Funds & CAN overnight tgt rate weekly closing values.

GOLDEN TIMES

(Stocks) Gold Stocks Outperform – July 27th to September 25th

Gold stocks were shunned for many years. It is only recently that interest has sparked again. What few investors know is that even during the twenty year bear market in gold that started in 1981, it was possible to make money in gold stocks.

7.1% when the S&P 500 has been negative

Gold stocks (XAU) Sector - Avg. Year 1984 to 2010

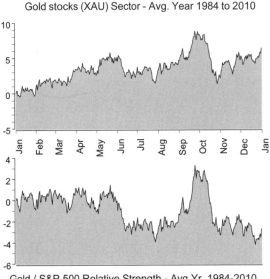

Gold / S&P 500 Relative Strength - Avg Yr. 1984-2010

XAU (Gold Stocks) vs S&P 500 1984 to 2010			
Jul 27 to		Positive	
Sep 25	S&P 500	XAU	Diff
1984	10.4 %	20.8 %	10.4 %
1985	-6.1	-5.5	0.6
1986	-3.5	36.9	40.4
1987	3.5	23.0	19.5
1988	1.7	-11.9	-13.7
1989	1.8	10.5	8.7
1990	-13.4	3.8	17.2
1991	1.6	-11.9	-13.5
1992	0.7	-3.8	-4.5
1993	1.9	-7.3	-9.2
1994	1.4	18.2	16.8
1995	3.6	-1.0	-4.6
1996	7.9	-1.0	-8.9
1997	-0.1	8.7	8.8
1998	-8.4	12.0	20.5
1999	-5.2	16.9	22.1
2000	-0.9	-2.8	-1.9
2001	-15.8	3.2	19.0
2002	-1.5	29.8	31.4
2003	0.5	11.0	10.5
2004	2.4	16.5	14.1
2005	-1.3	20.5	21.8
2006	4.6	-11.9	-16.8
2007	2.3	14.0	11.7
2008	-3.9	-18.5	-14.6
2009	6.7	6.0	-0.6
2010	3.0	14.7	11.7
Avg.	-0.2 %	7.1 %	7.3 %
Fq > 0	59 %	63 %	63 %

On average from 1984 (start of the XAU index) to 2010, gold stocks as represented by the XAU index, have outperformed the S&P 500 from July 27th to September 25th. One factor that has led to a rise in the price of gold stocks in August and September is the Indian festival and wedding season that starts in October and finishes in November during Diwali. The Asian culture places a great emphasis on gold as a store of value and a lot of it is "consumed" as jewellery during the festival and wedding season. The price of gold tends to increase in the months preceding this season as the jewellery fabricators purchase gold to make their final product.

The August-September increase in gold stocks coincides with the time that a lot of investors are pulling their money out of the broad market and are looking for a place to invest. If you believe in the merits of gold stocks, this is definitely a great time to consider.

Be careful. Just as the gold stocks tend to go up in August-September, they also tend to go down in October. Historically, this negative trend has been caused by European Central banks selling some of their gold holdings in autumn when their annual allotment of possible sales is renewed yearly. In recent years European Central banks have dramatically reduced gold sales. This has muted the negative trend in October.

In addition, investors can take advantage of the positive trend in gold from November 1st to December 31st. In this time period gold stocks (XAU) have produced an average return of 4.3%, been positive 52% of the time, and managed to beat the S&P 500 41% of the time (1984-2010). Seasonal investors should consider this trade if the fundamentals warrant it and gold has strong momentum at the time.

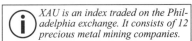
XAU is an index traded on the Philadelphia exchange. It consists of 12 precious metal mining companies.

16 MONDAY	198 / 168	**17** TUESDAY	199 / 167

18 WEDNESDAY	200 / 166	**19** THURSDAY	201 / 165

20 FRIDAY
202 / 164

Market Indices & Rates
Weekly Values**

Stock Markets	2009	2010
Dow	8,553	10,250
S&P500	924	1,084
Nasdaq	1,845	2,225
TSX	10,153	11,614
FTSE	4,307	5,226
DAX	4,874	6,055
Nikkei	9,264	9,308
Hang Seng	18,113	20,450

Commodities	2009	2010
Oil	61.27	77.60
Gold	928.8	1189.1

Bond Yields	2009	2010
USA 5 Yr Treasury	2.43	1.71
USA 10 Yr T	3.55	2.97
USA 20 Yr T	4.39	3.76
Moody's Aaa	5.44	4.69
Moody's Baa	7.19	5.96
CAN 5 Yr T	2.52	2.39
CAN 10 Yr T	3.43	3.19

Money Market	2009	2010
USA Fed Funds	0.25	0.25
USA 3 Mo T-B	0.18	0.16
CAN tgt overnight rate	0.25	0.70
CAN 3 Mo T-B	0.22	0.61

Foreign Exchange	2009	2010
USD/EUR	1.41	1.29
USD/GBP	1.63	1.53
CAN/USD	1.13	1.04
JPY/USD	93.77	87.13

2010 Strategy Performance

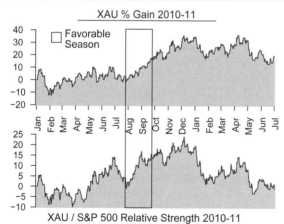

XAU % Gain 2010-11

Favorable Season

XAU / S&P 500 Relative Strength 2010-11

In 2010, gold stocks (XAU) started their seasonal run, right on cue, towards the end of July. Over their seasonally strong period they gained 14.7% compared to the 3.0% gain for the S&P 500. Gold stocks took a breather in October and then performed at market for the rest of the year. It is interesting to note that the gold stocks outperformed gold bullion when their seasonal times overlapped – which often happens.

** Weekly avg closing values- except Fed Funds & CAN overnight tgt rate weekly closing values.

JULY

M	T	W	T	F	S	S
						1
2	3	4	5	6	7	8
9	10	11	12	13	14	15
16	17	18	19	20	21	22
23	24	25	26	27	28	29
30	31					

AUGUST

M	T	W	T	F	S	S
	1	2	3	4	5
6	7	8	9	10	11	12
13	14	15	16	17	18	19
20	21	22	23	24	25	26
27	28	29	30	31		

SEPTEMBER

M	T	W	T	F	S	S
					1	2
3	4	5	6	7	8	9
10	11	12	13	14	15	16
17	18	19	20	21	22	23
24	25	26	27	28	29	30

In the past, my writings on the transportation sector have focused on the positive seasonal period. This is only half the story. Preceding transportation's positive seasonal period is a weak period, giving investors an opportunity to sell short the sector and profit from its decline. This weak period from August 1st to October 9 is followed by the strong period from October 10th to November 13th.

5.3% extra & positive 16 times out of 21

The transportation sector is very sensitive to economic expectations. Typically, when the economy is showing signs of improving, the transportation sector outperforms. When it is showing signs of deteriorating, the sector tends to underperform.

In the late summer months investors tend to question the strength of an economic run which in turn puts pressure on the transportation sector. On average since 1990, the transportation sector has lost 4.2% from August 1st to October 9th.

In autumn the market generally becomes positive about the expectations for the stock market's final months of the year which helps propel the transportation sector into positive territory. In addition, the price of oil tends to retreat in autumn. Since oil is one of the primary input costs for transportation, the sector benefits. From October 10th to November 13th, during the years 1990 to 2010, the transportation sector has gained an average of 6.3%.

ⓘ *The SP GICS Transportation Sector encompasses a wide range transportation based companies.*
For more information on the information technology sector, see www.standardandpoors.com

Transportation Sector vs. S&P 500 1990 to 2010
Negative ☐   Positive ▨

	SHORT Aug 1 to Oct 9		LONG Oct 10 to Nov 13		Compound Growth	
Year	S&P 500	Trans port	S&P 500	Trans port	S&P 500	Trans port
1990	-14.3 %	-19.2 %	4.1 %	3.3 %	19.0 %	23.1 %
1991	-2.8	0.5	5.5	9.6	8.5	9.1
1992	-5.1	-9.1	4.9	14.1	10.2	24.5
1993	2.7	-0.3	1.1	6.4	-1.6	6.8
1994	-0.7	-9.3	1.6	0.8	2.3	10.2
1995	2.9	-1.3	2.4	5.0	-0.6	6.4
1996	8.9	4.9	4.9	6.1	-4.4	0.9
1997	1.7	0.9	-5.6	-5.4	-7.2	-6.3
1998	-12.2	-16.5	14.4	12.5	28.3	31.0
1999	0.6	-11.0	4.5	4.0	3.9	15.4
2000	-2.0	-6.0	-3.6	13.0	-1.7	19.7
2001	-12.8	-20.0	7.8	14.1	21.5	36.9
2002	-14.8	-11.2	13.6	8.2	30.4	20.3
2003	4.9	4.9	1.9	8.0	-3.1	2.7
2004	1.9	6.6	5.5	11.1	3.6	3.7
2005	-3.1	-0.5	3.3	9.0	6.5	9.5
2006	5.8	6.4	2.5	3.8	-3.4	-2.9
2007	7.6	-0.2	-5.4	-2.9	-12.5	-2.7
2008	-28.2	-23.5	0.2	4.0	28.4	28.4
2009	8.5	6.7	2.1	5.9	-6.6	-1.2
2010	5.8	7.9	2.9	2.5	-3.0	-5.6
Avg.	-2.1 %	-4.2 %	3.3 %	6.3 %	5.6 %	10.9 %

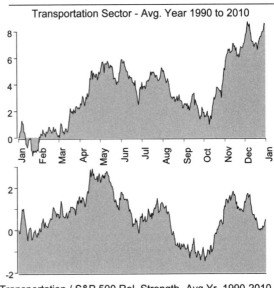

Transportation Sector - Avg. Year 1990 to 2010

Transportation / S&P 500 Rel. Strength- Avg Yr. 1990-2010

23 MONDAY	205 / 161	**24** TUESDAY	206 / 160

Market Indices & Rates
Weekly Values**

Stock Markets	2009	2010
Dow	8,962	10,499
S&P500	963	1,108
Nasdaq	1,938	2,271
TSX	10,570	11,720
FTSE	4,511	5,322
DAX	5,144	6,173
Nikkei	9,778	9,597
Hang Seng	19,611	21,006

Commodities	2009	2010
Oil	65.10	78.16
Gold	950.1	1168.0

Bond Yields	2009	2010
USA 5 Yr Treasury	2.48	1.73
USA 10 Yr T	3.62	3.02
USA 20 Yr T	4.46	3.83
Moody's Aaa	5.46	4.76
Moody's Baa	7.13	5.94
CAN 5 Yr T	2.57	2.41
CAN 10 Yr T	3.48	3.20

Money Market	2009	2010
USA Fed Funds	0.25	0.25
USA 3 Mo T-B	0.19	0.15
CAN tgt overnight rate	0.25	0.75
CAN 3 Mo T-B	0.23	0.64

Foreign Exchange	2009	2010
USD/EUR	1.42	1.30
USD/GBP	1.65	1.56
CAN/USD	1.10	1.03
JPY/USD	94.27	87.10

25 WEDNESDAY	207 / 159	**26** THURSDAY	208 / 158

27 FRIDAY	209 / 157

2010 Strategy Performance*

Transportation % Gain 2010-11

Transportation / S&P 500 Relative Strength 2010-11

In 2010, as a result of the Fed announcing their intention to re-lease another round of quantitative easing, the S&P 500 unchar-acteristically rose in late August through September. The transportation sector has a higher beta than the S&P 500 which caused it to rise even more than the market at a time when the sec-tor is normally negative. The transportation sector produced a gain during the period when it is best to have a "long" position in the sector, but it was not enough to overcome the loss on the "short" position from August to the beginning of October.

** Weekly avg closing values- except Fed Funds & CAN overnight tgt rate weekly closing values.

JULY

M	T	W	T	F	S	S
						1
2	3	4	5	6	7	8
9	10	11	12	13	14	15
16	17	18	19	20	21	22
23	24	25	26	27	28	29
30	31					

AUGUST

M	T	W	T	F	S	S
	1	2	3	4	5
6	7	8	9	10	11	12
13	14	15	16	17	18	19
20	21	22	23	24	25	26
27	28	29	30	31		

SEPTEMBER

M	T	W	T	F	S	S
					1	2
3	4	5	6	7	8	9
10	11	12	13	14	15	16
17	18	19	20	21	22	23
24	25	26	27	28	29	30

Seasonal Investment Time Line*

Investment	Season		2011 / 2012

Core Positions

Investment	Season	
S&P 500	Oct 28 - May 5	
TSX Comp	Oct 28 - May 5	
Cash	May 6 - Oct 27	

Primary Sectors

Investment	Season	
Consumer Staples	Jan 1 - Jan 22 (S)	Apr 23 - Oct 27
Financials	Jan 19 - Apr 13	
Energy	Feb 25 - May 9	Jul 24 - Oct 3
Utilities	Jul 17 - Oct 3	
Health Care	Aug 15 - Oct 18	
Information Tech	Oct 9 - Jan 17	
Consumer Disc.	Oct 28 - Apr 22	
Industrials	Oct 28 - Dec 31	Jan 23- May 5
Materials	Oct 28 - Jan 6	Jan 23 - May 5
Small Cap	Dec 19 - Mar 7	

Secondary Sectors

Investment	Season	
Silver Bullion	Jan - Mar & Sep & Nov	
Platinum	Jan 1 - May 31	
Canadian Dollar	Apr 1 - Apr 30	
Biotech	Jun 23 - Sep 13	
Gold Bullion	Jul 12 - Oct 9	
Gold Stocks (XAU)	Jul 27 - Sep 25	
Agriculture	Aug 1 - Dec 31	
Transportation	Aug 1 - Oct 9 (S)	Oct 10 - Nov 19
Natural Gas	Sep 6 - Dec 21	
Canadian Banks	Oct 10 - Dec 31	Jan 23 - Apr 13
Retail	Oct 28 - Nov 29	Jan 21 - Apr 12
Metals & Mining	Nov 19 - Jan 5	Jan 23 - May 5

Stocks

Investment	Season	
TJX Companies	Jan 22 - Mar 30	
DuPont	Jan 28 - May 14	
Suncor Energy	Feb 18 - May 9	
AMD	Feb 24 - May 5	May 6 - Jul 29 (S)
Intel	May 6 - Jul 29	
PotashCorp	Jun 23 - Jan 11	
Johnson & Johnson	Jul 14 - Oct 21	
Procter and Gamble	Aug 7 - Nov 19	
Alcoa Inc. (S)	Aug 23 - Sep 26	

Long Investment ▨▨▨   Short Investment (S) ▭

* Holiday, End of Month, Witches' Hangover, Yearly Cycles (Presidential Cycle), Predictor Trades (January Predictor), Value - Growth Trades - et al not included.

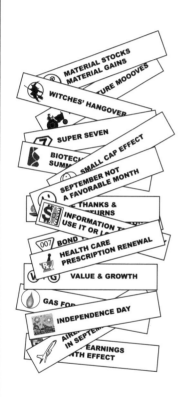

AUGUST

	MONDAY	TUESDAY	WEDNESDAY
WEEK 31	30	31	1 30
WEEK 32	6 25 CAN Market Closed- Civic Day	7 24	8 23
WEEK 33	13 18	14 17	15 16
WEEK 34	20 11	21 10	22 9
WEEK 35	27 4	28 3	29 2

THURSDAY	FRIDAY
2 29	**3** 28
9 22	**10** 21
16 15	**17** 14
23 8	**24** 7
30 1	**31**

SEPTEMBER

M	T	W	T	F	S	S
					1	2
3	4	5	6	7	8	9
10	11	12	13	14	15	16
17	18	19	20	21	22	23
24	25	26	27	28	29	30

OCTOBER

M	T	W	T	F	S	S
1	2	3	4	5	6	7
8	9	10	11	12	13	14
15	16	17	18	19	20	21
22	23	24	25	26	27	28
29	30	31				

NOVEMBER

M	T	W	T	F	S	S
			1	2	3	4
5	6	7	8	9	10	11
12	13	14	15	16	17	18
19	20	21	22	23	24	25
26	27	28	29	30		

DECEMBER

M	T	W	T	F	S	S
					1	2
3	4	5	6	7	8	9
10	11	12	13	14	15	16
17	18	19	20	21	22	23
24	25	26	27	28	29	30
31						

AUGUST
S U M M A R Y

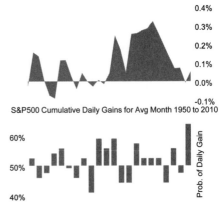

S&P500 Cumulative Daily Gains for Avg Month 1950 to 2010

	Dow Jones	S&P 500	Nasdaq	TSX Comp
Month Rank	10	9	10	10
# Up	35	34	21	14
# Down	26	27	18	12
% Pos	57	56	54	54
% Avg. Gain	0.0	0.1	0.2	-0.3

Dow & S&P 1950-June 2011, Nasdaq 1972-June 2011, TSX 1985-June 2011

August is typically a marginal month and has been the fourth worst month from 1950 to 2010, with an average gain of 0.1% ♦ If there is a summer rally, it is often in jeopardy in August. ♦ After a rally in July 2010, the S&P 500 pulled back substantially in August – until Bernanke hinted on August 27th of the possibility of a second quantitative easing round. At that point the market rallied strongly. Despite having a negative month, with the S&P 500 producing a loss of 4.7%, the market had very strong momentum going into the month of September.

BEST / WORST AUGUST BROAD MKTS. 2001-2010

BEST AUGUST MARKETS
- ♦ Russell 3000 Value (2009) 4.9%
- ♦ Russell 2000 (2003) 4.5%
- ♦ Nasdaq (2006) 4.4%

WORST AUGUST MARKETS
- ♦ Nasdaq (2001) -10.9%
- ♦ Russell 3000 Gr (2001) -8.1%
- ♦ Russell 2000 (2010) -7.5%

Index Values End of Month

	2001	2002	2003	2004	2005	2006	2007	2008	2009	2010
Dow	9,950	8,664	9,416	10,174	10,482	11,381	13,358	11,544	9,496	10,015
S&P 500	1,134	916	1,008	1,104	1,220	1,304	1,474	1,283	1,021	1,049
Nasdaq	1,805	1,315	1,810	1,838	2,152	2,184	2,596	2,368	2,009	2,114
TSX	7,399	6,612	7,510	8,377	10,669	12,074	13,660	13,771	10,868	11,914
Russell 1000	1,149	934	1,035	1,132	1,275	1,360	1,540	1,350	1,073	1,110
Russell 2000	1,165	972	1,236	1,362	1,656	1,791	1,970	1,838	1,422	1,496
Russell 3000 Growth	1,915	1,474	1,682	1,751	1,959	2,013	2,341	2,162	1,758	1,839
Russell 3000 Value	2,080	1,780	1,951	2,242	2,567	2,851	3,127	2,613	2,014	2,069

Percent Gain for August

	2001	2002	2003	2004	2005	2006	2007	2008	2009	2010
Dow	-5.4	-0.8	2.0	0.3	-1.5	1.7	1.1	1.5	3.5	-4.3
S&P 500	-6.4	0.5	1.8	0.2	-1.1	2.1	1.3	1.2	3.4	-4.7
Nasdaq	-10.9	-1.0	4.3	-2.6	-1.5	4.4	2.0	1.8	1.5	-6.2
TSX	-3.8	0.1	3.5	-1.0	2.4	2.1	-1.5	1.3	0.8	1.7
Russell 1000	-6.2	0.4	1.9	0.3	-1.1	2.2	1.1	1.2	3.4	-4.7
Russell 2000	-3.3	-0.4	4.5	-0.6	-1.9	2.8	2.2	3.5	2.8	-7.5
Russell 3000 Growth	-8.1	0.2	2.6	-0.8	-1.4	3.0	1.5	1.0	1.8	-5.1
Russell 3000 Value	-4.0	0.4	1.5	1.2	-0.9	1.5	0.9	1.7	4.9	-4.8

August Market Avg. Performance 2002 to 2011[1]

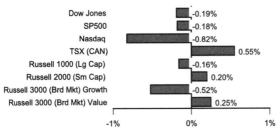

Dow Jones	-0.19%
SP500	-0.18%
Nasdaq	-0.82%
TSX (CAN)	0.55%
Russell 1000 (Lg Cap)	-0.16%
Russell 2000 (Sm Cap)	0.20%
Russell 3000 (Brd Mkt) Growth	-0.52%
Russell 3000 (Brd Mkt) Value	0.25%

Interest Corner Aug[2]

	Fed Funds % [3]	3 Mo. T-Bill % [4]	10 Yr % [5]	20 Yr % [6]
2010	0.25	0.14	2.47	3.23
2009	0.25	0.15	3.40	4.14
2008	2.00	1.72	3.83	4.47
2007	5.25	4.01	4.54	4.87
2006	5.25	5.05	4.74	4.95

(1) Russell Data provided by Russell (2) Federal Reserve Bank of St. Louis- end of month values (3) Target rate set by FOMC (4)(5)(6) Constant yield maturities.

THACKRAY SECTOR THERMOMETER

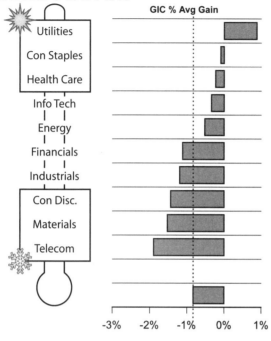

GIC[2] % Avg Gain	Fq % Gain >S&P 500	
SP GIC SECTOR 1990-2010[1]		
0.9 %	67 %	Utilities
-0.1	67	Consumer Staples
-0.2	71	Health Care
-0.3	52	Information Technology
-0.5	48	Energy
-1.1	38	Financials
-1.2	33	Industrials
-1.4	33	Consumer Discretionary
-1.5	43	Materials
-1.9 %	43 %	Telecom
-0.8 %	N/A %	S&P 500

Sector Commentary

♦ In August 2010 the *financial* sector was a large under performer as the problems within the European banking system affected the financial industry worldwide. The U.S. Financial sector produced a loss of 7.9%. ♦ This was followed closely by the *industrial* and *information technology* sectors which produced losses of 7.3% and 7.2% respectively. ♦ The only two sectors to produce gains were the defensive sectors, *telecom* and *utilities*, with gains of 2.3% and 0.9% respectively.

Sub-Sector Commentary

♦ In August 2010 the best performing sub-sectors were the *agriculture, gold* (London PM) and *gold* (XAU) sub-sectors. They produced gains of 12.5%, 9.1% and 6.6% respectively. These sub-sectors are typically the best performing sub-sectors in August ♦ *Biotech,* which in previous months had been performing well, slipped to market performance, producing a loss of 4.6%. ♦ *Airlines* and the *auto & components* were the worst performing sub-sectors, producing losses of 8.3% and 10.6% respectively.

SELECTED SUB-SECTORS 1990-2010[3]		
0.7 %	56 %	Biotech (93-2010)
0.7	53	Agriculture Products (94-2010)
0.6	57	Gold (XAU)
-0.1	48	Gold (London PM)
-0.2	50	Semiconductor (SOX) 95-2010
-0.3	67	Pharmaceuticals
-0.5	43	Integrated Oil & Gas
-0.7	57	Software & Services
-0.8	57	Retail
-0.9	43	Banks
-1.5	48	Metals & Mining
-2.9	29	Transportation
-3.6	29	Auto & Components
-5.2	24	Airlines

(1) Sector data provided by Standard and Poors (2) GIC is short form for Global Industry Classification (3) Sub Sector data provided by Standard and Poors, except where marked by symbol.

(Stocks)

Oil stocks tend to outperform the market from July 24th to October 3rd. Earlier in the year there is a first wave of outperformance from late February to early May. Although the first wave has had an incredible record of outperformance, the second wave in July is still noteworthy.

While the first wave has more to do with inventories during the switch from producing heating oil to gasoline, the second wave is more related to the conversion of production from gasoline to heating oil and the effects of the hurricane season.

Extra 2.5% &
59% of the time better than S&P 500

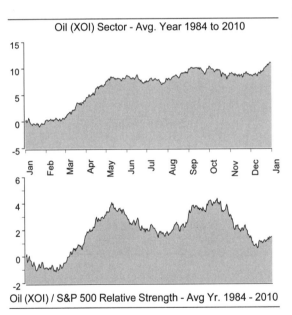

Oil (XOI) Sector - Avg. Year 1984 to 2010

Oil (XOI) / S&P 500 Relative Strength - Avg Yr. 1984 - 2010

XOI vs. S&P 500
1984 to 2010

Jul 24 to Oct 3	S&P 500	Positive XOI	Diff
1984	9.1 %	9.0 %	-0.1 %
1985	-4.3	6.7	11.0
1986	-2.1	15.7	17.7
1987	6.6	-1.2	-7.8
1988	3.0	-3.6	-6.6
1989	5.6	5.7	0.1
1990	-12.4	-0.5	11.8
1991	1.3	0.7	-0.7
1992	-0.4	2.9	3.3
1993	3.2	7.8	4.6
1994	1.9	-3.6	-5.5
1995	5.2	-2.2	-7.4
1996	10.5	7.7	-2.8
1997	3.0	8.9	5.9
1998	-12.0	1.4	13.5
1999	-5.5	-2.1	3.3
2000	-3.6	12.2	15.8
2001	-10.0	-5.1	4.8
2002	2.7	7.3	4.6
2003	4.2	5.5	1.4
2004	4.2	10.9	6.7
2005	-0.6	14.3	14.9
2006	7.6	-8.5	-16.9
2007	-0.1	-4.2	-4.1
2008	-14.3	-18.1	-3.8
2009	5.0	3.0	-2.0
2010	4.0	8.5	4.5
Avg	0.4 %	2.9 %	2.5 %
Fq > 0	59 %	63 %	59 %

start switching from gasoline to heating oil, dropping their inventory levels and boosting prices.

Second, hurricane season can play havoc with the production of oil and drive up prices substantially. The official duration of the hurricane season in the Gulf of Mexico is from June 1st to November 30th, but most major hurricanes occur in September and early October.

The threat of a strong hurricane can shut down the oil platforms temporarily, interrupting production. If a strong hurricane strikes the oil platforms it can do significant damage and put the platform out of commission for an extended period of time.

First, there is a large difference between how heating oil and gasoline are stored and consumed. For the average individual and business, gasoline is consumed in a fairly immediate fashion. It is stored by the local distributor and the supplies are drawn upon as needed. Heating oil, on the other hand is largely inventoried by individuals, farms and business operations in rural areas.

The inventory process starts well before the cold weather arrives. The production facilities have to

30 MONDAY	212 / 154	**31** TUESDAY	213 / 153

1 WEDNESDAY	214 / 152	**2** THURSDAY	215 / 151

3 FRIDAY   216 / 150

WEEK 31

Market Indices & Rates
Weekly Values**

Stock Markets	2009	2010
Dow	9,120	10,664
S&P500	982	1,124
Nasdaq	1,975	2,293
TSX	10,649	11,801
FTSE	4,580	5,376
DAX	5,278	6,305
Nikkei	10,162	9,610
Hang Seng	20,364	21,530

Commodities	2009	2010
Oil	67.07	81.81
Gold	940.4	1195.2

Bond Yields	2009	2010
USA 5 Yr Treasury	2.63	1.58
USA 10 Yr T	3.67	2.94
USA 20 Yr T	4.47	3.78
Moody's Aaa	5.40	4.73
Moody's Baa	6.91	5.86
CAN 5 Yr T	2.67	2.29
CAN 10 Yr T	3.54	3.11

Money Market	2009	2010
USA Fed Funds	0.25	0.25
USA 3 Mo T-B	0.19	0.16
CAN tgt overnight rate	0.25	0.75
CAN 3 Mo T-B	0.24	0.68

Foreign Exchange	2009	2010
USD/EUR	1.42	1.32
USD/GBP	1.65	1.59
CAN/USD	1.08	1.02
JPY/USD	94.99	85.98

AUGUST

M	T	W	T	F	S	S
	1	2	3	4	5
6	7	8	9	10	11	12
13	14	15	16	17	18	19
20	21	22	23	24	25	26
27	28	29	30	31		

SEPTEMBER

M	T	W	T	F	S	S
					1	2
3	4	5	6	7	8	9
10	11	12	13	14	15	16
17	18	19	20	21	22	23
24	25	26	27	28	29	30

OCTOBER

M	T	W	T	F	S	S
1	2	3	4	5	6	7
8	9	10	11	12	13	14
15	16	17	18	19	20	21
22	23	24	25	26	27	28
29	30	31				

2010 Strategy Performance*

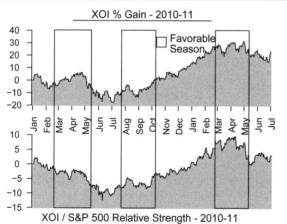

XOI % Gain - 2010-11

XOI / S&P 500 Relative Strength - 2010-11

In 2010, the energy sector (XOI) bottomed at the beginning of July, but investing in the sector on the seasonal buy date later in July still proved to be very profitable. In its seasonal period the energy sector gained 8.5% versus 4.0% for the S&P 500. The energy sector continued outperforming until the end of February.

** Weekly avg closing values- except Fed Funds & CAN overnight tgt rate weekly closing values.

Procter and Gamble
August 7th to November 19th

In investor's eyes, Procter and Gamble is a relatively defensive investment, as the company is in the consumer packaged goods business and its revenues are generated in over 180 countries. Defensive stocks have a reputation of producing sub par performance compared with the broad market. This is not the case with PG as on average it has outperformed the S&P 500 over the last twenty-one years.

11% & positive 86% of the time

Interestingly, on average, the gains have been produced largely in the second half of the year. In the first half of the year PG has been relatively flat and has under performed the S&P 500.

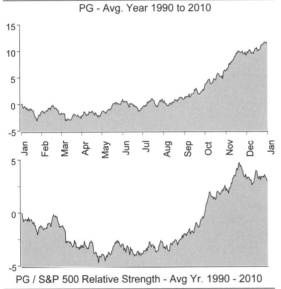

PG - Avg. Year 1990 to 2010

PG / S&P 500 Relative Strength - Avg Yr. 1990 - 2010

From a seasonal perspective, the best time to invest in PG has been from August 7th to November 19th. During this period, from 1990 to 2010, PG on average produced a gain of 11.0% and was positive 86% of the time. In addition it substantially outperformed the S&P 500, generating an extra profit of 9.6% and beating its performance 81% of the time.

Investors will often seek sanctuary in defensive stocks in late summer and early autumn. Although August is not typically the worst month of the year, it does have a weak risk reward profile. With the dreaded month of September falling right after August, investors become "gun shy" and start to become more conservative in August.

PG vs. S&P 500 - 1990 to 2010

Aug 7 to Nov19	S&P 500	PG	Positive Diff
1990	-4.5%	8.4%	13.0%
1991	-2.9	-2.1	0.8
1992	0.7	10.1	9.4
1993	3.1	17.7	14.6
1994	1.0	19.5	18.6
1995	7.4	27.8	20.5
1996	12.0	18.4	6.3
1997	-1.6	0.3	1.9
1998	5.8	14.0	8.2
1999	9.4	18.9	9.5
2000	-6.5	32.0	38.5
2001	-4.1	11.2	15.3
2002	4.3	-0.7	-5.0
2003	7.8	8.2	0.4
2004	10.0	2.5	-7.5
2005	1.8	6.2	4.4
2006	9.5	7.4	-2.1
2007	-2.3	12.0	14.4
2008	-37.4	-8.1	29.3
2009	9.8	20.8	11.0
2010	7.0	6.7	-0.3
Avg	1.4%	11.0%	9.6%
Fq > 0	67%	86%	81%

This trend benefits PG as more investors switch over to defensive companies. PG's outperformance on average starts to occur just after it releases its fourth quarter earnings in the beginning of August.

PG continues to outperform the S&P 500 through September and October. For the S&P 500, September on average is the worst month of the year and October is the most volatile month. The outperformance of PG continues into mid-November.

It is interesting to note that PG's seasonally strong period extends past the seasonal period for the consumer staples sector. It is possible that investors wait until after PG's first quarter results are released in the beginning of November before adjusting their portfolios.

ⓘ *The Procter and Gamble Company is a consumer packaged goods company. Its products are sold in more than 180 countries.*

6 MONDAY	219 / 147	**7** TUESDAY	220 / 146

8 WEDNESDAY	221 / 145	**9** THURSDAY	222 / 144

10 FRIDAY 223 / 143

WEEK 32

Market Indices & Rates
Weekly Values**

Stock Markets	2009	2010
Dow	9,303	10,469
S&P500	1,004	1,100
Nasdaq	1,997	2,231
TSX	10,936	11,667
FTSE	4,685	5,315
DAX	5,405	6,208
Nikkei	10,356	9,376
Hang Seng	20,675	21,349

Commodities	2009	2010
Oil	71.57	78.18
Gold	960.2	1205.7

Bond Yields	2009	2010
USA 5 Yr Treasury	2.73	1.48
USA 10 Yr T	3.77	2.76
USA 20 Yr T	4.50	3.65
Moody's Aaa	5.34	4.60
Moody's Baa	6.71	5.78
CAN 5 Yr T	2.68	2.19
CAN 10 Yr T	3.55	3.02

Money Market	2009	2010
USA Fed Funds	0.25	0.25
USA 3 Mo T-B	0.18	0.15
CAN tgt overnight rate	0.25	0.75
CAN 3 Mo T-B	0.26	0.67

Foreign Exchange	2009	2010
USD/EUR	1.44	1.30
USD/GBP	1.69	1.57
CAN/USD	1.07	1.04
JPY/USD	95.70	85.76

2010 Strategy Performance

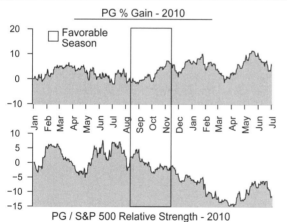

PG % Gain - 2010

PG / S&P 500 Relative Strength - 2010

In 2010, PG did not fall as much as the market as it corrected from late April into July, nor did it rise as much when the market started to rise during the summer months. Nevertheless, PG still produced a 6.7% gain from August 7th to November 19th. This compares to the S&P 500 which produced a 7% gain during the same time period. Historically, even when the S&P 500 is positive during the late summer, PG has been a solid investment.

AUGUST

M	T	W	T	F	S	S
		1	2	3	4	5
6	7	8	9	10	11	12
13	14	15	16	17	18	19
20	21	22	23	24	25	26
27	28	29	30	31		

SEPTEMBER

M	T	W	T	F	S	S
					1	2
3	4	5	6	7	8	9
10	11	12	13	14	15	16
17	18	19	20	21	22	23
24	25	26	27	28	29	30

OCTOBER

M	T	W	T	F	S	S
1	2	3	4	5	6	7
8	9	10	11	12	13	14
15	16	17	18	19	20	21
22	23	24	25	26	27	28
29	30	31				

** Weekly avg closing values- except Fed Funds & CAN overnight tgt rate weekly closing values.

AGRICULTURE MOOOVES
LAST 5 MONTHS OF THE YEAR – Aug to Dec

Agriculture, one of the hot sectors in recent years, has typically been hot during the last five months of the year (August to December).

This is the result of the major summer growing season in the northern hemisphere producing cash for the growers and subsequently increasing sales for the farming suppliers (fertilizer, farming machinery - see note at bottom of page for description of sector).

71% of the time
better than the S&P 500

Although this sector can represent a good opportunity, investors should be wary of the wide performance swings. Out of the fifteen cycles from 1994 to 2010, during August to December, there have been six years with absolute returns greater than +25% or less than -25%, and ten years of returns greater than +10% or less than -10%. In other words, this sector is very volatile.

Agriculture vs. S&P 500 1994 to 2010

Aug 1 to Dec 31	S&P 500	Positive Agri	Diff
1994 %	0.2 %	8.0 %	7.8 %
1995	9.6	31.7	22.1
1996	15.8	30.2	14.5
1997	1.7	14.7	13.0
1998	9.7	-3.4	-13.1
1999	10.6	-2.6	-13.2
2000	-7.7	68.0	75.7
2001	-5.2	12.5	17.7
2002	-3.5	6.0	9.5
2003	12.3	15.8	3.6
2004	10.0	44.6	34.6
2005	1.1	7.5	6.4
2006	11.1	-27.4	-38.5
2007	0.9	38.2	37.3
2008	-28.7	0.7	29.4
2009	12.9	4.0	-9.0
2010	14.2	9.9	-4.2
Avg.	3.8 %	15.2 %	11.4 %
Fq > 0	76 %	82 %	71 %

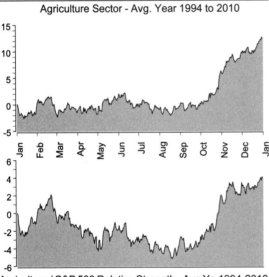

Agriculture Sector - Avg. Year 1994 to 2010

Agriculture / S&P 500 Relative Strength - Avg Yr. 1994-2010

On a year by year basis, the agriculture sector produced its biggest gain during its seasonally strong period in 2000, producing a gain of 68%. It is interesting to note that this is the same year that the technology sector bubble burst. The agriculture sector benefited from the market correction because investors were looking for a safe haven to invest in – people need to eat, regardless of the performance of worldwide stock markets.

After realizing that technology stocks were not going to grow to the sky, investors started to have an epiphany– that the world might be running out of food and as a result, interest in the agriculture sector started to pick up.

In the second half of 2006 the agriculture sector corrected after a strong run in the first half of the year. In 2007 and the first half of 2008, the agriculture sector once again rocketed upwards due to the increase in prices of agricultural products.

Although food prices have had some reprieve with the global slowdown, the world population is still increasing and imbalances in food supply and demand will continue to exist in the future.

Investors should consider "moooving" into the agriculture sector for the last five months of the year.

ⓘ *The SP GICS Agriculture Sector # 30202010*
For more information on the agriculture sector, see www.standardandpoors.com

13 MONDAY   226 / 140   **14** TUESDAY   227 / 139

15 WEDNESDAY   228 / 138   **16** THURSDAY   229 / 137

17 FRIDAY   230 / 136

WEEK 33

Market Indices & Rates
Weekly Values**

Stock Markets	2009	2010
Dow	9,332	10,322
S&P500	1,005	1,083
Nasdaq	1,991	2,193
TSX	10,751	11,699
FTSE	4,716	5,267
DAX	5,353	6,117
Nikkei	10,532	9,228
Hang Seng	20,839	21,065

Commodities	2009	2010
Oil	69.65	74.86
Gold	948.4	1224.9

Bond Yields	2009	2010
USA 5 Yr Treasury	2.65	1.44
USA 10 Yr T	3.67	2.61
USA 20 Yr T	4.42	3.42
Moody's Aaa	5.34	4.40
Moody's Baa	6.62	5.56
CAN 5 Yr T	2.62	2.16
CAN 10 Yr T	3.51	2.94

Money Market	2009	2010
USA Fed Funds	0.25	0.25
USA 3 Mo T-B	0.18	0.16
CAN tgt overnight rate	0.25	0.75
CAN 3 Mo T-B	0.23	0.66

Foreign Exchange	2009	2010
USD/EUR	1.42	1.28
USD/GBP	1.65	1.56
CAN/USD	1.09	1.04
JPY/USD	95.93	85.47

AUGUST

M	T	W	T	F	S	S
		1	2	3	4	5
6	7	8	9	10	11	12
13	14	15	16	17	18	19
20	21	22	23	24	25	26
27	28	29	30	31		

SEPTEMBER

M	T	W	T	F	S	S
					1	2
3	4	5	6	7	8	9
10	11	12	13	14	15	16
17	18	19	20	21	22	23
24	25	26	27	28	29	30

OCTOBER

M	T	W	T	F	S	S
1	2	3	4	5	6	7
8	9	10	11	12	13	14
15	16	17	18	19	20	21
22	23	24	25	26	27	28
29	30	31				

2010 Strategy Performance

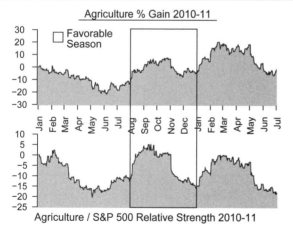

Agriculture % Gain 2010-11

Agriculture / S&P 500 Relative Strength 2010-11

During its seasonally strong period in 2010, the agriculture sector under performed the S&P 500, even though it gained 9.9%. The agriculture sector managed to have a strong run in late summer, but pulled back in autumn, erasing a large part of the earlier gains.

** Weekly avg closing values- except Fed Funds & CAN overnight tgt rate weekly closing values.

GAS FIRES UP IN SEPTEMBER
Natural Gas (Commodity) – Outperforms
Cash price increases from Sep 5th to Dec 21st

Note: Seasonal Date Change

In previous books the seasonally strong period for natural gas was stated as the beginning of August to December 21st. August can still be a good time to focus on natural gas investments, but the sweet spot for the trade starts in the first few days of September.

We may not use natural gas ourselves, but most of us depend on it in one way or another. It is used for furnaces and hot water tanks and is usually responsible for producing some portion of the electrical power that we consume.

As a result, there are two high consumption times for natural gas: winter and summer. The colder it gets in winter, the more natural gas is consumed to keep the furnaces going. The warmer it gets in the summer, the more natural gas is used to produce power for air conditioners.

On the supply side, weather also plays a large factor in determining price. During the hurricane season in the Gulf of Mexico, the price of natural gas is effected by the forecast for the number, severity and impact of hurricanes.

The tail end of the hurricane season occurs in late autumn and early winter, at the same time distributors are accumulating natural gas inventories for the winter heating season. As a result the price of natural gas tends to rise from the beginning of September. As the price is very dependent on the weather, it is also extremely volatile. Large percentage moves are not uncommon.

As a result of the hurricane season ending and the slowdown in accumulating natural gas inventories for winter heating, the price of natural gas frequently decreases during the last part of December.

Natural Gas (Cash) Henry Hub LA
Seasonal Gains 1995 to 2010

	Negative	Positive	Negative
	Jan 1 to Sep 4	Sep 5 to Dec 21	Dec 22 to Dec 31
1995		118 %	-24.0 %
1996	-38.4 %	159	-7.7
1997	-33.0	-13	-4.6
1998	-24.5	20	-5.6
1999	27.1	5	-10.8
2000	102.8	125	0.8
2001	-78.9	19	4.0
2002	14.5	61	-9.0
2003	2.4	47	-16.7
2004	-24.9	58	-11.9
2005	95.2	15	-29.8
2006	-45.0	16	-9.7
2007	-3.6	33	6.1
2008	-2.9	-22	-0.6
2009	-67.4	215	0.6
2010	-35.8	12	1.4
Avg.	-7.5 %	54 %	-7.5 %

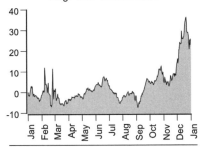

Natural Gas (Cash) Henry Hub LA
Avg. Year 1996 to 2010

Caution:
The cash price for natural gas is extremely volatile and extreme caution should be used. Care must be taken to ensure that investments are within risk tolerances.

Source: New York Mercantile Exchange. NYMX is an exchange provider of futures and options.

Natural Gas (Cash Price) Henry Hub Louisiana % Month Gain

	Jan	Feb	Mar	Apr	May	Jun	Jul	Aug	Sep	Oct	Nov	Dec	Year
1997	-28	-39	6	13	6	-6	3	22	16	3	-25	-6	-44
1998	-6	3	5	-5	-4	12	-22	-14	38	-19	18	18	-15
1999	-6	-8	19	13	0	4	10	13	-20	21	-22	6	19
2000	17	0	7	8	45	-4	-14	27	8	-15	46	64	353
2001	-44	-11	3	-12	-21	-21	12	-34	-17	68	-40	47	-74
2002	-21	16	28	15	-14	2	-6	3	31	7	-5	10	69
2003	22	94	-54	5	14	-11	-13	5	-4	-15	22	19	25
2004	1	-9	7	3	11	-7	0	-16	26	1	6	-11	5
2005	2	8	13	-11	-5	11	11	64	17	-18	-4	-19	58
2006	-8	-23	4	-5	-10	-2	38	-28	-37	81	25	-34	-42
2007	41	-7	4	3	1	-18	2	-16	12	18	0	-2	29
2008	9	12	8	10	6	15	-30	-11	-13	-13	4	-13	-21
2009	-15	-15	-11	-9	21	-5	-10	-28	34	27	7	32	3
2010	-10	-10	-17	0	9	5	6	-21	1	-13	24	1	-27
Avg	-1 %	0 %	1 %	0 %	4 %	-1 %	-2 %	-4 %	7 %	12 %	5 %	8 %	26 %

20 MONDAY	233 / 133	**21** TUESDAY	234 / 132

22 WEDNESDAY	235 / 131	**23** THURSDAY	236 / 130

24 FRIDAY 237 / 129

WEEK 34

Market Indices & Rates
Weekly Values**

Stock Markets	2009	2010
Dow	9,298	10,082
S&P500	1,000	1,057
Nasdaq	1,973	2,139
TSX	10,685	11,691
FTSE	4,726	5,172
DAX	5,292	5,942
Nikkei	10,276	8,971
Hang Seng	20,185	20,678

Commodities	2009	2010
Oil	70.84	72.87
Gold	940.8	1231.5

Bond Yields	2009	2010
USA 5 Yr Treasury	2.47	1.41
USA 10 Yr T	3.48	2.56
USA 20 Yr T	4.26	3.32
Moody's Aaa	5.24	4.31
Moody's Baa	6.56	5.51
CAN 5 Yr T	2.54	2.10
CAN 10 Yr T	3.42	2.84

Money Market	2009	2010
USA Fed Funds	0.25	0.25
USA 3 Mo T-B	0.17	0.16
CAN tgt overnight rate	0.25	0.75
CAN 3 Mo T-B	0.21	0.64

Foreign Exchange	2009	2010
USD/EUR	1.42	1.27
USD/GBP	1.65	1.55
CAN/USD	1.09	1.06
JPY/USD	94.37	84.66

AUGUST

M	T	W	T	F	S	S
	1	2	3	4	5
6	7	8	9	10	11	12
13	14	15	16	17	18	19
20	21	22	23	24	25	26
27	28	29	30	31		

SEPTEMBER

M	T	W	T	F	S	S
					1	2
3	4	5	6	7	8	9
10	11	12	13	14	15	16
17	18	19	20	21	22	23
24	25	26	27	28	29	30

OCTOBER

M	T	W	T	F	S	S
1	2	3	4	5	6	7
8	9	10	11	12	13	14
15	16	17	18	19	20	21
22	23	24	25	26	27	28
29	30	31				

2010 Strategy Performance*

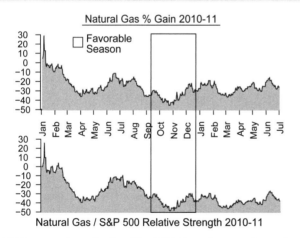

Natural Gas % Gain 2010-11

Natural Gas / S&P 500 Relative Strength 2010-11

In 2010, natural gas declined by 36% from January 1st to September 4th. This is the time period when natural gas tends to be negative. In its seasonally strong period, it managed a 12% increase. After the exit point on its strong seasonal period, it was essentially flat for the next six months.

** Weekly avg closing values- except Fed Funds & CAN overnight tgt rate weekly closing values.

HEALTH CARE
AUGUST PRESCRIPTION RENEWAL
August 15th to October 18th

Health care stocks have traditionally been classified as defensive stocks because of the stability of their earnings. Pharmaceutical and other health care companies typically still do well in an economic downturn.

Even in tough times, people still need to take their medication. As a result, investors have typically found comfort in this sector starting in the late summer doldrums and riding the momentum into early December.

> *2.9% more & 14 out of 21*
> *times better than the S&P 500*

Health Care vs. S&P 500
Performance 1990 to 2010

Aug 15 to Oct 18	S&P 500	Positive Health Care	Diff
1990	-9.9 %	-1.3 %	8.6 %
1991	0.7	1.3	0.6
1992	-1.9	-9.0	-7.1
1993	4.1	13.5	9.5
1994	1.2	7.2	6.0
1995	4.9	11.7	6.7
1996	7.4	9.4	2.1
1997	2.1	5.8	3.7
1998	-0.6	3.0	3.6
1999	-5.5	-0.5	5.0
2000	-10.0	6.9	16.9
2001	-10.0	-0.4	9.6
2002	-3.8	2.4	6.2
2003	4.9	-0.5	-5.4
2004	4.6	-0.8	-5.4
2005	-4.2	-3.1	1.2
2006	7.7	6.4	-1.3
2007	8.0	6.0	-2.0
2008	-27.3	-20.4	6.8
2009	8.3	5.1	-3.3
2010	9.8	8.2	-1.6
Avg	-0.5 %	2.4 %	2.9 %
Fq > 0	57 %	62 %	67 %

Health Care Sector - Avg. Year 1990 to 2010

Health Care / S&P 500 - Avg Yr. 1990 - 2010

The real benefit of investing in the health care sector has been the positive returns that have been generated when the market has typically been negative.

Since 1950, August and September have been the worst two-month combination for gains in the broad stock market.

Having an alternative sector to invest in during the summer and early autumn is a valuable asset.

From August 15th to October 18th (1990 to 2010), health care stocks have had a tendency to outperform the S&P 500 on a yearly basis.

During this time period, the broad market (S&P 500) produced a loss of 0.5%, compared with the health care stocks that produced a gain of 2.4%.

Despite competing with a runaway market in 2003 and legal problems which required drugs to be withdrawn from the market in 2004, the sector has beaten the S&P 500 fourteen out of twenty-one times from 1990 to 2010.

Alternate Strategy—As the health care sector has had a tendency to perform at par with the broad market from late October to early December, an alternative strategy is to continue holding the health care sector during this time period if the fundamentals or technicals are favorable.

Health Care SP GIC Sector# 35: An index designed to represent a cross section of utility companies.
For more information on the materials sector, see www.standardandpoors.com.

27 MONDAY	240 / 126	**28** TUESDAY	241 / 125

29 WEDNESDAY	242 / 124	**30** THURSDAY	243 / 123

31 FRIDAY   244 / 122

Market Indices & Rates
Weekly Values**

Stock Markets	2009	2010
Dow	9,543	10,212
S&P500	1,028	1,075
Nasdaq	2,025	2,169
TSX	10,907	12,014
FTSE	4,896	5,348
DAX	5,517	6,028
Nikkei	10,545	9,015
Hang Seng	20,354	20,748

Commodities	2009	2010
Oil	72.41	74.03
Gold	948.2	1245.4

Bond Yields	2009	2010
USA 5 Yr Treasury	2.48	1.41
USA 10 Yr T	3.46	2.59
USA 20 Yr T	4.18	3.36
Moody's Aaa	5.14	4.39
Moody's Baa	6.45	5.59
CAN 5 Yr T	2.61	2.11
CAN 10 Yr T	3.41	2.85

Money Market	2009	2010
USA Fed Funds	0.25	0.25
USA 3 Mo T-B	0.16	0.14
CAN tgt overnight rate	0.25	0.75
CAN 3 Mo T-B	0.20	0.71

Foreign Exchange	2009	2010
USD/EUR	1.43	1.28
USD/GBP	1.63	1.54
CAN/USD	1.09	1.05
JPY/USD	94.03	84.37

AUGUST

M	T	W	T	F	S	S
	1	2	3	4	5	
6	7	8	9	10	11	12
13	14	15	16	17	18	19
20	21	22	23	24	25	26
27	28	29	30	31		

SEPTEMBER

M	T	W	T	F	S	S
					1	2
3	4	5	6	7	8	9
10	11	12	13	14	15	16
17	18	19	20	21	22	23
24	25	26	27	28	29	30

OCTOBER

M	T	W	T	F	S	S
1	2	3	4	5	6	7
8	9	10	11	12	13	14
15	16	17	18	19	20	21
22	23	24	25	26	27	28
29	30	31				

2010 Strategy Performance*

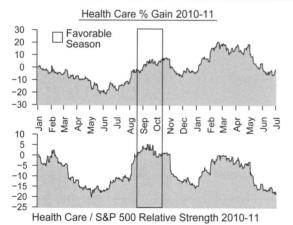

Health Care % Gain 2010-11

Favorable Season

Health Care / S&P 500 Relative Strength 2010-11

In 2010, the health care sector produced a return of 8.2% during its seasonally strong period, but it still under performed the S&P 500 which had a gain of 9.8% during the same period. Earlier in the summer when the market was in a free fall, the health care sector held up well. After the Federal Reserve hinted at launching a second quantitative easing program, the health care sector slipped in its relative performance.

** Weekly avg closing values- except Fed Funds & CAN overnight tgt rate weekly closing values.

SEPTEMBER

	MONDAY	TUESDAY	WEDNESDAY
WEEK 35	27	28	29
WEEK 36	**3** 27 USA Market Closed- Labour Day CAN Market Closed- Labour Day	**4** 26	**5** 25
WEEK 37	**10** 20	**11** 19	**12** 18
WEEK 38	**17** 13	**18** 12	**19** 11
WEEK 39	**24** 6	**25** 5	**26** 4

THURSDAY	FRIDAY
30	31
6 24	**7** 23
13 17	**14** 16
20 10	**21** 9
27 3	**28** 2

OCTOBER

M	T	W	T	F	S	S
1	2	3	4	5	6	7
8	9	10	11	12	13	14
15	16	17	18	19	20	21
22	23	24	25	26	27	28
29	30	31				

NOVEMBER

M	T	W	T	F	S	S
			1	2	3	4
5	6	7	8	9	10	11
12	13	14	15	16	17	18
19	20	21	22	23	24	25
26	27	28	29	30		

DECEMBER

M	T	W	T	F	S	S
					1	2
3	4	5	6	7	8	9
10	11	12	13	14	15	16
17	18	19	20	21	22	23
24	25	26	27	28	29	30
31						

JANUARY

M	T	W	T	F	S	S
	1	2	3	4	5	6
7	8	9	10	11	12	13
14	15	16	17	18	19	20
21	22	23	24	25	26	27
28	29	30	31			

SEPTEMBER
S U M M A R Y

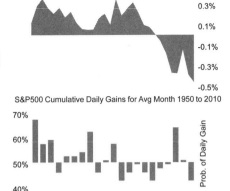

0.3%
0.1%
-0.1%
-0.3%
-0.5%

S&P500 Cumulative Daily Gains for Avg Month 1950 to 2010

	Dow Jones	S&P 500	Nasdaq	TSX Comp
Month Rank	12	12	12	12
# Up	24	27	21	10
# Down	37	34	18	16
% Pos	39	44	54	38
% Avg. Gain	-0.8	-0.5	-0.6	-1.5

Dow & S&P 1950-June 2011, Nasdaq 1972-June 2011, TSX 1985-June 2011

♦ From 1950 to 2010, on average September was the weakest month of the year with a loss of 0.5% and a positive frequency of 44%. ♦ September 2010 was an anomaly as the S&P 500 gained an incredible 8.8%. This strong performance was almost entirely due to Bernanke announcing his intentions to launch QE2. ♦ Although September can produce positive results, seasonal investors should be cautious and take advantage of sectors that have relative outperformance, such as *gold*, *health care* and *consumer staples*.

BEST / WORST SEPTEMBER BROAD MKTS. 2001-2010

BEST SEPTEMBER MARKETS
♦ Russell 2000 (2010) 12.3%
♦ Nasdaq (2010) 12.0%
♦ Russell 3000 Gr (2010) 10.8%

WORST SEPTEMBER MARKETS
♦ Nasdaq (2001) -17.0%
♦ TSX Comp (2008) -14.7%
♦ Russell 2000 (2001) -13.6%

Index Values End of Month

	2001	2002	2003	2004	2005	2006	2007	2008	2009	2010
Dow	8,848	7,592	9,275	10,080	10,569	11,679	13,896	10,851	9,712	10,788
S&P 500	1,041	815	996	1,115	1,229	1,336	1,527	1,166	1,057	1,141
Nasdaq	1,499	1,172	1,787	1,897	2,152	2,258	2,702	2,092	2,122	2,369
TSX	6,839	6,180	7,421	8,668	11,012	11,761	14,099	11,753	11,395	12,369
Russell 1000	1,050	833	1,023	1,145	1,285	1,391	1,597	1,219	1,115	1,211
Russell 2000	1,006	900	1,212	1,424	1,660	1,803	2,002	1,689	1,502	1,680
Russell 3000 Growth	1,714	1,322	1,660	1,772	1,967	2,063	2,434	1,910	1,834	2,037
Russell 3000 Value	1,925	1,584	1,928	2,277	2,595	2,901	3,220	2,420	2,090	2,230

Percent Gain for September

	2001	2002	2003	2004	2005	2006	2007	2008	2009	2010
Dow	-11.1	-12.4	-1.5	-0.9	0.8	2.6	4.0	-6.0	2.3	7.7
S&P 500	-8.2	-11.0	-1.2	0.9	0.7	2.5	3.6	-9.1	3.6	8.8
Nasdaq	-17.0	-10.9	-1.3	3.2	0.0	3.4	4.0	-11.6	5.6	12.0
TSX	-7.6	-6.5	-1.2	3.5	3.2	-2.6	3.2	-14.7	4.8	3.8
Russell 1000	-8.6	-10.9	-1.2	1.1	0.8	2.3	3.7	-9.7	3.9	9.0
Russell 2000	-13.6	-7.3	-2.0	4.6	0.2	0.7	1.6	-8.1	5.6	12.3
Russell 3000 Growth	-10.5	-10.3	-1.3	1.2	0.4	2.5	4.0	-11.7	4.3	10.8
Russell 3000 Value	-7.5	-11.0	-1.2	1.5	1.1	1.7	3.0	-7.4	3.8	7.8

September Market Avg. Performance 2001 to 2010[1]

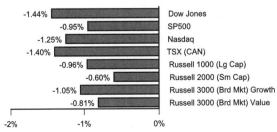

-1.44% Dow Jones
-0.95% SP500
-1.25% Nasdaq
-1.40% TSX (CAN)
-0.96% Russell 1000 (Lg Cap)
-0.60% Russell 2000 (Sm Cap)
-1.05% Russell 3000 (Brd Mkt) Growth
-0.81% Russell 3000 (Brd Mkt) Value

-2%   -1%   0%

Interest Corner Sep[2]

	Fed Funds %[3]	3 Mo. T-Bill %[4]	10 Yr %[5]	20 Yr %[6]
2010	0.25	0.16	2.53	3.38
2009	0.25	0.14	3.31	4.02
2008	2.00	0.92	3.85	4.43
2007	4.75	3.82	4.59	4.89
2006	5.25	4.89	4.64	4.84

(1) Russell Data provided by Russell (2) Federal Reserve Bank of St. Louis- end of month values (3) Target rate set by FOMC (4)(5)(6) Constant yield maturities.

THACKRAY SECTOR THERMOMETER

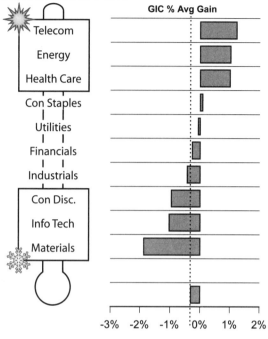

GIC(2) % Avg Gain	Fq % Gain >S&P 500	
SP GIC SECTOR 1990-2010(1)		
1.2 %	62 %	Telecom
1.0	62	Energy
1.0	62	Health Care
0.1	57	Consumer Staples
-0.1	33	Utilities
-0.3	57	Financials
-0.4	48	Industrials
-1.0	48	Consumer Discretionary
-1.0	67	Information Technology
-1.9 %	19 %	Materials
-0.3 %	N/A %	S&P 500

Sector Commentary

♦ In September 2010, *information technology* was the strongest sector with a gain of 12.1%, followed by the *industrials* and *consumer discretionary* sectors with gains of 11.2% and 11.0% respectively. These three sectors are typically at the bottom of the sector pack, but with an unusually strong September, the cyclicals outperformed. When the cyclical sectors outperform out of season, it is typically a sign of good markets ahead.

Sub-Sector Commentary

♦ Like the major sectors of the stock market, the sub-sectors got turned upside down as the typical under performers outperformed and vice versa in September 2010. ♦ The top three sub-sectors were *airlines, retail* and the *semiconductor* producing returns of 18.3%, 15.4% and 13.6% respectively. ♦ *Gold* usually leads the sub-sector list, but in 2010, both *gold (XAU)* and *gold (London PM)* were at the bottom of the list with gains of 6.4% and 4.9% respectively.

		SELECTED SUB-SECTORS 1990-2010(3)
5.8 %	71 %	Gold (XAU)
3.8	71	Gold (London PM)
1.7	61	Biotech (93-2010)
1.2	57	Integrated Oil & Gas
1.0	62	Pharmaceuticals
0.7	67	Software & Services
0.4	59	Agriculture Products (94-2010)
-0.6	52	Transportation
-0.6	43	Retail
-0.9	52	Banks
-1.3	43	Metals & Mining
-1.7	43	Airlines
-2.2	33	Auto & Components
-3.6	31	Semiconductor (SOX) 95-2010

(1) Sector data provided by Standard and Poors (2) GIC is short form for Global Industry Classification (3) Sub Sector data provided by Standard and Poors, except where marked by symbol.

SILVER — THREE BEST PERIODS
JAN to MAR, & SEP, & NOV

Very often sectors of the market have one period of strong seasonal performance in a year. Silver is different as on average it typically has three periods of seasonal strength — January to March, September and November.

The three periods of strength are the result of silver being both a precious metal and an industrial metal. With two strong influences affecting silver, opportunities are produced in the yearly trends.

The rise from January 1st to March 31st is mainly the result of increased economic activity at the start of the new year. Generally, this is the time of the year when positive expectations are formed for the economy over the next year and as a result investors focus on the industrial aspect of silver, pushing up its price.

11.7% and
positive 70% of the time

Silver tends to perform well in September because of its relationship with gold as a precious metal. Gold tends to rise at this time of year as the result of the large quantities of gold jewellery that gets consumed in the fourth quarter of the year (see *Gold Shines* strategy). As gold often has a weak month in October, so does silver.

The silver-gold relationship continues during the month of November as both metals tend to outperform the S&P 500. As investors adjust their yearend portfolios in December, both gold and silver tend to put in mediocre performances and under perform the S&P 500. Once again silver tends to outperform at the beginning of the year.

It is important to note that when silver is in a bull run with lots of momentum, it will bridge the gaps, performing well in both October and December. Investors can benefit from using technical analysis to fine tune their strategies in choosing the best buy and sell dates.

Source: Bank of England
London pricing is recognized as the world benchmark for silver prices.

Silver Performance
Jan-Mar, Sep & Nov 500- 1984-2010

	Jan1 to Mar31	Sep1 to Sep30	Nov1 to Nov30	Compound Growth
	Positive			
1984	8.3 %	-0.1 %	-2.0 %	6.0 %
1985	5.9	-3.1	0.1	2.7
1986	-3.2	6.8	-4.0	-0.7
1987	19.4	1.3	5.4	27.5
1988	0.8	-4.5	-3.8	-7.4
1989	-4.7	4.2	6.4	5.6
1990	-4.8	-0.7	-3.2	-8.5
1991	.8.5	8.4	-0.6	-1.4
1992	6.7	1.3	-0.8	7.2
1993	6.0	-16.8	1.5	-10.5
1994	12.1	4.9	-5.1	11.7
1995	6.4	3.9	-3.4	6.8
1996	7.3	-6.0	-1.7	-0.9
1997	6.9	9.4	10.0	28.7
1998	5.8	12.5	-2.6	16.1
1999	0.4	9.8	-2.1	7.9
2000	-7.4	-0.5	-2.3	-10.0
2001	-5.4	9.2	-3.2	0.1
2002	3.4	-0.7	-1.0	1.7
2003	-4.4	0.2	4.2	-0.2
2004	31.2	-1.1	8.3	40.5
2005	5.5	11.7	5.7	24.6
2006	33.1	-8.3	13.3	38.2
2007	3.5	14.2	-0.6	17.5
2008	21.9	-5.8	9.1	25.2
2009	21.5	13.1	9.5	50.5
2010	3.0	17.0	13.2	36.4
Avg	6.3 %	3.0 %	1.9 %	11.7 %
Fq>0	74 %	59 %	44 %	70 %

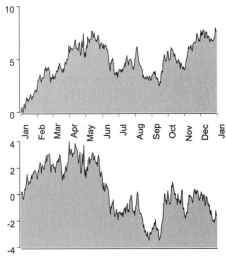

Silver (London) - Avg. Year 1984 to 2010

Silver / S&P 500 Rel. Strength- Avg Yr. 1984-2010

3 MONDAY	247 / 119	**4** TUESDAY	248 / 118

5 WEDNESDAY	249 / 117	**6** THURSDAY	250 / 116

7 FRIDAY 251 / 115

WEEK 36

Market Indices & Rates
Weekly Values**

Stock Markets	2009	2010
Dow	9,375	10,401
S&P500	1,007	1,101
Nasdaq	1,989	2,229
TSX	10,840	12,069
FTSE	4,821	5,455
DAX	5,360	6,175
Nikkei	10,341	9,178
Hang Seng	19,840	21,254

Commodities	2009	2010
Oil	68.41	74.87
Gold	972.9	1252.5

Bond Yields	2009	2010
USA 5 Yr Treasury	2.33	1.51
USA 10 Yr T	3.37	2.71
USA 20 Yr T	4.12	3.48
Moody's Aaa	5.12	4.50
Moody's Baa	6.37	5.67
CAN 5 Yr T	2.59	2.19
CAN 10 Yr T	3.35	2.93

Money Market	2009	2010
USA Fed Funds	0.25	0.25
USA 3 Mo T-B	0.14	0.14
CAN tgt overnight rate	0.25	0.90
CAN 3 Mo T-B	0.21	0.86

Foreign Exchange	2009	2010
USD/EUR	1.43	1.27
USD/GBP	1.63	1.54
CAN/USD	1.10	1.04
JPY/USD	92.78	83.97

SEPTEMBER

M	T	W	T	F	S	S
					1	2
3	4	5	6	7	8	9
10	11	12	13	14	15	16
17	18	19	20	21	22	23
24	25	26	27	28	29	30

OCTOBER

M	T	W	T	F	S	S
1	2	3	4	5	6	7
8	9	10	11	12	13	14
15	16	17	18	19	20	21
22	23	24	25	26	27	28
29	30	31				

NOVEMBER

M	T	W	T	F	S	S
			1	2	3	4
5	6	7	8	9	10	11
12	13	14	15	16	17	18
19	20	21	22	23	24	25
26	27	28	29	30		

2010 Strategy Performance

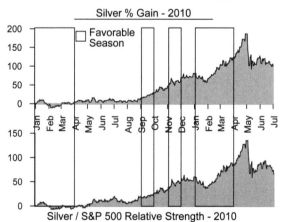

Silver % Gain - 2010

Silver / S&P 500 Relative Strength - 2010

All three periods of seasonal strength worked for silver in 2010. The compounded gains were a strong 36.4%. Silver became quite the rage in September as investors were looking for an alternative to gold. It also benefited from strong industrial demand. Many investors believe that silver is substantially underpriced relative to gold and as a result, look for silver to perform well during its seasonally strong periods in 2012.

** Weekly avg closing values- except Fed Funds & CAN overnight tgt rate weekly closing values.

Alcoa Inc. – SHORT SELL
August 23rd to September 26th

Alcoa has the distinction of "kicking off" the earnings season each quarter as it is the first large company to report. It typically reports in the second week of earnings months and the media covers its results with much fanfare.

As part of the metals and mining, Alcoa has a similar trend with a weak September. Alcoa's weak period from August 23rd to September 26th has provided investor's with a good opportunity to profit by taking a short position in the stock. From 1990 to 2010, shorting Alcoa during this time has produced an average gain of 6.4% (negative numbers in table represent a gain when shorting). The trade has also been both profitable 67% of the time and outperformed the S&P 500, 67% of the time.

6.4% gain & profitable 67% of the time

Although Alcoa can continue its negative performance until late October, it is generally prudent to exit the trade before Alcoa's Q4 earnings in early October.

Alcoa vs. S&P 500
Performance 1990 to 2010

Aug 23 to Sep 26	S&P 500	AA	Diff
		Negative	
1990	-3.6%	2.7%	6.3%
1991	-1.2	-3.2	-2.0
1992	-0.1	2.5	2.6
1993	0.3	-8.6	-8.9
1994	-0.3	10.5	10.8
1995	3.9	-14.3	-18.2
1996	2.3	-6.5	-8.8
1997	2.4	-5.3	-7.7
1998	-3.4	8.0	11.4
1999	-4.4	-11.5	-7.1
2000	-4.7	-27.5	-22.8
2001	-13.6	-23.9	-10.3
2002	-11.2	-27.4	-16.2
2003	0.4	-5.2	-5.5
2004	1.1	-3.2	-4.3
2005	-0.5	-14.7	-14.2
2006	2.9	-4.8	-7.7
2007	4.2	6.2	2.0
2008	-6.1	-27.1	-21.0
2009	1.8	4.1	2.4
2010	7.2	15.4	8.2
Avg	-1.1%	-6.4%	-5.3%
Fq > 0	48%	33%	33%

AA - Avg. Year 1990 to 2010

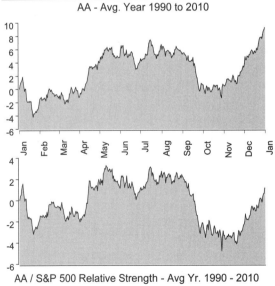

AA / S&P 500 Relative Strength - Avg Yr. 1990 - 2010

Generally the trade has not worked when the market has uncharacteristically rallied during the late summer and early autumn time period. More recently the trade did not work in 2009 and 2010 when the Fed's quantitative easing programs motivated investors to take on more stock market risk and pushed the market higher.

Despite the seasonal opportunity to profit from Alcoa's declining price, it has produced positive returns of 5% or greater four times since 1990. Investors should consider the magnitude of the potential loss before making a portfolio allocation decision.

Investors should also consider the current economic climate at the time and how cyclical stocks are responding. If the economy is showing signs of strong growth and the cyclical stocks are responding with strong momentum, investors should be extra cautious with this trade.

(i) ** Alcoa (AA) is engaged in the production and management of aluminium, fabricated aluminium, and alumina combined. Alcoa trades on the NYSE.*

10 MONDAY	254 / 112	**11** TUESDAY	255 / 111

12 WEDNESDAY	256 / 110	**13** THURSDAY	257 / 109

14 FRIDAY			258 / 108

WEEK 37

Market Indices & Rates
Weekly Values**

Stock Markets	2009	2010
Dow	9,569	10,569
S&P500	1,036	1,124
Nasdaq	2,066	2,299
TSX	11,128	12,165
FTSE	4,977	5,547
DAX	5,548	6,252
Nikkei	10,397	9,455
Hang Seng	20,956	21,748

Commodities	2009	2010
Oil	70.91	75.65
Gold	998.5	1264.6

Bond Yields	2009	2010
USA 5 Yr Treasury	2.34	1.47
USA 10 Yr T	3.41	2.74
USA 20 Yr T	4.18	3.55
Moody's Aaa	5.18	4.59
Moody's Baa	6.39	5.73
CAN 5 Yr T	2.60	2.24
CAN 10 Yr T	3.37	2.96

Money Market	2009	2010
USA Fed Funds	0.25	0.25
USA 3 Mo T-B	0.14	0.15
CAN tgt overnight rate	0.25	1.00
CAN 3 Mo T-B	0.21	0.91

Foreign Exchange	2009	2010
USD/EUR	1.45	1.30
USD/GBP	1.65	1.56
CAN/USD	1.08	1.03
JPY/USD	91.98	84.83

SEPTEMBER

M	T	W	T	F	S	S
					1	2
3	4	5	6	7	8	9
10	11	12	13	14	15	16
17	18	19	20	21	22	23
24	25	26	27	28	29	30

OCTOBER

M	T	W	T	F	S	S
1	2	3	4	5	6	7
8	9	10	11	12	13	14
15	16	17	18	19	20	21
22	23	24	25	26	27	28
29	30	31				

NOVEMBER

M	T	W	T	F	S	S
			1	2	3	4
5	6	7	8	9	10	11
12	13	14	15	16	17	18
19	20	21	22	23	24	25
26	27	28	29	30		

2010 Strategy Performance

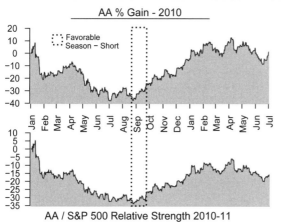

AA % Gain - 2010

AA / S&P 500 Relative Strength 2010-11

Alcoa started to consistently under perform the S&P 500 when the market peaked in April 2010. It was only when the Fed hinted in late August at launching another quantitative easing program that Alcoa started to perform positively and outperform the market. As a result, selling Alcoa short from August 23rd to September 26th did not work. When a macro event, such as a quantitative easing program, strongly influences the market it can easily overwhelm a seasonal tendency.

** Weekly avg closing values- except Fed Funds & CAN overnight tgt rate weekly closing values.

$$ SEPTEMBER PAIR TRADE
Long Gold – Short Sell Metals and Mining in September

How a pair trade works

The trade requires buying one security in the expectation that it will go up (long position) and buying a second security in the expectation that it will go down (short position). The short position can be achieved by selling a position short (selling a position before buying it), or buying a bear fund that buys the short positions.

Most retail investors shy away from taking a short position because of the perceived risk. But selling a position short can help reduce risk, especially when it is used in a pair trade.

Taking a long position in gold (expecting the price of gold to increase), and taking a short position in the metals and mining sector (expecting a decrease in price), has paid handsome rewards in the month of September from 1990 to 2010.

This trade has netted an average return of 3.8% and has been positive 81% of the time. The pair trade results have been better than if you just entered a long position for gold or a short position for the metals and mining sector.

There is a good reason that this pair trade makes sense. The metals and mining and the gold sector have a lot of the same factors driving their performance, at least on the supply side of the equation. If it costs more to get "stuff" out of the ground, then both sectors are effected.

Where the metals and mining sector and gold differ is in their demand cycle. Demand in the metals and mining sector slows down in the summer months as industrial production decreases during the holiday months. Gold, on the other hand, has a large spike in

demand in the late summer from the gold fabricators having to buy enough gold for the Indian wedding and festival season.

Over the long-term, gold and the metals and mining sector, have monthly averages that generally move together.

September presents an exception to this trend and a profitable opportunity for a pair trade.

Gold vs. Metals and Mining Performance 1990 to 2010

Sept	Gold	M&M	Diff
Positive when Long			
Negative when Short			
1990	5.3 %	-4.0 %	9.3 %
1991	2.2	-2.9	5.0
1992	2.6	-1.2	3.9
1993	-4.3	-8.0	3.6
1994	2.4	3.7	-1.4
1995	0.4	-1.7	2.1
1996	-1.9	-2.1	0.2
1997	2.1	1.3	0.8
1998	7.5	26.8	-19.3
1999	17.3	3.0	14.3
2000	-1.2	-15.3	14.1
2001	7.4	-13.0	20.4
2002	3.5	-16.7	20.1
2003	3.3	-4.2	7.5
2004	2.1	5.5	-3.4
2005	9.2	7.3	1.9
2006	-3.9	-5.4	1.5
2007	10.6	11.9	-1.3
2008	6.2	-31.1	37.3
2009	4.2	7.9	-3.7
2010	4.9	10.1	-5.2
Avg	3.8 %	-1.3 %	5.1 %
Fq Success	81 %	57 %	71 %

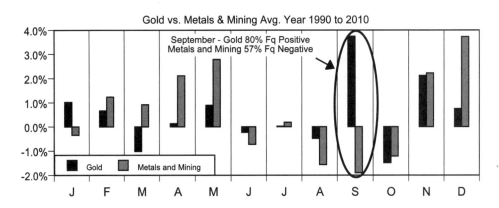

Gold vs. Metals & Mining Avg. Year 1990 to 2010

September - Gold 80% Fq Positive
Metals and Mining 57% Fq Negative

Gold   Metals and Mining

J F M A M J J A S O N D

17 MONDAY	261 / 105	**18** TUESDAY	262 / 104

19 WEDNESDAY	263 / 103	**20** THURSDAY	264 / 102

21 FRIDAY	265 / 101

WEEK 38

Market Indices & Rates
Weekly Values**

Stock Markets	2009	2010
Dow	9,741	10,755
S&P500	1,061	1,138
Nasdaq	2,117	2,350
TSX	11,472	12,172
FTSE	5,104	5,575
DAX	5,677	6,252
Nikkei	10,301	9,547
Hang Seng	21,319	22,037

Commodities	2009	2010
Oil	71.36	73.87
Gold	1008.3	1287.1

Bond Yields	2009	2010
USA 5 Yr Treasury	2.43	1.36
USA 10 Yr T	3.46	2.61
USA 20 Yr T	4.19	3.48
Moody's Aaa	5.15	4.55
Moody's Baa	6.36	5.66
CAN 5 Yr T	2.61	2.17
CAN 10 Yr T	3.37	2.88

Money Market	2009	2010
USA Fed Funds	0.25	0.25
USA 3 Mo T-B	0.11	0.16
CAN tgt overnight rate	0.25	1.00
CAN 3 Mo T-B	0.21	0.91

Foreign Exchange	2009	2010
USD/EUR	1.47	1.33
USD/GBP	1.65	1.57
CAN/USD	1.07	1.03
JPY/USD	91.06	84.77

SEPTEMBER

M	T	W	T	F	S	S
					1	2
3	4	5	6	7	8	9
10	11	12	13	14	15	16
17	18	19	20	21	22	23
24	25	26	27	28	29	30

OCTOBER

M	T	W	T	F	S	S
1	2	3	4	5	6	7
8	9	10	11	12	13	14
15	16	17	18	19	20	21
22	23	24	25	26	27	28
29	30	31				

NOVEMBER

M	T	W	T	F	S	S
			1	2	3	4
5	6	7	8	9	10	11
12	13	14	15	16	17	18
19	20	21	22	23	24	25
26	27	28	29	30		

2010 Strategy Performance

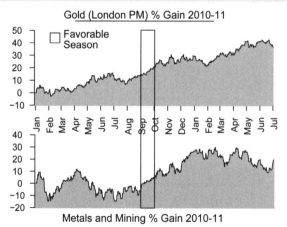

Gold (London PM) % Gain 2010-11

Metals and Mining % Gain 2010-11

In 2010, both the gold sector and the metals & mining sector produced positive returns during the month of September. The pair trade did not work because both sectors increased.

In the 2010, autumn and winter rally, most sectors went up in the market. It was just a matter of degree of which sectors went up more than the others.

** Weekly avg closing values- except Fed Funds & CAN overnight tgt rate weekly closing values.

CANADIAN BANKS — IN-OUT-IN AGAIN
➔IN (Oct 10 - Dec 31) ➔OUT ➔IN (Jan 23 - Apr 13)

During the financial crisis of 2007/08, the Canadian banks were touted as being the best in the world. Canadians love to invest in their banks because they operate in a regulated environment and for long periods of time have grown their earnings and dividends. Although a lot of sectors in the Canadian market have very similar seasonally strong periods compared with the US, the seasonality for Canadian banks starts earlier than the US banks.

The difference in seasonally strong periods is driven by the difference in fiscal year-ends. The US banks have their year-end on December 31st and the Canadian banks on October 31st. Why does this make a difference? Typically, banks clean up their "books" at their year-end, by announcing any bad news. In addition, this is often the time period when the banks announce their positive news, including increases in dividends.

CDN Banks* vs. S&P/TSX Comp 1989/90 to 2010/11   Positive ▢

| Year | Oct 10 to Dec 31 | | Jan 23 to Apr 13 | | Compound Growth | |
	TSX Comp	CDN Banks	TSX Comp	CDN Banks	TSX Comp	CDN Banks
1989/90	-1.7%	-1.8%	-6.3%	-9.1%	-7.9%	-10.8%
1990/91	3.7	8.9	9.8	14.6	13.9	24.8
1991/92	5.2	10.2	-6.8	-11.6	-2.0	-2.6
1992/93	4.1	2.5	10.7	14.4	15.2	17.3
1993/94	6.3	6.8	-5.6	-13.3	0.3	-7.4
1994/95	-1.8	3.4	5.0	10.0	3.1	13.8
1995/96	4.9	3.5	3.6	-3.2	8.6	0.1
1996/97	9.0	15.1	-6.2	0.7	2.3	15.9
1997/98	-6.1	7.6	19.9	38.8	12.6	49.4
1998/99	18.3	28.0	4.8	13.0	24.0	44.6
1999/00	18.2	5.1	3.8	22.1	22.8	28.3
2000/01	-14.4	1.7	-14.1	-6.7	-26.4	-5.1
2001/02	11.9	6.5	2.3	8.2	14.5	15.1
2002/03	16.1	21.3	-4.3	2.6	11.1	24.4
2003/04	8.1	5.1	2.0	2.1	10.3	7.4
2004/05	4.9	6.2	4.5	6.9	9.6	13.5
2005/06	6.2	8.4	5.5	2.7	12.1	11.3
2006/07	10.4	8.4	6.9	3.2	18.0	11.8
2007/08	-3.0	-10.4	8.2	-3.5	5.0	-13.5
2008/09	-6.4	-14.8	9.4	24.4	2.4	6.1
2009/10	2.7	2.4	6.7	15.2	9.6	18.0
2010/11	7.2	-0.2	4.3	9.1	11.9	8.9
Avg.	4.7%	5.6%	2.9%	6.4%	7.8%	12.3%
Fq > 0	73%	82%	73%	73%	86%	77%

4.6% extra & and positive 77% of the time

The Canadian Bank sector, from October 10th to December 31st for the years 1989 to 2010, has been positive 82% of the time and has produced an average gain of 5.6%. From January 23rd to April 13th, the sector has been positive 73% of the time and has produced an average gain of 6.4%. On a compounded basis, the strategy has been positive 77% of the time and produced an average gain of 12.3%.

Basically the strategy does well until mid-April which is the start of the earnings season. Investors have a choice of whether to bridge the two seasonal time periods for the Canadian Bank sector and hold for the entire October 10th to April 13th time period. Investors should consider that from January 1st to the 22nd, from 1990 to 2010, the sector has produced an average loss of 2.2% and has only been positive 40% of the time.

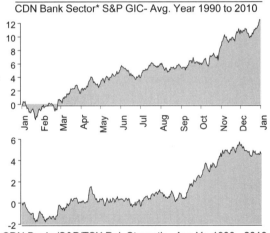

CDN Bank Sector* S&P GIC- Avg. Year 1990 to 2010

CDN Banks/S&P/TSX Rel. Strength - Avg Yr. 1990 - 2010

> *Alternate Strategy—*
> *Investors can bridge the gap between the two positive seasonal trends for the bank sector by holding from October 10th to April 13th. Longer term investors may prefer this strategy, shorter term investors can use technical tools to determine the appropriate strategy.*

> ** Banks SP GIC Canadian Sector Level 2*
> *An index designed to represent a cross section of banking companies. For more information on the bank sector, see www.standardandpoors.com.*

24 MONDAY	268 / 098	**25** TUESDAY	269 / 097

26 WEDNESDAY	270 / 096	**27** THURSDAY	271 / 095

28 FRIDAY   272 / 094

WEEK 39

Market Indices & Rates
Weekly Values**

Stock Markets	**2009**	**2010**
Dow	9,746	10,825
S&P500	1,058	1,144
Nasdaq	2,123	2,373
TSX	11,405	12,317
FTSE	5,116	5,573
DAX	5,653	6,248
Nikkei	10,405	9,486
Hang Seng	21,369	22,297

Commodities	**2009**	**2010**
Oil	68.32	78.42
Gold	1004.5	1304.4

Bond Yields	**2009**	**2010**
USA 5 Yr Treasury	2.41	1.27
USA 10 Yr T	3.43	2.52
USA 20 Yr T	4.15	3.38
Moody's Aaa	5.14	4.52
Moody's Baa	6.27	5.58
CAN 5 Yr T	2.63	2.04
CAN 10 Yr T	3.40	2.77

Money Market	**2009**	**2010**
USA Fed Funds	0.25	0.25
USA 3 Mo T-B	0.11	0.16
CAN tgt overnight rate	0.25	1.00
CAN 3 Mo T-B	0.23	0.88

Foreign Exchange	**2009**	**2010**
USD/EUR	1.47	1.36
USD/GBP	1.62	1.58
CAN/USD	1.08	1.03
JPY/USD	91.05	83.72

SEPTEMBER

M	T	W	T	F	S	S
					1	2
3	4	5	6	7	8	9
10	11	12	13	14	15	16
17	18	19	20	21	22	23
24	25	26	27	28	29	30

OCTOBER

M	T	W	T	F	S	S
1	2	3	4	5	6	7
8	9	10	11	12	13	14
15	16	17	18	19	20	21
22	23	24	25	26	27	28
29	30	31				

NOVEMBER

M	T	W	T	F	S	S
			1	2	3	4
5	6	7	8	9	10	11
12	13	14	15	16	17	18
19	20	21	22	23	24	25
26	27	28	29	30		

2010 Strategy Performance

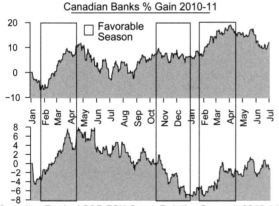

Canadian Banks % Gain 2010-11

Canadian Banks / S&P TSX Comp Relative Strength 2010-11

In 2010, the Canadian banking sector outperformed the S&P/ TSX Composite from the end of January to mid-April. Later in the year (mid-October to the end of the year) its performance was flat and under performed the TSX. In 2011, the Canadian banking sector strongly outperformed the TSX from the end of January to mid-April. In the total compounded combination, the Canadian Bank strategy was a success.

** Weekly avg closing values- except Fed Funds & CAN overnight tgt rate weekly closing values.

OCTOBER

	MONDAY	TUESDAY	WEDNESDAY
WEEK 40	**1** 30	**2** 29	**3** 28
WEEK 41	**8** 23 USA Bond Market Closed- Columbus Day CAN Market Closed- Thanksgiving Day	**9** 22	**10** 21
WEEK 42	**15** 16	**16** 15	**17** 14
WEEK 43	**22** 9	**23** 8	**24** 7
WEEK 44	**29** 2	**30** 1	**31**

THURSDAY		FRIDAY	
4	27	**5**	26
11	20	**12**	19
18	13	**19**	12
25	6	**26**	5
1		2	

NOVEMBER

M	T	W	T	F	S	S
			1	2	3	4
5	6	7	8	9	10	11
12	13	14	15	16	17	18
19	20	21	22	23	24	25
26	27	28	29	30		

DECEMBER

M	T	W	T	F	S	S
					1	2
3	4	5	6	7	8	9
10	11	12	13	14	15	16
17	18	19	20	21	22	23
24	25	26	27	28	29	30
31						

JANUARY

M	T	W	T	F	S	S
	1	2	3	4	5	6
7	8	9	10	11	12	13
14	15	16	17	18	19	20
21	22	23	24	25	26	27
28	29	30	31			

FEBRUARY

M	T	W	T	F	S	S
				1	2	3
4	5	6	7	8	9	10
11	12	13	14	15	16	17
18	19	20	21	22	23	24
25	26	27	28			

OCTOBER
S U M M A R Y

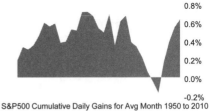

0.8%
0.6%
0.4%
0.2%
0.0%
-0.2%

S&P500 Cumulative Daily Gains for Avg Month 1950 to 2010

	Dow Jones	S&P 500	Nasdaq	TSX Comp
Month Rank	7	7	8	9
# Up	36	36	21	16
# Down	25	25	18	10
% Pos	59	59	54	62
% Avg. Gain	0.4	0.6	0.4	-0.3

Dow & S&P 1950-June 2011, Nasdaq 1972-June 2011, TSX 1985-June 2011

65%
55%
45%
35%

Prob. of Daily Gain

♦ October is very often a turnaround month when the market has been negative. It is the most volatile month of the year and often provides opportunities for short-term traders. ♦ The beginning part of October can provide positive returns if the market is expecting positive earnings announcements. ♦ October 9th can provide a good buying opportunity on a market pull back, especially for *technology* stocks. ♦ The market very often pulls back around the third week of the month and provides an excellent entry point around October 28th.

BEST / WORST OCTOBER BROAD MKTS. 2001-2010

BEST OCTOBER MARKETS
- ♦ Nasdaq (2002) 13.5%
- ♦ Nasdaq (2001) 12.8%
- ♦ Dow (2002) 10.6%

WORST OCTOBER MARKETS
- ♦ Russell 2000 (2008) -20.9%
- ♦ Russell 3000 Gr (2008) -18.0%
- ♦ Russell 3000 Value (2008) -17.8%

Index Values End of Month

	2001	2002	2003	2004	2005	2006	2007	2008	2009	2010
Dow	9,075	8,397	9,801	10,027	10,440	12,081	13,930	9,325	9,713	11,118
S&P 500	1,060	886	1,051	1,130	1,207	1,378	1,549	969	1,036	1,183
Nasdaq	1,690	1,330	1,932	1,975	2,120	2,367	2,859	1,721	2,045	2,507
TSX	6,886	6,249	7,773	8,871	10,383	12,345	14,625	9,763	10,911	12,676
Russell 1000	1,071	900	1,081	1,162	1,261	1,437	1,623	1,004	1,089	1,256
Russell 2000	1,064	928	1,313	1,451	1,607	1,906	2,058	1,336	1,399	1,748
Russell 3000 Growth	1,808	1,439	1,756	1,800	1,942	2,140	2,518	1,566	1,800	2,132
Russell 3000 Value	1,910	1,691	2,045	2,310	2,526	2,996	3,219	1,991	2,017	2,295

Percent Gain for October

	2001	2002	2003	2004	2005	2006	2007	2008	2009	2010
Dow	2.6	10.6	5.7	-0.5	-1.2	3.4	0.2	-14.1	0.0	3.1
S&P 500	1.8	8.6	5.5	1.4	-1.8	3.2	1.5	-16.9	-2.0	3.7
Nasdaq	12.8	13.5	8.1	4.1	-1.5	4.8	5.8	-17.7	-3.6	5.9
TSX	0.7	1.1	4.7	2.3	-5.7	5.0	3.7	-16.9	-4.2	2.5
Russell 1000	2.0	8.1	5.7	1.5	-1.9	3.3	1.6	-17.6	-2.3	3.8
Russell 2000	5.8	3.1	8.3	1.9	-3.2	5.7	2.8	-20.9	-6.9	4.0
Russell 3000 Growth	5.5	8.8	5.8	1.6	-1.3	3.7	3.4	-18.0	-1.9	4.7
Russell 3000 Value	-0.8	6.7	6.1	1.5	-2.7	3.3	-0.1	-17.8	-3.5	2.9

October Market Avg. Performance 2001 to 2010[1]

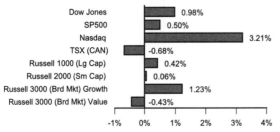

Dow Jones	0.98%
SP500	0.50%
Nasdaq	3.21%
TSX (CAN)	-0.68%
Russell 1000 (Lg Cap)	0.42%
Russell 2000 (Sm Cap)	0.06%
Russell 3000 (Brd Mkt) Growth	1.23%
Russell 3000 (Brd Mkt) Value	-0.43%

Interest Corner Oct[2]

	Fed Funds %[3]	3 Mo. T-Bill %[4]	10 Yr %[5]	20 Yr %[6]
2010	0.25	0.12	2.63	3.64
2009	0.25	0.05	3.41	4.19
2008	1.00	0.46	4.01	4.74
2007	4.50	3.94	4.48	4.79
2006	5.25	5.08	4.61	4.81

(1) Russell Data provided by Russell (2) Federal Reserve Bank of St. Louis- end of month values (3) Target rate set by FOMC (4)(5)(6) Constant yield maturities.

THACKRAY SECTOR THERMOMETER

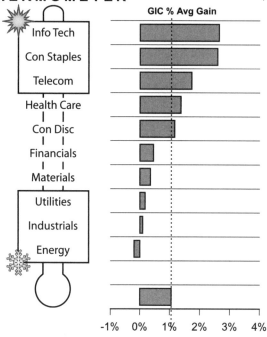

GIC[2] % Avg Gain	Fq % Gain >S&P 500	SP GIC SECTOR 1990-2010[1]
2.6 %	52 %	Information Technology
2.6	57	Consumer Staples
1.7	43	Telecom
1.4	48	Health Care
1.2	48	Consumer Discretionary
0.5	38	Financials
0.4	48	Materials
0.2	38	Utilities
0.1	29	Industrials
-0.2 %	43 %	Energy
1.1 %	N/A %	S&P 500

Sector Commentary

♦ *Consumer staples* and *information technology* live together in the top rank for this month (see *Odd Couple* strategy). ♦ *Information technology*, although it has a better average return than the S&P 500, outperforms the market less than half of the time during the month. The sector's outperformance has typically started after September's spell has worn off - October 9th (see *Information Technology Use It Or Lose It Strategy*). In 2010, the *consumer staples* sector under performed the S&P 500 with a return of 2.8% vs. the S&P's 3.7%, but the *information technology* sector produced a return of 6.5%, making the pair a winning combination again.

SELECTED SUB-SECTORS 1990-2010[3]		
6.2 %	76 %	Agriculture Products (94-2010)
4.4	71	Software & Services
3.7	67	Airlines
3.4	71	Transportation
2.1	57	Pharmaceuticals
1.4	44	Semiconductor (SOX) 95-2010
1.4	52	Retail
1.1	50	Biotech (93-2010)
0.5	43	Banks
0.1	43	Integrated Oil & Gas
-1.0	33	Metals & Mining
-1.1	38	Auto & Components
-1.3	29	Gold (London PM)
-4.8	33	Gold (XAU)

Sub-Sector Commentary

♦ The *agriculture* sub-sector is the top performing sub-sector producing an average gain of 6.2% for the month of October, from 1990 to 2010, and beating the S&P 500, 76% of the time. In 2010, it was the seventh best sub-sector and produced a gain of 4.4%. ♦ *Gold stocks (XAU)* typically do not do well in the month of October. In 2010 XAU performed approximately at market with a gain of 3.7%. *Gold (London PM)* produced a gain a slightly under market at 3.0%.

(1) Sector data provided by Standard and Poors (2) GIC is short form for Global Industry Classification (3) Sub Sector data provided by Standard and Poors, except where marked by symbol.

ODD COUPLE
CONSUMER STAPLES & INFO TECH
Live Together for the Month of October

The consumer staples and information technology sectors make an odd couple for the month of October.

Usually stocks of a similar type move together. For example, the growth sectors of the market tend to rise and fall together and defensive sectors tend to rise and fall together. Although this relationship is not always true, it is true more often than not.

1.5% extra and 71% of the time better than the S&P 500

October is considered a transition month, where the market bottoms and new sectors tend to rotate into positions of outperformance.

It also tends to be the most volatile month of the year. In this month, two unlikely sectors tend to outperform the market: consumer staples and information technology.

Consumer Staples & Information Technology
October Performance vs S&P 500- 1990-2010

	S&P 500	Info Tech	Cons Staples	Positive
				Cons Staples & Info Tech
1990	-0.7 %	-4.2 %	5.1 %	0.5 %
1991	1.2	-0.1	-0.1	-0.1
1992	0.2	-0.4	-0.1	-0.3
1993	1.9	2.6	6.8	4.7
1994	2.1	8.9	3.1	6.0
1995	-0.5	3.8	2.5	3.2
1996	2.6	1.1	1.5	1.3
1997	-3.4	-9.2	-2.1	-5.6
1998	8.0	6.7	14.9	10.8
1999	6.3	1.8	7.1	4.5
2000	-0.5	-5.8	11.6	2.9
2001	1.8	17.4	-0.6	8.4
2002	8.6	22.3	3.4	12.9
2003	5.5	8.1	4.8	6.5
2004	1.4	5.2	0.6	2.9
2005	-1.8	-2.2	-0.4	-1.3
2006	3.2	4.1	1.8	3.0
2007	1.5	7.1	1.7	4.4
2008	-16.9	-17.8	-11.1	-14.4
2009	-2.0	-0.4	1.0	0.3
2010	3.7	6.5	2.8	4.6
Avg	1.1 %	2.6 %	2.6 %	2.6 %
Fq > 0	67 %	62 %	76 %	71 %

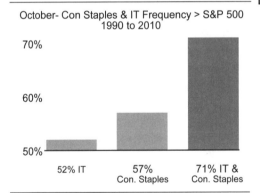

October- Con Staples & IT Frequency > S&P 500
1990 to 2010

| 52% IT | 57% Con. Staples | 71% IT & Con. Staples |

Why does this odd couple outperform? It is a combination of two factors.

First, investors seek the stability of earnings from the consumer staples sector during volatile times.

Second, investors desire to establish a position in information technology before the best three months of the market in a row- November, December and January.

In the transition month of October, the *Odd Couple* sectors of consumer staples and information technology have the same approximate gain, 2.6%. The real value of the odd couple comes in its combined performance of how often it outperforms the S&P 500. Information technology by itself has outperformed the S&P 500, 52% of the time from 1990 to 2010 and the consumer staples sector has outperformed 57% of the time. Together, the information technology sector and the consumer staples sector has outperformed the S&P 500, 71% of the time since 1990.

Historically, the *Odd Couple* strategy has added value by increasing diversification and the frequency of outperforming the S&P 500.

(i) *Odd Couple Strategy is similar to a Barbell Strategy- The term barbell strategy is usually reserved for fixed income managers who overweight both short-term and long-term bonds. The odd couple strategy is similar in that it combines sectors that are totally different.*

1 MONDAY	275 / 091	**2** TUESDAY	276 / 090

3 WEDNESDAY	277 / 089	**4** THURSDAY	278 / 088

5 FRIDAY			279 / 087

WEEK 40

Market Indices & Rates
Weekly Values**

Stock Markets	2009	2010
Dow	9,648	10,924
S&P500	1,047	1,156
Nasdaq	2,097	2,382
TSX	11,232	12,461
FTSE	5,099	5,639
DAX	5,629	6,238
Nikkei	9,991	9,573
Hang Seng	20,733	22,793

Commodities	2009	2010
Oil	68.99	82.37
Gold	997.1	1335.4

Bond Yields	2009	2010
USA 5 Yr Treasury	2.28	1.17
USA 10 Yr T	3.28	2.45
USA 20 Yr T	4.00	3.38
Moody's Aaa	5.00	4.56
Moody's Baa	6.14	5.59
CAN 5 Yr T	2.55	1.96
CAN 10 Yr T	3.30	2.74

Money Market	2009	2010
USA Fed Funds	0.25	0.25
USA 3 Mo T-B	0.12	0.13
CAN tgt overnight rate	0.25	1.00
CAN 3 Mo T-B	0.22	0.87

Foreign Exchange	2009	2010
USD/EUR	1.46	1.39
USD/GBP	1.59	1.59
CAN/USD	1.08	1.02
JPY/USD	89.77	82.77

OCTOBER

M	T	W	T	F	S	S
1	2	3	4	5	6	7
8	9	10	11	12	13	14
15	16	17	18	19	20	21
22	23	24	25	26	27	28
29	30	31				

NOVEMBER

M	T	W	T	F	S	S
			1	2	3	4
5	6	7	8	9	10	11
12	13	14	15	16	17	18
19	20	21	22	23	24	25
26	27	28	29	30		

DECEMBER

M	T	W	T	F	S	S
					1	2
3	4	5	6	7	8	9
10	11	12	13	14	15	16
17	18	19	20	21	22	23
24	25	26	27	28	29	30
31						

2010 Strategy Performance

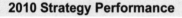

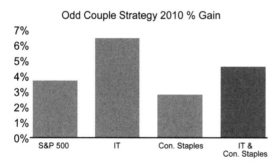

Odd Couple Strategy 2010 % Gain

In October 2010, the *Odd Couple* strategy worked once again, producing a gain of 4.6% compared with the S&P 500 which had a gain of 3.7%.

This combination worked once again because of the offsetting characteristics of both sectors. Although the consumer staples sector produced a gain, it under performed the S&P 500. The information technology sector's outperformance more than offset the under performance of the consumer staples sector. In the end, the *Odd Couple* strategy outperformed the S&P 500 by 0.9%.

** Weekly avg closing values- except Fed Funds & CAN overnight tgt rate weekly closing values.

INFORMATION TECHNOLOGY
USE IT OR LOSE IT
October 9th to January 17th

Information technology– the sector that investors love to love and love to hate. In recent times most investors have made and lost money in this sector. When the sector is good, it can be really good. When it is bad, it can be really bad.

5.6% extra compared with the S&P 500

Technology stocks get bid up at the end of the year for three reasons:

First, a lot of companies operate with year end budgets and if they do not spend the money in their budget, they lose it.

In the last few months of the year, whatever money they have, they spend. Hence, the saying "use it or lose it."

The number one purchase item for this budget flush is technology equipment. An upgrade in technology equipment is something which a large number of employees in the company can benefit from and is easy to justify.

Second, consumers indirectly help push up technology stocks by purchasing electronic items during the holiday season.

Retail sales ramp up significantly on Black Friday, the Friday after Thanksgiving. Investors anticipate the upswing in sales and buy technology stocks.

Third, the "Conference Effect" helps maintain the momentum in January. This phenomenon is the result of investors increasing positions ahead of major conferences in order to benefit from positive announcements.

In the case of Information Technology, investors increase their holdings ahead of the Las Vegas Consumer Electronics Conference that typically occurs in the second week of January.

Info Tech & Nasdaq vs S&P 500
Oct 9 to Jan 17, 1989/90-2010/11

	S&P 500	Info Tech	Nas daq	Diff IT to S&P	Diff Nas to S&P
1989/90	-6.0 %	-6.9 %	-9.3 %	-1.0 %	-3.3 %
1990/91	4.6	13.4	8.0	8.8	3.3
1991/92	10.0	16.4	21.2	6.4	11.2
1992/93	7.2	11.2	21.5	4.0	14.3
1993/94	2.8	12.5	3.7	9.7	0.8
1994/95	3.3	16.0	3.0	12.7	-0.3
1995/96	4.1	-8.9	-1.4	-13.0	-5.5
1996/97	10.8	21.2	8.8	10.4	-2.0
1997/98	-1.3	-14.2	-10.3	-12.9	-9.0
1998/99	29.6	71.8	65.5	42.2	35.9
1999/00	9.7	29.2	40.8	19.5	31.1
2001/01	-5.6	-21.7	-20.2	-16.1	-14.5
2001/02	7.2	26.8	23.7	19.6	16.5
2002/03	12.9	30.0	21.9	17.0	8.9
2003/04	10.3	14.2	13.0	4.0	2.8
2004/05	5.6	6.8	8.7	1.2	3.2
2005/06	7.3	9.7	10.2	2.4	2.9
2006/07	6.0	7.1	7.8	1.1	1.8
2007/08	-14.1	-14.9	-15.8	-0.7	-1.7
2008/09	-13.7	-12.0	-12.1	1.6	1.6
2009/10	6.6	9.9	7.7	3.3	1.1
2010/11	11.0	13.6	14.7	2.6	3.7
Avg	4.9 %	10.5 %	9.6 %	5.6 %	4.7 %
Fq > 0	77 %	73 %	73 %	77 %	68 %

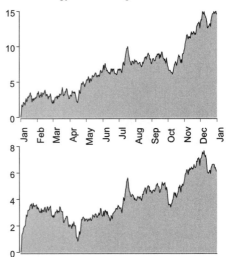

Technology Sector - Avg. Year 1990 to 2010

Technology / S&P 500 - Avg Yr. 1990 - 2010

(i) *Information Technology SP GIC Sector 45: An index designed to represent a cross section of information technology companies.*
For more information on the information technology sector, see www.standardandpoors.com.

8 MONDAY	282 / 084	**9** TUESDAY	283 / 083

10 WEDNESDAY	284 / 082	**11** THURSDAY	285 / 081

12 FRIDAY			286 / 080

WEEK 41

Market Indices & Rates
Weekly Values**

Stock Markets	2009	2010
Dow	9,742	11,057
S&P500	1,058	1,173
Nasdaq	2,109	2,433
TSX	11,324	12,619
FTSE	5,118	5,702
DAX	5,647	6,399
Nikkei	9,803	9,469
Hang Seng	21,095	23,479

Commodities	2009	2010
Oil	70.86	82.17
Gold	1036.2	1361.3

Bond Yields	2009	2010
USA 5 Yr Treasury	2.24	1.16
USA 10 Yr T	3.28	2.50
USA 20 Yr T	4.04	3.52
Moody's Aaa	5.06	4.71
Moody's Baa	6.22	5.74
CAN 5 Yr T	2.61	1.93
CAN 10 Yr T	3.34	2.74

Money Market	2009	2010
USA Fed Funds	0.25	0.25
USA 3 Mo T-B	0.08	0.14
CAN tgt overnight rate	0.25	1.00
CAN 3 Mo T-B	0.20	0.89

Foreign Exchange	2009	2010
USD/EUR	1.47	1.40
USD/GBP	1.59	1.59
CAN/USD	1.06	1.01
JPY/USD	89.03	81.71

2010-2011 Strategy Performance*

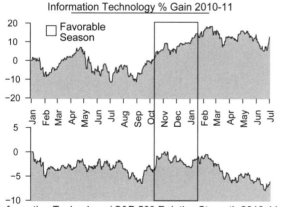

Information Technology % Gain 2010-11

☐ Favorable Season

Information Technology / S&P 500 Relative Strength 2010-11

OCTOBER

M	T	W	T	F	S	S
1	2	3	4	5	6	7
8	9	10	11	12	13	14
15	16	17	18	19	20	21
22	23	24	25	26	27	28
29	30	31				

NOVEMBER

M	T	W	T	F	S	S
			1	2	3	4
5	6	7	8	9	10	11
12	13	14	15	16	17	18
19	20	21	22	23	24	25
26	27	28	29	30		

In 2010, the information technology sector started its outperformance early at the beginning of September. It then went on to peak in mid-January 2011.

Exiting a trade at the right time is very important. This was true in 2011, as the information technology sector started to under perform the S&P 500 at the end of its seasonally strong period.

** Weekly avg closing values- except Fed Funds & CAN overnight tgt rate weekly closing values.

DECEMBER

M	T	W	T	F	S	S
					1	2
3	4	5	6	7	8	9
10	11	12	13	14	15	16
17	18	19	20	21	22	23
24	25	26	27	28	29	30
31						

CONSUMER SWITCH
SELL CONSUMER STAPLES
BUY CONSUMER DISCRETIONARY
Con. Discretionary Outperforms From Oct 28 to Apr 22

This is the time to sell the sector of "need" and buy the sector of "want."

Companies that are classified as consumer staples sell products to the consumer that they need for their everyday life.

Consumers will generally still buy products from a consumer staples company, such as a drugstore, even if the economy and the stock market turns down.

On the other hand, consumer discretionary companies sell products that consumers do not necessarily need, such as furniture.

Why is this important? Consumer discretionary companies tend to outperform in the six favorable months of the market.

The discretionary sector benefits from the positive market forces and positive market forecasts that tend to take place in this period.

The consumer staples and discretionary sectors average year graphs illustrate the individual trends of the sectors.

The discretionary sector tends to outperform strongly from the end of October to April. Although the staples sector in the summer months has a slightly average negative performance, it still outperforms the discretionary sector.

At the end of the year, both sectors do well, but investing in the right sector at the right time can make a substantial difference in an investor's profits.

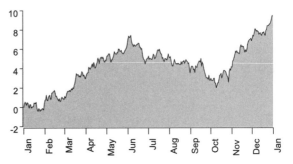

Consumer Discretionary Avg. Year 1990 to 2010

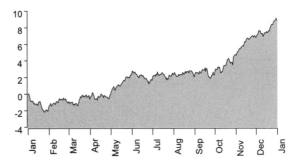

Consumer Staples Avg. Year 1990 to 2010

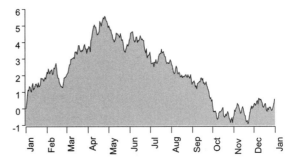

Con. Discretionary / Staples - Relative Strength Avg. Year 1990 to 2010

> *Alternate Strategy — The consumer discretionary stocks have dramatically outperformed the consumer staples stocks from December 27th to April 22nd. With both the discretionary and staples sectors performing well in November and December, depending on market conditions, investors can delay some or all of their allocation to the discretionary sector until the end of December.*

15 MONDAY   289 / 077   **16** TUESDAY   290 / 0764

17 WEDNESDAY   291 / 075   **18** THURSDAY   292 / 074

19 FRIDAY   293 / 073

WEEK 42

Market Indices & Rates
Weekly Values**

Stock Markets	2009	2010
Dow	9,966	11,102
S&P500	1,085	1,178
Nasdaq	2,156	2,463
TSX	11,489	12,618
FTSE	5,207	5,735
DAX	5,785	6,550
Nikkei	10,158	9,445
Hang Seng	21,716	23,591

Commodities	2009	2010
Oil	75.74	81.11
Gold	1055.4	1342.3

Bond Yields	2009	2010
USA 5 Yr Treasury	2.36	1.14
USA 10 Yr T	3.43	2.54
USA 20 Yr T	4.23	3.56
Moody's Aaa	5.21	4.71
Moody's Baa	6.38	5.76
CAN 5 Yr T	2.85	1.91
CAN 10 Yr T	3.51	2.74

Money Market	2009	2010
USA Fed Funds	0.25	0.25
USA 3 Mo T-B	0.07	0.14
CAN tgt overnight rate	0.25	1.00
CAN 3 Mo T-B	0.23	0.89

Foreign Exchange	2009	2010
USD/EUR	1.49	1.39
USD/GBP	1.61	1.58
CAN/USD	1.03	1.02
JPY/USD	90.09	81.33

OCTOBER

M	T	W	T	F	S	S
1	2	3	4	5	6	7
8	9	10	11	12	13	14
15	16	17	18	19	20	21
22	23	24	25	26	27	28
29	30	31				

NOVEMBER

M	T	W	T	F	S	S
			1	2	3	4
5	6	7	8	9	10	11
12	13	14	15	16	17	18
19	20	21	22	23	24	25
26	27	28	29	30		

DECEMBER

M	T	W	T	F	S	S
					1	2
3	4	5	6	7	8	9
10	11	12	13	14	15	16
17	18	19	20	21	22	23
24	25	26	27	28	29	30
31						

2010 Strategy Performance*

Consumer Discretionary vs. Consumer Staples 2010-11

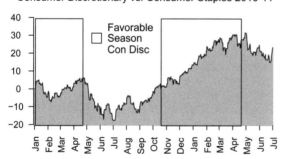

The consumer switch strategy worked well in 2010 and into 2011. The consumer discretionary sector started to outperform the consumer staples sector at the end of October and maintained its outperformance into April.

The above graph shows the ratio of outperformance between the two sectors. When the line is rising, the discretionary sector is outperforming. When it is falling, the staples sector is outperforming.

** Weekly avg closing values- except Fed Funds & CAN overnight tgt rate weekly closing values.

Although the *Retail – Shop Early* strategy is the second retail sector strategy of the year, it occurs before the biggest shopping season of the year – the Christmas holiday season.

3.0% extra & 77% of the time better than S&P 500

The time to go shopping for retail stocks is at the end of October, which is about one month before Thanksgiving. It is the time when two favorable influences happen at the same time.

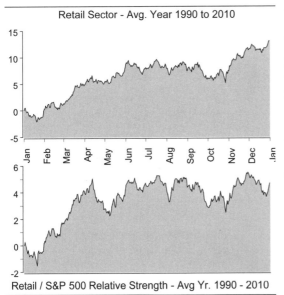

Retail Sector - Avg. Year 1990 to 2010

Retail / S&P 500 Relative Strength - Avg Yr. 1990 - 2010

First, historically the three best months in a row for the stock market have been November, December and January. The end of October usually represents an excellent buying opportunity, not only for the next three months, but the next six months.

Second, investors tend to buy retail stocks in anticipation of a strong holiday sales season. At the same time that the market tends to increase, investors are attracted back into the retail sector.

Retail sales tend to be lower in the summer and a lot of investors view investing in retail stocks at this time as dead money. During the summertime, investors prefer not to invest in this sector until it comes back

into favor towards the end of October.

The trick to investing is not to be too early, but early. If an investor gets into a sector too early, they can suffer from the frustration of having dead money– having an investment that goes nowhere, while the rest of the market increases.

If an investor moves into a sector too late, there is very little upside potential. In fact, this can be a dangerous strategy because if the sales or earnings numbers disappoint the analysts, the sector can severely correct.

For the *Retail – Shop Early* strategy the time to enter is approximately one month before Black Friday.

Coincidentally, the end of October is also typically a good time to enter the broad market.

Retail Sector vs. S&P 500 1990 to 2010

Oct 28 to Nov 29	Positive		
	S&P 500	Retail	Diff
1990	3.8 %	9.9 %	6.0 %
1991	-2.3	2.7	5.0
1992	2.8	5.5	2.8
1993	-0.6	6.3	6.9
1994	-2.3	0.4	2.7
1995	4.8	9.5	4.7
1996	8.0	0.4	-7.6
1997	8.9	16.9	7.9
1998	11.9	20.4	8.4
1999	8.6	14.1	5.5
2000	-2.7	9.9	12.6
2001	3.2	7.9	4.7
2002	4.3	-1.7	-6.0
2003	2.6	2.5	-0.1
2004	4.7	7.0	2.3
2005	6.7	9.9	3.2
2006	1.6	0.2	-1.4
2007	-4.3	-7.5	-3.2
2008	5.6	7.5	1.9
2009	2.6	3.6	1.0
2010	0.5	5.2	4.7
Avg.	3.3 %	6.2 %	3.0 %
Fq > 0	76 %	86 %	76 %

22 MONDAY	296 / 070	**23** TUESDAY	297 / 069

Market Indices & Rates
Weekly Values**

Stock Markets	2009	2010
Dow	10,027	11,138
S&P500	1,089	1,184
Nasdaq	2,162	2,501
TSX	11,487	12,631
FTSE	5,247	5,692
DAX	5,800	6,604
Nikkei	10,291	9,347
Hang Seng	22,341	23,340

Commodities	2009	2010
Oil	80.13	82.01
Gold	1056.2	1334.4

Bond Yields	2009	2010
USA 5 Yr Treasury	2.38	1.24
USA 10 Yr T	3.43	2.67
USA 20 Yr T	4.20	3.66
Moody's Aaa	5.17	4.77
Moody's Baa	6.31	5.80
CAN 5 Yr T	2.75	1.99
CAN 10 Yr T	3.47	2.83

24 WEDNESDAY	298 / 068	**25** THURSDAY	299 / 067

Money Market	2009	2010
USA Fed Funds	0.25	0.25
USA 3 Mo T-B	0.07	0.13
CAN tgt overnight rate	0.25	1.00
CAN 3 Mo T-B	0.22	0.91

Foreign Exchange	2009	2010
USD/EUR	1.50	1.39
USD/GBP	1.65	1.59
CAN/USD	1.04	1.02
JPY/USD	91.13	81.08

26 FRIDAY	300 / 066

2010 Strategy Performance*

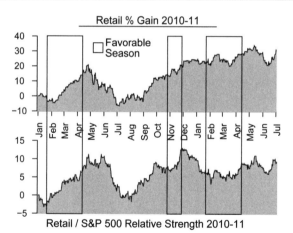

Retail % Gain 2010-11

□ Favorable Season

Retail / S&P 500 Relative Strength 2010-11

OCTOBER

M	T	W	T	F	S	S
1	2	3	4	5	6	7
8	9	10	11	12	13	14
15	16	17	18	19	20	21
22	23	24	25	26	27	28
29	30	31				

NOVEMBER

M	T	W	T	F	S	S
			1	2	3	4
5	6	7	8	9	10	11
12	13	14	15	16	17	18
19	20	21	22	23	24	25
26	27	28	29	30		

DECEMBER

M	T	W	T	F	S	S
					1	2
3	4	5	6	7	8	9
10	11	12	13	14	15	16
17	18	19	20	21	22	23
24	25	26	27	28	29	30
31						

The retail sector performed well in 2010. By the time autumn rolled around, it was quite evident that the consumer was not dead yet. The retail sector benefited from a drop in the market just before the start of its seasonal autumn period. On the bounce, it managed to outperform the S&P 500, as expected, until Black Friday. The above graph also includes the *Retail Post Holiday Bargain* strategy.

** Weekly avg closing values- except Fed Funds & CAN overnight tgt rate weekly closing values.

LAST 4 MARKET DAYS IN OCTOBER
The 1% Difference

The adage "buy at the beginning of November and sell at the end of April" has been around a long time. A lot of prudent investors believe in the merits of this strategy and have profited handsomely.

Nevertheless, if they entered the market four market days earlier they would have received, on average, an extra 1% per year from 1950 to 2010.

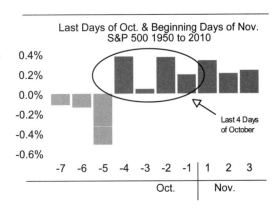

Last Days of Oct. & Beginning Days of Nov.
S&P 500 1950 to 2010

Last 4 Days of October

Average Return of 1% & Positive 57% of the time

It is not just the four days gain that is attractive; the seasonal safety net that follows has been very solid.

The last four days is followed by one of the best months: November. This month is also the first month of the best three months in a row and the first month of the six favorable months.

Although October has a reputation for being a "tough month," its average return has been positive from 1950 to 2010. It is October's volatility that shakes investors up.

The interesting fact is that almost all of the gains for October can be attributed to the last four market days. The average daily loss for all days in October, except the last four, is 0.02%. This pales in comparison to the average daily gain for the last four days of the market, 0.25%.

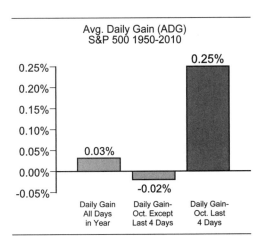

Avg. Daily Gain (ADG)
S&P 500 1950-2010

Daily Gain All Days in Year	Daily Gain- Oct. Except Last 4 Days	Daily Gain- Oct. Last 4 Days
0.03%	-0.02%	0.25%

Last 4 Market Days in October % Gain 1950 to 2010   Positive ☐

1950	-0.4 %	1960	2.3 %	1970	-0.1 %	1980	-0.3 %	1990	-2.0 %	2000	4.7 %	2010	0.0 %
1951	0.6	1961	0.4	1971	-0.9	1981	3.2	1991	2.1	2001	-3.7		
1952	1.8	1962	3.3	1972	0.8	1982	0.3	1992	0.1	2002	-1.3		
1953	0.9	1963	0.0	1973	-2.0	1983	-1.8	1993	0.8	2003	1.9		
1954	-0.9	1964	-0.2	1974	5.4	1984	-0.1	1994	2.3	2004	3.2		
1955	-0.7	1965	0.8	1975	-0.8	1985	1.2	1995	-0.2	2005	0.9		
1956	-0.6	1966	1.6	1976	2.8	1986	2.2	1996	0.6	2006	-0.3		
1957	1.2	1967	-1.3	1977	1.5	1987	10.6	1997	4.3	2007	2.3		
1958	1.8	1968	-0.4	1978	-4.3	1988	-1.2	1998	2.5	2008	14.1		
1959	1.0	1969	-0.9	1979	1.8	1989	-0.6	1999	5.4	2009	-2.9		
Avg.	0.5 %		0.6 %		0.4 %		1.3 %		1.6 %		1.9 %		0.0 %

29 MONDAY	303 / 063	**30** TUESDAY	304 / 062

31 WEDNESDAY	305 / 061	**1** THURSDAY	306 / 060

2 FRIDAY   307 / 059

WEEK 44

Market Indices & Rates
Weekly Values**

Stock Markets	2009	2010
Dow	9,838	11,281
S&P500	1,055	1,205
Nasdaq	2,092	2,547
TSX	11,016	12,764
FTSE	5,131	5,788
DAX	5,555	6,673
Nikkei	10,115	9,325
Hang Seng	21,737	24,176

Commodities	2009	2010
Oil	78.51	84.98
Gold	1040.6	1365.5

Bond Yields	2009	2010
USA 5 Yr Treasury	2.41	1.11
USA 10 Yr T	3.49	2.61
USA 20 Yr T	4.27	3.65
Moody's Aaa	5.22	4.75
Moody's Baa	6.34	5.79
CAN 5 Yr T	2.74	2.02
CAN 10 Yr T	3.48	2.85

Money Market	2009	2010
USA Fed Funds	0.25	0.25
USA 3 Mo T-B	0.07	0.13
CAN tgt overnight rate	0.25	1.00
CAN 3 Mo T-B	0.22	0.92

Foreign Exchange	2009	2010
USD/EUR	1.48	1.41
USD/GBP	1.64	1.61
CAN/USD	1.07	1.01
JPY/USD	91.25	80.84

NOVEMBER

M	T	W	T	F	S	S
			1	2	3	4
5	6	7	8	9	10	11
12	13	14	15	16	17	18
19	20	21	22	23	24	25
26	27	28	29	30		

DECEMBER

M	T	W	T	F	S	S
					1	2
3	4	5	6	7	8	9
10	11	12	13	14	15	16
17	18	19	20	21	22	23
24	25	26	27	28	29	30
31						

JANUARY

M	T	W	T	F	S	S
	1	2	3	4	5	6
7	8	9	10	11	12	13
14	15	16	17	18	19	20
21	22	23	24	25	26	27
28	29	30	31			

2010 Strategy Performance

October Last Days of Month and Beginning of Nov. S&P 500 (2010)

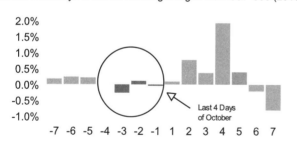

In 2010 the market was "flat" in the last four days of the month, but this hardly means that it was not a good time to get into the stock market. Starting on the first day of November, the market started to rally.

It is very difficult to pick the exact bottom of the market, but getting into the market four days before the end of October has proven to be a wise strategy over the long-term.

** Weekly avg closing values- except Fed Funds & CAN overnight tgt rate weekly closing values.

NOVEMBER

	MONDAY	TUESDAY	WEDNESDAY
WEEK 44	29	30	31
WEEK 45	5 25	6 24	7 23
WEEK 46	12 18	13 17	14 16
WEEK 47	19 11	20 10	21 9
WEEK 48	26 4	27 3	28 2

THURSDAY	FRIDAY
1 29	**2** 28
8 22	**9** 21
15 15	**16** 14
22 8 USA Market Closed- Thanksgiving Day	**23** 7 USA Early Market Close Thanksgiving
29 1	**30**

DECEMBER

M	T	W	T	F	S	S
					1	2
3	4	5	6	7	8	9
10	11	12	13	14	15	16
17	18	19	20	21	22	23
24	25	26	27	28	29	30
31						

JANUARY

M	T	W	T	F	S	S
	1	2	3	4	5	6
7	8	9	10	11	12	13
14	15	16	17	18	19	20
21	22	23	24	25	26	27
28	29	30	31			

FEBRUARY

M	T	W	T	F	S	S
				1	2	3
4	5	6	7	8	9	10
11	12	13	14	15	16	17
18	19	20	21	22	23	24
25	26	27	28			

MARCH

M	T	W	T	F	S	S
				1	2	3
4	5	6	7	8	9	10
11	12	13	14	15	16	17
18	19	20	21	22	23	24
25	26	27	28	29	30	31

NOVEMBER
SUMMARY

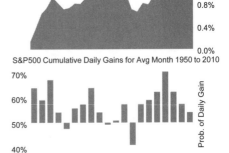

S&P500 Cumulative Daily Gains for Avg Month 1950 to 2010

	Dow Jones	S&P 500	Nasdaq	TSX Comp
Month Rank	3	2	3	8
# Up	40	21	26	16
# Down	21	40	13	10
% Pos	66	66	67	62
% Avg. Gain	1.5	1.6	1.7	0.8

Dow & S&P 1950-June 2011, Nasdaq 1972-June 2011, TSX 1985-June 2011

♦ The stock market in November typically performs well, but after a strong September and October in 2010, the S&P 500 lost a modest 0.2%. ♦ The day before and the day after the U.S. Thanksgiving tend to be very good (see *Thanksgiving - Give Thanks and Take Returns* strategy). In 2010, the *Thanksgiving* trade produced a gain. ♦ The *Metals and Mining* sector tends to start its ascent mid-November.

BEST / WORST NOVEMBER BROAD MKTS. 2001-2010

BEST NOVEMBER MARKETS
- ♦ Nasdaq (2001) 14.2%
- ♦ Nasdaq (2002) 11.2%
- ♦ Russell 3000 Gr (2001) 9.5%

WORST NOVEMBER MARKETS
- ♦ Russell 2000 (2008) -12.0%
- ♦ Nasdaq (2008) -10.8%
- ♦ Russell 3000 Gr (2008) -8.5%

Index Values End of Month

	2001	2002	2003	2004	2005	2006	2007	2008	2009	2010
Dow	9,852	8,896	9,782	10,428	10,806	12,222	13,372	8,829	10,345	11,006
S&P 500	1,139	936	1,058	1,174	1,249	1,401	1,481	896	1,096	1,181
Nasdaq	1,931	1,479	1,960	2,097	2,233	2,432	2,661	1,536	2,145	2,498
TSX	7,426	6,570	7,859	9,030	10,824	12,752	13,689	9,271	11,447	12,953
Russell 1000	1,152	952	1,093	1,210	1,306	1,464	1,550	925	1,150	1,258
Russell 2000	1,145	1,010	1,358	1,575	1,683	1,954	1,908	1,176	1,441	1,807
Russell 3000 Growth	1,979	1,520	1,776	1,868	2,026	2,180	2,415	1,433	1,903	2,158
Russell 3000 Value	2,018	1,795	2,072	2,429	2,601	3,057	3,046	1,834	2,121	2,283

Percent Gain for November

	2001	2002	2003	2004	2005	2006	2007	2008	2009	2010
Dow	8.6	5.9	-0.2	4.0	3.5	1.2	-4.0	-5.3	6.5	-1.0
S&P 500	7.5	5.7	0.7	3.9	3.5	1.6	-4.4	-7.5	5.7	-0.2
Nasdaq	14.2	11.2	1.5	6.2	5.3	2.7	-6.9	-10.8	4.9	-0.4
TSX	7.8	5.1	1.1	1.8	4.2	3.3	-6.4	-5.0	4.9	2.2
Russell 1000	7.5	5.7	1.0	4.1	3.5	1.9	-4.5	-7.9	5.6	0.1
Russell 2000	7.6	8.8	3.5	8.6	4.7	2.5	-7.3	-12.0	3.0	3.4
Russell 3000 Growth	9.5	5.6	1.1	3.7	4.3	1.9	-4.1	-8.5	5.7	1.2
Russell 3000 Value	5.7	6.1	1.3	5.1	3.0	2.0	-5.4	-7.9	5.2	-0.5

November Market Avg. Performance 2001 to 2010[1]

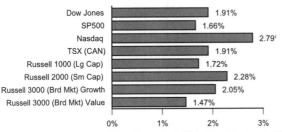

	Dow Jones	1.91%
SP500	1.66%
Nasdaq	2.79%
TSX (CAN)	1.91%
Russell 1000 (Lg Cap)	1.72%
Russell 2000 (Sm Cap)	2.28%
Russell 3000 (Brd Mkt) Growth	2.05%
Russell 3000 (Brd Mkt) Value	1.47%

Interest Corner Nov[2]

	Fed Funds %[3]	3 Mo. T-Bill %[4]	10 Yr %[5]	20 Yr %[6]
2010	0.25	0.17	2.81	3.80
2009	0.25	0.06	3.21	4.07
2008	1.00	0.01	2.93	3.71
2007	4.50	3.15	3.97	4.44
2006	5.25	5.03	4.46	4.66

(1) Russell Data provided by Russell (2) Federal Reserve Bank of St. Louis- end of month values (3) Target rate set by FOMC (4)(5)(6) Constant yield maturities.

THACKRAY SECTOR THERMOMETER

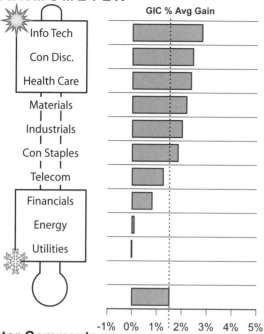

GIC(2) % Avg Gain	Fq % Gain >S&P 500	
SP GIC SECTOR 1990-2010(1)		
2.8 %	62 %	Information Technology
2.4	67	Consumer Discretionary
2.4	57	Health Care
2.2	57	Materials
2.0	67	Industrials
1.8	43	Consumer Staples
1.3	38	Telecom
0.8	33	Financials
0.1	29	Energy
0.0 %	33 %	Utilities
1.5 %	N/A %	S&P 500

Sector Commentary

◆ In 2010, *energy* which is usually at the bottom of the sector list in November, produced a strong gain of 5.1% in response to an improving economy. *Materials, consumer discretionary* and *industrials* produced gains of 0.9%, 2.4% and 0.9% respectively. All of the other sectors produced negative returns. *Utilities* produced the biggest loss of 3.6%.

Sub-Sector Commentary

◆ The *semiconductor* and *retail* sectors typically perform well in November. The *semiconductor* sector does well based upon the holiday sales expectations. In a similar vein, the *retail* sector also does well until the end of November (see *Retail Shop Early* strategy). In November 2010, both of these sectors were top performers with gains of 4.7% and 5.1% respectively.

		SELECTED SUB-SECTORS 1990-2010(3)
4.5 %	47 %	Agriculture Products (94-2010)
3.8	56	Semiconductor (SOX) 95-2010
3.5	67	Retail
2.5	67	Software & Services
2.2	57	Metals & Mining
2.2	57	Pharmaceuticals
2.1	57	Gold (London PM)
2.0	43	Transportation
1.8	43	Airlines
1.7	44	Biotech (93-2010)
1.5	48	Auto & Components
1.3	43	Gold (XAU)
0.7	43	Banks
0.5	33	Integrated Oil & Gas

(1) Sector data provided by Standard and Poors (2) GIC is short form for Global Industry Classification (3) Sub Sector data provided by Standard and Poors, except where marked by symbol.

Materials Composition – CAUTION

The U.S. materials sector is substantially different from the Canadian materials sector. The U.S. sector has over a 60% weight in chemical companies, versus the Canadian sector which has over a 60% weight in gold companies.

The materials sector (U.S.) generally does well during the favorable six months of the year, from the end of October to the beginning of May. The sector is economically sensitive and is leveraged to the economic forecasts. Generally, if the economy is expected to slow, the materials sector tends to decline, vice versa.

In the past I have focused my writings on the seasonal strength of the materials sector in the time period between the latter days of January to the first few days of May. Although the materials sector has done very well at this time of year, there is another time period when the materials sector has outperformed the broad markets – from October 28th to January 6th. During this time period, the sector has produced an average gain of 8.6% in the years from 1990 to 2010 and has been positive 81% of the time.

Positive 100% of the time

A lot of investors will ask the question: why not stay in the market for the entire October 28th to May 5th period? In fact, this is a very viable strategy, especially for investors looking to hold positions for a longer term.

The time period from January 7th to January 22nd has had an average loss of 3.4% and only been positive 27% of the time (1989/90 to 2010/11). The complete materials strategy is in the market from October 28th to January 6th, out of the market from January 7th to the 22nd, and back in on January 23rd to May 5th. This complete strategy has produced an average gain of 16.9% and has been positive 100% of the time.

Materials vs. S&P 500 1989/90 to 2010/11   Positive ▢

Year	Oct 28 to Jan6 S&P 500	Mat.	Jan 23 to May 5 S&P 500	Mat.	Compound Growth S&P 500	Mat.
1989/90	5.1 %	9.1 %	2.4 %	-3.1 %	7.7 %	5.7 %
1990/91	5.4	9.2	16.0	15.3	22.2	26.0
1991/92	8.8	1.5	-0.3	5.5	8.5	7.1
1992/93	3.8	5.6	1.9	4.3	5.8	10.2
1993/94	0.5	9.4	-4.9	-5.3	-4.4	3.6
1994/95	-1.1	-3.5	11.9	6.1	10.7	2.4
1995/96	6.4	7.6	4.6	11.1	11.3	19.5
1996/97	6.7	2.3	5.6	2.3	12.6	4.6
1997/98	10.2	1.4	15.8	20.9	27.7	22.6
1998/99	19.4	6.1	10.0	31.5	31.3	39.6
1999/00	8.2	15.7	-0.6	-7.1	7.6	7.5
2000/01	-5.9	19.2	-5.7	15.1	-11.2	37.2
2001/02	6.2	8.5	-4.1	14.9	1.8	24.7
2002/03	3.5	9.2	5.5	2.7	9.2	12.1
2003/04	9.0	16.6	-2.0	-3.0	6.8	13.1
2004/05	5.6	5.4	0.4	0.3	6.0	5.8
2005/06	9.0	16.3	5.1	14.7	14.6	33.5
2006/07	2.4	3.2	5.8	10.7	8.3	14.2
2007/08	-8.1	-5.1	7.4	16.7	-1.2	10.8
2008/09	10.1	12.0	9.2	23.3	20.3	38.1
2009/10	6.9	13.8	6.8	3.0	14.2	17.2
2010/11	7.7	11.7	4.0	4.2	12.1	16.4
Avg.	5.4 %	8.0 %	4.3 %	8.4 %	10.1 %	16.9 %
Fq > 0	86 %	91 %	72 %	82 %	86 %	100 %

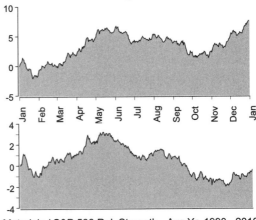

Materials Sector - Avg. Year 1990 to 2010

Materials / S&P 500 Rel. Strength - Avg Yr. 1990 - 2010

> **Ⴤ** *Alternate Strategy—*
> *Investors can bridge the gap between the two positive seasonal trends for the materials sector by holding from October 28th to May 5th. Longer term investors may prefer this strategy, shorter term investors can use technical tools to determine the appropriate strategy.*

> **ⓘ** *The SP GICS Materials Sector encompasses a wide range materials based companies.*
> *For more information on the information technology sector, see www.standardandpoors.com*

5 MONDAY	310 / 056	**6** TUESDAY	311 / 055

7 WEDNESDAY	312 / 054	**8** THURSDAY	313 / 053

9 FRIDAY   314 / 052

WEEK 45

Market Indices & Rates
Weekly Values**

Stock Markets	2009	2010
Dow	9,879	11,317
S&P500	1,054	1,214
Nasdaq	2,076	2,559
TSX	11,081	12,919
FTSE	5,104	5,831
DAX	5,440	6,743
Nikkei	9,789	9,769
Hang Seng	21,557	24,620

Commodities	2009	2010
Oil	79.04	86.86
Gold	1079.8	1397.4

Bond Yields	2009	2010
USA 5 Yr Treasury	2.35	1.25
USA 10 Yr T	3.53	2.68
USA 20 Yr T	4.32	3.81
Moody's Aaa	5.27	4.90
Moody's Baa	6.39	5.95
CAN 5 Yr T	2.71	2.19
CAN 10 Yr T	3.48	2.96

Money Market	2009	2010
USA Fed Funds	0.25	0.25
USA 3 Mo T-B	0.05	0.13
CAN tgt overnight rate	0.25	1.00
CAN 3 Mo T-B	0.22	0.94

Foreign Exchange	2009	2010
USD/EUR	1.48	1.38
USD/GBP	1.65	1.61
CAN/USD	1.07	1.01
JPY/USD	90.37	82.03

2010-2011 Strategy Performance

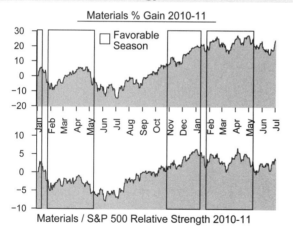

Materials % Gain 2010-11 — Favorable Season

Materials / S&P 500 Relative Strength 2010-11

The complete materials sector strategy worked extremely well in 2010 and 2011, keeping its perfect track record intact. Both parts of the strategy, October 28th to January 6th and January 23rd to May 5th, were successful, producing a compound gain of 16.4%.

NOVEMBER

M	T	W	T	F	S	S
			1	2	3	4
5	6	7	8	9	10	11
12	13	14	15	16	17	18
19	20	21	22	23	24	25
26	27	28	29	30		

DECEMBER

M	T	W	T	F	S	S
					1	2
3	4	5	6	7	8	9
10	11	12	13	14	15	16
17	18	19	20	21	22	23
24	25	26	27	28	29	30
31						

JANUARY

M	T	W	T	F	S	S
	1	2	3	4	5	6
7	8	9	10	11	12	13
14	15	16	17	18	19	20
21	22	23	24	25	26	27
28	29	30	31			

** Weekly avg closing values- except Fed Funds & CAN overnight tgt rate weekly closing values.

The industrial sector's seasonal trends are largely the same as the broad market, such as the S&P 500. Although the trends are similar, there still exists an opportunity to take advantage of the time period when the industrials tend to outperform.

3.4% extra & and positive 95% of the time

Industrials tend to outperform in the favorable six months, but there is an opportunity to temporarily get out of the sector to avoid a time period when the sector has, on average, decreased before turning positive again.

The overall strategy is to be invested in the industrial sector from October 28th to December 31st, sell at the end of the day on the 31st and reenter the sector to be invested from January 23rd to May 5th.

Using the IN-OUT-IN AGAIN strategy; from 1989/90 to 2010/11 the industrial sector has produced a total compounded average annual gain of 13.1%.

In addition, it has been positive 95% of the time and has outperformed the S&P 500, 81% of the time.

During the OUT time period from January 1st to January 22nd, the industrial sector has on average lost 1.3% and has only been positive 50% of the time.

It should be noted that longer term investors may decide to be invested during the whole time period from October 28th to May 5th.

Shorter term investors may decide to use technical analysis to determine if and when they should temporarily sell the industrials sector during its OUT time period.

	Oct 28 to Dec 31		Jan 23 to May 5		Compound Growth	
Year	S&P 500	Ind.	S&P 500	Ind.	S&P 500	Ind.
1989/90	5.5 %	6.9 %	2.4 %	5.5 %	8.0 %	12.7 %
1990/91	8.4	10.7	16.0	15.2	25.7	27.5
1991/92	8.6	7.2	-0.3	-1.0	8.2	6.1
1992/93	4.1	6.3	1.9	5.4	6.1	12.0
1993/94	0.4	5.1	-4.9	-6.7	-4.5	-2.0
1994/95	-1.4	-0.5	11.9	12.4	10.3	11.8
1995/96	6.3	10.7	4.6	7.6	11.1	19.1
1996/97	5.7	4.5	5.6	5.2	11.6	9.9
1997/98	10.7	10.5	15.8	11.5	28.2	23.2
1998/99	15.4	10.5	10.0	19.5	26.9	32.1
1999/00	13.3	10.8	-0.6	4.5	12.6	15.8
2000/01	-4.3	1.8	-5.7	4.7	-9.7	6.6
2001/02	3.9	8.1	-4.1	-5.3	-0.3	2.4
2002/03	-2.0	-1.3	5.5	8.6	3.4	7.1
2003/04	7.8	11.6	-2.0	-3.3	5.7	7.9
2004/05	7.7	8.7	0.4	0.2	8.1	8.9
2005/06	5.9	7.6	5.1	14.3	11.3	23.0
2006/07	3.0	3.1	5.8	6.8	9.0	10.1
2007/08	-4.4	-3.4	7.4	9.7	2.7	6.0
2008/09	6.4	7.1	9.2	6.1	16.2	13.7
2009/10	4.9	6.4	6.8	13.4	12.0	20.6
2010/11	6.4	8.1	4.0	4.9	10.6	13.5
Avg.	5.4 %	6.4 %	4.3 %	6.3 %	9.7 %	13.1 %
Fq > 0	82 %	86 %	73 %	82 %	86 %	95 %

Industrials vs. S&P 500 1989/90 to 2010/11 Positive

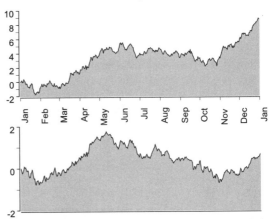

Industrial Sector - Avg. Year 1990 to 2010

Industrial / S&P 500 Rel. Strength - Avg Yr. 1990 - 2010

> *Alternate Strategy—*
> *Investors can bridge the gap between the two positive seasonal trends for the industrials sector by holding from October 28th to May 5th. Longer term investors may prefer this strategy, shorter term investors can use technical tools to determine the appropriate strategy.*

> ⓘ *The SP GICS Industrial Sector encompasses a wide range industrial based companies.*
> *For more information on the information technology sector, see www.standardandpoors.com*

12 MONDAY	317 / 049	**13** TUESDAY	318 / 048

14 WEDNESDAY 319 / 047

15 THURSDAY 320 / 046

16 FRIDAY 321 / 045

NOVEMBER

M	T	W	T	F	S	S
			1	2	3	4
5	6	7	8	9	10	11
12	13	14	15	16	17	18
19	20	21	22	23	24	25
26	27	28	29	30		

DECEMBER

M	T	W	T	F	S	S
					1	2
3	4	5	6	7	8	9
10	11	12	13	14	15	16
17	18	19	20	21	22	23
24	25	26	27	28	29	30
31						

JANUARY

M	T	W	T	F	S	S
	1	2	3	4	5	6
7	8	9	10	11	12	13
14	15	16	17	18	19	20
21	22	23	24	25	26	27
28	29	30	31			

2010-2011 Strategy Performance*

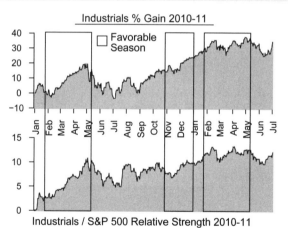

Industrials % Gain 2010-11

Industrials / S&P 500 Relative Strength 2010-11

In 2010-2011, both segments of the *Industrial Strength* strategy worked well. The first segment (Oct 28th to Dec 31st, 2010) produced a return of 8.1% and the second segment (Jan 23rd to May 5th, 2011) produced a gain of 4.9% for a compound gain of 13.5%. This compares very favorably to the S&P 500 compound gain during the same time period of 10.6%.

** Weekly avg closing values- except Fed Funds & CAN overnight tgt rate weekly closing values.

At the macro level, the metals and mining (M&M) sector is driven by future economic growth expectations. When worldwide growth expectations are increasing, there is a greater need for raw materials, when they are decreasing, the need is less.

Within the macro trend, the M&M sector has traditionally followed the overall market cycle of performing well from autumn until spring. This is the time of year that investors have a positive outlook on the economy and as a result, the cyclical sectors tend to outperform, including the metals and mining sector.

9.1% extra and positive 77% of the time

The metals and mining sector has two seasonal "sweet spots" – the first from November 19th to January 5th and the second from January 23rd to May 5th. Investors have the option to hold and "bridge the gap" across the two sweet spots, but over the long-term, nimble traders have been able to capture extra value by being out of the sector from January 6th to the 22nd. During this time period, the metals and mining sector has produced an average loss of 3.2% and has only been positive 45% of the time.

From a portfolio perspective, it is important to consider reducing exposure at the beginning of May. The danger of holding on too long is that the sector tends not to do well in the late summer, particularly in September. For more detail on why the metals and mining sector under performs in late summer, see the *September Pair Strategy - Long Gold and Short Metals and Mining Strategy*.

ⓘ *For more information on the metals and mining sector, see www.standardandpoors.com*

Metals & Mining Sector vs. S&P 500 1989/90 to 2010/11

Positive ▭

Year	Nov 19 to Jan 5		Jan 23 to May 5		Compound Growth	
	S&P 500	M&M	S&P 500	M&M	S&P 500	M&M
1989/90	3.1%	6.3%	2.4%	-4.6%	5.6%	1.4%
1990/91	1.2	6.4	16.0	7.1	17.4	13.9
1991/92	8.9	1.0	-0.3	-1.7	8.5	-0.7
1992/93	2.7	12.5	1.9	3.2	4.7	16.1
1993/94	0.9	9.0	-4.9	-11.1	-4.1	-3.1
1994/95	-0.2	-1.2	11.9	-3.0	11.6	-4.1
1995/96	2.8	8.3	4.6	5.8	7.5	14.6
1996/97	1.5	-1.9	5.6	-1.2	7.2	-3.0
1997/98	4.1	-4.5	15.8	19.3	20.6	13.9
1998/99	8.8	-7.9	10.0	31.0	19.6	20.6
1999/00	-1.6	21.7	-0.6	-10.4	-2.2	9.1
2000/01	-5.1	17.0	-5.7	19.6	-10.5	40.0
2001/02	3.0	5.5	-4.1	12.8	-1.3	19.0
2002/03	0.9	9.3	5.5	3.2	6.4	12.8
2003/04	8.5	18.2	-2.0	-12.1	6.4	3.9
2004/05	0.0	-8.4	0.4	-4.0	0.4	-12.0
2005/06	2.0	17.3	5.1	27.3	7.2	49.4
2006/07	0.6	3.0	5.8	17.2	6.5	20.8
2007/08	-3.2	0.9	7.4	27.4	3.9	28.5
2008/09	8.0	43.8	9.2	30.6	17.9	87.8
2009/10	2.4	6.3	6.8	4.8	9.4	11.3
2010/11	6.7	15.0	4.0	-1.6	11.0	13.1
Avg.	2.5%	8.1%	4.3%	7.3%	7.0%	16.1%
Fq > 0	77%	77%	73%	59%	82%	77%

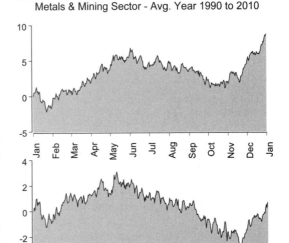

Metals & Mining Sector - Avg. Year 1990 to 2010

Metals & Mining / S&P 500 Rel. Strength- Avg Yr. 1990-2010

19 MONDAY	324 / 042	**20** TUESDAY	325 / 041

**Market Indices & Rates
Weekly Values****

Stock Markets	2009	2010
Dow	10,384	11,124
S&P500	1,103	1,192
Nasdaq	2,180	2,526
TSX	11,595	12,893
FTSE	5,318	5,657
DAX	5,747	6,816
Nikkei	9,649	10,066
Hang Seng	22,759	23,075

Commodities	2009	2010
Oil	78.36	82.24
Gold	1137.9	1367.0

21 WEDNESDAY	326 / 040	**22** THURSDAY	327 / 039

Bond Yields	2009	2010
USA 5 Yr Treasury	2.19	1.48
USA 10 Yr T	3.35	2.84
USA 20 Yr T	4.19	3.88
Moody's Aaa	5.16	4.90
Moody's Baa	6.27	5.95
CAN 5 Yr T	2.60	2.40
CAN 10 Yr T	3.39	3.13

23 FRIDAY		328 / 038

Money Market	2009	2010
USA Fed Funds	0.25	0.25
USA 3 Mo T-B	0.04	0.16
CAN tgt overnight rate	0.25	1.00
CAN 3 Mo T-B	0.22	0.99

Foreign Exchange	2009	2010
USD/EUR	1.49	1.34
USD/GBP	1.67	1.58
CAN/USD	1.06	1.02
JPY/USD	89.10	83.55

2010-2011 Strategy Performance

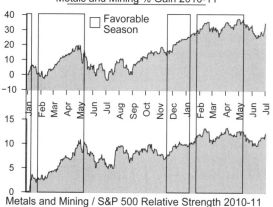

Metals and Mining % Gain 2010-11

Metals and Mining / S&P 500 Relative Strength 2010-11

NOVEMBER

M	T	W	T	F	S	S
			1	2	3	4
5	6	7	8	9	10	11
12	13	14	15	16	17	18
19	20	21	22	23	24	25
26	27	28	29	30		

DECEMBER

M	T	W	T	F	S	S
					1	2
3	4	5	6	7	8	9
10	11	12	13	14	15	16
17	18	19	20	21	22	23
24	25	26	27	28	29	30
31						

The metals and mining sector did well in the 2010/2011 trade. In the first sweet spot from November 19th to January 5th, the sector outperformed the S&P 500 by 8.3% (a substantial margin), and in the second sweet spot, from January 23rd to May 5th, the metals and mining sector under performed the S&P 500 by 5.6%. Not only did the Metals and Mining trade work, but investors using the strategy were able to avoid the weak time for the sector from January 6th to January 22nd.

** Weekly avg closing values- except Fed Funds & CAN overnight tgt rate weekly closing values.

JANUARY

M	T	W	T	F	S	S
	1	2	3	4	5	6
7	8	9	10	11	12	13
14	15	16	17	18	19	20
21	22	23	24	25	26	27
28	29	30	31			

THANKSGIVING
GIVE THANKS & TAKE RETURNS
Day Before and After – Two of the Best Days

We have a lot to be thankful for on Thanksgiving Day. As a bonus, the market day before and the market day after Thanksgiving have been two of the best days of the year in the stock market.

Each day by itself has produced spectacular results. From 1950 to 2010, the S&P 500 has had an average gain of 0.4% on the day before Thanksgiving and 0.4% on the day after.

The day before Thanksgiving and the day after have had an average cumulative return of 0.8% and together have been positive 85% of the time

To put the performance of these two days in perspective, the average daily return of the market over the same time period is 0.03%.

The gains the day before Thanksgiving and the day after are almost ten times better than the average market and have a much greater frequency of being positive.

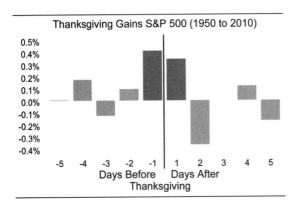

Thanksgiving Gains S&P 500 (1950 to 2010)

Days Before | Days After
Thanksgiving

Alternate Strategy — Although the focus has been on the performance of two specific days, the day before and the day after Thanksgiving, the holiday occurs at the end of November which tends to be a strong month. December, the next month is also strong. Investors have the good option of expanding their trade out to include the "Santa Arrives Early & Stays Late" Strategy.

History of Thanksgiving:
It was originally a "thanksgiving feast" by the pilgrims for surviving their first winter. Initially it was celebrated sporadically and the holiday, when it was granted, had its date changed several times. It was not until 1941 that it was proclaimed to be the 4th Thursday in November.

S&P500	Day Before	Day After
	Positive	
1950	1.4	0.8
1951	-0.2	-1.1
1952	0.6	0.5
1953	0.1	0.6
1954	0.6	1.0
1955	0.1	-0.1
1956	-0.5	1.1
1957	2.9	1.1
1958	1.7	1.1
1959	0.2	0.5
1960	0.1	0.6
1961	-0.1	0.2
1962	0.6	1.2
1963	-0.2	1.4
1964	-0.3	-0.3
1965	0.2	0.1
1966	0.7	0.8
1967	0.6	0.3
1968	0.5	0.6
1969	0.4	0.6
1970	0.4	1.0
1971	0.2	1.8
1972	0.6	0.3
1973	1.1	-0.3
1974	0.7	0.0
1975	0.3	0.3
1976	0.4	0.7
1977	0.4	0.2
1978	0.5	0.3
1979	0.2	0.8
1980	0.6	0.2
1981	0.4	0.8
1982	0.7	0.7
1983	0.1	0.1
1984	0.2	1.5
1985	0.9	-0.2
1986	0.2	0.2
1987	-0.9	-1.5
1988	0.7	-0.7
1989	0.7	0.6
1990	0.2	-0.3
1991	-0.4	-0.4
1992	0.4	0.2
1993	0.3	0.2
1994	0.0	0.5
1995	-0.3	0.3
1996	-0.1	0.3
1997	0.1	0.4
1998	0.3	0.5
1999	0.9	0.0
2000	-1.9	1.5
2001	-0.5	1.2
2002	2.8	-0.3
2003	0.4	0.0
2004	0.4	0.1
2005	0.3	0.2
2006	0.2	-0.4
2007	-1.6	1.7
2008	3.5	1.0
2009	0.5	-1.7
2010	1.5	-0.7
Total Avg %	0.4%	0.4%
Fq > 0	79%	75%

THANKSGIVING DAY

26 MONDAY 331 / 035

27 TUESDAY 332 / 034

28 WEDNESDAY 333 / 033

29 THURSDAY 334 / 032

30 FRIDAY 335 / 031

WEEK 48

Market Indices & Rates
Weekly Values**

Stock Markets	2009	2010
Dow	10,415	11,212
S&P500	1,104	1,204
Nasdaq	2,165	2,549
TSX	11,540	13,068
FTSE	5,297	5,647
DAX	5,735	6,832
Nikkei	9,327	10,080
Hang Seng	22,230	23,239

Commodities	2009	2010
Oil	76.15	86.76
Gold	1172.4	1383.7

Bond Yields	2009	2010
USA 5 Yr Treasury	2.12	1.59
USA 10 Yr T	3.30	2.93
USA 20 Yr T	4.14	3.91
Moody's Aaa	5.07	4.90
Moody's Baa	6.24	5.95
CAN 5 Yr T	2.43	2.41
CAN 10 Yr T	3.27	3.14

Money Market	2009	2010
USA Fed Funds	0.25	0.25
USA 3 Mo T-B	0.05	0.16
CAN tgt overnight rate	0.25	1.00
CAN 3 Mo T-B	0.22	1.01

Foreign Exchange	2009	2010
USD/EUR	1.50	1.32
USD/GBP	1.66	1.56
CAN/USD	1.06	1.01
JPY/USD	87.59	83.70

NOVEMBER

M	T	W	T	F	S	S
			1	2	3	4
5	6	7	8	9	10	11
12	13	14	15	16	17	18
19	20	21	22	23	24	25
26	27	28	29	30		

DECEMBER

M	T	W	T	F	S	S
					1	2
3	4	5	6	7	8	9
10	11	12	13	14	15	16
17	18	19	20	21	22	23
24	25	26	27	28	29	30
31						

JANUARY

M	T	W	T	F	S	S
	1	2	3	4	5	6
7	8	9	10	11	12	13
14	15	16	17	18	19	20
21	22	23	24	25	26	27
28	29	30	31			

2010 Strategy Performance

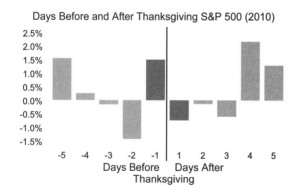

Days Before and After Thanksgiving S&P 500 (2010)

In 2010, the day before Thanksgiving was positive and the day after negative.

Fortunately, the gain from the day before Thanksgiving had a much bigger impact on the total strategy compared with the loss the day after Thanksgiving, making it a successful trade with a return of 0.8%.

** Weekly avg closing values- except Fed Funds & CAN overnight tgt rate weekly closing values.

DECEMBER

	MONDAY	TUESDAY	WEDNESDAY
WEEK 49	**3** 28	**4** 27	**5** 26
WEEK 50	**10** 21	**11** 20	**12** 19
WEEK 51	**17** 14	**18** 13	**19** 12
WEEK 52	**24** 7	**25** 6 CAN Market Closed- Christmas Day USA Market Closed- Christmas Day	**26** 5 CAN Market Closed- Boxing Day
WEEK 01	**31**	1	2

THURSDAY	FRIDAY
6 25	**7** 24
13 18	**14** 17
20 11	**21** 10
27 4	**28** 3
3	4

JANUARY

M	T	W	T	F	S	S
	1	2	3	4	5	6
7	8	9	10	11	12	13
14	15	16	17	18	19	20
21	22	23	24	25	26	27
28	29	30	31			

FEBRUARY

M	T	W	T	F	S	S
				1	2	3
4	5	6	7	8	9	10
11	12	13	14	15	16	17
18	19	20	21	22	23	24
25	26	27	28			

MARCH

M	T	W	T	F	S	S
				1	2	3
4	5	6	7	8	9	10
11	12	13	14	15	16	17
18	19	20	21	22	23	24
25	26	27	28	29	30	31

APRIL

M	T	W	T	F	S	S
1	2	3	4	5	6	7
8	9	10	11	12	13	14
15	16	17	18	19	20	21
22	23	24	25	26	27	28
29	30					

DECEMBER
S U M M A R Y

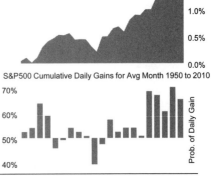

S&P500 Cumulative Daily Gains for Avg Month 1950 to 2010

	Dow Jones	S&P 500	Nasdaq	TSX Comp
Month Rank	2	1	2	1
# Up	43	47	23	24
# Down	18	14	16	2
% Pos	70	77	59	92
% Avg. Gain	1.7	1.8	1.9	2.5

Dow & S&P 1950-June 2011, Nasdaq 1972-June 2011, TSX 1985-June 2011

♦ December is one of the best months of the year and 2010 was no exception, as the S&P 500 produced a return of 6.5%. In December make sure your Christmas shopping includes stocks. ♦ Although the month tends to be positive, it is the second half of the month that tends to produce the biggest returns. ♦ The best method of participating in the Christmas rally has been to enter the stock market on December 15th (see *Santa Arrives Early & Stays Late* strategy). ♦ The US dollar has a habit of weakening in December for a rally in January.

BEST / WORST DECEMBER BROAD MKTS. 2001-2010

BEST DECEMBER MARKETS
♦ Russell 2000 (2009) 7.9%
♦ Russell 2000 (2010) 7.8%
♦ Russell 3000 Value (2010) 7.7%

WORST DECEMBER MARKETS
♦ Nasdaq (2002) -9.7%
♦ Russell 3000 Gr (2002) -7.0%
♦ Dow (2002) -6.2%

Index Values End of Month

	2001	2002	2003	2004	2005	2006	2007	2008	2009	2010
Dow	10,022	8,342	10,454	10,783	10,718	12,463	13,265	8,776	10,428	11,578
S&P 500	1,148	880	1,112	1,212	1,248	1,418	1,468	903	1,115	1,258
Nasdaq	1,950	1,336	2,003	2,175	2,205	2,415	2,652	1,577	2,269	2,653
TSX	7,688	6,615	8,221	9,247	11,272	12,908	13,833	8,988	11,746	13,443
Russell 1000	1,163	896	1,143	1,251	1,306	1,480	1,538	938	1,176	1,340
Russell 2000	1,214	952	1,384	1,619	1,673	1,958	1,904	1,241	1,554	1,948
Russell 3000 Growth	1,982	1,413	1,831	1,939	2,018	2,184	2,406	1,460	1,966	2,279
Russell 3000 Value	2,068	1,713	2,191	2,502	2,610	3,116	3,009	1,860	2,164	2,459

Percent Gain for December

	2001	2002	2003	2004	2005	2006	2007	2008	2009	2010
Dow	1.7	-6.2	6.9	3.4	-0.8	2.0	-0.8	-0.6	0.8	5.2
S&P 500	0.8	-6.0	5.1	3.2	-0.1	1.3	-0.9	0.8	1.8	6.5
Nasdaq	1.0	-9.7	2.2	3.7	-1.2	-0.7	-0.3	2.7	5.8	6.2
TSX	3.5	0.7	4.6	2.4	4.1	1.2	1.1	-3.1	2.6	3.8
Russell 1000	0.9	-5.8	4.6	3.5	0.0	1.1	-0.8	1.3	2.3	6.5
Russell 2000	6.0	-5.7	1.9	2.8	-0.6	0.2	-0.2	5.6	7.9	7.8
Russell 3000 Growth	0.1	-7.0	3.1	3.8	-0.4	0.2	-0.4	1.9	3.3	5.6
Russell 3000 Value	2.4	-4.5	5.7	3.0	0.3	1.9	-1.2	1.4	2.0	7.7

December Market Avg. Performance 2001 to 2010[1]

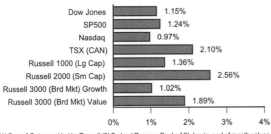

Dow Jones	1.15%
SP500	1.24%
Nasdaq	0.97%
TSX (CAN)	2.10%
Russell 1000 (Lg Cap)	1.36%
Russell 2000 (Sm Cap)	2.56%
Russell 3000 (Brd Mkt) Growth	1.02%
Russell 3000 (Brd Mkt) Value	1.89%

Interest Corner Dec[2]

	Fed Funds %[3]	3 Mo. T-Bill %[4]	10 Yr %[5]	20 Yr %[6]
2010	0.25	0.12	3.30	4.13
2009	0.25	0.06	3.85	4.58
2008	0.25	0.11	2.25	3.05
2007	4.25	3.36	4.04	4.50
2006	5.25	5.02	4.71	4.91

(1) Russell Data provided by Russell (2) Federal Reserve Bank of St. Louis- end of month values (3) Target rate set by FOMC (4)(5)(6) Constant yield maturities.

THACKRAY SECTOR THERMOMETER

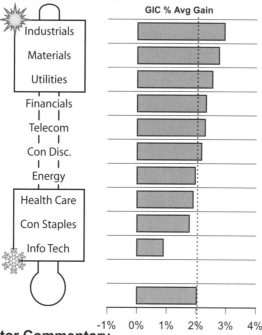

GIC[2] % Avg Gain	Fq % Gain >S&P 500	
SP GIC SECTOR 1990-2010[1]		
2.9 %	62 %	Industrials
2.7	48	Materials
2.5	52	Utilities
2.3	57	Financials
2.3	57	Telecom
2.2	52	Consumer Discretionary
2.0	43	Energy
1.9	52	Health Care
1.8	43	Consumer Staples
0.9 %	38 %	Information Technology
2.0 %	N/A %	S&P 500

Sector Commentary

♦ In December 2010, the economy was still printing decent economic numbers and the cyclical stocks outperformed. ♦ The *materials* sector was the strongest sector producing a return of 10.2%. The sector tends to do well in December, but starts to fall off at the beginning of January (see *Material Stocks - Material Gains*). ♦ The *U.S. financial* sector started its seasonal performance early with a gain of 10.6%. in December ♦ The *energy* sector continued to outperform past its typical seasonally strong period that ends in early October. It produced a gain of 8.9%. in December ♦ The worst performing sector for the month was the *health care* sector with a loss of 2.2%.

Sub-Sector Commentary

♦ In December 2010, the three best performing sub-sectors were *banks, metals* and *mining*, and *integrated oil & gas*. The sectors produced gains of 15.4% 14.4% and 8.8% respectively. ♦ The *banking* sector typically starts its seasonal run in mid-January, but if their prospects are improving, it can start its run in mid-December. This is particularly true if it has under performed in the months leading up to this time of year, as was the case in 2010.

		SELECTED SUB-SECTORS 1990-2010[3]
5.2 %	56 %	Biotech (93-2010)
4.2	62	Metals & Mining
4.0	52	Gold (XAU)
2.5	53	Agriculture Products (94-2010)
1.9	43	Software & Services
1.9	52	Banks
1.8	43	Integrated Oil & Gas
1.4	43	Pharmaceuticals
1.3	38	Auto & Components
1.3	33	Retail
1.2	33	Transportation
1.1	38	Semiconductor (SOX) 95-2010
0.8	33	Gold (London PM)
0.3	33	Airlines

(1) Sector data provided by Standard and Poors (2) GIC is short form for Global Industry Classification (3) Sub Sector data provided by Standard and Poors, except where marked by symbol.

SANTA ARRIVES EARLY & STAYS LATE
Dec 15th to Jan 6th

Every year investors wait for Santa Claus to come to town. They often get rewarded, but many leave with small returns because they focus on one or two days of outperformance. The best way to get the gift of Christmas is to get in early and stay late. The market typically makes a move up about halfway through December and continues through to the first week in January.

The first part of this move can be attributed to investors taking advantage of the *"January Effect,"* buying stocks that have been beaten down because of tax-loss selling (see *Small Company Effect* strategy).

The second part of the move, the start of January, benefits from the beginning of the month effect (see *Super Seven* strategy). The first few days in January are also boosted by money managers locking in their selections for the New Year.

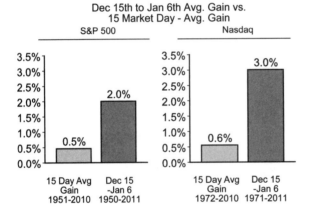

Dec 15th to Jan 6th Avg. Gain vs.
15 Market Day - Avg. Gain

S&P 500

- 15 Day Avg Gain 1951-2010: 0.5%
- Dec 15 -Jan 6 1950-2011: 2.0%

Nasdaq

- 15 Day Avg Gain 1972-2010: 0.6%
- Dec 15 -Jan 6 1971-2011: 3.0%

The *Santa Arrives Early & Stays Late* strategy starts on December 15th and ends January 6th. This Christmas strategy with the S&P 500 from 1950 to 2010 has on average lasted fifteen days and produced a return of 2.0%.

This compares to the 0.5% return for the average fifteen day period taken from any time period from 1951 to 2010 (year adjustment is used to more closely align strategy with benchmark years). The net result is that this Christmas strategy has been four times better than the average fifteen day period.

> **Alternate Strategy—The Extended Santa Rally:**
> The focus of the *"Santa Arrives Early Stays Late"* is around the Christmas days, but on average, after January 6th, the market tends to tread water for only a few days before rallying until the beginning of February (February 3rd).

	% Change Dec 15th to Jan 6th	
Date	S&P 500 Change	Nasdaq Change
50 / 51	7.5 %	N/A %
51 / 52	2.4	"
52 / 53	1.7	"
53 / 54	1.8	"
54 / 55	2.0	"
55 / 56	0.2	"
56 / 57	0.3	"
57 / 58	-0.1	"
58 / 59	4.5	"
59 / 60	1.8	"
60 / 61	2.7	"
61 / 62	-3.2	"
62 / 63	2.5	"
63 / 64	2.2	"
64 / 65	1.7	"
65 / 66	1.3	"
66 / 67	-0.6	"
67 / 68	0.5	"
68 / 69	-4.7	"
69 / 70	2.2	"
70 / 71	2.8	"
71 / 72	6.0	6.1
72 / 73	1.4	1.9
73 / 74	6.0	5.0
74 / 75	6.0	4.3
75 / 76	6.5	7.2
76 / 77	0.0	2.8
77 / 78	-2.6	-2.2
78 / 79	3.2	3.3
79 / 80	-2.2	-1.3
80 / 81	6.9	6.7
81 / 82	-2.9	-2.3
82 / 83	5.7	2.3
83 / 84	3.6	4.2
84 / 85	0.6	3.0
85 / 86	0.3	0.6
86 / 87	2.2	2.8
87 / 88	6.9	12.1
88 / 89	1.9	3.2
89 / 90	0.4	2.4
90 / 91	-1.8	-0.4
91 / 92	8.7	10.5
92 / 93	0.4	4.1
93 / 94	0.9	3.9
94 / 95	1.3	3.3
95 / 96	0.0	-0.5
96 / 97	2.6	2.5
97 / 98	1.4	2.8
98 / 99	11.5	18.0
99 / 00	0.0	4.4
00 / 01	-3.2	-11.8
01 / 02	4.4	5.4
02 / 03	4.4	4.3
03 / 04	4.6	5.6
04 / 05	-1.3	-3.2
05 / 06	1.0	1.9
06 / 07	-1.1	-0.8
07 / 08	-3.8	-5.0
08 / 09	6.2	7.2
09 / 10	2.1	4.0
10 / 11	2.6	3.1
AVG.	2.0 %	3.0 %

3 MONDAY · 338 / 028

4 TUESDAY · 339 / 027

5 WEDNESDAY · 340 / 026

6 THURSDAY · 341 / 025

7 FRIDAY · 342 / 024

WEEK 49

Market Indices & Rates
Weekly Values**

Stock Markets	2009	2010
Dow	10,405	11,375
S&P500	1,104	1,230
Nasdaq	2,175	2,611
TSX	11,616	13,217
FTSE	5,293	5,799
DAX	5,754	6,980
Nikkei	9,705	10,208
Hang Seng	22,255	23,219

Commodities	2009	2010
Oil	76.84	88.50
Gold	1196.0	1397.5

Bond Yields	2009	2010
USA 5 Yr Treasury	2.10	1.80
USA 10 Yr T	3.34	3.18
USA 20 Yr T	4.18	4.11
Moody's Aaa	5.11	5.03
Moody's Baa	6.29	6.09
CAN 5 Yr T	2.41	2.46
CAN 10 Yr T	3.26	3.23

Money Market	2009	2010
USA Fed Funds	0.25	0.25
USA 3 Mo T-B	0.06	0.14
CAN tgt overnight rate	0.25	1.00
CAN 3 Mo T-B	0.21	0.99

Foreign Exchange	2009	2010
USD/EUR	1.50	1.33
USD/GBP	1.65	1.58
CAN/USD	1.05	1.01
JPY/USD	87.86	83.58

2010-2011 Strategy Performance

Nasdaq & S&P 500 Santa Trade 2010-2011

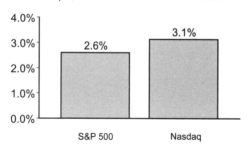

In 2010, Santa came early and stayed late. He treated both the Nasdaq and the S&P 500, but he gave more to the Nasdaq.

The media tends to focus on the S&P 500 when looking at stock market returns at the end of the year. Investors can typically increase their returns by using the Nasdaq instead. This was true in 2010-2011 when the Nasdaq produced a return of 3.1% compared with the S&P 500's return of 2.6%. Investors that switched out of the Nasdaq position in January benefited as the index started to under perform the S&P 500.

DECEMBER

M	T	W	T	F	S	S
					1	2
3	4	5	6	7	8	9
10	11	12	13	14	15	16
17	18	19	20	21	22	23
24	25	26	27	28	29	30
31						

JANUARY

M	T	W	T	F	S	S
	1	2	3	4	5	6
7	8	9	10	11	12	13
14	15	16	17	18	19	20
21	22	23	24	25	26	27
28	29	30	31			

FEBRUARY

M	T	W	T	F	S	S
				1	2	3
4	5	6	7	8	9	10
11	12	13	14	15	16	17
18	19	20	21	22	23	24
25	26	27	28			

** Weekly avg closing values- except Fed Funds & CAN overnight tgt rate weekly closing values.

SMALL CAP (SMALL COMPANY) EFFECT
Small Companies Outperform - Dec 19th to Mar 7th

At different stages of the business cycle, small capitalization companies (small caps represented by the Russell 2000), perform better than the large capitalization companies (large caps represented by the Russell 1000).

Evidence shows that the small caps relative outperformance also has a seasonal component as they typically outperform large caps from December 19th to March 7th.

3.3% extra & 23 times out of 32
better than the Russell 1000

Russell 2000 vs. Russell 1000 Gains
Dec 19th to Mar 7th 1979 to 2011
Positive ☐

Dec 19 - Mar7	Russell 1000	Russell 2000	Diff
79 / 80	-1.3 %	-0.4 %	0.9 %
80 / 81	-2.8	4.0	6.8
81 / 82	-12.4	-12.1	0.3
82 / 83	11.8	19.8	8.0
83 / 84	-6.4	-7.5	-1.1
84 / 85	7.7	17.1	9.4
85 / 86	8.2	11.7	3.5
86 / 87	17.2	21.3	4.1
87 / 88	8.3	16.4	8.0
88 / 89	6.9	9.1	2.5
89 / 90	-2.0	-1.9	0.2
90 / 91	14.6	29.0	14.4
91 / 92	6.0	16.8	10.8
92 / 93	1.4	5.0	3.5
93 / 94	0.5	5.7	5.3
94 / 95	5.3	5.5	0.2
95 / 96	8.3	7.8	-0.5
96 / 97	9.5	3.5	-6.0
97 / 98	10.2	10.3	0.1
98 / 99	7.3	0.2	-7.2
99 / 00	-1.7	27.7	29.4
00 / 01	-5.2	4.7	9.8
01 / 02	1.6	1.9	0.4
02 / 03	-6.7	-7.8	-1.0
03 / 04	6.4	9.6	3.3
04 / 05	2.8	0.3	-2.5
05 / 06	0.8	5.6	4.7
06 / 07	-1.6	-0.8	0.9
07 / 08	-10.9	-12.5	-1.5
08 / 09	-22.2	-26.7	-4.5
09 / 10	3.6	9.1	5.5
10 / 11	5.5	4.2	-1.3
Avg.	2.2 %	5.5 %	3.3 %
Fq > 0	66 %	75 %	72 %

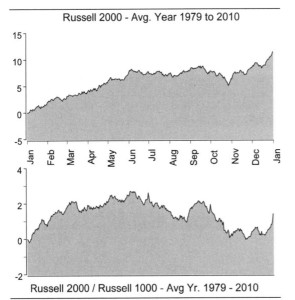

Russell 2000 - Avg. Year 1979 to 2010

Russell 2000 / Russell 1000 - Avg Yr. 1979 - 2010

The core part of the small cap seasonal strategy occurs in January and includes what has been described as the January Effect (Wachtel 1942, 184).

This well documented anomaly of superior performance of stocks in the month of January is based upon the tenet that investors sell stocks in December for tax loss reasons, artificially driving down prices, and creating a great opportunity for astute investors.

In recent times, the January Effect starts mid-December and is more pronounced for small caps as their prices are more volatile than large caps.

(i) *Russell 2000 (small cap index): The 2000 smallest companies in the Russell 3000 stock index (a broad market index). Russell 1000 (large cap index): The 1000 largest companies in the Russell 3000 stock index*

For more information on the Russell indexes, see www.Russell.com

Wachtel, S.B. 1942. Certain observations on seasonal movements in stock prices. The Journal of Business and Economics (Winter): 184.

10 MONDAY	345 / 021	**11** TUESDAY	346 / 020

Market Indices & Rates
Weekly Values**

Stock Markets	2009	2010
Dow	10,378	11,471
S&P500	1,100	1,241
Nasdaq	2,186	2,630
TSX	11,425	13,238
FTSE	5,249	5,877
DAX	5,717	7,016
Nikkei	10,057	10,307
Hang Seng	21,946	23,022

Commodities	2009	2010
Oil	71.53	88.25
Gold	1136.6	1382.8

12 WEDNESDAY	347 / 019	**13** THURSDAY	348 / 018

Bond Yields	2009	2010
USA 5 Yr Treasury	2.18	2.03
USA 10 Yr T	3.47	3.42
USA 20 Yr T	4.33	4.27
Moody's Aaa	5.25	5.08
Moody's Baa	6.37	6.18
CAN 5 Yr T	2.50	2.51
CAN 10 Yr T	3.33	3.27

14 FRIDAY		349 / 017

Money Market	2009	2010
USA Fed Funds	0.25	0.25
USA 3 Mo T-B	0.03	0.14
CAN tgt overnight rate	0.25	1.00
CAN 3 Mo T-B	0.21	0.98

Foreign Exchange	2009	2010
USD/EUR	1.47	1.33
USD/GBP	1.63	1.57
CAN/USD	1.06	1.01
JPY/USD	88.62	83.84

2010-2011 Strategy Performance

DECEMBER

M	T	W	T	F	S	S
					1	2
3	4	5	6	7	8	9
10	11	12	13	14	15	16
17	18	19	20	21	22	23
24	25	26	27	28	29	30
31						

Russell 2000 vs Russell 1000 Dec 19th to Mar 7th (2010-2011)

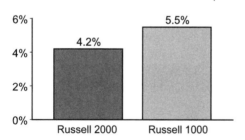

JANUARY

M	T	W	T	F	S	S
	1	2	3	4	5	6
7	8	9	10	11	12	13
14	15	16	17	18	19	20
21	22	23	24	25	26	27
28	29	30	31			

In 2010-11, despite the Russell 2000 providing a decent gain in the market of 4.2% during its strong seasonal period, it underperformed the large cap sector (Russell 1000).

The stock market rally at this time was still a relief rally supported by the liquidity that the Federal Reserve was pumping into the market. Large caps were the safer play for investors and as a result, small caps under performed.

FEBRUARY

M	T	W	T	F	S	S
				1	2	3
4	5	6	7	8	9	10
11	12	13	14	15	16	17
18	19	20	21	22	23	24
25	26	27	28			

** Weekly avg closing values- except Fed Funds & CAN overnight tgt rate weekly closing values.

DO THE "NAZ" WITH SANTA
Nasdaq gives more at Christmas – Dec 15th to Jan 23rd

One of the best times to invest in the major markets is Christmas time. What few investors know is that this seasonally strong time favors the Nasdaq market.

From December 15th to January 23rd, starting in 1972 and ending in 2011, the Nasdaq has outperformed the S&P 500 by an average 2.3% per year.

This rate of return is considered to be very high given that the length of favorable time is just over one month.

2.3% extra & 83% of time better than S&P 500

Looking for reasons that the Nasdaq outperforms? Interestingly, the Nasdaq starts to outperform at the same time as small companies in December (see *Small Company Effect* strategy).

As investors move into the market to scoop up bargains that have been sold for tax losses, smaller companies and stocks with greater volatility tend to outperform.

Compared with the S&P 500 and Dow Jones, the Nasdaq market, given its composition, tends to be a much greater recipient of the upward move created by investors picking up cheap stocks at this time of the year.

Nasdaq vs. S&P 500 Dec 15th to Jan 23rd 1971/72 To 2010/11

Dec 15 to Jan 23	S&P 500	Nasdaq	Diff
		Positive	
1971/72	6.1 %	7.5 %	1.3 %
1972/73	0.0	-0.7	-0.7
1973/74	4.1	6.8	2.8
1974/75	7.5	8.9	1.4
1975/76	13.0	13.8	0.9
1976/77	-1.7	2.8	4.5
1977/78	-5.1	-3.5	1.6
1978/79	4.7	6.2	1.4
1979/80	4.1	5.6	1.5
1980/81	0.8	3.3	2.5
1981/82	-6.0	-5.0	1.0
1982/83	4.7	5.5	0.8
1983/84	0.9	1.4	0.4
1984/85	9.0	13.3	4.3
1985/86	-2.7	0.8	3.5
1986/87	9.2	10.2	1.0
1987/88	1.8	9.1	7.3
1988/89	3.3	4.6	1.3
1989/90	-5.5	-3.8	1.7
1990/91	1.0	4.1	3.1
1991/92	7.9	15.2	7.2
1992/93	0.8	7.2	6.4
1993/94	2.5	5.7	3.2
1994/95	2.4	4.7	2.3
1995/96	-0.7	-1.0	-0.3
1996/97	6.7	7.3	0.6
1997/98	0.4	2.6	2.1
1998/99	7.4	18.9	11.6
1999/00	2.7	18.6	15.9
2000/01	1.5	4.1	2.6
2001/02	0.5	-1.6	-2.0
2002/03	-0.2	1.9	2.1
2003/04	6.3	9.0	2.7
2004/05	-3.0	-5.8	-2.9
2005/06	-0.7	-0.6	0.1
2006/07	0.2	-0.9	-1.1
2007/08	-8.8	-12.1	-3.3
2008/09	-5.4	-4.1	1.3
2009/10	-2.0	-0.3	1.7
2010/11	3.4	2.4	-1.0
Avg	1.8 %	4.0 %	2.3 %
Fq > 0	70 %	70 %	83 %

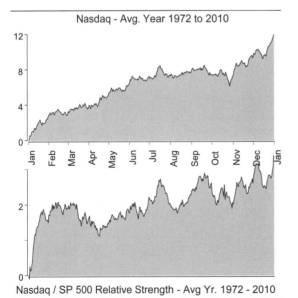

Nasdaq - Avg. Year 1972 to 2010

Nasdaq / SP 500 Relative Strength - Avg Yr. 1972 - 2010

Alternate Strategy — For those investors who favor the Nasdaq, an alternative strategy is to invest in the Nasdaq at an earlier date: October 28th. Historically, on average the Nasdaq has started its out performance at this time. The "Do the Naz with Santa" strategy focuses on the sweet spot of the Nasdaq's outperformance.

Nasdaq is a market with a number of sectors. It is more focused on technology and is typically more volatile than the S&P 500.

17 MONDAY · 352 / 014 · · **18** TUESDAY · 353 / 013

19 WEDNESDAY · 354 / 012 · · **20** THURSDAY · 355 / 011

21 FRIDAY · 356 / 010

WEEK 51

Market Indices & Rates
Weekly Values**

Stock Markets	2009	2010
Dow	10,406	11,536
S&P500	1,106	1,254
Nasdaq	2,202	2,664
TSX	11,532	13,339
FTSE	5,267	5,966
DAX	5,839	7,056
Nikkei	10,134	10,303
Hang Seng	21,607	22,883

Commodities	2009	2010
Oil	71.77	89.68
Gold	1121.0	1380.9

Bond Yields	2009	2010
USA 5 Yr Treasury	2.31	2.02
USA 10 Yr T	3.56	3.37
USA 20 Yr T	4.38	4.23
Moody's Aaa	5.26	5.01
Moody's Baa	6.33	6.10
CAN 5 Yr T	2.57	2.42
CAN 10 Yr T	3.40	3.17

Money Market	2009	2010
USA Fed Funds	0.25	0.25
USA 3 Mo T-B	0.04	0.14
CAN tgt overnight rate	0.25	1.00
CAN 3 Mo T-B	0.19	0.98

Foreign Exchange	2009	2010
USD/EUR	1.45	1.31
USD/GBP	1.62	1.54
CAN/USD	1.06	1.01
JPY/USD	89.70	83.38

2010-2011 Strategy Performance*

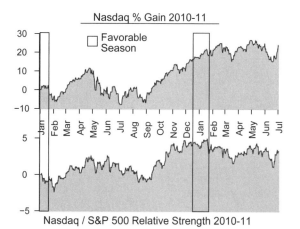

Nasdaq % Gain 2010-11

Nasdaq / S&P 500 Relative Strength 2010-11

DECEMBER

M	T	W	T	F	S	S
					1	2
3	4	5	6	7	8	9
10	11	12	13	14	15	16
17	18	19	20	21	22	23
24	25	26	27	28	29	30
31						

JANUARY

M	T	W	T	F	S	S
	1	2	3	4	5	6
7	8	9	10	11	12	13
14	15	16	17	18	19	20
21	22	23	24	25	26	27
28	29	30	31			

In 2010, the Nasdaq strongly outperformed the S&P 500 when the market started to rally in late August. This multi-month outperformance started to fade in December and the Nasdaq slightly under performed in the seasonal sweet spot from mid-December 2010 to mid-January 2011.

FEBRUARY

M	T	W	T	F	S	S
				1	2	3
4	5	6	7	8	9	10
11	12	13	14	15	16	17
18	19	20	21	22	23	24
25	26	27	28			

** Weekly avg closing values- except Fed Funds & CAN overnight tgt rate weekly closing values.

January has the reputation of being a strong month. Since 1950 the S&P 500 has produced an average gain of 1.1% and been positive 62% of the time. In the last ten years January has only been positive 40% of the time and has suffered some big drops.

-1.8% & negative 68% of the time

One of the weaker sectors in the market in January has been the consumer staples. From 1990 to 2010 the sector has produced a loss of 1.6% and has been negative 57% of the time.

The worst performance for the sector is focused on the time period from January 1st to January 22nd. In this time period the consumer staples sector has produced an average loss of 1.8% and has been negative 68% of the time.

Con. Staples vs. S&P 500 1990 to 2011

Jan 1 to Jan 22	S&P 500	Negative Staples	Diff
1990	-6.5 %	-8.3 %	-1.8 %
1991	-0.6	-1.1	-0.5
1992	0.3	-3.2	-3.4
1993	0.1	-3.5	-3.6
1994	1.8	-0.6	-2.4
1995	1.2	-1.1	-2.3
1996	-0.4	1.4	1.8
1997	6.1	6.2	0.0
1998	-0.8	-0.9	-0.1
1999	-0.3	-6.8	-6.4
2000	-1.9	-2.0	-0.1
2001	1.7	-8.4	-10.1
2002	-2.5	0.5	3.0
2003	-0.2	1.0	1.1
2004	2.9	-1.0	-3.9
2005	-3.6	0.4	4.1
2006	1.1	-0.8	-1.8
2007	0.3	1.7	1.4
2008	-10.8	-6.7	4.1
2009	-8.4	-4.9	3.5
2010	-2.1	-1.1	1.0
2011	2.0	0.2	-1.9
Avg.	-0.9 %	-1.8 %	-0.8 %
Fq Success	45 %	68 %	59 %

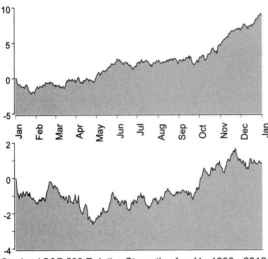

Consumer Staples Sector - Avg. Year 1990 to 2010

Staples / S&P 500 Relative Strength - Avg Yr. 1990 - 2010

The Consumer Staples vs. S&P 500 table illustrates the relationship between the two sectors. In general when the S&P 500 is positive or slightly negative the consumer staples sector tends to under perform. On the other hand, when the S&P 500 suffers large losses the consumer staples sector tends to outperform the S&P 500.

The direction of the US dollar has an impact on the performance of the consumer staples sector. When the US dollar is rising, the sector tends to fall and when the dollar is falling, the sector tends to increase.

The reason that this relationship exists is that consumer staples companies receive a higher percentage of their revenues from offshore companies compared with the S&P 500.

This means that if the US dollar is falling, then consumer staples companies will benefit from increased revenues because of the lower exchange rate and vice versa. This relationship is important because the US dollar tends to rise in January (see *U.S. Dollar – Short and Long* strategy) and therefore put downward pressure on the consumer staples sector.

> (i) The SP GICS Consumer Staples Sector encompasses a wide range consumer staples based companies. For more information on the information technology sector, see www.standardandpoors.com

24 MONDAY	359 / 007	**25** TUESDAY	360 / 006

Market Indices & Rates
Weekly Values**

Stock Markets	2009	2010
Dow	10,466	11,573
S&P500	1,120	1,258
Nasdaq	2,261	2,663
TSX	11,649	13,442
FTSE	5,349	5,956
DAX	5,945	6,963
Nikkei	10,398	10,306
Hang Seng	21,221	22,906

Commodities		
Oil	74.76	90.97
Gold	1091.6	1409.0

Bond Yields		
USA 5 Yr Treasury	2.50	2.07
USA 10 Yr T	3.76	3.38
USA 20 Yr T	4.53	4.21
Moody's Aaa	5.32	4.98
Moody's Baa	6.42	6.07
CAN 5 Yr T	2.72	2.45
CAN 10 Yr T	3.57	3.15

26 WEDNESDAY	361 / 005	**27** THURSDAY	362 / 004

Money Market		
USA Fed Funds	0.25	0.25
USA 3 Mo T-B	0.07	0.14
CAN tgt overnight rate	0.25	1.00
CAN 3 Mo T-B	0.19	0.97

Foreign Exchange		
USD/EUR	1.43	1.32
USD/GBP	1.60	1.55
CAN/USD	1.05	1.00
JPY/USD	91.50	81.89

28 FRIDAY	363 / 003

DECEMBER

M	T	W	T	F	S	S
					1	2
3	4	5	6	7	8	9
10	11	12	13	14	15	16
17	18	19	20	21	22	23
24	25	26	27	28	29	30
31						

2010-2011 Strategy Performance

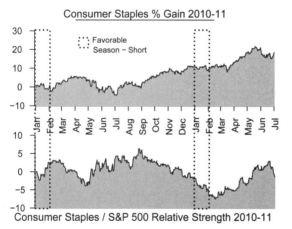

Consumer Staples % Gain 2010-11

Consumer Staples / S&P 500 Relative Strength 2010-11

JANUARY

M	T	W	T	F	S	S
	1	2	3	4	5	6
7	8	9	10	11	12	13
14	15	16	17	18	19	20
21	22	23	24	25	26	27
28	29	30	31			

In January 2010, the consumer staples sector fell along with the market. It also bottomed in February along with the rest of the market. It is important to note that although it rose with the rest of the market, it under performed the market into April. After the bottom of the market in February, it was much better to be invested in the consumer discretionary sector compared to the consumer staples sector. From February to April the discretionary sector strongly outperformed the staples sector.

FEBRUARY

M	T	W	T	F	S	S
				1	2	3
4	5	6	7	8	9	10
11	12	13	14	15	16	17
18	19	20	21	22	23	24
25	26	27	28			

** Weekly avg closing values- except Fed Funds & CAN overnight tgt rate weekly closing values.

FINANCIALS (U.S.) YEAR END CLEAN UP
Outperform January 19th to April 13th

The U.S. financial sector often starts its strong performance in October and then steps up its performance in mid-December and then really outperforms starting in mid-January.

If fundamental and technical indicators are favorable, then a justification to enter the market early can exist, otherwise a mid-January date represents the start of the seasonal sweet spot.

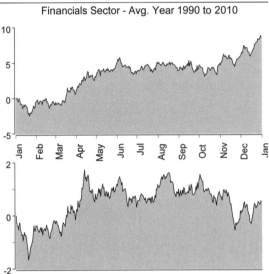

Financials Sector - Avg. Year 1990 to 2010

Financials / S&P 500 Relative Strength - Avg Yr. 1990-2010

Jan 19 to Apr 13	S&P 500	Positive Financials	Diff
1990	1.8 %	-4.3 %	-6.1 %
1991	14.5	27.7	13.2
1992	-3.1	-2.8	0.2
1993	2.8	11.3	8.5
1994	-5.9	-2.7	3.2
1995	8.4	10.4	1.9
1996	4.7	5.6	1.0
1997	-5.0	-2.6	2.4
1998	15.4	22.3	6.9
1999	8.6	13.2	4.6
1900	-1.0	5.9	6.9
2001	-12.2	-6.3	5.9
2002	-1.5	2.6	4.1
2003	-3.7	-5.2	-1.5
2004	-0.9	0.6	1.5
2005	-1.9	-6.2	-4.4
2006	0.9	1.1	0.2
2007	1.9	-3.1	-5.0
2008	0.6	-1.4	-2.0
2009	1.0	15.4	14.4
2010	5.4	11.2	5.8
2011	1.5	-2.1	-3.6
Avg.	1.5 %	4.1 %	2.6 %
Fq > 0	59 %	55 %	73 %

Financials Sector vs. S&P 500
1990 to 2011

Interest rates are at historic lows and although they may move lower over the next few years, it is not possible for them to have the same decline that they have had since the 1980s.

Given this situation investors should concentrate their financial investments during the strong seasonal period.

It should be noted that Canadian banks have their year-ends at the end of October (reporting in November) and as such, their seasonally strong period starts in October.

Extra 2.6% &
16 out of 22 times better than the S&P 500

In the 1990s and early 2000s, financial stocks benefited from the tailwind of falling interest rates. During this period, with a few exceptions, this sector has participated in both the rallies and the declines.

The real sweet spot on average each year, from 1989/90 to 2010/11, has been from mid-January to mid-April.

The main driver for the strong seasonal performance of the financial sector has been the year-end earnings of the banks that start to report in mid-January. A strong performance from mid-January has been the result of investors getting into the market early to take advantage of positive year-end earnings.

(i) *Financial SP GIC Sector # 40:*
An index that contains companies involved in activities such as banking, mortgage finance, consumer finance, specialized finance, investment banking and brokerage, asset management and custody, corporate lending, insurance, financial investment, and real estate, including REITs.

31 MONDAY   366 / 000   **1** TUESDAY

_____   _____
_____   _____
_____   _____
_____   _____
_____   _____
_____   _____

2 WEDNESDAY   **3** THURSDAY

_____   _____
_____   _____
_____   _____
_____   _____
_____   _____
_____   _____

4 FRIDAY

_____
_____
_____
_____
_____
_____

JANUARY

M	T	W	T	F	S	S
	1	2	3	4	5	6
7	8	9	10	11	12	13
14	15	16	17	18	19	20
21	22	23	24	25	26	27
28	29	30	31			

FEBRUARY

M	T	W	T	F	S	S
				1	2	3
4	5	6	7	8	9	10
11	12	13	14	15	16	17
18	19	20	21	22	23	24
25	26	27	28			

MARCH

M	T	W	T	F	S	S
				1	2	3
4	5	6	7	8	9	10
11	12	13	14	15	16	17
18	19	20	21	22	23	24
25	26	27	28	29	30	31

APRIL

M	T	W	T	F	S	S
1	2	3	4	5	6	7
8	9	10	11	12	13	14
15	16	17	18	19	20	21
22	23	24	25	26	27	28
29	30					

MAY

M	T	W	T	F	S	S
	1	2	3	4	5	
6	7	8	9	10	11	12
13	14	15	16	17	18	19
20	21	22	23	24	25	26
27	28	29	30	31		

JUNE

M	T	W	T	F	S	S
					1	2
3	4	5	6	7	8	9
10	11	12	13	14	15	16
17	18	19	20	21	22	23
24	25	26	27	28	29	30

2011 Strategy Performance

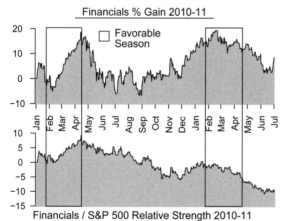

Financials % Gain 2010-11

Financials / S&P 500 Relative Strength 2010-11

The big question over the last few years has been the strength of the financial sector. It was the financial sector that lead the market down in 2007 so investors still focus on the strength of the sector to determine the direction of the market. In 2010, the sector started its outperformance on schedule and finished its run just days before the market started to collapse in April. In 2011, the European and U.S. debt crisis has had a large negative impact on the stock market and it has been all down hill for the financial sector.

** Weekly avg closing values- except Fed Funds & CAN overnight tgt rate weekly closing values.

APPENDIX

STOCK MARKET RETURNS

S&P 500
PERCENT CHANGES

	JAN	FEB	MAR	APR	MAY	JUN
1950	1.7 %	1.0 %	0.4 %	4.5 %	3.9 %	— 5.8 %
1951	6.1	0.6	— 1.8	4.8	— 4.1	— 2.6
1952	1.6	— 3.6	4.8	— 4.3	2.3	4.6
1953	— 0.7	— 1.8	— 2.4	— 2.6	— 0.3	— 1.6
1954	5.1	0.3	3.0	4.9	3.3	0.1
1955	1.8	0.4	— 0.5	3.8	— 0.1	8.2
1956	— 3.6	3.5	6.9	— 0.2	— 6.6	3.9
1957	— 4.2	— 3.3	2.0	3.7	3.7	— 0.1
1958	4.3	2.1	3.1	3.2	1.5	2.6
1959	0.4	— 0.1	0.1	3.9	1.9	— 0.4
1960	— 7.1	0.9	— 1.4	— 1.8	2.7	2.0
1961	6.3	2.7	2.6	0.4	1.9	— 2.9
1962	— 3.8	1.6	— 0.6	— 6.2	— 8.6	— 8.2
1963	4.9	— 2.9	3.5	4.9	1.4	— 2.0
1964	2.7	1.0	1.5	0.6	1.1	1.6
1965	3.3	— 0.1	— 1.5	3.4	— 0.8	— 4.9
1966	0.5	— 1.8	— 2.2	2.1	— 5.4	— 1.6
1967	7.8	0.2	3.9	4.2	— 5.2	1.8
1968	— 4.4	— 3.1	0.9	8.0	1.3	0.9
1969	— 0.8	— 4.7	3.4	2.1	0.2	— 5.6
1970	— 7.6	5.3	0.1	— 9.0	— 6.1	— 5.0
1971	4.0	0.9	3.7	3.6	— 4.2	— 0.9
1972	1.8	2.5	0.6	0.4	1.7	— 2.2
1973	— 1.7	— 3.7	— 0.1	— 4.1	— 1.9	— 0.7
1974	— 1.0	— 0.4	— 2.3	— 3.9	— 3.4	— 1.5
1975	12.3	6.0	2.2	4.7	4.4	4.4
1976	11.8	— 1.1	3.1	— 1.1	— 1.4	4.1
1977	— 5.1	— 2.2	— 1.4	0.0	— 2.4	4.5
1978	— 6.2	— 2.5	2.5	8.5	0.4	— 1.8
1979	4.0	— 3.7	5.5	0.2	— 2.6	3.9
1980	5.8	— 0.4	— 10.2	4.1	4.7	2.7
1981	— 4.6	1.3	3.6	— 2.3	— 0.2	— 1.0
1982	— 1.8	— 6.1	— 1.0	4.0	— 3.9	— 2.0
1983	3.3	1.9	3.3	7.5	— 1.2	3.2
1984	— 0.9	— 3.9	1.3	0.5	— 5.9	1.7
1985	7.4	0.9	— 0.3	— 0.5	5.4	1.2
1986	0.2	7.1	5.3	— 1.4	5.0	1.4
1987	13.2	3.7	2.6	— 1.1	0.6	4.8
1988	4.0	4.2	— 3.3	0.9	0.3	4.3
1989	7.1	— 2.9	2.1	5.0	3.5	— 0.8
1990	— 6.9	0.9	2.4	— 2.7	9.2	— 0.9
1991	4.2	6.7	2.2	0.0	3.9	— 4.8
1992	— 2.0	1.0	— 2.2	2.8	0.1	— 1.7
1993	0.7	1.0	1.9	— 2.5	2.3	0.1
1994	3.3	— 3.0	— 4.6	1.2	1.2	— 2.7
1995	2.4	3.6	2.7	2.8	3.6	2.1
1996	3.3	0.7	0.8	1.3	2.3	0.2
1997	6.1	0.6	— 4.3	5.8	5.9	4.3
1998	1.0	7.0	5.0	0.9	— 1.9	3.9
1999	4.1	— 3.2	3.9	3.8	— 2.5	5.4
2000	— 5.1	— 2.0	9.7	— 3.1	— 2.2	2.4
2001	3.5	— 9.2	— 6.4	7.7	0.5	— 2.5
2002	— 1.6	— 2.1	3.7	— 6.1	— 0.9	— 7.2
2003	— 2.7	— 1.7	0.8	8.1	5.1	1.1
2004	1.7	1.2	— 1.6	— 1.7	1.2	1.8
2005	— 2.5	1.9	— 1.9	— 2.0	3.0	0.0
2006	2.5	0.0	1.1	1.2	— 3.1	0.0
2007	1.4	— 2.2	1.0	4.3	3.3	— 1.8
2008	— 6.1	— 3.5	— 0.6	4.8	1.1	— 8.6
2009	— 8.6	— 11.0	8.5	9.4	5.3	0.0
2010	— 3.7	2.9	5.9	1.5	— 8.2	— 5.4
FQ POS*	37 / 61	32 / 61	40 / 61	42 / 61	35 / 61	31 / 61
% FQ POS*	61 %	52 %	66 %	69 %	57 %	51 %
AVG GAIN*	1.0 %	-0.2 %	1.2 %	1.5 %	0.3 %	— 0.1 %
RANK GAIN*	5	11	4	3	8	10

JUL	AUG	SEP	OCT	NOV	DEC		YEAR
0.8 %	3.3 %	5.6 %	0.4 %	— 0.1 %	4.6 %	1950	21.8 %
6.9	— 0.1	— 1.4	— 0.3	3.9	3.9	1951	16.5
1.8	— 1.5	— 2.0	— 0.1	4.6	3.5	1952	11.8
2.5	— 5.8	0.1	5.1	0.9	0.2	1953	— 6.6
5.7	— 3.4	8.3	— 1.9	8.1	5.1	1954	45.0
6.1	— 0.8	1.1	— 3.0	7.5	— 0.1	1955	26.4
5.2	— 3.8	— 4.5	0.5	— 1.1	3.5	1956	2.6
1.1	— 5.6	— 6.2	— 3.2	1.6	— 4.1	1957	— 14.3
4.3	1.2	4.8	2.5	2.2	5.2	1958	38.1
3.5	— 1.5	— 4.6	1.1	1.3	2.8	1959	8.5
— 2.5	2.6	— 6.0	— 0.2	4.0	4.6	1960	— 3.0
3.3	2.0	— 2.0	2.8	3.9	0.3	1961	23.1
6.4	1.5	— 4.8	0.4	10.2	1.3	1962	— 11.8
— 0.3	4.9	— 1.1	3.2	— 1.1	2.4	1963	18.9
1.8	— 1.6	2.9	0.8	— 0.5	0.4	1964	13.0
1.3	2.3	3.2	2.7	— 0.9	0.9	1965	9.1
— 1.3	— 7.8	— 0.7	4.8	0.3	— 0.1	1966	— 13.1
4.5	— 1.2	3.3	— 3.5	0.8	2.6	1967	20.1
— 1.8	1.1	3.9	0.7	4.8	— 4.2	1968	7.7
— 6.0	4.0	— 2.5	4.3	— 3.4	— 1.9	1969	— 11.4
7.3	4.4	3.4	— 1.2	4.7	5.7	1970	0.1
— 3.2	3.6	— 0.7	— 4.2	— 0.3	8.6	1971	10.8
0.2	3.4	— 0.5	0.9	4.6	1.2	1972	15.6
3.8	— 3.7	4.0	— 0.1	— 11.4	1.7	1973	— 17.4
— 7.8	— 9.0	— 11.9	16.3	— 5.3	— 2.0	1974	— 29.7
— 6.8	— 2.1	— 3.5	6.2	2.5	— 1.2	1975	31.5
— 0.8	— 0.5	2.3	— 2.2	— 0.8	5.2	1976	19.1
— 1.6	— 2.1	— 0.2	— 4.3	2.7	0.3	1977	— 11.5
5.4	2.6	— 0.7	— 9.2	1.7	1.5	1978	1.1
0.9	5.3	0.0	— 6.9	4.3	1.7	1979	12.3
6.5	0.6	2.5	1.6	10.2	— 3.4	1980	25.8
— 0.2	— 6.2	— 5.4	4.9	3.7	— 3.0	1981	— 9.7
— 2.3	11.6	0.8	11.0	3.6	1.5	1982	14.8
— 3.0	1.1	1.0	— 1.5	1.7	— 0.9	1983	17.3
— 1.6	10.6	— 0.3	0.0	— 1.5	2.2	1984	1.4
— 0.5	— 1.2	— 3.5	4.3	6.5	4.5	1985	26.3
— 5.9	7.1	— 8.5	5.5	2.1	— 2.8	1986	14.6
4.8	3.5	— 2.4	— 21.8	— 8.5	7.3	1987	2.0
— 0.5	— 3.9	4.0	2.6	— 1.9	1.5	1988	12.4
8.8	1.6	— 0.7	— 2.5	1.7	2.1	1989	27.3
— 0.5	— 9.4	— 5.1	— 0.7	6.0	2.5	1990	— 6.6
4.5	2.0	— 1.9	1.2	— 4.4	11.2	1991	26.3
3.9	— 2.4	0.9	0.2	3.0	1.0	1992	4.5
— 0.5	3.4	— 1.0	1.9	— 1.3	1.0	1993	7.1
3.1	3.8	— 2.7	2.1	— 4.0	1.2	1994	— 1.5
3.2	0.0	4.0	— 0.5	4.1	1.7	1995	34.1
— 4.6	1.9	5.4	2.6	7.3	— 2.2	1996	20.3
7.8	— 5.7	5.3	— 3.4	4.5	1.6	1997	31.0
— 1.2	— 14.6	6.2	8.0	5.9	5.6	1998	26.7
— 3.2	— 0.6	— 2.9	6.3	1.9	5.8	1999	19.5
— 1.6	6.1	— 5.3	— 0.5	— 8.0	0.4	2000	— 10.1
— 1.1	— 6.4	— 8.2	1.8	7.5	0.8	2001	— 13.0
— 7.9	0.5	— 11.0	8.6	5.7	— 6.0	2002	— 23.4
1.6	1.8	— 1.2	5.5	0.7	5.1	2003	26.4
-3.4	0.2	0.9	1.4	3.9	3.2	2004	9.0
3.6	— 1.1	0.7	— 1.8	3.5	— 0.1	2005	3.0
0.5	2.1	2.5	3.2	1.6	1.3	2006	13.6
— 3.2	1.3	3.6	1.5	— 4.4	— 0.9	2007	3.5
— 1.0	1.2	— 9.2	— 16.8	— 7.5	0.8	2008	-38.5
7.4	3.4	3.6	— 2.0	5.7	1.8	2009	23.5
6.9	— 4.7	8.8	3.7	— 0.2	6.5	2010	12.8
33 / 61	34 / 61	27 / 61	36 / 61	40 / 61	47 / 61		45 / 61
54 %	56 %	44 %	59 %	66 %	77 %		74 %
1.0 %	0.1 %	— 0.5 %	0.6 %	1.6 %	1.8 %		8.8 %
6	9	12	7	2	1		

S&P 500 MONTH CLOSING VALUES

	JAN	FEB	MAR	APR	MAY	JUN
1950	17	17	17	18	19	18
1951	22	22	21	22	22	21
1952	24	23	24	23	24	25
1953	26	26	25	25	25	24
1954	26	26	27	28	29	29
1955	37	37	37	38	38	41
1956	44	45	48	48	45	47
1957	45	43	44	46	47	47
1958	42	41	42	43	44	45
1959	55	55	55	58	59	58
1960	56	56	55	54	56	57
1961	62	63	65	65	67	65
1962	69	70	70	65	60	55
1963	66	64	67	70	71	69
1964	77	78	79	79	80	82
1965	88	87	86	89	88	84
1966	93	91	89	91	86	85
1967	87	87	90	94	89	91
1968	92	89	90	97	99	100
1969	103	98	102	104	103	98
1970	85	90	90	82	77	73
1971	96	97	100	104	100	99
1972	104	107	107	108	110	107
1973	116	112	112	107	105	104
1974	97	96	94	90	87	86
1975	77	82	83	87	91	95
1976	101	100	103	102	100	104
1977	102	100	98	98	96	100
1978	89	87	89	97	97	96
1979	100	96	102	102	99	103
1980	114	114	102	106	111	114
1981	130	131	136	133	133	131
1982	120	113	112	116	112	110
1983	145	148	153	164	162	168
1984	163	157	159	160	151	153
1985	180	181	181	180	190	192
1986	212	227	239	236	247	251
1987	274	284	292	288	290	304
1988	257	268	259	261	262	274
1989	297	289	295	310	321	318
1990	329	332	340	331	361	358
1991	344	367	375	375	390	371
1992	409	413	404	415	415	408
1993	439	443	452	440	450	451
1994	482	467	446	451	457	444
1995	470	487	501	515	533	545
1996	636	640	646	654	669	671
1997	786	791	757	801	848	885
1998	980	1049	1102	1112	1091	1134
1999	1280	1238	1286	1335	1302	1373
2000	1394	1366	1499	1452	1421	1455
2001	1366	1240	1160	1249	1256	1224
2002	1130	1107	1147	1077	1067	990
2003	856	841	848	917	964	975
2004	1131	1145	1126	1107	1121	1141
2005	1181	1204	1181	1157	1192	1191
2006	1280	1281	1295	1311	1270	1270
2007	1438	1407	1421	1482	1531	1503
2008	1379	1331	1323	1386	1400	1280
2009	826	735	798	873	919	919
2010	1074	1104	1169	1187	1089	1031

S&P 500 MONTH CLOSING VALUES

STOCK MKT

JUL	AUG	SEP	OCT	NOV	DEC	
18	18	19	20	20	20	1950
22	23	23	23	23	24	1951
25	25	25	25	26	27	1952
25	23	23	25	25	25	1953
31	30	32	32	34	36	1954
44	43	44	42	46	45	1955
49	48	45	46	45	47	1956
48	45	42	41	42	40	1957
47	48	50	51	52	55	1958
61	60	57	58	58	60	1959
56	57	54	53	56	58	1960
67	68	67	69	71	72	1961
58	59	56	57	62	63	1962
69	73	72	74	73	75	1963
83	82	84	85	84	85	1964
85	87	90	92	92	92	1965
84	77	77	80	80	80	1966
95	94	97	93	94	96	1967
98	99	103	103	108	104	1968
92	96	93	97	94	92	1969
78	82	84	83	87	92	1970
96	99	98	94	94	102	1971
107	111	111	112	117	118	1972
108	104	108	108	96	98	1973
79	72	64	74	70	69	1974
89	87	84	89	91	90	1975
103	103	105	103	102	107	1976
99	97	97	92	95	95	1977
101	103	103	93	95	96	1978
104	109	109	102	106	108	1979
122	122	125	127	141	136	1980
131	123	116	122	126	123	1981
107	120	120	134	139	141	1982
163	164	166	164	166	165	1983
151	167	166	166	164	167	1984
191	189	182	190	202	211	1985
236	253	231	244	249	242	1986
319	330	322	252	230	247	1987
272	262	272	279	274	278	1988
346	351	349	340	346	353	1989
356	323	306	304	322	330	1990
388	395	388	392	375	417	1991
424	414	418	419	431	436	1992
448	464	459	468	462	466	1993
458	475	463	472	454	459	1994
562	562	584	582	605	616	1995
640	652	687	705	757	741	1996
954	899	947	915	955	970	1997
1121	957	1017	1099	1164	1229	1998
1329	1320	1283	1363	1389	1469	1999
1431	1518	1437	1429	1315	1320	2000
1211	1134	1041	1060	1139	1148	2001
912	916	815	886	936	880	2002
990	1008	996	1051	1058	1112	2003
1102	1104	1115	1130	1174	1212	2004
1234	1220	1229	1207	1249	1248	2005
1277	1304	1336	1378	1401	1418	2006
1455	1474	1527	1549	1481	1468	2007
1267	1283	1165	969	896	903	2008
987	1021	1057	1036	1096	1115	2009
1102	1049	1141	1183	1181	1258	2010

DOW JONES PERCENT
MONTH CHANGES

	JAN	FEB	MAR	APR	MAY	JUN
1950	0.8 %	0.8 %	1.3 %	4.0 %	4.2 %	— 6.4 %
1951	5.7	1.3	— 1.7	4.5	— 3.6	— 2.8
1952	0.6	— 3.9	3.6	— 4.4	2.1	4.3
1953	— 0.7	— 2.0	— 1.5	— 1.8	— 0.9	— 1.5
1954	4.1	0.7	3.1	5.2	2.6	1.8
1955	1.1	0.8	— 0.5	3.9	— 0.2	6.2
1956	— 3.6	2.8	5.8	0.8	— 7.4	3.1
1957	— 4.1	— 3.0	2.2	4.1	2.1	— 0.3
1958	3.3	— 2.2	1.6	2.0	1.5	3.3
1959	1.8	1.6	— 0.3	3.7	3.2	0.0
1960	— 8.4	1.2	— 2.1	— 2.4	4.0	2.4
1961	5.2	2.1	2.2	0.3	2.7	— 1.8
1962	— 4.3	1.2	— 0.2	— 5.9	— 7.8	— 8.5
1963	4.7	— 2.9	3.0	5.2	1.3	— 2.8
1964	2.9	1.9	1.6	— 0.3	1.2	1.3
1965	3.3	0.1	— 1.6	3.7	— 0.5	— 5.4
1966	1.5	— 3.2	— 2.8	1.0	— 5.3	— 1.6
1967	8.2	— 1.2	3.2	3.6	— 5.0	0.9
1968	— 5.5	— 1.8	0.0	8.5	— 1.4	— 0.1
1969	0.2	— 4.3	3.3	1.6	— 1.3	— 6.9
1970	— 7.0	4.5	1.0	— 6.3	— 4.8	— 2.4
1971	3.5	1.2	2.9	4.1	— 3.6	— 1.8
1972	1.3	2.9	1.4	1.4	0.7	— 3.3
1973	— 2.1	— 4.4	— 0.4	— 3.1	— 2.2	— 1.1
1974	0.6	0.6	— 1.6	— 1.2	— 4.1	0.0
1975	14.2	5.0	3.9	6.9	1.3	5.6
1976	14.4	— 0.3	2.8	— 0.3	— 2.2	2.8
1977	— 5.0	— 1.9	— 1.8	0.8	— 3.0	2.0
1978	— 7.4	— 3.6	2.1	10.5	0.4	— 2.6
1979	4.2	— 3.6	6.6	— 0.8	— 3.8	2.4
1980	4.4	— 1.5	— 9.0	4.0	4.1	2.0
1981	— 1.7	2.9	3.0	— 0.6	— 0.6	— 1.5
1982	— 0.4	— 5.4	— 0.2	3.1	— 3.4	— 0.9
1983	2.8	3.4	1.6	8.5	— 2.1	1.8
1984	— 3.0	— 5.4	0.9	0.5	— 5.6	2.5
1985	6.2	— 0.2	— 1.3	— 0.7	4.6	1.5
1986	1.6	8.8	6.4	— 1.9	5.2	0.9
1987	13.8	3.1	3.6	— 0.8	0.2	5.5
1988	1.0	5.8	— 4.0	2.2	— 0.1	5.4
1989	8.0	— 3.6	1.6	5.5	2.5	— 1.6
1990	— 5.9	1.4	3.0	— 1.9	8.3	0.1
1991	3.9	5.3	1.1	— 0.9	4.8	— 4.0
1992	1.7	1.4	— 1.0	3.8	1.1	— 2.3
1993	0.3	1.8	1.9	— 0.2	2.9	— 0.3
1994	6.0	— 3.7	— 5.1	1.3	2.1	— 3.5
1995	0.2	4.3	3.7	3.9	3.3	2.0
1996	5.4	1.7	1.9	— 0.3	1.3	0.2
1997	5.7	0.9	— 4.3	6.5	4.6	4.7
1998	0.0	8.1	3.0	3.0	— 1.8	0.6
1999	1.9	— 0.6	5.2	10.2	— 2.1	3.9
2000	— 4.5	— 7.4	7.8	— 1.7	— 2.0	— 0.7
2001	0.9	— 3.6	— 5.9	8.7	1.6	— 3.8
2002	— 1.0	1.9	2.9	— 4.4	— 0.2	— 6.9
2003	— 3.5	— 2.0	1.3	6.1	4.4	1.5
2004	0.3	0.9	— 2.1	— 1.3	— 0.4	2.4
2005	— 2.7	2.6	— 2.4	— 3.0	2.7	— 1.8
2006	1.4	1.2	1.1	2.3	— 1.7	— 0.2
2007	1.3	— 2.8	0.7	5.7	4.3	— 1.6
2008	— 4.6	— 3.0	0.0	4.5	— 1.4	— 10.2
2009	— 8.8	— 11.7	7.7	7.3	4.1	— 0.6
2010	— 3.5	2.6	5.1	1.4	— 7.9	— 3.6
FQ POS	39 / 61	34 / 61	39 / 61	39 / 61	31 / 61	28 / 61
% FQ POS	64 %	56 %	64 %	64 %	51 %	46 %
AVG GAIN	1.0 %	0.0 %	1.1 %	2.0 %	0.0 %	— 0.4 %
RANK GAIN	6	10	5	1	8	11

DOW JONES PERCENT MONTH CHANGES — STOCK MKT

JUL	AUG	SEP	OCT	NOV	DEC	YEAR	
0.1 %	3.6 %	4.4 %	− 0.6 %	1.2 %	3.4 %	1950	17.6 %
6.3	4.8	0.3	− 3.2	− 0.4	3.0	1951	14.4
1.9	− 1.6	− 1.6	− 0.5	5.4	2.9	1952	8.4
2.6	− 5.2	1.1	4.5	2.0	− 0.2	1953	− 3.8
4.3	− 3.5	7.4	− 2.3	9.9	4.6	1954	44.0
3.2	0.5	− 0.3	− 2.5	6.2	1.1	1955	20.8
5.1	− 3.1	− 5.3	1.0	− 1.5	5.6	1956	2.3
1.0	− 4.7	− 5.8	− 3.4	2.0	− 3.2	1957	− 12.8
5.2	1.1	4.6	2.1	2.6	4.7	1958	34.0
4.9	− 1.6	− 4.9	2.4	1.9	3.1	1959	16.4
− 3.7	1.5	− 7.3	0.1	2.9	3.1	1960	− 9.3
3.1	2.1	− 2.6	0.4	2.5	1.3	1961	18.7
6.5	1.9	− 5.0	1.9	10.1	0.4	1962	− 10.8
− 1.6	4.9	0.5	3.1	− 0.6	1.7	1963	17.0
1.2	− 0.3	4.4	− 0.3	0.3	− 0.1	1964	14.6
1.6	1.3	4.2	3.2	− 1.5	2.4	1965	10.9
− 2.6	− 7.0	− 1.8	4.2	− 1.9	− 0.7	1966	− 18.9
5.1	− 0.3	2.8	− 5.1	− 0.4	3.3	1967	15.2
− 1.6	1.5	4.4	1.8	3.4	− 4.2	1968	4.3
− 6.6	2.6	− 2.8	5.3	− 5.1	− 1.5	1969	15.2
7.4	4.2	− 0.5	− 0.7	5.1	5.6	1970	4.8
− 3.7	4.6	− 1.2	− 5.4	− 0.9	7.1	1971	6.1
− 0.5	4.2	− 1.1	0.2	6.6	0.2	1972	14.6
3.9	− 4.2	6.7	1.0	− 14.0	3.5	1973	− 16.6
− 5.6	− 10.4	− 10.4	9.5	− 7.0	− 0.4	1974	− 27.6
− 5.4	0.5	− 5.0	5.3	3.0	− 1.0	1975	38.3
− 1.8	− 1.1	1.7	− 2.6	− 1.8	6.1	1976	17.9
− 2.9	− 3.2	− 1.7	− 3.4	1.4	0.2	1977	− 17.3
5.3	1.7	− 1.3	− 8.5	0.8	0.8	1978	− 3.2
0.5	4.9	− 1.0	− 7.2	0.8	2.0	1979	4.2
7.8	− 0.3	0.0	− 0.8	7.4	− 2.9	1980	14.9
− 2.5	− 7.4	− 3.6	0.3	4.3	− 1.6	1981	− 9.2
− 0.4	11.5	− 0.6	10.6	4.8	0.7	1982	19.6
− 1.9	1.4	1.4	− 0.6	4.1	− 1.4	1983	20.3
− 1.5	9.8	− 1.4	0.1	− 1.5	1.9	1984	− 3.7
0.9	− 1.0	− 0.4	3.4	7.1	5.1	1985	27.7
− 6.2	6.9	− 6.9	6.2	1.9	− 1.0	1986	22.6
6.4	3.5	− 2.5	− 23.2	− 8.0	5.7	1987	2.3
− 0.6	− 4.6	4.0	1.7	− 1.6	2.6	1988	11.9
9.0	2.9	− 1.6	− 1.8	2.3	1.7	1989	27.0
0.9	− 10.0	− 6.2	− 0.4	4.8	2.9	1990	− 4.3
4.1	0.6	− 0.9	1.7	− 5.7	9.5	1991	20.3
2.3	− 4.0	0.4	− 1.4	2.4	− 0.1	1992	4.2
0.7	3.2	− 2.6	3.5	0.1	1.9	1993	13.7
3.8	4.0	− 1.8	1.7	− 4.3	2.5	1994	2.1
3.3	− 2.1	3.9	− 0.7	6.7	0.8	1995	33.5
− 2.2	1.6	4.7	2.5	8.2	− 1.1	1996	26.0
7.2	− 7.3	4.2	− 6.3	5.1	1.1	1997	22.6
− 0.8	− 15.1	4.0	9.6	6.1	0.7	1998	16.1
− 2.9	1.6	− 4.5	3.8	1.4	5.3	1999	24.7
0.7	6.6	− 5.0	3.0	− 5.1	3.6	2000	− 5.8
0.2	− 5.4	− 11.1	2.6	8.6	1.7	2001	− 7.1
− 5.5	− 0.8	− 12.4	10.6	5.9	− 6.2	2002	− 16.8
2.8	2.0	− 1.5	5.7	− 0.2	6.9	2003	25.3
− 2.8	0.3	− 0.9	− 0.5	4.0	3.4	2004	3.1
3.6	− 1.5	0.8	− 1.2	3.5	− 0.8	2005	− 0.6
0.3	1.7	2.6	3.4	1.2	2.0	2006	16.3
− 1.5	1.1	4.0	0.2	− 4.0	− 0.8	2007	6.4
0.2	1.5	− 6.0	− 14.1	− 5.3	− 0.6	2008	− 33.8
8.6	3.5	2.3	0.0	6.5	0.8	2009	18.8
7.1	− 4.3	7.7	3.1	− 1.0	5.2	2010	11.0
38 / 61	35 / 61	24 / 61	36 / 61	40 / 61	43 / 61		43 / 61
62 %	57 %	39 %	59 %	66 %	70 %		70 %
1.2 %	0.0 %	− 0.8 %	0.4 %	1.5 %	1.7 %		8.2 %
4	9	12	7	3	2		

DOW JONES
MONTH CLOSING VALUES

	JAN	FEB	MAR	APR	MAY	JUN
1950	202	203	206	214	223	209
1951	249	252	248	259	250	243
1952	271	260	270	258	263	274
1953	290	284	280	275	272	268
1954	292	295	304	319	328	334
1955	409	412	410	426	425	451
1956	471	484	512	516	478	493
1957	479	465	475	494	505	503
1958	450	440	447	456	463	478
1959	594	604	602	624	644	644
1960	623	630	617	602	626	641
1961	648	662	677	679	697	684
1962	700	708	707	665	613	561
1963	683	663	683	718	727	707
1964	785	800	813	811	821	832
1965	903	904	889	922	918	868
1966	984	952	925	934	884	870
1967	850	839	866	897	853	860
1968	856	841	841	912	899	898
1969	946	905	936	950	938	873
1970	744	778	786	736	700	684
1971	869	879	904	942	908	891
1972	902	928	941	954	961	929
1973	999	955	951	921	901	892
1974	856	861	847	837	802	802
1975	704	739	768	821	832	879
1976	975	973	1000	997	975	1003
1977	954	936	919	927	899	916
1978	770	742	757	837	841	819
1979	839	809	862	855	822	842
1980	876	863	786	817	851	868
1981	947	975	1004	998	992	977
1982	871	824	823	848	820	812
1983	1076	1113	1130	1226	1200	1222
1984	1221	1155	1165	1171	1105	1132
1985	1287	1284	1267	1258	1315	1336
1986	1571	1709	1819	1784	1877	1893
1987	2158	2224	2305	2286	2292	2419
1988	1958	2072	1988	2032	2031	2142
1989	2342	2258	2294	2419	2480	2440
1990	2591	2627	2707	2657	2877	2881
1991	2736	2882	2914	2888	3028	2907
1992	3223	3268	3236	3359	3397	3319
1993	3310	3371	3435	3428	3527	3516
1994	3978	3832	3636	3682	3758	3625
1995	3844	4011	4158	4321	4465	4556
1996	5395	5486	5587	5569	5643	5655
1997	6813	6878	6584	7009	7331	7673
1998	7907	8546	8800	9063	8900	8952
1999	9359	9307	9786	10789	10560	10971
2000	10941	10128	10922	10734	10522	10448
2001	10887	10495	9879	10735	10912	10502
2002	9920	10106	10404	9946	9925	9243
2003	8054	7891	7992	8480	8850	8985
2004	10488	10584	10358	10226	10188	10435
2005	10490	10766	10504	10193	10467	10275
2006	10865	10993	11109	11367	11168	11150
2007	12622	12269	12354	13063	13628	13409
2008	12650	12266	12263	12820	12638	11350
2009	8001	7063	7609	8168	8500	8447
2010	10067	10325	10857	11009	10137	9774

DOW JONES
MONTH CLOSING VALUES
STOCK MKT

JUL	AUG	SEP	OCT	NOV	DEC	
209	217	226	225	228	235	**1950**
258	270	271	262	261	269	**1951**
280	275	271	269	284	292	**1952**
275	261	264	276	281	281	**1953**
348	336	361	352	387	404	**1954**
466	468	467	455	483	488	**1955**
518	502	475	480	473	500	**1956**
509	484	456	441	450	436	**1957**
503	509	532	543	558	584	**1958**
675	664	632	647	659	679	**1959**
617	626	580	580	597	616	**1960**
705	720	701	704	722	731	**1961**
598	609	579	590	649	652	**1962**
695	729	733	755	751	763	**1963**
841	839	875	873	875	874	**1964**
882	893	931	961	947	969	**1965**
847	788	774	807	792	786	**1966**
904	901	927	880	876	905	**1967**
883	896	936	952	985	944	**1968**
816	837	813	856	812	800	**1969**
734	765	761	756	794	839	**1970**
858	898	887	839	831	890	**1971**
925	964	953	956	1018	1020	**1972**
926	888	947	957	822	851	**1973**
757	679	608	666	619	616	**1974**
832	835	794	836	861	852	**1975**
985	974	990	965	947	1005	**1976**
890	862	847	818	830	831	**1977**
862	877	866	793	799	805	**1978**
846	888	879	816	822	839	**1979**
935	933	932	925	993	964	**1980**
952	882	850	853	889	875	**1981**
809	901	896	992	1039	1047	**1982**
1199	1216	1233	1225	1276	1259	**1983**
1115	1224	1207	1207	1189	1212	**1984**
1348	1334	1329	1374	1472	1547	**1985**
1775	1898	1768	1878	1914	1896	**1986**
2572	2663	2596	1994	1834	1939	**1987**
2129	2032	2113	2149	2115	2169	**1988**
2661	2737	2693	2645	2706	2753	**1989**
2905	2614	2453	2442	2560	2634	**1990**
3025	3044	3017	3069	2895	3169	**1991**
3394	3257	3272	3226	3305	3301	**1992**
3540	3651	3555	3681	3684	3754	**1993**
3765	3913	3843	3908	3739	3834	**1994**
4709	4611	4789	4756	5075	5117	**1995**
5529	5616	5882	6029	6522	6448	**1996**
8223	7622	7945	7442	7823	7908	**1997**
8883	7539	7843	8592	9117	9181	**1998**
10655	10829	10337	10730	10878	11453	**1999**
10522	11215	10651	10971	10415	10788	**2000**
10523	9950	8848	9075	9852	10022	**2001**
8737	8664	7592	8397	8896	8342	**2002**
9234	9416	9275	9801	9782	10454	**2003**
10140	10174	10080	10027	10428	10783	**2004**
10641	10482	10569	10440	10806	10718	**2005**
11186	11381	11679	12801	12222	12463	**2006**
13212	13358	13896	13930	13372	13265	**2007**
11378	11544	10851	9325	8829	8776	**2008**
9172	9496	9712	9713	10345	10428	**2009**
10466	10015	10788	11118	11006	11578	**2010**

NASDAQ PERCENT MONTH CHANGES

	JAN	FEB	MAR	APR	MAY	JUN
1972	4.2	5.5	2.2	2.5	0.9	— 1.8
1973	— 4.0	— 6.2	— 2.4	— 8.2	— 4.8	— 1.6
1974	3.0	— 0.6	— 2.2	— 5.9	— 7.7	— 5.3
1975	16.6	4.6	3.6	3.8	5.8	4.7
1976	12.1	3.7	0.4	— 0.6	— 2.3	2.6
1977	— 2.4	— 1.0	— 0.5	1.4	0.1	4.3
1978	— 4.0	0.6	4.7	8.5	4.4	0.0
1979	6.6	— 2.6	7.5	1.6	— 1.8	5.1
1980	7.0	— 2.3	— 17.1	6.9	7.5	4.9
1981	— 2.2	0.1	6.1	3.1	3.1	— 3.5
1982	— 3.8	— 4.8	— 2.1	5.2	— 3.3	— 4.1
1983	6.9	5.0	3.9	8.2	5.3	3.2
1984	— 3.7	— 5.9	— 0.7	— 1.3	— 5.9	2.9
1985	12.8	2.0	— 1.8	0.5	3.6	1.9
1986	3.4	7.1	4.2	2.3	4.4	1.3
1987	12.4	8.4	1.2	— 2.9	— 0.3	2.0
1988	4.3	6.5	2.1	1.2	— 2.3	6.6
1989	5.2	— 0.4	1.8	5.1	4.3	— 2.4
1990	— 8.6	2.4	2.3	— 3.5	9.3	0.7
1991	10.8	9.4	6.4	0.5	4.4	— 6.0
1992	5.8	2.1	— 4.7	— 4.2	1.1	— 3.7
1993	2.9	— 3.7	2.9	— 4.2	5.9	0.5
1994	3.0	— 1.0	— 6.2	— 1.3	0.2	— 4.0
1995	0.4	5.1	3.0	3.3	2.4	8.0
1996	0.7	3.8	0.1	8.1	4.4	— 4.7
1997	6.9	— 5.1	— 6.7	3.2	11.1	3.0
1998	3.1	9.3	3.7	1.8	— 4.8	6.5
1999	14.3	— 8.7	7.6	3.3	— 2.8	8.7
2000	— 3.2	19.2	— 2.6	— 15.6	— 11.9	16.6
2001	12.2	— 22.4	— 14.5	15.0	— 0.3	2.4
2002	— 0.8	— 10.5	6.6	— 8.5	— 4.3	— 9.4
2003	— 1.1	1.3	0.3	9.2	9.0	1.7
2004	3.1	— 1.8	— 1.8	— 3.7	3.5	3.1
2005	— 5.2	— 0.5	— 2.6	— 3.9	7.6	— 0.5
2006	4.6	— 1.1	2.6	— 0.7	— 6.2	— 0.3
2007	2.0	— 1.9	0.2	4.3	3.1	0.0
2008	— 9.9	— 5.0	0.3	5.9	4.6	— 9.1
2009	— 6.4	— 6.7	10.9	12.3	3.3	3.4
2010	— 5.4	4.2	7.1	2.6	— 8.3	— 6.5
FQ POS	25/39	19/39	25/39	25/39	24/39	23/39
% FQ POS	64 %	49 %	64 %	64 %	62 %	59 %
AVG GAIN	2.7 %	0.2 %	0.7 %	1.4 %	1.1 %	0.8 %
RANK GAIN	1	9	7	4	5	6

NASDAQ PERCENT MONTH CHANGES 🇺🇸 STOCK MKT

JUL	AUG	SEP	OCT	NOV	DEC		YEAR
− 1.8	1.7	− 0.3	0.5	2.1	0.6	**1972**	17.2
7.6	− 3.5	6.0	− 0.9	− 15.1	− 1.4	**1973**	− 31.1
− 7.9	− 10.9	− 10.7	17.2	− 3.5	− 5.0	**1974**	− 35.1
− 4.4	− 5.0	− 5.9	3.6	2.4	− 1.5	**1975**	29.8
1.1	− 1.7	1.7	− 1.0	0.9	7.4	**1976**	26.1
0.9	− 0.5	0.7	− 3.3	5.8	1.8	**1977**	7.3
5.0	6.9	− 1.6	− 16.4	3.2	2.9	**1978**	12.3
2.3	6.4	− 0.3	− 9.6	6.4	4.8	**1979**	28.1
8.9	5.7	3.4	2.7	8.0	− 2.8	**1980**	33.9
− 1.9	− 7.5	− 8.0	8.4	3.1	− 2.7	**1981**	− 3.2
− 2.3	6.2	5.6	13.3	9.3	0.0	**1982**	18.7
− 4.6	− 3.8	1.4	− 7.4	4.1	− 2.5	**1983**	19.9
− 4.2	10.9	− 1.8	− 1.2	− 1.9	1.9	**1984**	− 11.3
1.7	− 1.2	− 5.8	4.4	7.4	3.5	**1985**	31.5
− 8.4	3.1	− 8.4	2.9	− 0.3	− 3.0	**1986**	7.4
2.4	4.6	− 2.4	− 27.2	− 5.6	8.3	**1987**	− 5.2
− 1.9	− 2.8	2.9	− 1.3	− 2.9	2.7	**1988**	15.4
4.2	3.4	0.8	− 3.7	0.1	− 0.3	**1989**	19.2
− 5.2	− 13.0	− 9.6	− 4.3	8.9	4.1	**1990**	− 17.8
5.5	4.7	0.2	3.1	− 3.5	11.9	**1991**	56.9
3.1	− 3.0	3.6	3.8	7.9	3.7	**1992**	15.5
0.1	5.4	2.7	2.2	− 3.2	3.0	**1993**	14.7
2.3	6.0	− 0.2	1.7	− 3.5	0.2	**1994**	− 3.2
7.3	1.9	2.3	− 0.7	2.2	− 0.7	**1995**	39.9
− 8.8	5.6	7.5	− 0.4	5.8	− 0.1	**1996**	22.7
10.5	− 0.4	6.2	− -5.5	0.4	− 1.9	**1997**	21.6
− 1.2	− 19.9	13.0	4.6	10.1	12.5	**1998**	39.6
− 1.8	3.8	0.2	8.0	12.5	22.0	**1999**	85.6
− 5.0	11.7	− 12.7	− 8.3	− 22.9	− 4.9	**2000**	− 39.3
− 6.2	− 10.9	− 17.0	12.8	14.2	1.0	**2001**	− 21.1
− 9.2	− 1.0	− 10.9	13.5	11.2	− 9.7	**2002**	− 31.5
6.9	4.3	− 1.3	8.1	1.5	2.2	**2003**	50.0
− 7.8	− 2.6	3.2	4.1	6.2	3.7	**2004**	8.6
6.2	− 1.5	0.0	− 1.5	5.3	− 1.2	**2005**	1.4
− 3.7	4.4	3.4	4.8	2.7	− 0.7	**2006**	9.5
− 2.2	2.0	4.0	5.8	− 6.9	− 0.3	**2007**	9.8
1.4	1.8	− 11.6	− 17.7	− 10.8	2.7	**2008**	− 40.5
7.8	1.5	5.6	− 3.6	4.9	5.8	**2009**	43.9
6.9	− 6.2	12.0	5.9	− 0.4	6.2	**2010**	16.9
20/39	21/39	21/39	21/39	26/39	23/39		28/39
51 %	54 %	54 %	54 %	67 %	59 %		72 %
0.1 %	0.2 %	− 0.6 %	0.4 %	1.7 %	1.9 %		11.9 %
11	10	12	8	3	2		

NASDAQ MONTH
CLOSING VALUES

	JAN	FEB	MAR	APR	MAY	JUN
1972	119	125	128	131	133	130
1973	128	120	117	108	103	101
1974	95	94	92	87	80	76
1975	70	73	76	79	83	87
1976	87	90	91	90	88	90
1977	96	95	94	95	96	100
1978	101	101	106	115	120	120
1979	126	123	132	134	131	138
1980	162	158	131	140	150	158
1981	198	198	210	217	223	216
1982	188	179	176	185	179	171
1983	248	261	271	293	309	319
1984	268	253	251	247	233	240
1985	279	284	279	281	291	296
1986	336	360	375	383	400	406
1987	392	425	430	418	417	425
1988	345	367	375	379	370	395
1989	401	400	407	428	446	435
1990	416	426	436	420	459	462
1991	414	453	482	485	506	476
1992	620	633	604	579	585	564
1993	696	671	690	661	701	704
1994	800	793	743	734	735	706
1995	755	794	817	844	865	933
1996	1060	1100	1101	1191	1243	1185
1997	1380	1309	1222	1261	1400	1442
1998	1619	1771	1836	1868	1779	1895
1999	2506	2288	2461	2543	2471	2686
2000	3940	4697	4573	3861	3401	3966
2001	2773	2152	1840	2116	2110	2161
2002	1934	1731	1845	1688	1616	1463
2003	1321	1338	1341	1464	1596	1623
2004	2066	2030	1994	1920	1987	2048
2005	2062	2052	1999	1922	2068	2057
2006	2306	2281	2340	2323	2179	2172
2007	2464	2416	2422	2525	2605	2603
2008	2390	2271	2279	2413	2523	2293
2009	1476	1378	1529	1717	1774	1835
2010	2147	2238	2398	2461	2257	2109

NASDAQ MONTH CLOSING VALUES

STOCK MKT

JUL	AUG	SEP	OCT	NOV	DEC	
128	130	130	130	133	134	**1972**
109	105	111	110	94	92	**1973**
70	62	56	65	63	60	**1974**
83	79	74	77	79	78	**1975**
91	90	91	90	91	98	**1976**
101	100	101	98	103	105	**1977**
126	135	133	111	115	118	**1978**
141	150	150	136	144	151	**1979**
172	182	188	193	208	202	**1980**
212	196	180	195	201	196	**1981**
167	178	188	213	232	232	**1982**
304	292	297	275	286	279	**1983**
230	255	250	247	242	247	**1984**
301	298	280	293	314	325	**1985**
371	383	351	361	360	349	**1986**
435	455	444	323	305	331	**1987**
387	377	388	383	372	381	**1988**
454	469	473	456	456	455	**1989**
438	381	345	330	359	374	**1990**
502	526	527	543	524	586	**1991**
581	563	583	605	653	677	**1992**
705	743	763	779	754	777	**1993**
722	766	764	777	750	752	**1994**
1001	1020	1044	1036	1059	1052	**1995**
1081	1142	1227	1222	1293	1291	**1996**
1594	1587	1686	1594	1601	1570	**1997**
1872	1499	1694	1771	1950	2193	**1998**
2638	2739	2746	2966	3336	4069	**1999**
3767	4206	3673	3370	2598	2471	**2000**
2027	1805	1499	1690	1931	1950	**2001**
1328	1315	1172	1330	1479	1336	**2002**
1735	1810	1787	1932	1960	2003	**2003**
1887	1838	1897	1975	2097	2175	**2004**
2185	2152	2152	2120	2233	2205	**2005**
2091	2184	2258	2367	2432	2415	**2006**
2546	2596	2702	2859	2661	2652	**2007**
2326	2368	2092	1721	1536	1577	**2008**
1979	2009	2122	2045	2145	2269	**2009**
2255	2114	2369	2507	2498	2653	**2010**

S&P/TSX MONTH PERCENT CHANGES

	JAN	FEB	MAR	APR	MAY	JUN
1985	8.1	0.0	0.7	0.8	3.8	— 0.8
1986	— 1.7	0.5	6.7	1.1	1.4	— 1.2
1987	9.2	4.5	6.9	— 0.6	— 0.9	1.5
1988	— 3.3	4.8	3.4	0.8	— 2.7	5.9
1989	6.7	— 1.2	0.2	1.4	2.2	1.5
1990	— 6.7	— 0.5	— 1.3	— 8.2	6.7	— 0.6
1991	0.5	5.8	1.0	-0.8	2.2	— 2.3
1992	2.4	— 0.4	— 4.7	— 1.7	1.0	0.0
1993	— 1.3	4.4	4.4	5.2	2.5	2.2
1994	5.4	— 2.9	— 2.1	— 1.4	1.4	— 7.0
1995	— 4.7	2.7	4.6	— -0.8	4.0	1.8
1996	5.4	— 0.7	0.8	3.5	1.9	— 3.9
1997	3.1	0.8	— 5.0	2.2	6.8	0.9
1998	0.0	5.9	6.6	1.4	— 1.0	— 2.9
1999	3.8	— 6.2	4.5	6.3	— 2.5	2.5
2000	0.8	7.6	3.7	— 1.2	— 1.0	10.2
2001	4.3	— 13.3	— 5.8	4.5	2.7	— 5.2
2002	— 0.5	— 0.1	2.8	— 2.4	— 0.1	— 6.7
2003	— 0.7	— 0.2	— 3.2	3.8	4.2	1.8
2004	3.7	3.1	— 2.3	— 4.0	2.1	1.5
2005	— 0.5	5.0	— 0.6	— 3.5	3.6	3.1
2006	6.0	— 2.2	3.6	0.8	— 3.8	— 1.1
2007	1.0	0.1	0.9	1.9	4.8	— 1.1
2008	— 4.9	3.3	— 1.7	4.4	5.6	— 1.7
2009	— 3.3	— 6.6	7.4	6.9	11.2	0.0
2010	— 5.5	4.8	3.5	1.4	— 3.7	— 4.0
FQ POS	15/26	14/26	17/26	16/26	18/26	12/26
% FQ POS	58 %	54 %	65 %	62 %	69 %	46 %
AVG GAIN	1.0 %	0.7 %	1.3 %	0.8 %	2.0 %	-0.3 %
RANK GAIN	4	8	3	6	2	9

S&P/TSX MONTH PERCENT CHANGES · STOCK MKT

JUL	AUG	SEP	OCT	NOV	DEC	YEAR	
2.4	1.5	− 6.7	1.6	6.8	1.3	**1985**	20.5
− 4.9	3.2	− 1.6	1.6	0.7	0.6	**1986**	6.0
7.8	− 0.9	− 2.3	− 22.6	− 1.4	6.1	**1987**	3.1
− 1.9	− 2.7	− 0.1	3.4	− 3.0	2.9	**1988**	7.3
5.6	1.0	− 1.7	− 0.6	0.6	0.7	**1989**	17.1
0.5	− 6.0	− 5.6	− 2.5	2.3	3.4	**1990**	− 18.0
2.1	− 0.6	− 3.7	3.8	− 1.9	1.9	**1991**	7.8
1.6	− 1.2	− 3.1	1.2	− 1.6	2.1	**1992**	− 4.6
0.0	4.3	− 3.6	6.6	− 1.8	3.4	**1993**	29.0
3.8	4.1	0.1	− 1.4	− 4.6	2.9	**1994**	− 2.5
1.9	− 2.1	0.3	− 1.6	4.5	1.1	**1995**	11.9
− 2.3	4.3	2.9	5.8	7.5	− 1.5	**1996**	25.7
6.8	− 3.9	6.5	− 2.8	− 4.8	2.9	**1997**	13.0
− 5.9	− 20.2	1.5	10.6	2.2	2.2	**1998**	− 3.2
1.0	− 1.6	− 0.2	4.3	3.6	11.9	**1999**	29.7
2.1	8.1	− 7.7	− 7.1	− 8.5	1.3	**2000**	6.2
− 0.6	− 3.8	− 7.6	0.7	7.8	3.5	**2001**	− 13.9
− 7.6	0.1	− 6.5	1.1	5.1	0.7	**2002**	− 14.0
3.9	3.6	− 1.3	4.7	1.1	4.6	**2003**	24.3
− 1.0	− 1.0	3.5	2.3	1.8	2.4	**2004**	12.5
5.3	2.4	3.2	− 5.7	4.2	4.1	**2005**	21.9
1.9	2.1	− 2.6	5.0	3.3	1.2	**2006**	14.5
− 0.3	− 1.5	3.2	3.7	− 6.4	1.1	**2007**	7.2
− 6.0	1.3	− 14.7	− 16.9	− 5.0	− 3.1	**2008**	− 35.0
4.0	0.8	4.8	− 4.2	4.9	2.6	**2009**	30.7
3.7	1.7	3.8	2.5	2.2	3.8	**2010**	14.4
17/26	14/26	10/26	16/26	16/26	24/26		19/26
65 %	54 %	38 %	62 %	62 %	92 %		73 %
0.9 %	− 0.3 %	− 1.5 %	− 0.3 %	0.8 %	2.5 %		8.1 %
5	11	12	10	7	1		

S&P/TSX MONTH CLOSING VALUES

	JAN	FEB	MAR	APR	MAY	JUN
1985	2595	2595	2613	2635	2736	2713
1986	2843	2856	3047	3079	3122	3086
1987	3349	3499	3739	3717	3685	3740
1988	3057	3205	3314	3340	3249	3441
1989	3617	3572	3578	3628	3707	3761
1990	3704	3687	3640	3341	3565	3544
1991	3273	3462	3496	3469	3546	3466
1992	3596	3582	3412	3356	3388	3388
1993	3305	3452	3602	3789	3883	3966
1994	4555	4424	4330	4267	4327	4025
1995	4018	4125	4314	4280	4449	4527
1996	4968	4934	4971	5147	5246	5044
1997	6110	6158	5850	5977	6382	6438
1998	6700	7093	7559	7665	7590	7367
1999	6730	6313	6598	7015	6842	7010
2000	8481	9129	9462	9348	9252	10196
2001	9322	8079	7608	7947	8162	7736
2002	7649	7638	7852	7663	7656	7146
2003	6570	6555	6343	6586	6860	6983
2004	8521	8789	8586	8244	8417	8546
2005	9204	9668	9612	9275	9607	9903
2006	11946	11688	12111	12204	11745	11613
2007	13034	13045	13166	13417	14057	13907
2008	13155	13583	13350	13937	14715	14467
2009	8695	8123	8720	9325	10370	10375
2010	11094	11630	12038	12211	11763	11294

S&P/TSX PERCENT CLOSING VALUES

JUL	AUG	SEP	OCT	NOV	DEC	
2779	2820	2632	2675	2857	2893	**1985**
2935	3028	2979	3027	3047	3066	**1986**
4030	3994	3902	3019	2978	3160	**1987**
3377	3286	3284	3396	3295	3390	**1988**
3971	4010	3943	3919	3943	3970	**1989**
3561	3346	3159	3081	3151	3257	**1990**
3540	3518	3388	3516	3449	3512	**1991**
3443	3403	3298	3336	3283	3350	**1992**
3967	4138	3991	4256	4180	4321	**1993**
4179	4350	4354	4292	4093	4214	**1994**
4615	4517	4530	4459	4661	4714	**1995**
4929	5143	5291	5599	6017	5927	**1996**
6878	6612	7040	6842	6513	6699	**1997**
6931	5531	5614	6208	6344	6486	**1998**
7081	6971	6958	7256	7520	8414	**1999**
10406	11248	10378	9640	8820	8934	**2000**
7690	7399	6839	6886	7426	7688	**2001**
6605	6612	6180	6249	6570	6615	**2002**
7258	7517	7421	7773	7859	8221	**2003**
8458	8377	8668	8871	9030	9247	**2004**
10423	10669	11012	10383	10824	11272	**2005**
11831	12074	11761	12345	12752	12908	**2006**
13869	13660	14099	14625	13689	13833	**2007**
13593	13771	11753	9763	9271	8988	**2008**
10787	10868	11935	10911	11447	11746	**2009**
11713	11914	12369	12676	12953	13443	**2010**

10 BEST

YEARS

	Close	Change	Change
1954	36	11 pt	45.0 %
1958	55	15	38.1
1995	616	157	34.1
1975	90	22	31.5
1997	970	230	31.0
1989	353	76	27.3
1998	1229	259	26.7
1955	45	10	26.4
2003	1112	232	26.4
1985	211	44	26.3

MONTHS

	Close	Change	Change
Oct 1974	74	10 pt	16.3 %
Aug 1982	120	12	11.6
Dec 1991	417	42	11.2
Oct 1982	134	13	11.0
Aug 1984	167	16	10.6
Nov 1980	141	13	10.2
Nov 1962	62	6	10.2
Mar 2000	1499	132	9.7
Apr 2009	798	75	9.4
May 1990	361	30	9.2

DAYS

		Close	Change	Change
Mon	2008 Oct 13	1003	104 pt	11.6 %
Tue	2008 Oct 28	941	92	10.8
Wed	1987 Oct 21	258	22	9.1
Mon	2009 Mar 23	883	54	7.1
Thu	2008 Nov 13	911	59	6.9
Mon	2008 Nov 24	852	52	6.5
Tues	2009 Mar 10	720	43	6.4
Fri	2008 Nov 21	800	48	6.3
Wed	2002 Jul 24	843	46	5.7
Tue	2008 Sep 30	1166	60	5.4

10 WORST

YEARS

	Close	Change	Change
2008	903	− 566 pt	− 38.5 %
1974	69	− 29	− 29.7
2002	880	− 268	− 23.4
1973	98	− 21	− 17.4
1957	40	− 7	− 14.3
1966	80	− 12	− 13.1
2001	1148	− 172	− 13.0
1962	63	− 8	− 11.8
1977	95	− 12	− 11.5
1969	92	− 12	− 11.4

MONTHS

	Close	Change	Change
Oct 1987	252	− 70 pt	− 21.8 %
Oct 2008	969	− 196	− 16.8
Aug 1998	957	− 163	− 14.6
Sep 1974	64	− 9	− 11.9
Nov 1973	96	− 12	− 11.4
Sep 2002	815	− 101	− 11.0
Feb 2009	735	− 91	− 11.0
Mar 1980	102	− 12	− 10.2
Aug 1990	323	− 34	− 9.4
Feb 2001	1240	− 126	− 9.2

DAYS

		Close	Change	Change
Mon	1987 Oct 19	225	− 58 pt	− 20.5 %
Wed	2008 Oct 15	908	− 90	− 9.0
Mon	2008 Dec 01	816	− 80	− 8.9
Mon	2008 Sep 29	1106	− 107	− 8.8
Mon	1987 Oct 26	228	− 21	− 8.3
Thu	2008 Oct 09	910	− 75	− 7.6
Mon	1997 Oct 27	877	− 65	− 6.9
Mon	1998 Aug 31	957	− 70	− 6.8
Fri	1988 Jan 8	243	− 18	− 6.8
Thu	2008 Nov 20	752	− 54	− 6.7

10 BEST

10 WORST

YEARS

	Close	Change	Change
1954	404	124 pt	44 %
1975	852	236	38.3
1958	584	148	34.0
1995	5117	1283	33.5
1985	1547	335	27.7
1989	2753	585	27.0
1996	6448	1331	26.0
2003	10454	2112	25.3
1999	11453	2272	25.2
1997	7908	1460	22.6

YEARS

	Close	Change	Change
2008	8776	− 4488 pt	− 33.8 %
1974	616	− 235	− 27.6
1966	786	− 184	− 18.9
1977	831	− 174	− 17.3
2002	8342	− 1680	− 16.8
1973	851	− 169	− 16.6
1969	800	− 143	− 15.2
1957	436	− 64	− 12.8
1962	652	− 79	− 10.8
1960	616	− 64	− 9.3

MONTHS

	Close	Change	Change
Aug 1982	901	93 pt	11.5 %
Oct 1982	992	95	10.6
Oct 2002	8397	805	10.6
Apr 1978	837	80	10.5
Apr 1999	10789	1003	10.2
Nov 1962	649	60	10.1
Nov 1954	387	35	9.9
Aug 1984	1224	109	9.8
Oct 1998	8592	750	9.6
Oct 1974	666	58	9.5

MONTHS

	Close	Change	Change
Oct 1987	1994	− 603 pt	− 23.2 %
Aug 1998	7539	− 1344	− 15.1
Oct 2008	9325	− 1526	− 14.1
Nov 1973	822	− 134	− 14.0
Sep 2002	7592	− 1072	− 12.4
Feb 2009	7063	− 938	− 11.7
Sep 2001	8848	− 1102	− 11.1
Sep 1974	608	− 71	− 10.4
Aug 1974	679	− 79	− 10.4
Jun 2008	11350	− 1288	− 10.2

DAYS

		Close	Change	Change
Mon	2008 Oct 13	9388	936 pt	11.1 %
Tue	2008 Oct 28	9065	889	10.9
Wed	1987 Oct 21	2028	187	10.2
Mon	2009 Mar 23	7776	497	6.8
Thu	2008 Nov 13	8835	553	6.7
Fri	2008 Nov 21	8046	494	6.5
Wed	2002 Jul 24	8191	489	6.3
Tue	1987 Oct 20	1841	102	5.9
Tue	2009 Mar 10	6926	379	5.8
Mon	2002 Jul 29	8712	448	5.4

DAYS

		Close	Change	Change
Mon	1987 Oct 19	1739	− 508 pt	− 22.6 %
Mon	1987 Oct 26	1794	− 157	− 8.0
Wed	2008 Oct 15	8578	− 733	− 7.9
Mon	2008 Dec 01	8149	− 680	− 7.7
Thu	2008 Oct 09	8579	− 679	− 7.3
Mon	1997 Oct 27	8366	− 554	− 7.2
Mon	2001 Sep 17	8921	− 685	− 7.1
Mon	2008 Sep 29	10365	− 778	− 7.0
Fri	1989 Oct 13	2569	− 191	− 6.9
Fri	1988 Jan 8	1911	− 141	− 6.9

10 BEST

YEARS

	Close	Change	Change
1999	4069	1877 pt	85.6 %
1991	586	213	56.9
2003	2003	668	50.0
2009	2269	692	43.9
1995	1052	300	39.9
1998	2193	622	39.6
1980	202	51	33.9
1985	325	78	31.5
1975	78	18	29.8
1979	151	33	28.1

MONTHS

	Close	Change	Change
Dec 1999	4069	733 pt	22.0 %
Feb 2000	4697	756	19.2
Oct 1974	65	10	17.2
Jun 2000	3966	565	16.6
Apr 2001	2116	276	15.0
Nov 2001	1931	240	14.2
Oct 2002	1330	158	13.5
Oct 1982	1771	25	13.3
Sep 1998	1694	195	13.0
Oct 2001	1690	191	12.8

DAYS

		Close	Change	Change
Wed	2001 Jan 3	2617	325 pt	14.2 %
Mon	2008 Oct 13	1844	195	11.8
Tue	2000 Dec 5	2890	274	10.5
Tue	2008 Oct 28	1649	144	9.5
Thu	2001 Apr 5	1785	146	8.9
Wed	2001 Apr 18	2079	156	8.1
Tue	2000 May 30	3459	254	7.9
Fri	2000 Oct 13	3317	242	7.9
Thu	2000 Oct 19	3419	247	7.8
Wed	2002 May 8	1696	122	7.8

10 WORST

YEARS

	Close	Change	Change
2008	1577	– 1075 pt	– 40.5 %
2000	2471	– 1599	– 39.3
1974	60	– 32	– 35.1
2002	1336	– 615	– 31.5
1973	92	– 42	– 31.1
2001	1950	– 520	– 21.1
1990	374	– 81	– 17.8
1984	247	– 32	– 11.3
1987	331	– 18	– 5.2
1981	196	– 7	– 3.2

MONTHS

	Close	Change	Change
Oct 1987	323	– 121 pt	– 27.2 %
Nov 2000	2598	– 772	– 22.9
Feb 2001	2152	– 621	– 22.4
Aug 1998	1499	– 373	– 19.9
Oct 2008	1721	– 371	– 17.7
Mar 1980	131	– 27	– 17.1
Sep 2001	1499	– 307	– 17.0
Oct 1978	111	– 22	– 16.4
Apr 2000	3861	– 712	– 15.6
Nov 1973	94	– 17	– 15.1

DAYS

		Close	Change	Change
Mon	1987 Oct 19	360	– 46 pt	– 11.3 %
Fri	2000 Apr 14	3321	– 355	– 9.7
Mon	2008 Sep 29	1984	– 200	– 9.1
Mon	1987 Oct 26	299	– 30	– 9.0
Tue	1987 Oct 20	328	– 32	– 9.0
Mon	2008 Dec 01	1398	– 138	– 9.0
Mon	1998 Aug 31	1499	– 140	– 8.6
Wed	2008 Oct 15	1628	– 151	– 8.5
Mon	2000 Apr 03	4224	– 349	– 7.6
Tue	2001 Jan 02	2292	– 179	– 7.2

10 BEST

10 WORST

YEARS

	Close	Change	Change
2009	8414	2758 pt	30.7 %
1999	4321	1928	29.7
1993	5927	971	29.0
1996	8221	1213	25.7
2003	11272	1606	24.3
2005	2893	2026	21.9
1985	3970	500	20.8
1989	12908	580	17.1
2006	6699	1636	14.5
2010	13433	1697	14.4

YEARS

	Close	Change	Change
2008	8988	− 4845 pt	35.0 %
1990	3257	− 713	− 18.0
2002	6615	− 1074	− 14.0
2001	7688	− 1245	− 13.9
1992	3350	− 162	− 4.6
1998	6486	− 214	− 3.2
1994	4214	− 108	− 2.5
1987	3160	94	3.1
1986	3066	173	6.0
2000	8934	520	6.2

MONTHS

	Close	Change	Change
Dec 1999	8414	891 pt	11.8 %
May 2009	8500	1045	11.2
Oct 1998	6208	594	10.6
Jun 2000	10196	943	10.2
Jan 1985	2595	195	8.1
Aug 2000	11248	842	8.1
Nov 2001	7426	540	7.8
Jul 1987	4030	290	7.8
Feb 2000	9129	648	7.6
Nov 1996	6017	418	7.5

MONTHS

	Close	Change	Change
Oct 1987	3019	− 883 pt	− 22.6 %
Aug 1998	5531	− 1401	− 20.2
Oct 2008	9763	− 1990	− 16.9
Sep 2008	11753	− 2018	− 14.7
Feb 2001	8079	− 1243	− 13.3
Nov 2000	8820	− 820	− 8.5
Apr 1990	3341	− 299	− 8.2
Sep 2000	10378	− 870	− 7.7
Sep 2001	6839	− 561	− 7.6
Jul 2002	6605	− 540	− 7.6

DAYS

		Close	Change	Change
Tue	2008 Oct 14	9956	891 pt	9.8 %
Wed	1987 Oct 21	3246	269	9.0
Mon	2008 Oct 20	10251	689	7.2
Tue	2008 Oct 28	9152	614	7.2
Fri	2008 Sep 19	12913	848	7.0
Fri	2008 Nov 28	9271	517	5.9
Fri	2008 Nov 21	8155	431	5.6
Mon	2008 Dec 08	8567	450	5.5
Mon	2009 Mar 23	8959	452	5.3
Fri	1987 Oct 30	3019	147	5.1

DAYS

		Close	Change	Change
Mon	1987 Oct 19	3192	− 407 pt	− 11.3 %
Mon	2008 Dec 01	8406	− 864	− 9.3
Thu	2008 Nov 20	7725	− 766	− 9.0
Mon	2008 Oct 27	8537	− 757	− 8.1
Wed	2000 Oct 25	9512	− 840	− 8.1
Mon	1987 Oct 26	2846	− 233	− 7.6
Thu	2008 Oct 02	10901	− 814	− 6.9
Mon	2008 Sep 29	11285	− 841	− 6.9
Tue	1987 Oct 20	2977	− 215	− 6.7
Fri	2001 Feb 16	8393	− 574	− 6.4

BOND YIELDS

BOND YIELDS 🇺🇸 10 YEAR TREASURY*

	JAN	FEB	MAR	APR	MAY	JUN
1954	2.48	2.47	2.37	2.29	2.37	2.38
1955	2.61	2.65	2.68	2.75	2.76	2.78
1956	2.9	2.84	2.96	3.18	3.07	3
1957	3.46	3.34	3.41	3.48	3.6	3.8
1958	3.09	3.05	2.98	2.88	2.92	2.97
1959	4.02	3.96	3.99	4.12	4.31	4.34
1960	4.72	4.49	4.25	4.28	4.35	4.15
1961	3.84	3.78	3.74	3.78	3.71	3.88
1962	4.08	4.04	3.93	3.84	3.87	3.91
1963	3.83	3.92	3.93	3.97	3.93	3.99
1964	4.17	4.15	4.22	4.23	4.2	4.17
1965	4.19	4.21	4.21	4.2	4.21	4.21
1966	4.61	4.83	4.87	4.75	4.78	4.81
1967	4.58	4.63	4.54	4.59	4.85	5.02
1968	5.53	5.56	5.74	5.64	5.87	5.72
1969	6.04	6.19	6.3	6.17	6.32	6.57
1970	7.79	7.24	7.07	7.39	7.91	7.84
1971	6.24	6.11	5.7	5.83	6.39	6.52
1972	5.95	6.08	6.07	6.19	6.13	6.11
1973	6.46	6.64	6.71	6.67	6.85	6.9
1974	6.99	6.96	7.21	7.51	7.58	7.54
1975	7.5	7.39	7.73	8.23	8.06	7.86
1976	7.74	7.79	7.73	7.56	7.9	7.86
1977	7.21	7.39	7.46	7.37	7.46	7.28
1978	7.96	8.03	8.04	8.15	8.35	8.46
1979	9.1	9.1	9.12	9.18	9.25	8.91
1980	10.8	12.41	12.75	11.47	10.18	9.78
1981	12.57	13.19	13.12	13.68	14.1	13.47
1982	14.59	14.43	13.86	13.87	13.62	14.3
1983	10.46	10.72	10.51	10.4	10.38	10.85
1984	11.67	11.84	12.32	12.63	13.41	13.56
1985	11.38	11.51	11.86	11.43	10.85	10.16
1986	9.19	8.7	7.78	7.3	7.71	7.8
1987	7.08	7.25	7.25	8.02	8.61	8.4
1988	8.67	8.21	8.37	8.72	9.09	8.92
1989	9.09	9.17	9.36	9.18	8.86	8.28
1990	8.21	8.47	8.59	8.79	8.76	8.48
1991	8.09	7.85	8.11	8.04	8.07	8.28
1992	7.03	7.34	7.54	7.48	7.39	7.26
1993	6.6	6.26	5.98	5.97	6.04	5.96
1994	5.75	5.97	6.48	6.97	7.18	7.1
1995	7.78	7.47	7.2	7.06	6.63	6.17
1996	5.65	5.81	6.27	6.51	6.74	6.91
1997	6.58	6.42	6.69	6.89	6.71	6.49
1998	5.54	5.57	5.65	5.64	5.65	5.5
1999	4.72	5	5.23	5.18	5.54	5.9
2000	6.66	6.52	6.26	5.99	6.44	6.1
2001	5.16	5.1	4.89	5.14	5.39	5.28
2002	5.04	4.91	5.28	5.21	5.16	4.93
2003	4.05	3.9	3.81	3.96	3.57	3.33
2004	4.15	4.08	3.83	4.35	4.72	4.73
2005	4.22	4.17	4.5	4.34	4.14	4.00
2006	4.42	4.57	4.72	4.99	5.11	5.11
2007	4.76	4.72	4.56	4.69	4.75	5.10
2008	3.74	3.74	3.51	3.68	3.88	4.10
2009	2.52	2.87	2.82	2.93	3.29	3.72
2010	3.73	3.69	3.73	3.85	3.42	3.20

* Source: Federal Reserve Bank of St. Louis, monthly data calculated as average of business days

JUL	AUG	SEP	OCT	NOV	DEC	
2.3	2.36	2.38	2.43	2.48	2.51	**1954**
2.9	2.97	2.97	2.88	2.89	2.96	**1955**
3.11	3.33	3.38	3.34	3.49	3.59	**1956**
3.93	3.93	3.92	3.97	3.72	3.21	**1957**
3.2	3.54	3.76	3.8	3.74	3.86	**1958**
4.4	4.43	4.68	4.53	4.53	4.69	**1959**
3.9	3.8	3.8	3.89	3.93	3.84	**1960**
3.92	4.04	3.98	3.92	3.94	4.06	**1961**
4.01	3.98	3.98	3.93	3.92	3.86	**1962**
4.02	4	4.08	4.11	4.12	4.13	**1963**
4.19	4.19	4.2	4.19	4.15	4.18	**1964**
4.2	4.25	4.29	4.35	4.45	4.62	**1965**
5.02	5.22	5.18	5.01	5.16	4.84	**1966**
5.16	5.28	5.3	5.48	5.75	5.7	**1967**
5.5	5.42	5.46	5.58	5.7	6.03	**1968**
6.72	6.69	7.16	7.1	7.14	7.65	**1969**
7.46	7.53	7.39	7.33	6.84	6.39	**1970**
6.73	6.58	6.14	5.93	5.81	5.93	**1971**
6.11	6.21	6.55	6.48	6.28	6.36	**1972**
7.13	7.4	7.09	6.79	6.73	6.74	**1973**
7.81	8.04	8.04	7.9	7.68	7.43	**1974**
8.06	8.4	8.43	8.14	8.05	8	**1975**
7.83	7.77	7.59	7.41	7.29	6.87	**1976**
7.33	7.4	7.34	7.52	7.58	7.69	**1977**
8.64	8.41	8.42	8.64	8.81	9.01	**1978**
8.95	9.03	9.33	10.3	10.65	10.39	**1979**
10.25	11.1	11.51	11.75	12.68	12.84	**1980**
14.28	14.94	15.32	15.15	13.39	13.72	**1981**
13.95	13.06	12.34	10.91	10.55	10.54	**1982**
11.38	11.85	11.65	11.54	11.69	11.83	**1983**
13.36	12.72	12.52	12.16	11.57	11.5	**1984**
10.31	10.33	10.37	10.24	9.78	9.26	**1985**
7.3	7.17	7.45	7.43	7.25	7.11	**1986**
8.45	8.76	9.42	9.52	8.86	8.99	**1987**
9.06	9.26	8.98	8.8	8.96	9.11	**1988**
8.02	8.11	8.19	8.01	7.87	7.84	**1989**
8.47	8.75	8.89	8.72	8.39	8.08	**1990**
8.27	7.9	7.65	7.53	7.42	7.09	**1991**
6.84	6.59	6.42	6.59	6.87	6.77	**1992**
5.81	5.68	5.36	5.33	5.72	5.77	**1993**
7.3	7.24	7.46	7.74	7.96	7.81	**1994**
6.28	6.49	6.2	6.04	5.93	5.71	**1995**
6.87	6.64	6.83	6.53	6.2	6.3	**1996**
6.22	6.3	6.21	6.03	5.88	5.81	**1997**
5.46	5.34	4.81	4.53	4.83	4.65	**1998**
5.79	5.94	5.92	6.11	6.03	6.28	**1999**
6.05	5.83	5.8	5.74	5.72	5.24	**2000**
5.24	4.97	4.73	4.57	4.65	5.09	**2001**
4.65	4.26	3.87	3.94	4.05	4.03	**2002**
3.98	4.45	4.27	4.29	4.3	4.27	**2003**
4.5	4.28	4.13	4.1	4.19	4.23	**2004**
4.18	4.26	4.20	4.46	4.54	4.47	**2005**
5.09	4.88	4.72	4.73	4.60	4.56	**2006**
5.00	4.67	4.52	4.53	4.15	4.10	**2007**
4.01	3.89	3.69	3.81	3.53	2.42	**2008**
3.56	3.59	3.40	3.39	3.40	3.59	**2009**
3.01	2.70	2.65	2.54	2.76	3.29	**2010**

	JAN	FEB	MAR	APR	MAY	JUN
1954	2.17	2.04	1.93	1.87	1.92	1.92
1955	2.32	2.38	2.48	2.55	2.56	2.59
1956	2.84	2.74	2.93	3.20	3.08	2.97
1957	3.47	3.39	3.46	3.53	3.64	3.83
1958	2.88	2.78	2.64	2.46	2.41	2.46
1959	4.01	3.96	3.99	4.12	4.35	4.50
1960	4.92	4.69	4.31	4.29	4.49	4.12
1961	3.67	3.66	3.60	3.57	3.47	3.81
1962	3.94	3.89	3.68	3.60	3.66	3.64
1963	3.58	3.66	3.68	3.74	3.72	3.81
1964	4.07	4.03	4.14	4.15	4.05	4.02
1965	4.10	4.15	4.15	4.15	4.15	4.15
1966	4.86	4.98	4.92	4.83	4.89	4.97
1967	4.70	4.74	4.54	4.51	4.75	5.01
1968	5.54	5.59	5.76	5.69	6.04	5.85
1969	6.25	6.34	6.41	6.30	6.54	6.75
1970	8.17	7.82	7.21	7.50	7.97	7.85
1971	5.89	5.56	5.00	5.65	6.28	6.53
1972	5.59	5.69	5.87	6.17	5.85	5.91
1973	6.34	6.60	6.80	6.67	6.80	6.69
1974	6.95	6.82	7.31	7.92	8.18	8.10
1975	7.41	7.11	7.30	7.99	7.72	7.51
1976	7.46	7.45	7.49	7.25	7.59	7.61
1977	6.58	6.83	6.93	6.79	6.94	6.76
1978	7.77	7.83	7.86	7.98	8.18	8.36
1979	9.20	9.13	9.20	9.25	9.24	8.85
1980	10.74	12.60	13.47	11.84	9.95	9.21
1981	12.77	13.41	13.41	13.99	14.63	13.95
1982	14.65	14.54	13.98	14.00	13.75	14.43
1983	10.03	10.26	10.08	10.02	10.03	10.63
1984	11.37	11.54	12.02	12.37	13.17	13.48
1985	10.93	11.13	11.52	11.01	10.34	9.60
1986	8.68	8.34	7.46	7.05	7.52	7.64
1987	6.64	6.79	6.79	7.57	8.26	8.02
1988	8.18	7.71	7.83	8.19	8.58	8.49
1989	9.15	9.27	9.51	9.30	8.91	8.29
1990	8.12	8.42	8.60	8.77	8.74	8.43
1991	7.70	7.47	7.77	7.70	7.70	7.94
1992	6.24	6.58	6.95	6.78	6.69	6.48
1993	5.83	5.43	5.19	5.13	5.20	5.22
1994	5.09	5.40	5.94	6.52	6.78	6.70
1995	7.76	7.37	7.05	6.86	6.41	5.93
1996	5.36	5.38	5.97	6.30	6.48	6.69
1997	6.33	6.20	6.54	6.76	6.57	6.38
1998	5.42	5.49	5.61	5.61	5.63	5.52
1999	4.60	4.91	5.14	5.08	5.44	5.81
2000	6.58	6.68	6.50	6.26	6.69	6.30
2001	4.86	4.89	4.64	4.76	4.93	4.81
2002	4.34	4.30	4.74	4.65	4.49	4.19
2003	3.05	2.90	2.78	2.93	2.52	2.27
2004	3.12	3.07	2.79	3.39	3.85	3.93
2005	3.71	3.77	4.17	4.00	3.85	3.77
2006	4.35	4.57	4.72	4.90	5.00	5.07
2007	4.75	4.71	4.48	4.59	4.67	5.03
2008	2.98	2.78	2.48	2.84	3.15	3.49
2009	1.60	1.87	1.82	1.86	2.13	2.71
2010	2.48	2.36	2.43	2.58	2.18	2.00

* Source: Federal Reserve Bank of St. Louis, monthly data calculated as average of business days

5 YEAR TREASURY BOND YIELDS

JUL	AUG	SEP	OCT	NOV	DEC	
1.85	1.90	1.96	2.02	2.09	2.16	1954
2.72	2.86	2.85	2.76	2.81	2.93	1955
3.12	3.41	3.47	3.40	3.56	3.70	1956
4.00	4.00	4.03	4.08	3.72	3.08	1957
2.77	3.29	3.69	3.78	3.70	3.82	1958
4.58	4.57	4.90	4.72	4.75	5.01	1959
3.79	3.62	3.61	3.76	3.81	3.67	1960
3.84	3.96	3.90	3.80	3.82	3.91	1961
3.80	3.71	3.70	3.64	3.60	3.56	1962
3.89	3.89	3.96	3.97	4.01	4.04	1963
4.03	4.05	4.08	4.07	4.04	4.09	1964
4.15	4.20	4.25	4.34	4.46	4.72	1965
5.17	5.50	5.50	5.27	5.36	5.00	1966
5.23	5.31	5.40	5.57	5.78	5.75	1967
5.60	5.50	5.48	5.55	5.66	6.12	1968
7.01	7.03	7.57	7.51	7.53	7.96	1969
7.59	7.57	7.29	7.12	6.47	5.95	1970
6.85	6.55	6.14	5.93	5.78	5.69	1971
5.97	6.02	6.25	6.18	6.12	6.16	1972
7.33	7.63	7.05	6.77	6.92	6.80	1973
8.38	8.63	8.37	7.97	7.68	7.31	1974
7.92	8.33	8.37	7.97	7.80	7.76	1975
7.49	7.31	7.13	6.75	6.52	6.10	1976
6.84	7.03	7.04	7.32	7.34	7.48	1977
8.54	8.33	8.43	8.61	8.84	9.08	1978
8.90	9.06	9.41	10.63	10.93	10.42	1979
9.53	10.84	11.62	11.86	12.83	13.25	1980
14.79	15.56	15.93	15.41	13.38	13.60	1981
14.07	13.00	12.25	10.80	10.38	10.22	1982
11.21	11.63	11.43	11.28	11.41	11.54	1983
13.27	12.68	12.53	12.06	11.33	11.07	1984
9.70	9.81	9.81	9.69	9.28	8.73	1985
7.06	6.80	6.92	6.83	6.76	6.67	1986
8.01	8.32	8.94	9.08	8.35	8.45	1987
8.66	8.94	8.69	8.51	8.79	9.09	1988
7.83	8.09	8.17	7.97	7.81	7.75	1989
8.33	8.44	8.51	8.33	8.02	7.73	1990
7.91	7.43	7.14	6.87	6.62	6.19	1991
5.84	5.60	5.38	5.60	6.04	6.08	1992
5.09	5.03	4.73	4.71	5.06	5.15	1993
6.91	6.88	7.08	7.40	7.72	7.78	1994
6.01	6.24	6.00	5.86	5.69	5.51	1995
6.64	6.39	6.60	6.27	5.97	6.07	1996
6.12	6.16	6.11	5.93	5.80	5.77	1997
5.46	5.27	4.62	4.18	4.54	4.45	1998
5.68	5.84	5.80	6.03	5.97	6.19	1999
6.18	6.06	5.93	5.78	5.70	5.17	2000
4.76	4.57	4.12	3.91	3.97	4.39	2001
3.81	3.29	2.94	2.95	3.05	3.03	2002
2.87	3.37	3.18	3.19	3.29	3.27	2003
3.69	3.47	3.36	3.35	3.53	3.60	2004
3.98	4.12	4.01	4.33	4.45	4.39	2005
5.04	4.82	4.67	4.69	4.58	4.53	2006
4.88	4.43	4.20	4.20	3.67	3.49	2007
3.30	3.14	2.88	2.73	2.29	1.52	2008
2.46	2.57	2.37	2.33	2.23	2.34	2009
1.76	1.47	1.41	1.18	1.35	1.93	2010

3 MONTH TREASURY

	JAN	FEB	MAR	APR	MAY	JUN
1982	12.92	14.28	13.31	13.34	12.71	13.08
1983	8.12	8.39	8.66	8.51	8.50	9.14
1984	9.26	9.46	9.89	10.07	10.22	10.26
1985	8.02	8.56	8.83	8.22	7.73	7.18
1986	7.30	7.29	6.76	6.24	6.33	6.40
1987	5.58	5.75	5.77	5.82	5.85	5.85
1988	6.00	5.84	5.87	6.08	6.45	6.66
1999	8.56	8.84	9.14	8.96	8.74	8.43
1990	7.90	8.00	8.17	8.04	8.01	7.99
1991	6.41	6.12	6.09	5.83	5.63	5.75
1992	3.91	3.95	4.14	3.84	3.72	3.75
1993	3.07	2.99	3.01	2.93	3.03	3.14
1994	3.04	3.33	3.59	3.78	4.27	4.25
1995	5.90	5.94	5.91	5.84	5.85	5.64
1996	5.15	4.96	5.10	5.09	5.15	5.23
1997	5.17	5.14	5.28	5.30	5.20	5.07
1998	5.18	5.23	5.16	5.08	5.14	5.12
1999	4.45	4.56	4.57	4.41	4.63	4.72
2000	5.50	5.73	5.86	5.82	5.99	5.86
2001	5.29	5.01	4.54	3.97	3.70	3.57
2002	1.68	1.76	1.83	1.75	1.76	1.73
2003	1.19	1.19	1.15	1.15	1.09	0.94
2004	0.90	0.94	0.95	0.96	1.04	1.29
2005	2.37	2.58	2.80	2.84	2.90	3.04
2006	4.34	4.54	4.63	4.72	4.84	4.92
2007	5.11	5.16	5.08	5.01	4.87	4.74
2008	2.82	2.17	1.28	1.31	1.76	1.89
2009	0.13	0.30	0.22	0.16	0.18	0.18
2010	0.06	0.11	0.15	0.16	0.16	0.12

* Source: Federal Reserve Bank of St. Louis, monthly data calculated as average of business days

3 MONTH TREASURY BOND YIELDS

JUL	AUG	SEP	OCT	NOV	DEC	
11.86	9.00	8.19	7.97	8.35	8.20	**1982**
9.45	9.74	9.36	8.99	9.11	9.36	**1983**
10.53	10.90	10.80	10.12	8.92	8.34	**1984**
7.32	7.37	7.33	7.40	7.48	7.33	**1985**
6.00	5.69	5.35	5.32	5.50	5.68	**1986**
5.88	6.23	6.62	6.35	5.89	5.96	**1987**
6.95	7.30	7.48	7.60	8.03	8.35	**1988**
8.15	8.17	8.01	7.90	7.94	7.88	**1999**
7.87	7.69	7.60	7.40	7.29	6.95	**1990**
5.75	5.50	5.37	5.14	4.69	4.18	**1991**
3.28	3.20	2.97	2.93	3.21	3.29	**1992**
3.11	3.09	3.01	3.09	3.18	3.13	**1993**
4.46	4.61	4.75	5.10	5.45	5.76	**1994**
5.59	5.57	5.43	5.44	5.52	5.29	**1995**
5.30	5.19	5.24	5.12	5.17	5.04	**1996**
5.19	5.28	5.08	5.11	5.28	5.30	**1997**
5.09	5.04	4.74	4.07	4.53	4.50	**1998**
4.69	4.87	4.82	5.02	5.23	5.36	**1999**
6.14	6.28	6.18	6.29	6.36	5.94	**2000**
3.59	3.44	2.69	2.20	1.91	1.72	**2001**
1.71	1.65	1.66	1.61	1.25	1.21	**2002**
0.92	0.97	0.96	0.94	0.95	0.91	**2003**
1.36	1.50	1.68	1.79	2.11	2.22	**2004**
3.29	3.52	3.49	3.79	3.97	3.97	**2005**
5.08	5.09	4.93	5.05	5.07	4.97	**2006**
4.96	4.32	3.99	4.00	3.35	3.07	**2007**
1.66	1.75	1.15	0.69	0.19	0.03	**2008**
0.18	0.17	0.12	0.07	0.05	0.05	**2009**
0.16	0.16	0.15	0.13	0.14	0.14	**2010**

MOODY'S SEASONED CORPORATE Aaa*

	JAN	FEB	MAR	APR	MAY	JUN
1950	2.57	2.58	2.58	2.60	2.61	2.62
1951	2.66	2.66	2.78	2.87	2.89	2.94
1952	2.98	2.93	2.96	2.93	2.93	2.94
1953	3.02	3.07	3.12	3.23	3.34	3.40
1954	3.06	2.95	2.86	2.85	2.88	2.90
1955	2.93	2.93	3.02	3.01	3.04	3.05
1956	3.11	3.08	3.10	3.24	3.28	3.26
1957	3.77	3.67	3.66	3.67	3.74	3.91
1958	3.60	3.59	3.63	3.60	3.57	3.57
1959	4.12	4.14	4.13	4.23	4.37	4.46
1960	4.61	4.56	4.49	4.45	4.46	4.45
1961	4.32	4.27	4.22	4.25	4.27	4.33
1962	4.42	4.42	4.39	4.33	4.28	4.28
1963	4.21	4.19	4.19	4.21	4.22	4.23
1964	4.39	4.36	4.38	4.40	4.41	4.41
1965	4.43	4.41	4.42	4.43	4.44	4.46
1966	4.74	4.78	4.92	4.96	4.98	5.07
1967	5.20	5.03	5.13	5.11	5.24	5.44
1968	6.17	6.10	6.11	6.21	6.27	6.28
1969	6.59	6.66	6.85	6.89	6.79	6.98
1970	7.91	7.93	7.84	7.83	8.11	8.48
1971	7.36	7.08	7.21	7.25	7.53	7.64
1972	7.19	7.27	7.24	7.30	7.30	7.23
1973	7.15	7.22	7.29	7.26	7.29	7.37
1974	7.83	7.85	8.01	8.25	8.37	8.47
1975	8.83	8.62	8.67	8.95	8.90	8.77
1976	8.60	8.55	8.52	8.40	8.58	8.62
1977	7.96	8.04	8.10	8.04	8.05	7.95
1978	8.41	8.47	8.47	8.56	8.69	8.76
1979	9.25	9.26	9.37	9.38	9.50	9.29
1980	11.09	12.38	12.96	12.04	10.99	10.58
1981	12.81	13.35	13.33	13.88	14.32	13.75
1982	15.18	15.27	14.58	14.46	14.26	14.81
1983	11.79	12.01	11.73	11.51	11.46	11.74
1984	12.20	12.08	12.57	12.81	13.28	13.55
1985	12.08	12.13	12.56	12.23	11.72	10.94
1986	10.05	9.67	9.00	8.79	9.09	9.13
1987	8.36	8.38	8.36	8.85	9.33	9.32
1988	9.88	9.40	9.39	9.67	9.90	9.86
1989	9.62	9.64	9.80	9.79	9.57	9.10
1990	8.99	9.22	9.37	9.46	9.47	9.26
1991	9.04	8.83	8.93	8.86	8.86	9.01
1992	8.20	8.29	8.35	8.33	8.28	8.22
1993	7.91	7.71	7.58	7.46	7.43	7.33
1994	6.92	7.08	7.48	7.88	7.99	7.97
1995	8.46	8.26	8.12	8.03	7.65	7.30
1996	6.81	6.99	7.35	7.50	7.62	7.71
1997	7.42	7.31	7.55	7.73	7.58	7.41
1998	6.61	6.67	6.72	6.69	6.69	6.53
1999	6.24	6.40	6.62	6.64	6.93	7.23
2000	7.78	7.68	7.68	7.64	7.99	7.67
2001	7.15	7.10	6.98	7.20	7.29	7.18
2002	6.55	6.51	6.81	6.76	6.75	6.63
2003	6.17	5.95	5.89	5.74	5.22	4.97
2004	5.54	5.50	5.33	5.73	6.04	6.01
2005	5.36	5.20	5.40	5.33	5.15	4.96
2006	5.29	5.35	5.53	5.84	5.95	5.89
2007	5.40	5.39	5.30	5.47	5.47	5.79
2008	5.33	5.53	5.51	5.55	5.57	5.68
2009	5.05	5.27	5.50	5.39	5.54	5.61
2010	5.26	5.35	5.27	5.29	4.96	4.88

* Source: Federal Reserve Bank of St. Louis, monthly data calculated as average of business days

MOODY'S SEASONED CORPORATE Aaa 🇺🇸 BOND YIELDS

JUL	AUG	SEP	OCT	NOV	DEC	
2.65	2.61	2.64	2.67	2.67	2.67	**1950**
2.94	2.88	2.84	2.89	2.96	3.01	**1951**
2.95	2.94	2.95	3.01	2.98	2.97	**1952**
3.28	3.24	3.29	3.16	3.11	3.13	**1953**
2.89	2.87	2.89	2.87	2.89	2.90	**1954**
3.06	3.11	3.13	3.10	3.10	3.15	**1955**
3.28	3.43	3.56	3.59	3.69	3.75	**1956**
3.99	4.10	4.12	4.10	4.08	3.81	**1957**
3.67	3.85	4.09	4.11	4.09	4.08	**1958**
4.47	4.43	4.52	4.57	4.56	4.58	**1959**
4.41	4.28	4.25	4.30	4.31	4.35	**1960**
4.41	4.45	4.45	4.42	4.39	4.42	**1961**
4.34	4.35	4.32	4.28	4.25	4.24	**1962**
4.26	4.29	4.31	4.32	4.33	4.35	**1963**
4.40	4.41	4.42	4.42	4.43	4.44	**1964**
4.48	4.49	4.52	4.56	4.60	4.68	**1965**
5.16	5.31	5.49	5.41	5.35	5.39	**1966**
5.58	5.62	5.65	5.82	6.07	6.19	**1967**
6.24	6.02	5.97	6.09	6.19	6.45	**1968**
7.08	6.97	7.14	7.33	7.35	7.72	**1969**
8.44	8.13	8.09	8.03	8.05	7.64	**1970**
7.64	7.59	7.44	7.39	7.26	7.25	**1971**
7.21	7.19	7.22	7.21	7.12	7.08	**1972**
7.45	7.68	7.63	7.60	7.67	7.68	**1973**
8.72	9.00	9.24	9.27	8.89	8.89	**1974**
8.84	8.95	8.95	8.86	8.78	8.79	**1975**
8.56	8.45	8.38	8.32	8.25	7.98	**1976**
7.94	7.98	7.92	8.04	8.08	8.19	**1977**
8.88	8.69	8.69	8.89	9.03	9.16	**1978**
9.20	9.23	9.44	10.13	10.76	10.74	**1979**
11.07	11.64	12.02	12.31	12.97	13.21	**1980**
14.38	14.89	15.49	15.40	14.22	14.23	**1981**
14.61	13.71	12.94	12.12	11.68	11.83	**1982**
12.15	12.51	12.37	12.25	12.41	12.57	**1983**
13.44	12.87	12.66	12.63	12.29	12.13	**1984**
10.97	11.05	11.07	11.02	10.55	10.16	**1985**
8.88	8.72	8.89	8.86	8.68	8.49	**1986**
9.42	9.67	10.18	10.52	10.01	10.11	**1987**
9.96	10.11	9.82	9.51	9.45	9.57	**1988**
8.93	8.96	9.01	8.92	8.89	8.86	**1989**
9.24	9.41	9.56	9.53	9.30	9.05	**1990**
9.00	8.75	8.61	8.55	8.48	8.31	**1991**
8.07	7.95	7.92	7.99	8.10	7.98	**1992**
7.17	6.85	6.66	6.67	6.93	6.93	**1993**
8.11	8.07	8.34	8.57	8.68	8.46	**1994**
7.41	7.57	7.32	7.12	7.02	6.82	**1995**
7.65	7.46	7.66	7.39	7.10	7.20	**1996**
7.14	7.22	7.15	7.00	6.87	6.76	**1997**
6.55	6.52	6.40	6.37	6.41	6.22	**1998**
7.19	7.40	7.39	7.55	7.36	7.55	**1999**
7.65	7.55	7.62	7.55	7.45	7.21	**2000**
7.13	7.02	7.17	7.03	6.97	6.77	**2001**
6.53	6.37	6.15	6.32	6.31	6.21	**2002**
5.49	5.88	5.72	5.70	5.65	5.62	**2003**
5.82	5.65	5.46	5.47	5.52	5.47	**2004**
5.06	5.09	5.13	5.35	5.42	5.37	**2005**
5.85	5.68	5.51	5.51	5.33	5.32	**2006**
5.73	5.79	5.74	5.66	5.44	5.49	**2007**
5.67	5.64	5.65	6.28	6.12	5.05	**2008**
5.41	5.26	5.13	5.15	5.19	5.26	**2009**
4.72	4.49	4.53	4.68	4.87	5.02	**2010**

MOODY'S SEASONED CORPORATE Baa*

	JAN	FEB	MAR	APR	MAY	JUN
1950	3.24	3.24	3.24	3.23	3.25	3.28
1951	3.17	3.16	3.23	3.35	3.40	3.49
1952	3.59	3.53	3.51	3.50	3.49	3.50
1953	3.51	3.53	3.57	3.65	3.78	3.86
1954	3.71	3.61	3.51	3.47	3.47	3.49
1955	3.45	3.47	3.48	3.49	3.50	3.51
1956	3.60	3.58	3.60	3.68	3.73	3.76
1957	4.49	4.47	4.43	4.44	4.52	4.63
1958	4.83	4.66	4.68	4.67	4.62	4.55
1959	4.87	4.89	4.85	4.86	4.96	5.04
1960	5.34	5.34	5.25	5.20	5.28	5.26
1961	5.10	5.07	5.02	5.01	5.01	5.03
1962	5.08	5.07	5.04	5.02	5.00	5.02
1963	4.91	4.89	4.88	4.87	4.85	4.84
1964	4.83	4.83	4.83	4.85	4.85	4.85
1965	4.80	4.78	4.78	4.80	4.81	4.85
1966	5.06	5.12	5.32	5.41	5.48	5.58
1967	5.97	5.82	5.85	5.83	5.96	6.15
1968	6.84	6.80	6.85	6.97	7.03	7.07
1969	7.32	7.30	7.51	7.54	7.52	7.70
1970	8.86	8.78	8.63	8.70	8.98	9.25
1971	8.74	8.39	8.46	8.45	8.62	8.75
1972	8.23	8.23	8.24	8.24	8.23	8.20
1973	7.90	7.97	8.03	8.09	8.06	8.13
1974	8.48	8.53	8.62	8.87	9.05	9.27
1975	10.81	10.65	10.48	10.58	10.69	10.62
1976	10.41	10.24	10.12	9.94	9.86	9.89
1977	9.08	9.12	9.12	9.07	9.01	8.91
1978	9.17	9.20	9.22	9.32	9.49	9.60
1979	10.13	10.08	10.26	10.33	10.47	10.38
1980	12.42	13.57	14.45	14.19	13.17	12.71
1981	15.03	15.37	15.34	15.56	15.95	15.80
1982	17.10	17.18	16.82	16.78	16.64	16.92
1983	13.94	13.95	13.61	13.29	13.09	13.37
1984	13.65	13.59	13.99	14.31	14.74	15.05
1985	13.26	13.23	13.69	13.51	13.15	12.40
1986	11.44	11.11	10.50	10.19	10.29	10.34
1987	9.72	9.65	9.61	10.04	10.51	10.52
1988	11.07	10.62	10.57	10.90	11.04	11.00
1989	10.65	10.61	10.67	10.61	10.46	10.03
1990	9.94	10.14	10.21	10.30	10.41	10.22
1991	10.45	10.07	10.09	9.94	9.86	9.96
1992	9.13	9.23	9.25	9.21	9.13	9.05
1993	8.67	8.39	8.15	8.14	8.21	8.07
1994	7.65	7.76	8.13	8.52	8.62	8.65
1995	9.08	8.85	8.70	8.60	8.20	7.90
1996	7.47	7.63	8.03	8.19	8.30	8.40
1997	8.09	7.94	8.18	8.34	8.20	8.02
1998	7.19	7.25	7.32	7.33	7.30	7.13
1999	7.29	7.39	7.53	7.48	7.72	8.02
2000	8.33	8.29	8.37	8.40	8.90	8.48
2001	7.93	7.87	7.84	8.07	8.07	7.97
2002	7.87	7.89	8.11	8.03	8.09	7.95
2003	7.35	7.06	6.95	6.85	6.38	6.19
2004	6.44	6.27	6.11	6.46	6.75	6.78
2005	6.02	5.82	6.06	6.05	6.01	5.86
2006	6.24	6.27	6.41	6.68	6.75	6.78
2007	6.34	6.28	6.27	6.39	6.39	6.70
2008	6.54	6.82	6.89	6.97	6.93	7.07
2009	8.14	8.08	8.42	8.39	8.06	7.50
2010	6.25	6.34	6.27	6.25	6.05	6.23

* Source: Federal Reserve Bank of St. Louis, monthly data calculated as average of business days

MOODY'S SEASONED CORPORATE Baa* BOND YIELDS

JUL	AUG	SEP	OCT	NOV	DEC	
3.32	3.23	3.21	3.22	3.22	3.20	**1950**
3.53	3.50	3.46	3.50	3.56	3.61	**1951**
3.50	3.51	3.52	3.54	3.53	3.51	**1952**
3.86	3.85	3.88	3.82	3.75	3.74	**1953**
3.50	3.49	3.47	3.46	3.45	3.45	**1954**
3.52	3.56	3.59	3.59	3.58	3.62	**1955**
3.80	3.93	4.07	4.17	4.24	4.37	**1956**
4.73	4.82	4.93	4.99	5.09	5.03	**1957**
4.53	4.67	4.87	4.92	4.87	4.85	**1958**
5.08	5.09	5.18	5.28	5.26	5.28	**1959**
5.22	5.08	5.01	5.11	5.08	5.10	**1960**
5.09	5.11	5.12	5.13	5.11	5.10	**1961**
5.05	5.06	5.03	4.99	4.96	4.92	**1962**
4.84	4.83	4.84	4.83	4.84	4.85	**1963**
4.83	4.82	4.82	4.81	4.81	4.81	**1964**
4.88	4.88	4.91	4.93	4.95	5.02	**1965**
5.68	5.83	6.09	6.10	6.13	6.18	**1966**
6.26	6.33	6.40	6.52	6.72	6.93	**1967**
6.98	6.82	6.79	6.84	7.01	7.23	**1968**
7.84	7.86	8.05	8.22	8.25	8.65	**1969**
9.40	9.44	9.39	9.33	9.38	9.12	**1970**
8.76	8.76	8.59	8.48	8.38	8.38	**1971**
8.23	8.19	8.09	8.06	7.99	7.93	**1972**
8.24	8.53	8.63	8.41	8.42	8.48	**1973**
9.48	9.77	10.18	10.48	10.60	10.63	**1974**
10.55	10.59	10.61	10.62	10.56	10.56	**1975**
9.82	9.64	9.40	9.29	9.23	9.12	**1976**
8.87	8.82	8.80	8.89	8.95	8.99	**1977**
9.60	9.48	9.42	9.59	9.83	9.94	**1978**
10.29	10.35	10.54	11.40	11.99	12.06	**1979**
12.65	13.15	13.70	14.23	14.64	15.14	**1980**
16.17	16.34	16.92	17.11	16.39	16.55	**1981**
16.80	16.32	15.63	14.73	14.30	14.14	**1982**
13.39	13.64	13.55	13.46	13.61	13.75	**1983**
15.15	14.63	14.35	13.94	13.48	13.40	**1984**
12.43	12.50	12.48	12.36	11.99	11.58	**1985**
10.16	10.18	10.20	10.24	10.07	9.97	**1986**
10.61	10.80	11.31	11.62	11.23	11.29	**1987**
11.11	11.21	10.90	10.41	10.48	10.65	**1988**
9.87	9.88	9.91	9.81	9.81	9.82	**1989**
10.20	10.41	10.64	10.74	10.62	10.43	**1990**
9.89	9.65	9.51	9.49	9.45	9.26	**1991**
8.84	8.65	8.62	8.84	8.96	8.81	**1992**
7.93	7.60	7.34	7.31	7.66	7.69	**1993**
8.80	8.74	8.98	9.20	9.32	9.10	**1994**
8.04	8.19	7.93	7.75	7.68	7.49	**1995**
8.35	8.18	8.35	8.07	7.79	7.89	**1996**
7.75	7.82	7.70	7.57	7.42	7.32	**1997**
7.15	7.14	7.09	7.18	7.34	7.23	**1998**
7.95	8.15	8.20	8.38	8.15	8.19	**1999**
8.35	8.26	8.35	8.34	8.28	8.02	**2000**
7.97	7.85	8.03	7.91	7.81	8.05	**2001**
7.90	7.58	7.40	7.73	7.62	7.45	**2002**
6.62	7.01	6.79	6.73	6.66	6.60	**2003**
6.62	6.46	6.27	6.21	6.20	6.15	**2004**
5.95	5.96	6.03	6.30	6.39	6.32	**2005**
6.76	6.59	6.43	6.42	6.20	6.22	**2006**
6.65	6.65	6.59	6.48	6.40	6.65	**2007**
7.16	7.15	7.31	8.88	9.21	8.43	**2008**
7.09	6.58	6.31	6.29	6.32	6.37	**2009**
6.01	5.66	5.66	5.72	5.92	6.10	**2010**

COMMODITIES

OIL - WEST TEXAS INTERMEDIATE
CLOSING VALUES $ / bbl

	JAN	FEB	MAR	APR	MAY	JUN
1950	2.6	2.6	2.6	2.6	2.6	2.6
1951	2.6	2.6	2.6	2.6	2.6	2.6
1952	2.6	2.6	2.6	2.6	2.6	2.6
1953	2.6	2.6	2.6	2.6	2.6	2.8
1954	2.8	2.8	2.8	2.8	2.8	2.8
1955	2.8	2.8	2.8	2.8	2.8	2.8
1956	2.8	2.8	2.8	2.8	2.8	2.8
1957	2.8	3.1	3.1	3.1	3.1	3.1
1958	3.1	3.1	3.1	3.1	3.1	3.1
1959	3.0	3.0	3.0	3.0	3.0	3.0
1960	3.0	3.0	3.0	3.0	3.0	3.0
1961	3.0	3.0	3.0	3.0	3.0	3.0
1962	3.0	3.0	3.0	3.0	3.0	3.0
1963	3.0	3.0	3.0	3.0	3.0	3.0
1964	3.0	3.0	3.0	3.0	3.0	3.0
1965	2.9	2.9	2.9	2.9	2.9	2.9
1966	2.9	2.9	2.9	2.9	2.9	2.9
1967	3.0	3.0	3.0	3.0	3.0	3.0
1968	3.1	3.1	3.1	3.1	3.1	3.1
1969	3.1	3.1	3.3	3.4	3.4	3.4
1970	3.4	3.4	3.4	3.4	3.4	3.4
1971	3.6	3.6	3.6	3.6	3.6	3.6
1972	3.6	3.6	3.6	3.6	3.6	3.6
1973	3.6	3.6	3.6	3.6	3.6	3.6
1974	10.1	10.1	10.1	10.1	10.1	10.1
1975	11.2	11.2	11.2	11.2	11.2	11.2
1976	11.2	12.0	12.1	12.2	12.2	12.2
1977	13.9	13.9	13.9	13.9	13.9	13.9
1978	14.9	14.9	14.9	14.9	14.9	14.9
1979	14.9	15.9	15.9	15.9	18.1	19.1
1980	32.5	37.0	38.0	39.5	39.5	39.5
1981	38.0	38.0	38.0	38.0	38.0	36.0
1982	33.9	31.6	28.5	33.5	35.9	35.1
1983	31.2	29.0	28.8	30.6	30.0	31.0
1984	29.7	30.1	30.8	30.6	30.5	30.0
1985	25.6	27.3	28.2	28.8	27.6	27.1
1986	22.9	15.4	12.6	12.8	15.4	13.5
1987	18.7	17.7	18.3	18.6	19.4	20.0
1988	17.2	16.8	16.2	17.9	17.4	16.5
1989	18.0	17.8	19.4	21.0	20.0	20.0
1990	22.6	22.1	20.4	18.6	18.2	16.9
1991	25.0	20.5	19.9	20.8	21.2	20.2
1992	18.8	19.0	18.9	20.2	20.9	22.4
1993	19.1	20.1	20.3	20.3	19.9	19.1
1994	15.0	14.8	14.7	16.4	17.9	19.1
1995	18.0	18.5	18.6	19.9	19.7	18.4
1996	18.9	19.1	21.4	23.6	21.3	20.5
1997	25.2	22.2	21.0	19.7	20.8	19.2
1998	16.7	16.1	15.0	15.4	14.9	13.7
1999	12.5	12.0	14.7	17.3	17.8	17.9
2000	27.2	29.4	29.9	25.7	28.8	31.8
2001	29.6	29.6	27.2	27.4	28.6	27.6
2002	19.7	20.7	24.4	26.3	27.0	25.5
2003	32.9	35.9	33.6	28.3	28.1	30.7
2004	34.3	34.7	36.8	36.7	40.3	38.0
2005	46.8	48.0	54.3	53.0	49.8	56.3
2006	65.5	61.6	62.9	69.7	70.9	71.0
2007	54.6	59.3	60.6	64.0	63.5	67.5
2008	93.0	95.4	105.6	112.6	125.4	133.9
2009	41.7	39.2	48.0	49.8	59.2	69.7
2010	78.2	76.4	81.2	84.5	73.8	75.4

* Source: Federal Reserve

OIL - WEST TEXAS INTERMEDIATE CLOSING VALUES $ / bbl COMMODITIES

JUL	AUG	SEP	OCT	NOV	DEC	
2.6	2.6	2.6	2.6	2.6	2.6	1950
2.6	2.6	2.6	2.6	2.6	2.6	1951
2.6	2.6	2.6	2.6	2.6	2.6	1952
2.8	2.8	2.8	2.8	2.8	2.8	1953
2.8	2.8	2.8	2.8	2.8	2.8	1954
2.8	2.8	2.8	2.8	2.8	2.8	1955
2.8	2.8	2.8	2.8	2.8	2.8	1956
3.1	3.1	3.1	3.1	3.1	3.0	1957
3.1	3.1	3.1	3.1	3.0	3.0	1958
3.0	3.0	3.0	3.0	3.0	3.0	1959
3.0	3.0	3.0	3.0	3.0	3.0	1960
3.0	3.0	3.0	3.0	3.0	3.0	1961
3.0	3.0	3.0	3.0	3.0	3.0	1962
3.0	3.0	3.0	3.0	3.0	3.0	1963
2.9	2.9	2.9	2.9	2.9	2.9	1964
2.9	2.9	2.9	2.9	2.9	2.9	1965
2.9	2.9	3.0	3.0	3.0	3.0	1966
3.0	3.1	3.1	3.1	3.1	3.1	1967
3.1	3.1	3.1	3.1	3.1	3.1	1968
3.4	3.4	3.4	3.4	3.4	3.4	1969
3.3	3.3	3.3	3.3	3.3	3.6	1970
3.6	3.6	3.6	3.6	3.6	3.6	1971
3.6	3.6	3.6	3.6	3.6	3.6	1972
3.6	4.3	4.3	4.3	4.3	4.3	1973
10.1	10.1	10.1	11.2	11.2	11.2	1974
11.2	11.2	11.2	11.2	11.2	11.2	1975
12.2	12.2	13.9	13.9	13.9	13.9	1976
13.9	14.9	14.9	14.9	14.9	14.9	1977
14.9	14.9	14.9	14.9	14.9	14.9	1978
21.8	26.5	28.5	29.0	31.0	32.5	1979
39.5	38.0	36.0	36.0	36.0	37.0	1980
36.0	36.0	36.0	35.0	36.0	35.0	1981
34.2	34.0	35.6	35.7	34.2	31.7	1982
31.7	31.9	31.1	30.4	29.8	29.2	1983
28.8	29.3	29.3	28.8	28.1	25.4	1984
27.3	27.8	28.3	29.5	30.8	27.2	1985
11.6	15.1	14.9	14.9	15.2	16.1	1986
21.4	20.3	19.5	19.8	18.9	17.2	1987
15.5	15.5	14.5	13.8	14.0	16.3	1988
19.6	18.5	19.6	20.1	19.8	21.1	1989
18.6	27.2	33.7	35.9	32.3	27.3	1990
21.4	21.7	21.9	23.2	22.5	19.5	1991
21.8	21.4	21.9	21.7	20.3	19.4	1992
17.9	18.0	17.5	18.1	16.7	14.5	1993
19.7	18.4	17.5	17.7	18.1	17.2	1994
17.3	18.0	18.2	17.4	18.0	19.0	1995
21.3	22.0	24.0	24.9	23.7	25.4	1996
19.6	19.9	19.8	21.3	20.2	18.3	1997
14.1	13.4	15.0	14.4	12.9	11.3	1998
20.1	21.3	23.9	22.6	25.0	26.1	1999
29.8	31.2	33.9	33.1	34.4	28.5	2000
26.5	27.5	25.9	22.2	19.7	19.3	2001
26.9	28.4	29.7	28.9	26.3	29.4	2002
30.8	31.6	28.3	30.3	31.1	32.2	2003
40.7	44.9	46.0	53.1	48.5	43.3	2004
58.7	65.0	65.6	62.4	58.3	59.4	2005
74.4	73.1	63.9	58.9	59.4	62.0	2006
74.2	72.4	79.9	86.2	94.6	91.7	2007
133.4	116.6	103.9	76.7	57.4	41.0	2008
64.1	71.1	69.5	75.6	78.1	74.3	2009
76.4	76.8	75.3	81.9	84.1	89.0	2010

GOLD $US/OZ LONDON PM
MONTH CLOSE

	JAN	FEB	MAR	APR	MAY	JUN
1970	34.9	35.0	35.1	35.6	36.0	35.4
1971	37.9	38.7	38.9	39.0	40.5	40.1
1972	45.8	48.3	48.3	49.0	54.6	62.1
1973	65.1	74.2	84.4	90.5	102.0	120.1
1974	129.2	150.2	168.4	172.2	163.3	154.1
1975	175.8	181.8	178.2	167.0	167.0	166.3
1976	128.2	132.3	129.6	128.4	125.5	123.8
1977	132.3	142.8	148.9	147.3	143.0	143.0
1978	175.8	182.3	181.6	170.9	184.2	183.1
1979	233.7	251.3	240.1	245.3	274.6	277.5
1980	653.0	637.0	494.5	518.0	535.5	653.5
1981	506.5	489.0	513.8	482.8	479.3	426.0
1982	387.0	362.6	320.0	361.3	325.3	317.5
1983	499.5	408.5	414.8	429.3	437.5	416.0
1984	373.8	394.3	388.5	375.8	384.3	373.1
1985	306.7	287.8	329.3	321.4	314.0	317.8
1986	350.5	338.2	344.0	345.8	343.2	345.5
1987	400.5	405.9	405.9	453.3	451.0	447.3
1988	458.0	426.2	457.0	449.0	455.5	436.6
1989	394.0	387.0	383.2	377.6	361.8	373.0
1990	415.1	407.7	368.5	367.8	363.1	352.2
1991	366.0	362.7	355.7	357.8	360.4	368.4
1992	354.1	353.1	341.7	336.4	337.5	343.4
1993	330.5	327.6	337.8	354.3	374.8	378.5
1994	377.9	381.6	389.2	376.5	387.6	388.3
1995	374.9	376.4	392.0	389.8	384.3	387.1
1996	405.6	400.7	396.4	391.3	390.6	382.0
1997	345.5	358.6	348.2	340.2	345.6	334.6
1998	304.9	297.4	301.0	310.7	293.6	296.3
1999	285.4	287.1	279.5	286.6	268.6	261.0
2000	283.3	293.7	276.8	275.1	272.3	288.2
2001	264.5	266.7	257.7	263.2	267.5	270.6
2002	282.3	296.9	301.4	308.2	326.6	318.5
2003	367.5	347.5	334.9	336.8	361.4	346.0
2004	399.8	395.9	423.7	388.5	393.3	395.8
2005	422.2	435.5	427.5	435.7	414.5	437.1
2006	568.8	556.0	582.0	644.0	653.0	613.5
2007	650.5	664.2	661.8	677.0	659.1	650.5
2008	923.3	971.5	933.5	871.0	885.8	930.3
2009	919.5	952.0	916.5	883.3	975.5	934.5
2010	1078.5	1108.3	1115.5	1179.3	1207.5	1244.0

* Source: Bank of England

GOLD $US/OZ LONDON PM MONTH CLOSE

COMMODITIES

JUL	AUG	SEP	OCT	NOV	DEC	
35.3	35.4	36.2	37.5	37.4	37.4	**1970**
41.0	42.7	42.0	42.5	42.9	43.5	**1971**
65.7	67.0	65.5	64.9	62.9	63.9	**1972**
120.2	106.8	103.0	100.1	94.8	106.7	**1973**
143.0	154.6	151.8	158.8	181.7	183.9	**1974**
166.7	159.8	141.3	142.9	138.2	140.3	**1975**
112.5	104.0	116.0	123.2	130.3	134.5	**1976**
144.1	146.0	154.1	161.5	160.1	165.0	**1977**
200.3	208.7	217.1	242.6	193.4	226.0	**1978**
296.5	315.1	397.3	382.0	415.7	512.0	**1979**
614.3	631.3	666.8	629.0	619.8	589.8	**1980**
406.0	425.5	428.8	427.0	414.5	397.5	**1981**
342.9	411.5	397.0	423.3	436.0	456.9	**1982**
422.0	414.3	405.0	382.0	405.0	382.4	**1983**
342.4	348.3	343.8	333.5	329.0	309.0	**1984**
327.5	333.3	326.5	325.1	325.3	326.8	**1985**
357.5	384.7	423.2	401.0	383.5	388.8	**1986**
462.5	453.4	459.5	468.8	492.5	484.1	**1987**
436.8	427.8	397.7	412.4	422.6	410.3	**1988**
368.3	359.8	366.5	375.3	408.2	398.6	**1989**
372.3	387.8	408.4	379.5	384.9	386.2	**1990**
362.9	347.4	354.9	357.5	366.3	353.2	**1991**
357.9	340.0	349.0	339.3	334.2	332.9	**1992**
401.8	371.6	355.5	369.6	370.9	391.8	**1993**
384.0	385.8	394.9	383.9	383.1	383.3	**1994**
383.4	382.4	384.0	382.7	387.8	387.0	**1995**
385.3	386.5	379.0	379.5	371.3	369.3	**1996**
326.4	325.4	332.1	311.4	296.8	290.2	**1997**
288.9	273.4	293.9	292.3	294.7	287.8	**1998**
255.6	254.8	299.0	299.1	291.4	290.3	**1999**
276.8	277.0	273.7	264.5	269.1	274.5	**2000**
265.9	273.0	293.1	278.8	275.5	276.5	**2001**
304.7	312.8	323.7	316.9	319.1	347.2	**2002**
354.8	375.6	388.0	386.3	398.4	416.3	**2003**
391.4	407.3	415.7	425.6	453.4	435.6	**2004**
429.0	433.3	473.3	470.8	495.7	513.0	**2005**
632.5	623.5	599.3	603.8	646.7	632.0	**2006**
665.5	672.0	743.0	789.5	783.5	833.8	**2007**
918.0	833.0	884.5	730.8	814.5	869.8	**2008**
939.0	955.5	995.8	1040.0	1175.8	1087.5	**2009**
1169.0	1246.0	1307.0	1346.8	1383.5	1405.5	**2010**

FOREIGN EXCHANGE

US DOLLAR vs CDN DOLLAR MONTHLY AVG. VALUES*

	JAN		FEB		MAR		APR		MAY		JUN	
	US / CDN	CDN / US	US / CDN	CDN / US	US / CDN	CDN /US	US / CDN	CDN / US	US / CDN	CDN / US	US / CDN	CDN / US
1971	1.01	0.99	1.01	0.99	1.01	0.99	1.01	0.99	1.01	0.99	1.02	0.98
1972	1.01	0.99	1.00	1.00	1.00	1.00	1.00	1.00	0.99	1.01	0.98	1.02
1973	1.00	1.00	1.00	1.00	1.00	1.00	1.00	1.00	1.00	1.00	1.00	1.00
1974	0.99	1.01	0.98	1.02	0.97	1.03	0.97	1.03	0.96	1.04	0.97	1.03
1975	0.99	1.01	1.00	1.00	1.00	1.00	1.01	0.99	1.03	0.97	1.03	0.97
1976	1.01	0.99	0.99	1.01	0.99	1.01	0.98	1.02	0.98	1.02	0.97	1.03
1977	1.01	0.99	1.03	0.97	1.05	0.95	1.05	0.95	1.05	0.95	1.06	0.95
1978	1.10	0.91	1.11	0.90	1.13	0.89	1.14	0.88	1.12	0.89	1.12	0.89
1979	1.19	0.84	1.20	0.84	1.17	0.85	1.15	0.87	1.16	0.87	1.17	0.85
1980	1.16	0.86	1.16	0.87	1.17	0.85	1.19	0.84	1.17	0.85	1.15	0.87
1981	1.19	0.84	1.20	0.83	1.19	0.84	1.19	0.84	1.20	0.83	1.20	0.83
1982	1.19	0.84	1.21	0.82	1.22	0.82	1.23	0.82	1.23	0.81	1.28	0.78
1983	1.23	0.81	1.23	0.81	1.23	0.82	1.23	0.81	1.23	0.81	1.23	0.81
1984	1.25	0.80	1.25	0.80	1.27	0.79	1.28	0.78	1.29	0.77	1.30	0.77
1985	1.32	0.76	1.35	0.74	1.38	0.72	1.37	0.73	1.38	0.73	1.37	0.73
1986	1.41	0.71	1.40	0.71	1.40	0.71	1.39	0.72	1.38	0.73	1.39	0.72
1987	1.36	0.73	1.33	0.75	1.32	0.76	1.32	0.76	1.34	0.75	1.34	0.75
1988	1.29	0.78	1.27	0.79	1.25	0.80	1.24	0.81	1.24	0.81	1.22	0.82
1989	1.19	0.84	1.19	0.84	1.20	0.84	1.19	0.84	1.19	0.84	1.20	0.83
1990	1.17	0.85	1.20	0.84	1.18	0.85	1.16	0.86	1.17	0.85	1.17	0.85
1991	1.16	0.87	1.15	0.87	1.16	0.86	1.15	0.87	1.15	0.87	1.14	0.87
1992	1.16	0.86	1.18	0.85	1.19	0.84	1.19	0.84	1.20	0.83	1.20	0.84
1993	1.28	0.78	1.26	0.79	1.25	0.80	1.26	0.79	1.27	0.79	1.28	0.78
1994	1.32	0.76	1.34	0.74	1.36	0.73	1.38	0.72	1.38	0.72	1.38	0.72
1995	1.41	0.71	1.40	0.71	1.41	0.71	1.38	0.73	1.36	0.73	1.38	0.73
1996	1.37	0.73	1.38	0.73	1.37	0.73	1.36	0.74	1.37	0.73	1.37	0.73
1997	1.35	0.74	1.36	0.74	1.37	0.73	1.39	0.72	1.38	0.72	1.38	0.72
1998	1.44	0.69	1.43	0.70	1.42	0.71	1.43	0.70	1.45	0.69	1.47	0.68
1999	1.52	0.66	1.50	0.67	1.52	0.66	1.49	0.67	1.46	0.68	1.47	0.68
2000	1.45	0.69	1.45	0.69	1.46	0.68	1.47	0.68	1.50	0.67	1.48	0.68
2001	1.50	0.67	1.52	0.66	1.56	0.64	1.56	0.64	1.54	0.65	1.52	0.66
2002	1.60	0.63	1.60	0.63	1.59	0.63	1.58	0.63	1.55	0.65	1.53	0.65
2003	1.54	0.65	1.51	0.66	1.48	0.68	1.46	0.69	1.38	0.72	1.35	0.74
2004	1.30	0.77	1.33	0.75	1.33	0.75	1.34	0.75	1.38	0.73	1.36	0.74
2005	1.22	0.82	1.24	0.81	1.22	0.82	1.24	0.81	1.26	0.80	1.24	0.81
2006	1.16	0.86	1.15	0.87	1.16	0.86	1.14	0.87	1.11	0.90	1.11	0.90
2007	1.18	0.85	1.17	0.85	1.17	0.86	1.14	0.88	1.10	0.91	1.07	0.94
2008	1.01	0.99	1.00	1.00	1.00	1.00	1.01	0.99	1.00	1.00	1.02	0.98
2009	1.22	0.82	1.25	0.80	1.26	0.79	1.22	0.82	1.15	0.87	1.13	0.89
2010	1.04	0.96	1.06	0.95	1.02	0.98	1.01	0.99	1.04	0.96	1.04	0.96

Source: Federal Reserve: Avg of daily rates, noon buying rates in New York City for cable transfers payable in foreign currencies

US DOLLAR vs CDN DOLLAR
MONTHLY AVG. VALUES

JUL US / CDN	JUL CDN / US	AUG US / CDN	AUG CDN / US	SEP US / CDN	SEP CDN / US	OCT US / CDN	OCT CDN / US	NOV US / CDN	NOV CDN / US	DEC US / CDN	DEC CDN / US	
1.02	0.98	1.01	0.99	1.01	0.99	1.00	1.00	1.00	1.00	1.00	1.00	1971
0.98	1.02	0.98	1.02	0.98	1.02	0.98	1.02	0.99	1.01	1.00	1.00	1972
1.00	1.00	1.00	1.00	1.01	0.99	1.00	1.00	1.00	1.00	1.00	1.00	1973
0.98	1.02	0.98	1.02	0.99	1.01	0.98	1.02	0.99	1.01	0.99	1.01	1974
1.03	0.97	1.04	0.97	1.03	0.97	1.03	0.98	1.01	0.99	1.01	0.99	1975
0.97	1.03	0.99	1.01	0.98	1.03	0.97	1.03	0.99	1.01	1.02	0.98	1976
1.06	0.94	1.08	0.93	1.07	0.93	1.10	0.91	1.11	0.90	1.10	0.91	1977
1.12	0.89	1.14	0.88	1.17	0.86	1.18	0.85	1.17	0.85	1.18	0.85	1978
1.16	0.86	1.17	0.85	1.17	0.86	1.18	0.85	1.18	0.85	1.17	0.85	1979
1.15	0.87	1.16	0.86	1.16	0.86	1.17	0.86	1.19	0.84	1.20	0.84	1980
1.21	0.83	1.22	0.82	1.20	0.83	1.20	0.83	1.19	0.84	1.19	0.84	1981
1.27	0.79	1.25	0.80	1.23	0.81	1.23	0.81	1.23	0.82	1.24	0.81	1982
1.23	0.81	1.23	0.81	1.23	0.81	1.23	0.81	1.24	0.81	1.25	0.80	1983
1.32	0.76	1.30	0.77	1.31	0.76	1.32	0.76	1.32	0.76	1.32	0.76	1984
1.35	0.74	1.36	0.74	1.37	0.73	1.37	0.73	1.38	0.73	1.40	0.72	1985
1.38	0.72	1.39	0.72	1.39	0.72	1.39	0.72	1.39	0.72	1.38	0.72	1986
1.33	0.75	1.33	0.75	1.32	0.76	1.31	0.76	1.32	0.76	1.31	0.76	1987
1.21	0.83	1.22	0.82	1.23	0.82	1.21	0.83	1.22	0.82	1.20	0.84	1988
1.19	0.84	1.18	0.85	1.18	0.85	1.17	0.85	1.17	0.85	1.16	0.86	1989
1.16	0.86	1.14	0.87	1.16	0.86	1.16	0.86	1.16	0.86	1.16	0.86	1990
1.15	0.87	1.15	0.87	1.14	0.88	1.13	0.89	1.13	0.88	1.15	0.87	1991
1.19	0.84	1.19	0.84	1.22	0.82	1.25	0.80	1.27	0.79	1.27	0.79	1992
1.28	0.78	1.31	0.76	1.32	0.76	1.33	0.75	1.32	0.76	1.33	0.75	1993
1.38	0.72	1.38	0.73	1.35	0.74	1.35	0.74	1.36	0.73	1.39	0.72	1994
1.36	0.73	1.36	0.74	1.35	0.74	1.35	0.74	1.35	0.74	1.37	0.73	1995
1.37	0.73	1.37	0.73	1.37	0.73	1.35	0.74	1.34	0.75	1.36	0.73	1996
1.38	0.73	1.39	0.72	1.39	0.72	1.39	0.72	1.41	0.71	1.43	0.70	1997
1.49	0.67	1.53	0.65	1.52	0.66	1.55	0.65	1.54	0.65	1.54	0.65	1998
1.49	0.67	1.49	0.67	1.48	0.68	1.48	0.68	1.47	0.68	1.47	0.68	1999
1.48	0.68	1.48	0.67	1.49	0.67	1.51	0.66	1.54	0.65	1.52	0.66	2000
1.53	0.65	1.54	0.65	1.57	0.64	1.57	0.64	1.59	0.63	1.58	0.63	2001
1.55	0.65	1.57	0.64	1.58	0.63	1.58	0.63	1.57	0.64	1.56	0.64	2002
1.38	0.72	1.40	0.72	1.36	0.73	1.32	0.76	1.31	0.76	1.31	0.76	2003
1.32	0.76	1.31	0.76	1.29	0.78	1.25	0.80	1.20	0.84	1.22	0.82	2004
1.22	0.82	1.20	0.83	1.18	0.85	1.18	0.85	1.18	0.85	1.16	0.86	2005
1.13	0.89	1.12	0.89	1.12	0.90	1.13	0.89	1.14	0.88	1.15	0.87	2006
1.05	0.95	1.06	0.95	1.03	0.97	0.98	1.03	0.97	1.03	1.00	1.00	2007
1.01	0.99	1.05	0.95	1.06	0.95	1.18	0.84	1.22	0.82	1.23	0.81	2008
1.12	0.89	1.09	0.92	1.08	0.92	1.05	0.95	1.06	0.94	1.05	0.95	2009
1.04	0.96	1.04	0.96	1.03	0.97	1.02	0.98	1.01	0.99	1.01	0.99	2010

FOREIGN EXCHANGE — U.S. DOLLAR vs EURO MONTHLY AVG. VALUES

	JAN		FEB		MAR		APR		MAY		JUN	
	EUR / US	US / EUR	EUR / US	US / EUR	EUR / US	US / EUR	EUR / US	US / EUR	EUR / US	US / EUR	EUR / US	US / EUR
1999	1.16	0.86	1.12	0.89	1.09	0.92	1.07	0.93	1.06	0.94	1.04	0.96
2000	1.01	0.99	0.98	1.02	0.96	1.04	0.94	1.06	0.91	1.10	0.95	1.05
2001	0.94	1.07	0.92	1.09	0.91	1.10	0.89	1.12	0.88	1.14	0.85	1.17
2002	0.88	1.13	0.87	1.15	0.88	1.14	0.89	1.13	0.92	1.09	0.96	1.05
2003	1.06	0.94	1.08	0.93	1.08	0.93	1.09	0.92	1.16	0.87	1.17	0.86
2004	1.26	0.79	1.26	0.79	1.23	0.82	1.20	0.83	1.20	0.83	1.21	0.82
2005	1.31	0.76	1.30	0.77	1.32	0.76	1.29	0.77	1.27	0.79	1.22	0.82
2006	1.21	0.82	1.19	0.84	1.20	0.83	1.23	0.81	1.28	0.78	1.27	0.79
2007	1.30	0.77	1.31	0.76	1.32	0.75	1.35	0.74	1.35	0.74	1.34	0.75
2008	1.47	0.68	1.48	0.68	1.55	0.64	1.58	0.63	1.56	0.64	1.56	0.64
2009	1.32	0.76	1.28	0.78	1.31	0.77	1.32	0.76	1.36	0.73	1.40	0.71
2010	1.43	0.70	1.37	0.73	1.36	0.74	1.34	0.75	1.26	0.80	1.22	0.82

Source: Federal Reserve: Avg of daily rates, noon buying rates in New York City for cable transfers payable in foreign currencies

US DOLLAR vs EURO
MONTHLY AVG. VALUES

	JUL		AUG		SEP		OCT		NOV		DEC	
	EUR / US	US / EUR	EUR / US	US / EUR	EUR / US	US / EUR	EUR / US	US / EUR	EUR / US	US / EUR	EUR / US	US / EUR	
	1.04	0.96	1.06	0.94	1.05	0.95	1.07	0.93	1.03	0.97	1.01	0.99	**1999**
	0.94	1.07	0.90	1.11	0.87	1.15	0.85	1.17	0.86	1.17	0.90	1.11	**2000**
	0.86	1.16	0.90	1.11	0.91	1.10	0.91	1.10	0.89	1.13	0.89	1.12	**2001**
	0.99	1.01	0.98	1.02	0.98	1.02	0.98	1.02	1.00	1.00	1.02	0.98	**2002**
	1.14	0.88	1.12	0.90	1.13	0.89	1.17	0.85	1.17	0.85	1.23	0.81	**2003**
	1.23	0.82	1.22	0.82	1.22	0.82	1.25	0.80	1.30	0.77	1.34	0.75	**2004**
	1.20	0.83	1.23	0.81	1.22	0.82	1.20	0.83	1.18	0.85	1.19	0.84	**2005**
	1.27	0.79	1.28	0.78	1.27	0.79	1.26	0.79	1.29	0.78	1.32	0.76	**2006**
	1.37	0.73	1.36	0.73	1.39	0.72	1.42	0.70	1.47	0.68	1.46	0.69	**2007**
	1.58	0.63	1.50	0.67	1.43	0.70	1.33	0.75	1.27	0.78	1.35	0.74	**2008**
	1.41	0.71	1.43	0.70	1.46	0.69	1.48	0.67	1.49	0.67	1.46	0.69	**2009**
	1.28	0.78	1.29	0.78	1.31	0.76	1.39	0.72	1.37	0.73	1.32	0.76	**2010**